W9-BXP-872

Ernst Jünger and Germany

Ernst Jünger and Germany

Into the Abyss, 1914–1945

Thomas Nevin

Duke University Press · Durham 1996

© 1996 Duke University Press
All rights reserved
Printed in the United States of America on acid-free paper ∞
Typeset in Monotype Garamond by Tseng Information Systems, Inc.
Library of Congress Cataloging-in-Publication Data appear
on the last printed page of this book.

For Karl Zangerle

Der Irrniss und der Leiden
Pfade kam ich

Contents

Acknowledgments

Much I owe many. Nigel Jones and Jean-François Valet were wonderfully helpful in getting me started. For their advice and references early in the writing I wish to thank James Albisetti, Gordon Craig, Bruce Gudmundsson, Konrad Jarausch, Gerhard Loose, and Dennis Showalter; thanks, too, to Jost Hermand and Fritz Stern later in this process. A very special debt I owe to the late Hermann Broch de Rothermann, who kindly encouraged me from the first and who was a model of equanimous judgment about Jünger and his writing.

Klaus Jonas read and sent me criticisms of the first and second chapters. George Mosse took valuable time from his own work to provide a very helpful reading of the third chapter. Karl Zangerle, a sharp-eyed reader who is also exceptionally knowledgeable about Jünger, read the entire work in its initial draft, caught many errors, and afforded many insightful criticisms. My debt to him is inadequately recorded on another page. I am immeasurably grateful to my keen-eyed readers for Duke University Press, who combed the manuscript, saved me from countless errors, and provided many valuable suggestions for revision. Whatever the shortcomings of perspective in this book, all are mine alone.

I wish to thank the many librarians who gave me their help unstintingly: Drs. Regina Mahlke and Jörg Jacoby of the Preussischer Kulturbesitz, Berlin; Ulrich Ott and the staff of the Deutsches Literaturarchiv, Marbach; Christa Sammons, curator of German books, the Beinecke Library, Yale University; the staff of the Militärgeschichtliches Forschungsamt and Dr. Fleischer's colleagues at the Militärarchiv, Freiburg-im-Breisgau; the staff of the photo documents and printed books departments, especially Martin Taylor, at the Imperial War Museum, London; Agnes Peterson at the Hoover Institution on War, Revolution, and Peace,

Stanford; Donald Wright at the Library of Congress; and, for securing me a rare edition of *Feuer und Blut,* Dorothy Christiansen, librarian at the State University of New York, Albany. Caron Knapp was untiringly helpful in filling innumerable interlibrary loan requests. Roger Woods generously supplied me with rare copies of Ernst Jünger's essays for *Arminius.*

I wish to thank also the sponsors of papers I have given on Jünger: Alain Blayac at the Université Paul Valéry, Montpellier; Hugh Cecil and Peter Liddle at Leeds University; Laszlo Géfin at Concordia University, Montreal; and Terri Apter at Clare Hall, Cambridge University. On all of these occasions I have been immeasurably stimulated by lively discussions about Ernst Jünger. I am particularly indebted to my colleagues of many disciplines at Clare Hall, where I composed much of this work, and above all to Antony and Belle Low, who helped to make the academic year of 1992–1993 so pleasurable and productive.

I have benefited from many conversations with a longtime and fairminded reader of Jünger, my colleague Wilhelm Bartsch. For other talks and insights I am grateful to Brian Bond, Hugh Cecil, the late Alister Kershaw, Keith Simpson, Zara Steiner, and Jay Winter.

John Carroll University generously granted me a leave of absence for 1992–93 which allowed me to complete the first draft of this work. The George F. Grauel Foundation I thank for its financial support during that year. The Graduate School of John Carroll University kindly contributed a subvention toward the publication of this book.

I wish to thank Klett-Cotta for permission to reproduce photos from *Ernst Jünger: Sein Leben und Werk in Bildern und Texten,* ed. Heimo Schwilk (1988). I am also grateful to Ian Carter and the Imperial War Museum for permission to reproduce photos from the First and Second World War archives.

I am profoundly indebted to the editorial staff of Duke University Press and especially to Valerie Millholland and Pamela Morrison for the highest professionalism, enthusiasm, and courage.

I can never adequately express to my wife, friend, and fellow scholar Caroline Zilboorg my appreciation for all the support and invaluable writing time she has given me over the past seven years. I owe a similar debt to our four children, who have so understandingly put up with their academic parents.

Finally, I wish to thank the subject of this book and his wife, Frau Doktor Liselotte Jünger, for admitting me to their home in July 1992.

Introduction: Why Jünger?

Ernst Jünger's life and writing span one hundred years and five periods of modern German history: the late Wilhelmine era, the Weimar Republic, the Third Reich, Germany divided, and the new Germany. This book addresses the first three periods and Jünger's first fifty years: his formation as a writer, his endurance in the two World Wars, and the crystallization of his reputation.

Jünger is one of this century's foremost writers. His first memoir, *In Storms of Steel,* was published seventy-five years ago. George Steiner has said that "it remains the most remarkable piece of writing to come out of the First World War." Since then Jünger has remained controversial: extolled, despised, denounced, admired. Now in his one hundred and first year and still writing, he holds Germany's highest literary awards, the Goethe Prize and the Schiller Memorial Prize, yet he is regularly disparaged in Germany's foremost weekly journal, *Der Spiegel.* His writings, as this book indicates, put him at an unimpeachable remove from the Nazis, but neo-Nazi rightists in Germany have rushed to embrace him. He served in the military occupation of France from 1940 to 1944, but he is an honorary citizen of Montpellier, has received the Médaille de la Paix of Verdun, and has a street named after him in Cambrai. At the Franco-German reconciliation ceremonies at Verdun in September 1984 he was the guest speaker of the French president and the German chancellor. Helmut Kohl and François Mitterrand have visited him at his home in the Black Forest; so have estimable fellow writers, Borges and Moravia among them. Mitterrand has said that had Jünger lived in the age of Napoleon he would have been one of Bonaparte's marshals. Pope John Paul II has given him a citation, and to observe Jünger's centenary a leftist director bitterly attacked him in an obscene musical, "Ernst Jünger's Storm of Steel," which played for weeks in East Berlin.

Neither celebration nor defamation has affected him. "I am immune to praise," he once said over German radio. "Like Till Eulenspiegel, no sooner have I set one foot down in the valley than my other is leaping to the next peak." About the legion of haters he has said little, but his estimate of the "world improvers" among them is on record. "They like to call themselves Marxists or humanitarians but they are just power wielders."

If he has helped the cause of Franco-German reconciliation, he has furthered political divisions in Germany itself. His detractors see him as a fascist, an embarrassing offense to Germany in its generations-long search for self-restoration. His apologists claim he is a Christian humanist or an adventurer. They suppose that his violent writings of the 1920s were not a prescription for Hitlerism but a seismograph of the tremors that shook and finally destroyed the Weimar Republic. Jünger's friends and foes can agree that Germany after fifty years in the wilderness of its search for identity has yet to come to terms with the man who is its distant past articulated in variously dark and luminous tones. As Heinrich Böll was Germany's postwar "conscience," Jünger is, by fate's leave, its still living pre-Hitler conscience, one that many Germans would rather not carry.

The militant mentality that makes the word *teutonic* so unsettling has its primary representative in Jünger because his writing is, with some historical exceptions, so poised and detached that the tone seems impersonal and objective. He is a naturalist of war who sees in it both chaos and order. He challenges us by his eerie equanimity and his refusal to moralize, thus forcing us to consider or reconsider assumptions that may in fact be only illusions or prejudices. What is one to say of a decorated veteran who scorned Hitler but affirmed war? "Combat is one of the truly great experiences, and I have yet to find someone for whom the moment of victory was not one of devastating exhilaration."

Fellow veterans have been radically divided in their estimate of Jünger. Edmund Blunden believed that "for the whole affair of trench and shellhole life, Lieutenant Jünger is a spokesman of the highest order, fresh and distinct in detail, balanced in judgment and reflection, eloquent and richly allusive. He obtains our absolute trust." Of this same man, Richard Aldington observed that Jünger was almost unrivaled in his idolatry of destruction.

With his slim figure and metallic blue eyes he looks like Hitler's ideal warrior, "sleek as a gazelle and hard as the steel of Krupp," but he has the severe remoteness of a Roman patrician in his bearing. It is his capacity for final distance that saved him from the allure of Nazism in the twenties and thirties when Hitler and Goebbels courted him, and it is that same distance that since 1945 has kept him unperturbed about Germany, its past and its future. Jünger's Olympian reserve is notorious even among those who know him well. A woman friend from the Paris days of the Second World War has described him as "a statue of ice," and his publisher of forty years, Ernst Klett, says that a friendship with Jünger is "not one of embraces." Jünger's distancing even from himself is not only a capacity; it is a disposition which suggests his great difficulty in establishing any deep emotional relationships with anyone. His wife and sons are all but phantoms in this study.

His angles of vision are distinctive, often outrageous. Goebbels, for example, was of "an inferior niveau" of intelligence; the Nazis, not sufficiently metaphysical. When I talked with him about the Second World War, he remarked, "There were only two contestants in that war, Hitler and Stalin. All the others—Churchill, Roosevelt, Mussolini, De Gaulle—they were supporting characters (Nebenfiguren)." Jünger belongs at the farthest remove from writers who have bewailed or reveled in life's seeming meaninglessness and our supposedly godless freedom. "I hate him," said Sartre. Jünger has carried out a mission far more arduous than his death-dealing in enemy trenches: he affirms an intelligible cosmos of constantly unfolding mystery and beauty, and he affirms the human mind as its worthy celebrant. That is so from his first writing to the present, and the more remarkably since he has experienced the terror and tyranny that could justify a negative verdict on humanity and its future. The record of terror and tyranny, in his journals of the Occupation of Paris, 1940–1944, still awaits English translation. Of that work a Jewish refugee from the Nazis, Hannah Arendt, has written: "Jünger's war diaries constitute without doubt the best and most honest proof of the enormous difficulties to which the individual is exposed when he wants to keep whole his idea of moral values and his conception of truth in a world where truth and morality have lost the very possibility of being perceived and identified."

Jünger, a nineteenth-century mind, points at twenty-first-century problems, chiefly the hubristic powers with which we shall use technology. He writes seemingly oblivious to the great modern revolutions of intellect, as though, contra Galileo, we still occupy the center of the universe; as though, contra Darwin, we are fit to discern divine harmonies; as though, contra Freud, we are still in charge of our own house. There is an almost priestly steadfastness in Jünger's mind and his best writing, and it is that assurance of self and tone that has distinguished him from conservative Germans who are much younger and who salute him as a way out of their anxieties. He embodies for them and many others the myth of an old yet unsullied Germany. By the immovable strength of his character, he is the ideal carrier of that myth. On his ninetieth birthday he characterized himself as "a field marshal of ideas," but he calls no philosophical system to attention. His mind works by intuitive flashes and synthetic imagery, with a precise diction that is frequently colored by ambiguity. He has the poet's gift for seeking out what is hidden behind the ordinary and apparent, and he has a perceptive interest in finding evil in seeming good, especially in technology.

This study is not a book of praises, nor is it a blackwash. Jünger does not need the one nor deserve the other. It is an attempt first to find him within the historical milieux for which his writing provides us a series of refractory lenses. His optic includes memoir, diary, essay, and fiction. His primary themes are that warfaring is an ineradicable part of our psyche, that technology's gifts to us are sinister, and that the beauty in nature's order is our stay against confusion and despair. In reading Jünger we are reminded of Baudelaire's dictum that "only three men are worthy of respect: the priest, the warrior, and the poet. To know, to kill, to create." This book is the study of three men in one.

Lofty poise of style and a studied ambiguity argue literary mastery, but the relation of style to substance assumes weighty implications in Jünger's case. On the downside of the myth he carries, he might be called Germany's "calamity of so long life," for no other writer in modern German history has been so tethered to its sinister course. Although in its formality his diction shows he owes more to the Wilhelmine era than to the twentieth century, his writing has become forever embedded in the disasters of 1914–1945 which it obliquely registers. Because over the past generation his memoirs and fictions alike have been politicized, this acutely individual writer has become a standard-bearer of German nationalism, a role he did not achieve even in the tempestuous Weimar years when he was writing in right-wing militarist journals against the republican experiment. As though attaining an acme of political incorrectness, Jünger's writings on his hazards in the Great War have been reduced to a celebration of war, and his bizarre fictions to dandyism in expressionist garb. In Jeffrey Herf's recent characterization, Jünger has become "an ideal typical aesthete of the Right."

More subtly, J. P. Stern, in the most penetrating English essay on Jünger since the Second World War, suggests that Jünger's very diction, his "embattled style" of calculated abstraction from human experience and his penchant for "cruel metaphors" reveal a contempt for life and an inability to love. In Jünger's "abstraction" Stern sees an intensification of a decline in the German language itself, as though Jünger's "defective sensibility" were symptomatic of a general linguistic barbarism. Stern allows that this barbarism is not simply a German phenomenon; he joins Jünger to Orwell, indicting both for an inability to respond humanly to the horrors they so vividly focus. Indeed, through Jünger, Stern seems to be indicting us all so far as, by embracing or acceding to fetishisms of violence, whether martial or rhetorical, we fall short of vital affirmations of experience and compassionate responses to suffering. In reading what Stern calls Jünger's "language of unfeeling" we find a means to test our own language and feeling.

Shall we find Jünger an all too representative voice? Or, contra Stern, shall we see in him not the amoralist but a moral writer alone in the forbidding privacy of ethical considerations? Jünger's is the reticent probity of German Protestantism taking refuge in a catch-me-if-you-can style, an artful distancing from masses and masters and from critics, too. Will this elusive Jünger succeed in persuading his fellow Germans that he is the model for their much desired disculpation from collective and personal guilt? It may well be that his final importance and his strongest influence will be revealed within the next generation. Thus, a writer deemed by detractors to be second rate may be of the first importance. As to the tag of second rate, I would submit that literature, like any other art form, is not a horse race.

The sequence of chapters is historical. The first finds Jünger not at home with an extraordinary father and absent-mindedly in the Kaiser's schools. The indifferent student's resort to fantasy in literature receives particular attention, for I assume that a child's true life lies in the quality of his imagination. Jünger's is reflected in the books he walked through as though they were enchanted lands. They provided signposts for him far into adulthood.

The second chapter looks at his fantastic education in war. There I establish that Jünger is not the glorifier of war he is so often labeled, chiefly by those who know his work only in translation or through the sort of superstition that passes for critical consensus. It is upon Jünger's Great War memoirs, chiefly *In Stahlgewittern* (In Storms of Steel), that his current and perhaps lasting reputation rests. As Jünger is a notorious re-writer, I have had to address the several versions of each memoir.

Chapter 3 takes up Jünger's journalism during the Weimar years. It examines essays, many of which have never been republished and none translated, that indicate the character of his opposition to "Western" parliamentary democracy. Although as a member of the "Conservative Revolution" he is firmly situated among the deadly enemies of the repub-lic, his assessment of National Socialism and "the Jewish question" may surprise those who presume he was a virtual Nazi.

The next chapter examines Jünger's heraldic claim that totalitarianism belongs not to political ideology but to technology and its manipulators. His formidable tract *Der Arbeiter* (The Worker) has sometimes been de-fended as a description, not prescription, of a coming military-industrial statism, but it will be clear in these pages that Jünger was no mere sooth-sayer. Like Pygmalion, he was all too fond of his vision and confident that a new iron order would globally displace the bourgeois world and its prewar values. A bannerless revolution manifested outwardly in tech-nology and mysteriously in human consciousness became his version of a fascism in the human future.

In the fifth chapter we enter the Third Reich and leave it three times to follow Jünger abroad. His travel journals, completely neglected by critics and scholars, show him an invaluable witness to and critic of life under Hitler. The concluding section addresses his surreal fictions and the masterwork, *Auf den Marmorklippen* (On the Marble Cliffs). This dis-cussion addresses the question of how a nationally esteemed writer evaded the suffocative conformism of the time and composed a parable against the regime that had tried to enlist him.

The final chapter situates Jünger in Paris during the German occu-pation. We see a subjugated Gallic culture through the eyes of a Ger-man who had assimilated it with articulate sympathy and sophistication.

Although eternalizing the war experience by his detachment, he registers in his most important work, the Paris diaries, the official terrorists' degradations. This chapter looks at the controversial Jünger, alleged aesthete of barbarism, and considers the virtually unknown devotee of biblical apocalypse. Here the reader will find Jünger's unequivocal recognition of Germany's responsibility for Hitler and the ruin he brought.

A postlude is given to Jünger's secret tract "The Peace," his contribution to the July 1944 conspiracy against Hitler. This document is vital to an understanding of how Jünger kept himself clear of Nazism's contaminants and sought to reclaim through Christendom a benign authoritarian order for a postwar Europe. Had the Gestapo found this work, Jünger would have become one of the July 20 "martyrs."

This study's framework is historical, but to a lively degree the issues it examines are current. Reunified Germany, groping for identity and direction, has yet to come to full terms with a savage legacy. Jünger's acutely refined sensibility opens for us a window and casts prismatic rays on that past. The sibyl proclaimed to Aeneas a future of wars. Jünger's is a monitory voice that says the same thing to Germany about its past. That is perhaps the most forceful reason that so many hate him.

Jünger poses the old question of a writer's relation to society, to its shifting consensus and its vested powers. If, as Graham Greene submits, the writer has a duty to be disloyal, we must determine the nature of Jünger's disloyalty. That may be as important as a determination of his supposed allegiances. Irony has shaped an essential fact about Jünger: he has admitted to being a godfather of fascism yet as a writer he has always been disdainful of political partisanship, including rightist varieties. If he speaks for the individual on behalf of aristocracy, we can afford indulgence; this century has produced few aristocrats in literature, or elsewhere. The salient feature of Jünger's aristocratic posture is a fatalism that forbids cheer at our human prospect. Dispassionate, he vexes the human need of solace. A participant and scribe of Germany's grim errancies in this century, he seems entrenched in a Stoic immobility. In the sixth chapter of this book, however, the reader will discover a Jünger who knew what guilt meant and said so.

Yearly, the chess masters arrived at his father's house, and they stayed for six weeks. They played according to tournament rules: recorded moves and clocks in stern tempo as the phalanxes of pawns and their noble overseers moved about the close-patterned world. From early morning until evening the contestants, champions and amateurs alike, hovered.

The chessboard offered no mere occasion of leisure for the elder Jünger. Far more than a pastime for this chemical engineer, so affluent that he was able to retire from his business while in his forties, chess served as an analogue to the world at large, which he knew, robustly engaged, and confidently overcame. It was a world of successive challenges, of problems that lured by hiding well their solutions. Here, a never flagging acuity of observation and calculation would be certain of reward. In a sense, this kind of chess had no losers; it could only vouchsafe the triumph of reason's advance upon apparent chaos. So, too, did the world, as it seemed.

When Ernst Jünger was born (March 29, 1895), Germany had been for over a generation one of the most advanced industrial communities of Europe. Yet, during that time the national economy had failed to grow or even to recover from a depression precipitated by a financial crash in 1873. The Social Democratic Party, blessed by the First International and threatening revolution, seemed to Bismarck all but a traitor to the Wilhelmine imperial state. There were unemployed even among the graduates of the elitist Gymnasia. Bismarck feared that these young men, clever and restive—they were known as the *Abiturproletariat*—were or would become nihilists. However, neither political rumbling nor economic stagnation had reached a crisis, in part because Bismarck, a relentless foe of the socialists, co-opted some of their program by enacting legislation for workers' health and disability insurance. He satisfied industry and agriculture by protective tariffs, and he promoted nonpartisan commercial leagues. While forestalling revolution, if not its rhetoric, he began to tame the Social Democrats themselves into a reformist party. In the fin de siècle the newly arrived petite bourgeoisie of white-collared urban employees joined the older petite bourgeoisie of shopkeepers, artisans, and small businessmen as an emergent political force which the established political parties, Conservative and Socialist, and new nationalistic pressure groups attempted to secure.

The last twenty years of Wilhelmine peace, from 1895 to 1914, were generally prosperous. The advent of new technologies on a massive scale —electrification, the wireless, automobiles—begot parvenus among the bourgeoisie and raised the expectations of workers. They, too, became consumers. This expansive, progressive world seemed reliably to vouchsafe the confidence and élan of the father.

Jünger was born in Heidelberg but grew up in and around Hanover, where the family had lived for two generations. His paternal grandfather had come to Hanover as a teacher. He had two sons, one of whom died in early maturity. The other, Ernst, shrugged off everything that did not suit him. At the municipal lyceum, renowned for its humanistic tradition, he studied Greek, excelled in physics, and was most inclined to natural sciences, especially chemistry and pharmacy. Upon graduation he served as an apothecary's assistant in Pyrmont, southwest of Hanover. When he came home after three years, he was dismayed to find that his former friends had drifted away and created new bonds of which he had no part. The experience stung him and left in him a permanent residue of mistrust and coldness.[1]

He went to work at a pharmaceutical laboratory in Munich, and considered study toward a university degree. But, finding he could not bear the subordinate position of an assistant lectureship, he returned to Hanover and set up his own laboratory in the nearby town of Schwarzenberg. He bought it with money sent by a distant relative after his wife insisted he ask for help.

The family's first home, at Schwarzenberg, had been a cloister before the Reformation. Its many deep passageways, cellars, and wells prompted the Jünger children (after Ernst came a sister and three brothers) to believe that spirits, dwarfs, and marvelous animals had lived there. Perhaps they had. Schwarzenberg, an ancient walled city, impressed upon Jünger's childhood (he lived there from 1902 to 1904) the image of an ever receding and irrecoverable past. In counterpoint to that stable but vanishing world, schooling was erratic: between his sixth and eleventh year, young Ernst was obliged to change school residence several times, as his parents moved or as poor grades required.

Schwarzenberg offered Jünger a flood of sensuous memorabilia that enforced in him a melancholic sense not of loss but of losing: "It is the feeling of being very near to the spirit of a time the reality of which has forever disappeared." Whatever of the past seems apprehensible assumes a dream image: if we attempt to grasp it, it passes. This yearning in Jünger—every child who has lost a home has some sense of it—served as a powerful companion to the exuberant urge of his adolescence to seek faraway places. It also opens a window upon his lifelong inclination to esteem the past at the expense of the present. Recalling the inhabitants of Schwarzenberg, his "ancient little town," he once wrote:

> There were no individuals such as the whirlpool of the masses pushes fleeting upon us, with faces so masked that out of many thousands not one is grafted to our memory. They were personalities, each singular, people of character, and even of the curious little barber, who ran from his shop into the street, shining razor in hand, whenever he heard a clamor, it was said that even if he hadn't a good character, even so he had a character.[2]

In 1907, Jünger's father sold his pharmacy and moved the family back toward Hanover, settling in a house on a high meadow, near Rehburg. The Jüngers' home, at Brunnenstrasse 9, overlooked the moors that border the Steinhuder Meer, the site of nearly all the wonder and danger of Jünger's early adolescence.

Young Ernst was proud of this boggy terrain. It seemed to have defeated history. Indeed, the Romans had been unable to penetrate it, and not far distant was the Teutoburg Forest, where in the year 9 C.E. the survivors of three legions of Caesar Augustus had been roasted alive in cages. When Germanicus entered that wood a generation after, he found moss-covered skulls of men and horses on the trees, a tableau of terror Jünger's pen would match in his forest by marble cliffs on the eve of Hitler's war. The moor near Rehburg was "more being than becoming, a grey and brown web of the Norns."[3] Thus hallowed in Jünger's mnemonic preserve, this land became through his writing a domain that furnished him an occult source of power, as though he had become a genie summoning childhood's lone illimitability.

The family's life was dominated by its authoritarian center. The father held forth regularly at table on various topics, usually historical or biographical. The children could have written a life of Bismarck based upon his table talk. More than forty years after he was gone, his son paid him this tribute:

> I consider what my father related at table more important than all my scholastic education: my taste for history and my judgments of value came in a sense from him. He was typical of the nineteenth century in that he appreciated great personalities, beginning with Achilles, then Alexander the Great, and going up to the conquistadores and Napoleon. . . . He never had breakfast or dinner without speaking in detail on these subjects.[4]

Despite (or because of) an evangelical Protestant upbringing, his father did not believe in eternal life; he felt that one lives on through one's children. His calculated distance from people included a talent for looking through them as though they were made of glass. Yet he was an exuberant man, and he loved to whistle and sing. His light baritone's repertoire was primarily Mozart, and it was not unusual for his children to hear Papageno on the stairs as their father descended in the morning.

This eccentric cultivated in his children a rugged independence. He prided himself on being enlightened, which meant that he proceeded in a rigorously scientific fashion to tackle any problem, scorning along the way all predecessors who might have made it easier. Jünger has suggested that his father "was in effect an anarchist. One example among a hundred: one day my grandfather took my grandmother into a café outside of town so that she couldn't make a scene, and told her, 'I have something disagreeable to tell you, Hermine. Our Ernst—my father—is married, and already has a four-year-old boy.'"[5]

To the fact that his father was an Aries in the zodiac Jünger ascribed his eager, rapacious response to something once he became interested in it. His enthusiasms were neither caprices nor dilettantisms but passions that would involve him for as long as a decade, day and night. Once mastery of the passion's subject had been attained, he tended to lose interest: when, for example, moneymaking became easy, or when driving an automobile became safe and the roads smooth. During the 1920s he became engaged in telescopics and astronomy: the house gained a new roof.

Chess, unlike money and cars, is inexhaustible, but it is also exclusive: "The force of irrational elements and ideas discomforted him," says Jünger of his father, "as did excesses, especially incalculable ones. He would take a great store of facts and extract mathematical details from them."[6] Like other pharmacists, the elder Jünger had made some experiments with morphine, but they were so unpleasant his son did not feel free to inquire about them. Transports of this sort were not to his father's liking, the effect of chemicals upon one's sensibility being, after all, unpredictable. Chess, an infinity of challenges within a narrow space, remained a passion to life's end. (Jünger never dared to play chess with his father. It would have been a totemic disaster had he ever beaten him.[7])

The family made regular outings into the woods, and would bathe in cold forest streams. These wanderings and the visits to the zoo in Hanover cultivated in young Ernst a fascination for plant and animal life that never left him. He shared this enthusiasm with only one of his brothers, Friedrich-Georg, who was also fated to share with Ernst service in war and a career in writing.

Their father encouraged the boys' interest in gathering insects (plants and stones, being inert, were less challenging but nothing was overlooked) and often at Christmas the necessary equipment for this adventure was provided with all attention to thoroughness: "net, needle, flask, a box whose bottom was lined with peat and covered with glazed paper." Ernst also carried a child's book on coleoptera, *Der Käferfreund* (The Beetle's Friend), its pictures suggesting the bait. The boy was captured before the beetle. Recalling the first of his "subtle hunts," Jünger once compared insect hunting to his father's chess playing, noting that the enticement was greater for the son because he spent as much time (or more) in the field as his father over the board. Besides, the hunter and the elusive hunted were quite other: "The partners did not exhaust themselves in pure combinations, rather an inexhaustible field of vision was open." Because the assaults of this "beetle's friend" came to success only gradually, "the little objects took on a magical glow. I never lacked time for them; the strange thing was rather that I had time for anything else."[8] Within a few weeks, the box of magic would be filled with a booty of specimens (snail shells, insects, some fossils), the nomenclature of Linnaeus would be steadily absorbed, and Ernst would have to ask his father for another box.

Jünger's boyish attraction to the teeming, furtive animal life of the moors gained impetus, perhaps inspiration, from his father's informed and precisely trained eye. He very early apprehended "the intellectual charm of zoology in the study of its prismatic deviation, which undergoes an invisible life in the unending variety of the community." And he recalled, "What enchantment I felt as a child when my father opened such a secret to me." [9] He learned, too, that exceptions not only prove the rule, they enlighten it. For Jünger this realization entailed a poetic lesson, that in every species observed, intricate figural lines are drawn which contribute to the grand arabesques of nature's mystery. The point merits emphasis. Thanks to the moors and his father, Jünger became an aesthete in his earliest years, and remained one, but he was never the cringing, hypersensitive sort usually connoted in the term. He was a perceiver of the sensible world. That is not all, but that is already much.

In the last weeks of the Second World War, when Germany lay in nearly total dissolution, Jünger mused on his childhood's longing for the natural world as a seeking out of anarchy, because then "the horrible burden, the atmospheric pressure of civilization vanished. Things became more dangerous but also more simple. Thoughts lost their embroidery. Life became more sumptuous." [10] The pathway to this luxuriant danger lay directly before the family doorstep. The house stood only a few minutes' walk from marshes where men had been known to disappear. En route lay a Jewish cemetery populated with the families of tanners and butchers (young Ernst was enthralled by the indecipherable script on the slabs) and beyond, a row of old barns where he and brother Fritz would scale ladders and lie hidden in the hay of irascible farmers.

The Steinhuder Meer flowed into the countryside west of Hanover in dark-water streams. Beyond the villages, the landscape was desolate; there were only bulrushes, marsh, pinewood, peat bogs. Uninhibited, Ernst and brother Fritz made the moor their own. Playing Adam's game in Eden, they named everything they discovered. The boys would go naked through the marsh, covering themselves with mud to keep off the summer's flies. Friedrich-Georg recalled that this sporting was exhilarated by its dangers:

It was no innocuous pastime. Often our feet would break through and we sank to our thighs in the black slime that lay under the turf. Many a shudder ran down our backs. Here we bathed, sunned ourselves, and chatted for hours. . . . We never met a soul here, for the place was so shunned that not once did the herdsmen search in it. So this midland, half secure, half flowing, was left to us alone, and we crossed it on a hundred paths which were known only to us.[11]

While the flora and fauna of the Steinhuder Meer initiated Ernst into his father's world of adventurously pursued precision, an adventure at home furnished him no less abundantly and exclusively. This was literature. It armed him, so he later reckoned, against what he regarded as life's greatest danger, ordinariness. Sherlock Holmes, "the thin nervous hero with the short pipe between his teeth," the Count of Monte Cristo, "this friend of cottages and enemy of palaces," Karl May's Old Shatterhand, Captain Morgan, who carried a death's head on a black pennant— "all these adventurers, fairy tale princes, sea pirates, and magnanimous criminals, I don't complain that they have passed on but I would wish that they might find with every new orbit that life affords us successors on whom the whole sum of love and belief dedicated to them might be carried on."[12]

The devotion to literature Ernst owed to his mother, Karoline. Her family's name was Lampl, from Westphalia. In her youth she had become a free spirit. Because as a child she had been forced to attend church, she revolted. She read Ibsen (once met him) and socialist literature. She was delighted when a suffragette assaulted a masterwork in the British Museum, and the incident in which Lady Pankhurst was borne under police constraint through a London street (as known through the famous photograph) offered more delight.

She read Goethe and Schiller passionately, and made annual pilgrimages to Weimar, at times taking her children with her. One of Ernst's fondest childhood memories came from Goethe's enormous home and his *Gartenhaus* which sits splendid and solitary across the river. Before the Jünger children were able to read, their mother read to them, in a high voice. When delivering Schiller's ballad "Das Lied von der Glocke" (The Song of the Clock), she would break down at the lines telling of the dear mother carried off by the black prince of shadows from her spouse's arms and those of her tender babes. We are left to speculate on what manner of anxieties this histrionic performance and its inspirational text caused the young listeners.

It may be too easy to oppose to the rigorously scientific and rational father the image of an irrational mother brooding over belles lettres. In his memoirs, Friedrich-Georg tells an illuminating story of how his father acquired the pharmacy at Schwarzenberg:

> He didn't have the amount of money needed for the purchase, and he saw no way of getting it. He was firmly convinced that no one on earth would advance it to him. My mother, once involved in this matter, reminded him that an older well-off relative might help. Although he considered it unthinkable, she wrote to the woman and immediately received a willing and friendly assurance of help. To my father's great astonishment, everything went smoothly: a letter sufficed, the money came, and the business was bought. My mother told this story many times, and took it as proof that nothing is difficult if we don't make it so, and that difficulties lie in the views we import into things.[13]

This mother was doing something more: she was asserting again and again her central role in starting her husband's successful career, and she was instructing her children in her variety of willfulness. A one-time free spirit submerged in domesticity—the familiar story tells itself.

Jünger credited to her not only a love of literature that he made his own, but also the ability to speak "a remarkable German."

> It is always important, no matter to what country one may belong, to have parents who speak their language well. Language is virtually the most precious good which parents can leave their children. However far the spirit of egalitarianism may go, on the first words someone utters you know whom you are dealing with. And when one has a literary culture, with the mention of two or three writers, it's clear whether a dialogue is worth pursuing and may be fecund.[14]

Jünger's aristocracy of the tongue may be bookish but it was born of a household where youthful will was tempered only by refined solicitudes. He owed his parents richly.

He paid them tribute in a scholastic essay he wrote in 1913. The subject for exposition was Goethe's idyllic poem *Hermann und Dorothea,* which is also an epic on the coming of the French Revolutionary war to a peaceful Rhine Valley community:

> Above all, I like the characterization of Hermann, the innkeeper's son. He has inherited the good qualities of his parents, on whom he hangs with childlike love. He's the very image of the noble German youth who unites within himself courageous power and physical beauty with inwardness of mind and refinement of soul. With tender piety he honors his parents' viewpoints and habits. . . . We see that here Goethe has portrayed an ideal household. May every family be blessed with such delightful and spiritual qualities as those of the valiant innkeeper.[15]

Pious, perhaps—this deference is what a schoolmaster would have expected a good pupil to show—but not cloying. One senses that Jünger wrote sincerely because he had in his own home life the "delightful and spiritual qualities" he praised in Hermann's. From his father he had gained acuity of vision and the will to assert it; from his mother, the inspiration of language and its artful impress. Science and magic: Jünger's struggle into manhood, his creation of himself, was to be primarily the art of keeping these qualities in tandem and equipoise.

The Jünger home, like most in the German upper middle class, was blessed with the toy accoutrements of domestic technology: it had a sciopticon (also known as a stereopticon or stereoscope) and a kaleidoscope. These magic lanterns were not wasted on Jünger's eye, and he would later attribute to them a revelatory and redemptive power, but the magic that mattered most to his childhood lay within books. Even if we did not have his not infrequent homage to their effect within his mature writings, it would be impossible to overestimate the sway that books exerted upon his sensibility, his imagination, and his will. Some attempt to retrieve, however refractorily, the open sesame of the child's realm of literature from an age innocent of radio and television affords one avenue—one so important Jünger himself has shown us its direction—to some understanding of a man who has been esteemed and hated for mostly wrong reasons.

His childhood was suffused with heroic literary fantasies, but none was so compelling to him as the exotic tales of Arabia, *A Thousand and One Nights,* which he discovered in his ninth year.[16] Favorite among these stories were two. "The Story of the City of Brass," "for whose magic my father early sharpened my eyes," relates the desert search of Emir-Musa for fabled bottles of brass in which spirits had been imprisoned. In the course of his treasure hunt, the emir comes upon a succession of inscriptions warning that every great culture of the past, no matter how splendid, how glorious, was overtaken by death. The emir manages to find a city in the desert that is indeed a necropolis: corpses there are bedecked and surrounded with inestimable gems; chambers are fantastically appointed with precious metals and brilliant embroideries. He is careful not to despoil this place of all its treasure, but he delivers to his master, Prince of the Islamic faithful, the brass bottles. The spirits released from them demand repentance. The Prince observes to the emir, "Would that I had been with you to behold what you beheld."[17]

It remains uncertain whether he had learned the lesson, but Jünger had. "Emir Musa is a profound mind. He is a connoisseur of the melancholy of ruins, of the bitter pride preceding downfall, as he presents to us the heart of archaeological endeavor and becomes there more pure, contemplative, and sensitive."[18] This story fed Jünger's youthful Wanderlust, but, more important, it early informed with its oriental fatalism his antinomian heritage in Protestantism. Both of these spiritualities set the lone soul before an awesome, immitigable fate. The story of Emir Musa was to cast its prophetic force across Jünger's own life.

His other favorite story from Scheherazade concerns a sultan's three sons in love with their beautiful cousin. Their father dispatches them on a year's journey to find the most extraordinary item they can. The eldest finds a magic carpet; the second, an ivory tile in which one can observe anybody one wishes. The youngest, Prince Ahmad, acquires a magical fruit that can cure all diseases. When the brothers meet, the tile shows their far-off cousin lying near death. The brothers fly to her on the carpet, and Ahmad gives her the fruit. The sultan then sets another simpler contest: whoever shoots the farthest arrow shall win the bride. Ahmad's overshoots the others' but disappears, so the bride is awarded to the second brother. Ahmad searches for his arrow along a rock cliff, finds it, and is led into a sumptuous grotto, home of Pari-Banou. It was she, disguised as a vendor, who had provided the carpet, tile, and fruit to the brothers. Learning of her love for him, Ahmad consents to marry this spirit, who is immeasurably more beautiful than his cousin. They live blissfully together amid Pari-Banou's subterranean riches, but Ahmad fears that the sultan is grieving for his absence. Besides, his hidden marriage and residence inspire intriguers at court. They prompt the sultan to learn of Pari-Banou and to test her powers as a *jinn*. Of course she meets every test handily but finally calls upon her fearsome brother (he is eighteen inches tall and sports a thirty-foot beard), who kills all the intriguers—even the sultan!—and sets up Ahmad and Pari-Banou as rulers of all India.

Jünger found in this story "the model of the exalted love-adventure, for the sake of which inherited power is gladly renounced. It is beautiful how the young prince in this kingdom disappears as into a more spiritual world." Also celebrated is the contest of the bow, "which is a life symbol assuming with Prince Ahmad a metaphysical tension. His arrow flies forth incomparably into the unknown, above and beyond the others." Pari-Banou's castle is, in Jünger's view, a spiritual Venusberg: "The invisible flame bestows, the visible consumes." [19]

These words come from Jünger's maturity. No ten year old would likely recognize Ahmad and Musa as "princes of the old Indo-Germanic realms," nor impose upon the story of Pari-Banou an apparatus of metaphysical symbols. Yet, given the anxieties that beset Jünger's childhood (derived only in part from school), we might assume that Ahmad's story served as a talisman in those green, uncertain years. Ahmad enjoys not only a comforting withdrawal into the womblike grotto, not only the fairy's unconditional love: he wins release from paternally high expectations of him—the predicate of Jünger's own unease and loneliness. It would be some years before he realized that his own Pari-Banou was the muse guiding his pen. With her he was destined to live comfortably, richly, and long.

Upon the sensitive first child the contrast between the two exotic tales must have left a profound impress. The dark destiny in the emir's story, the threat of futility which indwells all endeavor and achievement, above all the masculinity of this tale (there are no women) and the telltale fact that Jünger's father, otherwise the insistent rationalist and problem solver, introduced it to him—all of this speaks eloquently. Over and dramatically against this story is Pari-Banou, who comes to the rescue of a youth, secures him from the totem of male authority (sultan and court), and provides him with the undying love of which only a mother is capable.

These stories offer in a refractory light the domestic tensions, the family dramaturgy, which Jünger had to confront and reconcile within himself: the punitive, menacing figure of fatherly authority in the guise of Fate and the salvific figure of feminine envelopment. That Jünger as a child was aware of the totemic politics of fathers and sons is dubious; the same may be said of his awareness of incest, even though in maturity he argued that its force is universal and exclusive.[20]

Of particular value in childhood were two books by military veterans which only such as they could have written. Both provided in "their thoroughly warlike works" a wondrous feeling of adventure, "a decisive lesson in the form of a great and singular pleasure."[21] Jünger refers to Grimmelshausen's narrative set during the Thirty Years' War, *Der abenteuerliche Simplicissimus* (The Adventures of Simplicissimus), and to *Don Quixote*.

Simplicissimus, a work that every German schoolchild knows (or once knew), traverses a series of picaresque episodes and arrives at a surreal vision of divine justice. Like the *Aeneid,* it is both adventure and theodicy, and it passes in one sentence the definitive condemnation of martial glory: "The splendid deeds of the heroic would be glorious to celebrate if they hadn't been achieved by other men's ruin and loss."[22] The polymathic hero, rather like Jünger, never settles down to anything but writing.

Cervantes's most unwarlike book is almost primarily a book about books. "The Knight of the Lions" takes his inspiration from a vast library of chivalric fantasies. Jünger first read Cervantes when he was ten "and with a truly Spanish seriousness." It did not seem madness to him when Quixote, in the dreamt battle with a giant, assaulted wineskins with a dagger. Reading "straight," "I was proud of my Lord of La Mancha every time he drew sword from scabbard or couched his lance."[23] Jünger was charmed that Quixote was an old man, nearly fifty. "At that time I believed one had to be old to comprehend such great and worthy deeds, and today (at 30) I know that old fools are the best."[24]

Cervantes tells us that Quixote's friends "one moment thought him a man of sense, and the next he slipped into craziness; nor could they decide what degree to assign him between wisdom and folly."[25] The quixotic optics dissolving the boundary between reality and fantasy persisted into Jünger's adulthood. It informs his psychology throughout, as when he regards animals as though they were human and sees people as particular animals, or bids us consider life one dream among thousands and every dream as a special elucidation of reality.[26] Of the avenues to understanding Jünger's character, the most engaging and most hazardous puts us in the company he treasured, with Aladdin and the Don.

Whatever the pull of the Eastern tales and knightly fictions, Jünger did not confine his juvenile enthusiasm to them. One of his favorite German

authors in youth deserves notice on two counts: Hermann Löns characterized wistfully, sometimes lyrically, the medieval Germany which Jünger already at Schwarzenberg had learned to lament, and he wrote with
a naturalist's keen eye about the Saxon landscape. Löns had grown up in
Lower Saxony. His best-known work, *Der Wehrwolf* (The Werewolf, 1910),
he wrote in the dialect of its Lüneberger Heide, the wild expanse south of
Hamburg. That historical novel of peasant resistance to marauders during
the Thirty Years' War does not rise much above an adolescent indulgence
of violence and sentimentality—no match for Grimmelshausen's lively
and contemporaneous account of the same war. But this work's appeal
lay partly (and may still) in the nostalgia it provided for the rustic life of
rugged simple virtues that urbanization and modern industry had forever
displaced. A journalist in Hanover when Jünger was growing up in its
neighborhoods, Löns was an accomplished satirist of city life but felt at
home only in the open air, and his best writing describes the Lüneberger
landscape with inspired, exquisite attention. It was this writing—especially *Mein braunes Buch* (My Brown Book, 1907)—that Jünger treasured.
As a writer, Löns can fairly be called the mentor of Jünger's youth.

In his journal of wanderings, Löns shows a descriptive power of almost
photographic acuity. The heath, to whose rhythms of fruition and decay
he shows himself minutely sensitive, assumes a personality. One might say
it is Löns's Pari-Banou. Commingled with the naturalist's logs are some
pieces of folkish propaganda, most remarkably one called "Teufelswerk"
("The Devil's Doing"). The devil, outraged by the heath's harmony and
peace, plots to destroy it: disguised as a land developer he has the heath
opened to industry. Within a year monstrous black towers have filled the
landscape with noise and smoke. The peasant family, forced to the city,
becomes thoroughly degenerate. In another condemnation of the urban
age, "Das stumme Dorf" ("The Silent Village"), the peasants' dwelling
has lost the vitality of its primeval spirits, who in simpler (preindustrial)
days blessed the land with laughter and its seed with fruit. Löns finds
no remedy for the present, but his despair speaks poignantly for many.
A generation after his death his work was enlisted to serve the cheerless
nostalgia of National Socialism.[27]

Of *Mein braunes Buch* Jünger has written:

> If you read a book like this, you feel for the first time what bind-
> ing power the soil possesses. . . . If I were asked who Löns was, it

would be hard for me to answer. Beneath a simplicity that creates the same effect as water, to which one comes after all other drinks, deeper complexities are concealed which found expression in the destiny of his life as well as in many of his books. But the essential thing in him is his German core, and this finally allowed him to triumph over the troubles of his time and of his own life.[28]

The personal troubles included two failed marriages and a nervous breakdown when Löns was forty-five. His "destiny" came near Rheims in September 1914: he was shot during a night patrol. Well beyond the age of most volunteers, at forty-seven he had found in the Great War an idealized conduit for his nationalism and the perfect escape from a tepid, aimless life.

Löns had shown the way for a national art by rooting his work in the land he knew and loved. That bond, according to Jünger, exalts Löns above admittedly superior stylists: "He knows what we should never forget, that Germany's power lies in its peoples (Stämme), and from that he attempts to penetrate his own, the Lower Saxon, and to pursue its relations to saga, history, and landscape into the finest details."[29] But, contrary to Jünger's asseverations, it is not the people of Lower Saxony who matter most to Löns; it is the primeval solitudes of their boggy landscapes, where, in Jünger's own characterization, one finds "a confusion of sounds, an unfolding of movement, color, and fragrance, a millionfold will to live, a gay flame that dances over the earth . . . so that to press one's body between flowers and grass seems a heathen pleasure, a pantheistic intoxication, the feel of which perhaps only the American Walt Whitman knows how to convey in words."[30]

Löns was also an avid hunter. He wrote of a terrain over which his eye was often keen for prey. Of the moments after sunset in the wood, for example, he says, "Nothing brings us so near to nature as this quarter hour between day and night, and only hunting teaches us to understand this short span in its great solemnity and its secretive devotion."[31] These words seem perilously close to mummery, but Jünger from his postwar vantage could rationalize Löns's murderous sport into a sacrifice to some deity of manhood, that the prey, dead, "becomes a symbol through which we are bound to the primitive passions from which everything proceeds."[32] Jünger accepts as wholly natural that Löns in his death was the hunter hunted down. This end, he submits, Löns himself would have found worthy.

Löns's career complements the conjunction of Jünger's youth, his "subtle hunts" for coleoptera on the moors, and his maturity, when he learned to hunt men. Foremost, however, remains Jünger's primary experience in childhood of Löns as a writer. If the *Thousand and One Nights* released him into the delicious holds of fantasy, Löns taught him how to articulate his youthful grasp of the immediate and tactile world, which admits its own fantasies to the attentive eye.

Jünger, aged ten, used to walk to school burdened with a brooding sense of abandonment. "I was tormented with the thought of what would happen to me if my mother were to die, and then also the feeling that I was so different from what was expected of me."[33] This so-called separation anxiety (as in Schiller's ballad) is a horror common to countless children, perhaps to first sons foremostly. Jünger was no exception. What did make him exceptional was his recourse to his mother's example. He learned from her the invaluable lessons of autodidacticism, that in the final reckoning one cultivates within oneself what one truly cares for. Because he was already in his very green years developing what would become his lifelong passions, his excursions into literature and biology, he was armored against the dictates of schoolmasters.

Like many intelligent children, he balked at the scholastic regimen, but passively: he was inclined to dream. Teachers' reports charged him with inattention, which he admits: "I had contrived a kind of distant indifference which allowed me to be bound to reality only by an invisible thread, like that of a spider."[34] With a father who could render other people invisible, Jünger must have developed his own knack rather easily. This revolt serves as the initial biographical sign of Jünger's aristocratic temper, a kind of casualness he would cultivate throughout his life. One might presume it came from his mother, but it complements Jünger's stringent diction and his insistence upon elevated discourse—the certain legacy of his exacting father. That Jünger survived the lockstep austerities of a Prussian education without succumbing to them is yet another tribute to the bonds and thrusts of his home life. His ease of assurance had its budding grove there. School was incarceration.

In the late Wilhelmine years, Germany's school system was reputed to be the most efficient in Europe. It was also "Prussian": hierarchic, conservative, authoritarian. Schools, from the first levels through the collegiate, marched in tandem with the Kaiser's nationalistic dicta: education, whatever the discipline, was supposed to include fear of God (Wotan), love of country (the Kaiser), and the confounding of socialism (whatever threatened Wotan and the Kaiser). It was not so much the militarization of academic disciplines, but school life itself, the heavy curriculum and even the building that proved the deadweights upon students' minds and bodies. Schools were notoriously ill-ventilated. In midyear (the German school year ran from Easter to Easter) the rooms would become so stifling by early afternoon that students would have to be dismissed. Lighting was poor, too, and contributed to an almost pervasive near-sightedness among upper-school students. The ocular crisis became so acute that even the Kaiser complained of it when calling for soldiers.[35]

Jünger claims he was aware of the schoolroom's horror before he was enrolled. As the eldest child he lacked reliable reconnaissance, and his only recourse was to image school as a very disagreeable place: "Apparently, my parents, or the maid, or someone else had threatened me, 'Just wait a while, you'll see when you get to school!' and I figured school was an invention." But then he saw older children passing along the street carrying their satchels. He no sooner conceded that perhaps there was such a thing as school than he concluded that, no, his parents had staged the children's walk just to make him believe there was a school. "It was my first philosophical reflection!"[36] He first attended school in Hanover, at Lyceum II in the Goethestrasse, where his paternal grandfather was teaching natural history. But his parents' moves and his poor marks forced a number of changes of venue. From 1905 to 1907 he went to private boarding schools, first in Hanover, then in Braunschweig: "Those people had rather harsh ways. They did not spare blows; and the students who found themselves there were either too bestial or too lazy."[37]

For four years (1907–1911) after the family settled in Rehburg, he regularly took a train along the shores of the Steinhuder Meer to Wunstorf and the Scharnhorst-Realschule. (The old building is still there but is no longer used as a school.) In 1912 he took the examination required of all male students who wished to serve as one-year volunteers in the army. The certificate on passing would have enabled him to leave school two years in advance of final graduation, but Jünger, despite his desultory performance and still under his father's expectant eye, went to a Reformschule in Hameln. It was there he wrote of "Hermann und Dorothea," and there that his German teacher evaluated the initial efforts of one of German literature's most fastidious masters. Jünger's work, his parents learned, was showing "an affected and pretentious way of expression which, carried further, would pose a considerable danger to his style." He was warned, "Therefore observe moderation in verbal adornment! B (noch gut)."[38] Was Jünger's pretentious diction a mere adolescent self-indulgence, or was it an attempt through rhetoric to approach the magical world of extravagant action in which he as reader had immersed himself? Lonely and incorrigible, he joined a rower's club, a haven for rowdy youths, but he had no taste for the teamwork of oars. He preferred the solitary work of a kayak on the Weser River and idling at the boathouse.

Whatever his apprehensions, Jünger's youth seems to have been abundantly normal, if a norm can still be taken from "wanderings through forest and field, where a secret is hidden behind every tree and every hedge; the wild, romping play in the dim corners of town; the glow of friendship, and reverence for ideals." Adolescence proved no less vigorous. Jünger compares youth's inchoate awareness of its potential to a landscape one senses through a mist, with bright mountain peaks shining in morning sun. Of his generation he has claimed: "Much awaited us, and everyone was worried about coming too late, because marvel perpetually called out and enticed us like the dilated cry, shrill and bold, of a predatory bird, resounding over the solitude of great forests."[39]

Although in adolescence Jünger and his schoolmates passed from their callings as sea pirates, trappers, and hunters toward the more lofty professions of bank director, general, professor, and minister, they were still pledged to freedom. His was a generation of the earnest and dedicated, not from any intention or habit but "from the immediate propulsion of the heart that seeks to hang on to something and longs for great words."[40] It was a generation predisposed to the romantic intoxicants of myth, of fulfillment in belief itself. Young men before 1914 felt all possibilities were open to them, many beckoning from afar.

Such cloud-free idealism carried many youths into the Wandervögel, a kind of boy scout movement that delivered the young from the oppressive monotony of their urban lives. The Wandervögel have sometimes been condemned in caricature as predecessors of the Hitler Jugend. Scions of an age when anti-Semitism was coming into the open, they occasionally rejected Jewish applicants, but they were more drawn to the amorphous enthusiasms of youth than to the dreary racism of their elders. They were fueled mostly by the urge to get away:

> By that time the teachers partly tolerated, partly favored the Wandervögel; each high school had a troop. The ideals were blurry, deter-

mined more by feeling than by fact, and without academic, military, or political intent. "To be on the way," to wander romantically, cook out, sit by the campfire, sing, pitch tents, or pass the night in barns—a good deal was gained by all that, yet still more was sloughed off.[41]

In July 1911 Jünger and his brother Fritz joined a troop centered at Wunstorf. With some twelve members and two youthful guides—Werner (the inspiring "born" leader) and Robby (petulant and fussy)—the Wunstorf pack in the month the Jüngers enrolled sponsored two two-week trips, one through the Weser-Wena province, from Hameln to Eisenach and back, another through the moorland, from Hanover to Hamburg. On one outing the troop stopped at the Porta Westfalica and greeted the Kaiser's statue, then went on to a brewery where they were given a tour lecture, followed by continuous rounds of beer and cigars. Having passed a bibulous afternoon with songs as payment to their host, they resumed the woodland way but found it difficult to secure lodgings. A barn would have sufficed but the only one in sight proved inhospitable (an angry dog), so Werner decided to make a night's walk. "Marching it should be called, because it was strenuous. In the early morning hours, as it was just becoming gray, I learned to recognize the visions one might call the magic of exhaustion: the dreams of endless roads, the hallucination of the night watch."[42]

The Wandervögel itineraries through woods and mountain paths could not finally satisfy Jünger's need to roam, because they were bounded by roads and towns and because they were collective, organized efforts. Yet to their exhilarations he owed his first appearance in print: five months after he joined, he contributed a poem, "Our Life," to the journal of Lower Saxony's Wandervögel, *Hannoverland*. Its sixteen lines celebrate straightforwardly the hikes, campfires, and songs as, to paraphrase the final verse, a cornucopia that makes daily living bearable and adorns through memory the course of one's life.

In the following year, as a lower-school graduate (*Einjähriger*), Jünger went through the eternal curriculum of youth: visits to taverns, drinking contests, and revelry in the streets as late as eleven o'clock. School regulations did include a curfew; time for playing the bohemian or dandy was all but chaperoned.

Some of Jünger's most vivid memories of his youth are private and sensuous, as when in early summer's heat the foliage had not completely lost its light green, the sky was cloud-free, and the fragrance of mountain meadows reached to the town. Another pleasure awaited him as the season progressed: "The Gymnasium often closed its doors by eleven o'clock [in the morning], and the festive sense of joy in turning one's back on the two-winged, very solemn building of yellow tile at such a time was all the greater when it was the mathematics class that had been sacrificed to the heat." The next morning, on waking, he realized everything was transformed—room, walls, furniture—and that "life emerged from its own emptiness, streaming out upon the smallest details."[43] By sixteen he had overcome childhood's insular delights and that awkward time of torturous disparity between self and the world.

Jünger's youth was peculiarly informed by two spectacular events. First of these was the passing of Halley's Comet in May 1910. One night, his father gathered the five children and told them while they were observing that perhaps Wolfgang (the youngest) would live to see it once again. This positivist's calculation for the comet's next appearance, seventy-six years later, went amiss. Of the five children, Wolfgang was the first to die, and the others followed in a sequence inverse to their births. Only Ernst lived to see Halley come again, in 1986, over Kuala Lampur.

More momentous was an event that profoundly influenced Jünger's "prognostic," as he calls it, of technology in the twentieth century: the sinking of the luxury liner *Titanic* after it was struck by an iceberg, in April 1912. This "convergence of the twain," a manifestation of indomitable nature in which we seek to find some volition or intent, and of the hubristic impulses at work within mechanized culture, Jünger came to understand as a prophetic emblem of our modern fate, set on its irreversible course. The very name of Titan says enough, and in Jünger's metaphysical magnum opus, *Der Arbeiter,* which appeared twenty years later, the eponymous hero in the world's workshop is laboring to achieve a higher and quite impersonal order but to no foreseeable end. Negatively construed, this titanism is a blind and pointless assault upon the Olympus of nature itself. Positively, it is the effect of humankind forced to look to its own resources after Nietzsche's subversion of civilization and its ethos of progress. That grappling with the elemental power of nature Max Beckmann captured in his painting (itself gigantic) of the *Titanic*'s survivors struggling amid the lifeboats, a twentieth-century *Raft of the Medusa.* The human will fashioning cataclysm for itself and enduring it, disaster and triumph in disaster: such was the *Titanic*'s cautionary tale, a cosmic morality play, that Jünger absorbed in his adolescence.

Neither marshlands nor Arabia's literature could satisfy Jünger's longing for autonomy. Neither could the Wandervögel, even if, in one critic's words, their recidivist cult of nature proclaimed "impetuous reaction against an unjust, inefficient, and hypocritical social order and an unnatural form of living." [44] Jünger was hardly immune to the idealistic suasions of his generation, but he was resolutely set upon going his own way. A revolt against his father's world was inevitable, since his father himself had been a model rebel and surely, if not altogether deliberately, instilled rebellion in his first-born son.

Learning about Africa gave Jünger his cue. "I had read a lot of books about travels in this realm, Stanley, *The Dark Continent,* works of that sort. I represented this land to myself as very beautiful; it had to be always very hot there, and then there were the animals, the primitive life." [45] Henry Stanley did not, however, imbue this young German reader with the uplifting urges of British colonialism. Jünger in fact read around Stanley's decrying of the Muslims' slave trade, and once admitted some preference of the overlords to those they exploited.

As warmth was to Jünger "the very element of life, the bearer of a peculiarly palpable fullness which like grace gives itself effortlessly," so Africa became in his youthful apprehension a kind of intensification of life impulses. It was also the ground he chose to satisfy his adolescent need of self-testing. He found a makeshift passage in his parents' greenhouse, where during long summer hours free of school he would withdraw at midday, "and many times when the glowing air trembled over the glass roof, I thought with a strange pleasure that it probably couldn't be much hotter even in Africa. It had to be somewhat hotter there in any case because what was nearly unbearable and not yet experienced was indeed enticing. Africa was for me the epitome of the wild and aboriginal, the only possible place for a life according to the plan by which I intended to live." [46]

Jünger, at least in reminiscence, was not content to have found a mere release from the unspeakably ordinary and predictable. He wanted a wilderness that insured menace, if not death. He delighted to read of the sleeping sickness which befell intruders to Africa's coast, but pictures of railroad construction or newspaper accounts of progress against the tsetse fly annoyed him.⁴⁷ Such presumed conquests of nature were the patent of that confident rationalism in his father which he needed to escape. His protest he aimed, however, not at the patriarch but at the technology that threatened to level all the distinctions he believed natural. Africa should be left in peace, if only so that somewhere on earth one could move freely "without stumbling upon a stone barracks or a prohibition sign."⁴⁸

Whatever the thrill in reading Stanley's topographical descriptions or his lists of flora and fauna on the plain of the Luwamberri, Jünger disliked the Welshman's apparent condescension to this subject, that he was bringing light to darkness. Tracing the sources of fabled rivers, mapping the landscape, these were vexing signs of "American-European energy":

> It was no accident that this man was a reporter: his dispatches do not rise above a dry mediocrity, and the foul smell of the record-book was traceable in them everywhere. The secret of the landscape, the soul of the wild man, the reality of animals in their uniqueness and diversity, yes even the feeling of his own heart which was at war with a hostile and puzzling world—of all this his conception affords scarcely a trace.⁴⁹

The foil to this prosaic mentality Jünger found in the splendid ethnographies of Herodotus, but even within Stanley's account he could find inspiration, precisely where Stanley might have feared to provoke the reader's disdain, in those encounters with the Arab slaveowners. In fact, Stanley's estimate of the Arabs he met in Zanzibar and the interior is temperate and judicious, but for Jünger these men were the worthy descendants of Sinbad; they were fully entitled "to burn villages, chase down slaves, and send heads rolling in the sand." He dismisses Western objections to them, "pronounced in the loathsome tone of puritans," as hypocritical, since enslavement of whites in the factories of modern industry is "a thousand times more devilish or, worse, a thousand times more tedious."⁵⁰

Africa was both an occasion for Jünger's need of independence and a place he presumed to find agreeable to his sensibility. It was an emblem of "the magnificent anarchy of life which even in its wild manifestation fulfills a profound and tragic order, and toward which every young person feels drawn at some time."⁵¹ He had already arrived in Africa in his mind, and perhaps already too there was inchoately formed within his youthful awareness the intimation that order lies fundamentally beyond anything that can be set or controlled, in the incalculable world of dreams, the inimitable vitality of insects, the so-called primitive world of Stanley's "savages" with their "superlatively hideous gestures." [52]

Had Jünger not been resident in a boarding school in Hameln but closer to home, he might not have been so audacious as to plot a permanent truancy. In Hameln's lending library he found the adventure stories of Karl May. The woodcuts in thrillers like *Captain Nobody* and *A Chase around the Globe* fired him. "The librarian in Hameln didn't put them on her list; she pressed them surreptitiously into my hand. Undoubtedly they had a lot to do with my entering the Foreign Legion." [53] In the fall of 1913, less than six months before he was to face his qualifying examinations for graduation, he bolted. The account of his departure from home and school, from Germany and from Europe, he wrote over twenty years after the fact, when he was an "internal emigrant" of the Third Reich. By then well established as a memoirist of the Great War, and displaced as a polemicist of late Weimar, he was free to return to the childhood he had mused upon in his first volume known as *Das abenteuerliche Herz* (The Adventurous Heart), which appeared in 1929. He veils his story with the fiction of a persona, Herbert Berger, and so gives himself the reins of fantasy to embellish an already exceptional venture. It would be impossible and pointless, not to say captious, to try to determine in all particulars the correspondence between what Jünger lived out in that autumn of 1913 and what he fashioned (from the journal he was keeping at the time) into a charming narrative of adolescent rites of passage. From the most renowned of all autobiographies since Augustine's he could have taken warrant for putting *Dichtung* before *Wahrheit,* fiction before truth. However, a substantial portion of the truth is there and deserves a place within this early chronology.[54]

With money for school fees he bought himself a six-shot revolver, a volume of Stanley, and a railroad ticket to Verdun. In leaving his parents no word about his departure, itinerary, or destination he was setting his rationally enterprising father the challenge of a catch-me-if-you-can. At Verdun he enlisted in the French Foreign Legion. He had no intention of going off to some distant war; service in the Legion simply guaranteed that he would be posted to North Africa. However, in his fictionalized memoir, *Afrikanische Spiele* (African Games), he has Berger naively speak of going on the warpath (*Kriegspfad*) and rationalize the diversion of school money as a contribution from the enemy. Assuming the Nietzschean posturing of his generation, this adventurer proclaims, "In war, as you know of course, everything is permitted." [55]

Berger's motivation for leaving home is identical to Jünger's: school meant tedium. He was so listless that the instructor tried to punish him by pretending that he was not there, but this contrived distancing merely ratified Berger's self-seclusion in fantasy. Oddly, in contrast to the memoirs of *Das abenteuerliche Herz,* where the parents have some profile, in *Afrikanische Spiele* their virtual absence from the narrative makes the reader wonder at how feeble the bonds of affection might have been. When Jünger departed home, he was leaving not only the "royal expectations" of professional training in succession to his father. He was also abandoning what he likes to call the "muse's culture," the refined nurturing from his mother. It is a small, plain irony that the fruit of this desertion was, finally, a book.

In Verdun he trashed what little money he had so that he would not be able to return home. When he asked for directions to the Foreign Legion's recruiting offices, a policeman remonstrated with him not to join a society of miscreants and ne'er-do-wells, but Jünger joined anyway. He fibbed about his age, adding two years to his eighteen. Immediately he fell in with a youthful underworld of confidence tricksters, brutes, and shiftless subliterates, the detritus of the life he so wanted to escape. Drinking freely (wine and absinthe), dodging blows, and remaining open to every next experience, he arrived in Marseille. He met a military doctor, a middle-aged melancholic with considerable literary sophistication, who gave him his second cautionary lecture, one more shrewdly to the point than the gendarme's at Verdun: "You're at the age when the reality of books is overestimated. There's a wonderful geography there but, believe me, flights of this sort are best undertaken when you're lying comfortably in a chair, smoking Turkish cigarettes." The diseases Africa offers are not the stuff of adventure, he warned. The central admonition came at the end:

> You're still too young to know that you live in a world one cannot escape. You want to discover extraordinary things there but you'll find nothing but a deadly boredom. Today there's nothing but exploitation, and the person who has special inclinations is only conceiving of special kinds of exploitation. It is the particular shape, the great theme of our century, exploitation, and anyone with other ideas falls into it most easily and cheaply. The colonies are Europe, too, little

European provinces where one does business a bit more openly and unreflectingly. You won't get through the wall on which Rimbaud was wrecked. So go back to your books, and quickly, tomorrow![56]

This caveat, from a writer by then self-secluded within the Third Reich, succeeded no better than the earlier warning, but both serve in this work to break into the illusion-filled world Jünger was drifting through in 1913. He has called his recollection "a final sentimental journey," but it is more aptly a picaresque fiction, a vividly episodic account of a life cast low, become marginal and flirtatious with crime. It parodies the youthful adventure by continually dissolving its dream into the coarse reality for which the benevolent doctor makes apology. Jünger remembered his Cervantes.

When he debarked on the North African coast he found the port city, Oran, no different from any in Europe. Confined within Legion quarters, he dreamt of leaping its walls by night and setting off along the coast where there was some promise of meeting deadly snakes, but he overslept and had to face the garish light of day and, worst of all, a transfer to an inland post by railroad. Even his expectation that he and his newly met companions from Marseille would be lodged in tents was dashed: another barracks. The good doctor's cautions were all too well confirmed:

> I was inclined to regard life above every particular of its circumstances as a journey that you could interrupt at any point where it took your fancy. There seemed to me no sufficient reason at hand for staying on in some oppressive or discomforting situation when the world was so great and resourceful. But I didn't know that such a simple thought as this is so hard to realize. Things obtrude about which you never read in books: apprehension, exhaustion, or even the heart that pounds in your throat.[57]

Fortunately, Jünger holds such confessional passages to a shrewd minimum, and employs his persona, Berger, as a character witness among the rowdies who confer upon the tedious barracks world its rude vitality.[58] The fire-eater who demonstrates his immunity to pain by grinding glass under his hand; the tobacco addict who falls asleep in the midst of a suicide attempt; the ex-waiter who instructs his bunkmates in the thievish arts; the dolt whose face is so puffed from fisticuffs "that one might almost speak with Lamarck of an acquired characteristic that had become physiognomic"[59]—from such delightful fellows, the zanies of despair, Jünger learned to read his own vague and pointless seeking: "As a novel properly starts off where it usually ends, so too there's a dramatic point of resolution in another, rather dismal realm, one where hopelessness reigns, a realm of prisons, rubbish heaps, and slow ruin. In this zone one no longer performs the movements of the fighter but those of the intoxicated." [60]

However much or little this reflection weighed upon Jünger in 1913— it is also about Germany in 1936—he continued to plot his own release from the Legion's confines. Two routes lay open: the railroad back to Oran or the wasteland west to Morocco. Hearing that to the west lived peoples who cut the throat of any foreigner they met, he resolved to go west. Getting free of the Legion barracks was no problem. Staying free was a task propelled by reconnaissance Jünger had gathered from deserters; he was dismayed that they were all former deserters, returned as by some ineluctable rite to quarters. He likens them to the ten men in *A Thousand and One Nights* who to gain the key to a certain room must each submit to an adventure resulting in the loss of one eye. Each adventure involves its own intricacies but all ten end in this calamity. Thus, for all their several motives, plots, and itineraries, the deserters ended alike in the barracks' prison.

At last good fortune gave him a hand, or seemed to, in posing an unexpected challenge: he received a letter from his father. The Marseille doctor, having failed to convince Jünger to abandon his blind enthusiasm for the unknown, had contacted his parents through the Foreign Office in Berlin. Jünger's father, having spent three days there, sent his son a detailed agenda and one hundred marks: he was to learn to speak French, to shoot, to drill; he was to enroll in a school for corporals. His son was expected to return to home and school (it was now early December) directly after the Christmas holidays. The paternal instructions included not a word of reproach. "Unfortunately, I've lost this letter. For a long time I preserved it as one of the masterworks of the positivist generation, and it was in its way perhaps comparable to the performance of a chess player who analyzes an unexpected move." [61]

Jünger ignored his father's outrageously reasonable proposal. The corporal's school, as everyone locally knew, was for *Dummköpfe*. Sensible of the need for a companion on the trip west, he secured him in a person he calls Charles Benoit, a veteran of oriental service who had regaled him with tales of Annamite jungles, tigers, and opium's paradise. On the way through town before their nocturnal rendezvous, Jünger was distracted by the Lamarckian specimen, who dragged him along to a brothel. Shocked when a prostitute undressed before him, he ran out, "less from a sense of virtue than from an overwhelming sense of embarrassment." [62] It is Jünger's only encounter with a woman in this book, and one of very few in his early writing, an episode that is brief, awkward, and furtive.

Armed with wine and inedible figs, Jünger and Benoit set out under moonlight for Morocco. Toward dawn they discovered some haystacks, and burrowed into one to sleep out the day. Jünger awoke to hear Benoit cursing in all the languages he knew. Loud laughter ensued: "All the greater was the merriment which greeted me when unsuspecting I appeared, still half dreaming and covered head to foot with straw. Gradually I perceived fifty brown faces. . . . For me in any case, that was the moment when I began to curse my African adventure." [63] The nearby village was much frequented by legionnaire deserters, and there was a standing reward for turning them in. A small post there included a jail where Benoit and Jünger spent three days before their retrieval.

Back at quarters, he was given ten days in jail. By the end of that time his father had, through considerable effort, secured his discharge from the Legion. Conviction for insubordination in that day entailed six months in prison. Had Jünger been tried and imprisoned, he would never have been admitted to officer's training during the war that was soon to come. His father was shrewd enough to enlist a lawyer who convinced the court at Metz that young Ernst's enlistment was at best "une folie de jeunesse." [64]

Jünger was plotting a second desertion when his father's second message arrived, December 13: "The French government has released you. Get yourself photographed." (He did so, and the photograph captures the naive resilience of a young *gallant.*) His father pledged no further interference in his son's plans if only Ernst would return home and complete his preparation for graduation, the Abitur. His father also promised to sponsor him on a trip to Kilimanjaro, an irresistible bait. On arrival at Marseille, he learned the good doctor was on leave but had left him a letter with a gnomic remark, "which I have remembered because I've often found it confirmed: One experiences everything, including its contrary." [65]

The intended self-initiation into a violent, primitive otherness had farcically misfired. If not a rite of passage into adulthood, it was in effect a farewell to youth. Jünger's concluding estimate of his "African games" is sober:

One's rush into lawlessness is instructive, like one's first love affair or one's first experience of combat; the common denominator of these early collisions is the defeat which awakens new and greater strengths. We're born a bit too wild, and we cure the fever at work in us through draughts of a bitter kind.

Still, for a long time I felt myself abandoned in my pride and I didn't want to talk of my flight. It was like a wound that's late in healing. "Each can live as he pleases," goes the familiar saying, but it's more accurate to say that no one can.[66]

To feel abandoned and proud, yet not free: this, cloaked within the account of a sentimental journey, was Jünger's letter to the world in 1936, that pindaric year for the Reich as it opened its capital to the Olympic games. The "African games" were an oxymoron, the predication of unbounded adventure lost in triviality.

To complete his secondary education, Jünger was sent to Hanover's Gildemeister Institut, a cramming school he caricatured sixty years later in another fictional guise, *Die Zwille* (1973). The young protagonist of that work, pale and withdrawn, is an orphan adopted at the story's close by one of his professors. In biographical fact, Jünger, along with millions of other young men, was presently adopted by, in Heraclitus's words, "the father of all things." That father arrived in August 1914.

Because, on one end, his African excursion had shortchanged his Unterprimaner (first term, senior year), and on the other, war was imminent, Jünger's Abitur late in July was a rushed affair. To these exceptional circumstances could be added the fact that Jünger was a son of the upper middle class: social standing, whatever the professed egalitarianism of the schools, still counted mightily: prior to graduation, one was in effect what one's father was.[67]

It is worth pausing to look once more into Germany's schoolrooms just before chaos came. What had they given to those who were about to die at Langemarck and Tannenburg? Some of the topics and questions posed for class essays (*Klassenaufsätze*) and graduation exercises (*Reifeprüfungsaufsätze*) in the Hanover district offer us a glimpse. Consider these topics for a senior essay: "The Kaiser's words, 'I am a citizen of the German Reich,' words of pride and duty," or "War is as terrible as plagues from heaven, but it is good, it is a fate like them." Or these: "How authentic is the saying of Frederick the Great, 'Life means being a warrior'?"[68] "The bow when bent first shows its power," "My favorite hero in the *Nibelungenlied*," "A nation is worthless if it doesn't set everything upon its honor."[69]

To attend only to these issues of militarist ideology would distort the facts. The schools maintained their humanistic heritage, and students had the option to write on "the significance of Goethe's second Swiss journey," "the exposition of Lessing's *Nathan der Weise*," favorite characters in Schiller's dramas, the interpretation of Dürer's woodcuts, the psychological effect of looking at the sea, and even "books are our friends and our enemies,"[70] as well as an old stand-by, "what I did on my vacation." In view of the schools' poor ventilation, poor lighting, and the authoritarian way, we can only imagine the written responses to the statement, "Do not forget school; it has done you good."[71] We might presume it had. That holds especially at the point where the humanist tradition and the cult of the military had their scholastic nexus: in Homer. Many senior essay topics were based upon readings from the *Iliad*: how does Homer depict Agamemnon in the first seven books? how can the failure of the embassy to Achilles be explained? how, among the epic's heroes, does Hector stir our particular sympathy?

The answer to this last question came in an address to graduates at the Gymnasium of Meppen. The director, Dr. Joseph Riehemann, told them that "apart from the light of Christianity, nothing will penetrate your future life with a brighter and warmer glow than Homer's sun." He warned them about people like Thersites, who would seek to turn them "against God and religion, against monarch and law." Jünger cared for none of these, and yet in his own adolescent void he would learn far sooner than he could have foreseen the lesson of Hector, model of princes, fighters, men: "And if you must in fact be someone's opponent," said Riehemann, "do not despise and slight his person but seek rather to learn even from him in ready recognition of his brave striving and will."[72] Whatever may be said against the Germans who fought in the Great War, if Jünger's writing on the war can be admitted as evidence, they carried out this ethic of honorable opposition.[73]

Jünger did not hear Riehemann's address, but he knew his Homer, having read him in Wunstorf, Hameln, and at the Gildemeister Institut.[74] And yet fidelity, obedience, bravery—the passwords of German military life—must have seemed unlikely to secure so desultory, not to say deficient, a student as he was in 1914. Jünger's candidacy for graduation from the Gildemeister Institut must have appeared something out of the ordinary: here was the grandson of a higher school instructor, a renegade to Africa, a dreamer about to enlist in the Imperial Army, and they were examining him not according to the school calendar, at Easter's commencement, but in the summer's heat. Everyone knew that something colossally more imposing than quadratics or grammar was about to happen. Perhaps in normally stringent conditions, Jünger would have not survived these exams. In the event, he passed with marks sufficient to gain him formal admission to the University at Heidelberg, his home town. He never went.

Of the writing for which Jünger is best known, the books on his service in the First World War, foremost remains the first, *In Stahlgewittern* (In Storms of Steel). Upon his father's urging, it was published privately in 1920 by the Jüngers' family gardener, Robert Meier. The issue ran to two thousand copies. Composed from Jünger's war diaries, it enjoyed wide circulation among army officers and quickly became known abroad.[1] The Berlin publishing house of E. S. Mittler, long established as the Reichswehr's press, issued two editions of it, in 1922 and 1924.

In October 1924 Mittler published a second memoir, *Das Wäldchen 125* (Copse 125), subscribed as "a chronicle from the trench battles of 1918," and the following year the Stahlhelm's press at Magdeburg published *Feuer und Blut* (Fire and Blood), "a small excerpt from a great battle," the March 21 offensive, Ludendorff's first, in 1918. The latter two works differ markedly from *Stahlgewitter;* besides reminiscences, they contain lengthy reflections on the war's conduct and meaning. As such they complement Jünger's expressionistic essay of 1922, *Der Kampf als Inneres Erlebnis* (Battle as Inner Experience), which is sometimes mistaken as yet another memoir of the war.

In order to distinguish memoir from reflection, I first review Jünger's experiences in the war as given in *Stahlgewitter* and (for 1918) *Wäldchen 125* and *Feuer und Blut,* with some background on the war's course and circumstances of the engagements in which Jünger was active. We then pass to *Der Kampf als Inneres Erlebnis* and Jünger's remarks on the soldier's life and the war's meaning.

My division of texts establishes the two ways in which Jünger is read: even his most hostile readers have conceded that *Stahlgewitter* is a masterly narrative. Here is the soldier's soldier. What they abhor is the ideological Jünger thereafter, the apparent glorifier of war and slaughter, the proto-Nazi criminal. "I see many death worshippers in the world," wrote war veteran Richard Aldington in 1930, "but Herr Junger (*sic*) is certainly an almost unrivalled fanatic in the idolatry of destruction."[2] This chapter weighs not the charge but the facts of writing and the nature of the memories that that writing reflects.

As the war's experience receded into an ignoble peace, Jünger's memory became more vivid by the iterations of its exercise in writing. His record of warfare is marked by two integral facts: he emerged personally triumphant in the very time of Germany's humiliation, and he became a brilliant chronicler of his experience, a singular victor by sword and pen. This conjunction of endurance and lucidity in its retrieval puts Jünger in the rare company which includes Ulysses Grant and T. E. Lawrence.

Jünger's remembrance of war and reflections on it I introduce by considering Homeric epic as the archetype to which he reverted, both by his education and by the exceptional nature of his war service. As the veteran lieutenant of an elite company of storm troops, he was able to renew the *Iliad*'s scenario of martial violence and its chivalric ἀρετή or performing excellence.[3] Some seventy years after the Great War began, Jünger wrote, "It takes a long while before we learn from experience; and often the gain, which we might have been able to draw from its instruction, is by then already used up. Thus we were able to bring the First World War to an end without noting that the actual fronts went right through the positions and that we no longer had to do with war either in the Homeric or the nineteenth century sense."[4] The instruction is far less important here than the illusion it tardily overcame. For the illusion points to an essential yet easily overlooked datum of 1914–1918: those who entered that war had in their minds' eyes the epic wars of their fathers in the ages of Frederick the Great, Napoleon, and Bismarck. Those who went to war in 1914 had no more the intention of waging a battle mechanized to the proportions of a behemoth than of spawning fascism or national socialism.

The "Homeric sense" of war—the contest of chieftains for their own martial renown, the ruthless exaltation of honor over life, a forcefulness that, in Rachel Bespaloff's words, "is divine insofar as it represents a superabundance of life flashing out in contempt of death and the ecstasy of self-sacrifice"[5]—all this as a preconception would have mattered only to that minute fraction of soldiers on either side who had the inestimable, elitist benefits of a classical education: the scions of Rugby and Eton, of the lycées Louis le Grand and Henri IV, and of the gymnasia. Everyone else would have belonged, like Homer's enlistees, to a faceless herdlike host driven hither and yon by fate and the "betters."

Jünger stood securely among the ἄριστοι, the foremost. Besides the "folk memory" of Friedrich II and the nineteenth-century wars, his education gave him the imperishable literary model of the warrior. As John Keegan has shrewdly observed, war confuses, "and confronted with the need to make sense of something he does not understand, even the cleverest, indeed pre-eminently the cleverest man, realizing his need for a language and metaphor he does not possess, will turn to look at what someone else has already made of a similar set of events as a guide for his own pen."[6] Objectively considered, every war is its own spectacle, but the Homeric scenario informed Jünger to a fateful degree because his experience of the Great War had an objective correlation in the Greek epic. In Homer, the waging of war overwhelms the purported goal itself. There is no promise of eventual peace or an everlasting dominion for the victors. Like the warriors before Troy, Jünger was engaged in fighting for its own sake. This final pointlessness is at the heart of Jünger's war memoirs.

When he entered the war, he was in no position to consider it Homeric. Like many others, he felt the gladiatorial *Morituristimmung,* "we who are about to die salute you," addressed perhaps to that emperor of old, Barbarossa, who was to come awake on Mount Kyffhaüsen in Thuringia and lead the Germans to victory. But Jünger's elevation to the rank of lieutenant of a storm troopers' company individualized his perception of the war. It gave him Homeric bearings: like Odysseus or Ajax, he was a chieftain. His sheer endurance in the front line became an oblique performance of those deeds of singular renown known as *aristeia.* His merits accrued with his wounds, as the war assumed an ever more imposing, metallic indifference, of which the coming of tanks served as emblem. The introduction of steel helmets (1916) conferred a hard, uniform dullness, the tarnhelm under which all individuality disappeared, but Jünger proved himself a splendid anomaly amidst all the mechanization and the rutted trenches. All the storm troops were to a degree anomalies, autonomous bands of marauders, adept at individual combat and its stylized violence of pistols and egglike grenades.

Jünger was different even from these, his own men, on two counts. He had already been in uniform and had already served—in Africa. His picaresque journey to the French Foreign Legion had certified him in the very qualities he would be called to as a junior officer: independence and initiative. He had observed, as *Afrikanische Spiele* shows, the character of men under the constraints of authority, their vim and vulnerability, their truculence, the endless spin of their fantasy, the press of dissipation. It was a forceful schooling in control, the more eloquent for its random vitality.

The lure of Africa had lain in his desire to find nature as yet untrammeled by commerce and to live out his own 1001 Nights. To reconcile literature with experience, he discovered, required only his pen: the act of writing gave him a genie's control over his life. It made experience tolerable by a choreographic recast. The literary fantasies of childhood had availed little. Jünger could never recover by experience the naïveté of the Arabian tales, and Africa taught him he could not even recover Stanley. But Homer proved true, a vouchsafement to experience and sensibility that informed and elevated both. The *Iliad* foretold to him the baleful dues that fear and rage would exact, the casual terror of battle, the sudden caprices of death, and the loftiness of valor.

Still, the Great War was not Homer's. Agamemnon and Aeneas did not have to contend with weapons that had a life of their own. The shafts of the ancient warriors, like their patrimony, belonged only to them. In the Great War, steel, by the inventive leaps and bounds of industrial cunning, gained a forcefully eloquent independence of single human initiative. That was not a new story in 1914 but it became a definitive one. Marx had asked, "Is Achilles possible with gunpowder and lead?"[7] Jünger has answered, "That was my problem."[8]

In Storms of Steel records personal triumph. Its compass is necessarily limited to the immediate and contingent realm of war's hazards. Jünger provides no objective overview of the war, of its causes or aims. He and his fellows are placed in the war's midst but even those men quickly recede from the subjective optics of the account; Jünger does not speak for others. His daybook style informs the matter: concentration upon circumstance gives it a seeming irremediability akin to fatalism; whatever is straight before him he uncritically accepts and never presumes to change. Yet, the individual alone counts because in him are concentrated the antinomies of patience and boldness, and the storm troop leader counts above all because in him we find "the feeling of exalted duty and honor, the sportslike joy in danger, the chivalric push to continue the battle," all of this rare in the trench's common soldiers.[9]

One summer day in 1914 Jünger was on the roof of his father's house, talking with a repairman and the family's gardener, Robert Meier. His parents were at a seaside resort. The postman came at the usual time with unusual news: Germany was mobilizing for war. Like hundreds of thousands of others, Jünger resolved at once to volunteer for military service. He went to Rehburg's city hall, where orders for mobilization were posted. There was no noticeable response to the news—excitement is foreign to the Lower Saxon peasantry—but at the Ernst August Platz in Hanover Jünger saw women pass into the ranks of a marching regiment, garlanding the troops: "Since then, I've seen many inspired crowds, but no inspiration was deeper and mightier than on that day. It was an impression of blood, roses, and splendid tears that went to the very core of oneself."[10] From the train car to the city he had noticed effigies of Czar Nicholas II hanging on poles in the wind.

From October into December Jünger was trained in the Ersatz (reserve) battalion of Hanover's Seventy-third Regiment, the corps of fusilliers renowned since the Gibraltar campaign against the French and Spanish (1779–1783). He had initially tried to enlist in the Seventy-fourth Regiment but the lines were lengthy, and he was enrolled in the Seventy-third after only three days of waiting. Two days after Christmas, he was dispatched to Champagne. In two months of training Jünger learned to march, shoot, and appreciate the Prussian discipline "against the edges and corners of which I initially hurled myself violently and to which yet I owe more than to all the schoolmasters and books in the world."[11]

The war was already five months old when he entered it, much older than any of the contestant nations had anticipated. Initially, the psychology on both sides was anachronistic. It was commonly presumed that the war would be the brief work of professional armies. As is well known, both sides made fateful blunders that precluded early victory. The French were entranced with an offensive strategy through long-lost Alsace and Lorraine; they presumed a quick thrust into Germany's industrial heart, the Ruhr Valley, would suffice. They underestimated German strength and the value of defensive action. The Germans had inherited from Graf von Schlieffen, head of the General Staff from 1891 to 1906, the bold plan of a two-front war in which Russia, the vast yet weaker foe, would be held at bay while France was overwhelmed by a German right-wing advance through neutral Holland and Belgium, a swing wide to attack Paris, and, moving east, an encirclement of the French army. This plan went awry because Schlieffen's successor, Helmut von Moltke, changed it substantially by fortifying the eastern or left wing at the expense of the right, and by passing the right wing east, then south of Paris rather than besieging the capital. Besides, the Germans had underestimated the Belgians, whose army resisted the invasion at Liège, a stall that allowed the British to land and rescue the French at Mons.

Both the Allied and Central Powers had planned their strategies on the assumption of maximal mobility and maneuver, but the stalemate that resulted by November 1914 was primarily the triumph of firepower. The Germans learned at Langemarck what the French learned in Alsace: the insuperable defensive power of machine gunnery. Precipitous attempts of each side to outflank the other, the so-called rush to the sea, resulted in a trench war, the line extending from the Swiss frontier to the Channel. The last gesture of chivalric war was made across the trenches in the famous Christmas fraternization of English and Lower Saxon troops.

No one in this first season knew the war would quickly pass from a professional to a national effort, drawing in each nation's technology, industry, and science. Jünger, like many others trained in the reserves, was anxious lest the war end in the assured victory before he could be engaged. (German patrols had already reported seeing the Eiffel Tower.) He missed Langemarck and the Christmas fraternity, but the war and its distant audience in the rear were still fresh enough in December to send off troops with August fervor:

> We had left lecture rooms, school benches, and work tables behind and in the short weeks of instruction we'd been melted together into a great, inspired body, the carrier of German idealism since 1870. Grown up in a materialistic age, we all longed for the unusual, for great danger. The war had gripped us like an intoxicant.[12]

In these first notes, Jünger catches the curious exuberance of his generation toward the war, the vaguely idealistic breakout from ease—Wandervögel flown from their coop—and the inebriatory affirmation of death. As one of the war songs intoned in an odd variant on Horace's *dulce et decorum,* "There's no death more beautiful than to be slain before the enemy."

Why such fervor for death? and did Jünger share it? The cult of death had an ancient pedigree in Germany. Death's celebration and glorifica-tion rested firmly on a paradox: not only integral to life, death is, as the Baroque mysticism of Jacob Boehme affirmed, the source of life, and the avenue of its release to eternal freedom. Whether the medium of per-sonality's extinction, as Boehme prescribed, or of its exertion, as Luther preached, death was life's supreme occasion for creative transformation and for access to the unlimited. The German youths who marched in happy consciousness of imminent death in Flanders that first autumn of the war were armed with more than this metaphysical imperative. Besides a Dionysian intoxication to which the young are always susceptible,[13] the irrational courting of death carried a religiosity that Schleiermacher had hailed a century before the war: not thought nor act but intuition and feeling are all. The late Romantic period in Germany gave primacy to the will only so that the will could cultivate "an artful sense of death."[14] Christianity was embraced as a religion of death: Christ was the over-comer of death who leads to the immeasurable life beyond. Death itself, in the Protestant evangelical view, was payment for sin, yet it also held the promise of oneness with God. "Stirb und Werde," die and become: death is the completion of humanity, the victory over life's abiding sick-ness, the deliverance to an absolute life.

German Romanticism sported with this final absurdity in a giddy aban-don. "Todeslust ist Kriegergeist," Novalis had written: the spirit of a war-rior is pleasure in death, and the collective expression of death-longing, at once nationalistic and religious, was Friedrich Schlegel's poem on the legend of Roland: God's will is fulfilled in heroic battles, and martyrs' deaths win laurels from heaven. Other hortatory texts could be cited: from Hölderlin, whose Empedocles heroically sacrifices himself that he may pass to his true self, and whose Socrates makes death a summons of youth to rebirth; from Kleist, who believed that self-realization comes with the sublime act of throwing life away; from Jean Paul, for whom death was an eternal dying and arising (*Verleben und Überleben*). The en-chantment of this mad transcendence is perhaps best rendered by Achim von Arnim: "We live to die, we die to live," a proclamation Mahler re-sumed with his "Resurrection" symphony, which premiered in March 1895, the month Jünger was born.

It will never be known whether Novalis, von Arnim, or Schlegel's Roland was on the minds of young volunteers slaughtered by British in-fantry near Langemarck, November 10, 1914. The mystification of death seems not to have been on Jünger's mind when he entered the war a few months later. If the sixteen pocket-sized notebooks he filled over the next four years contained any literary injunctions to embrace death, they did not find their way into *Storms of Steel*. His fellows he describes in one of his forewords as "patient, iron-laden day-laborers of death,"[15] who endured their time in the earth's bowels, surrounded by mildew and rats, finding only occasional release through night forays into the desolation of *Niemandsland*. Often enough, amid the cracking of shots "a cry blew away into the unknown,"[16] but it was a cry far from any worked-up erotic of the soul yearning for passage to the beyond. Jünger's view of life's end is unsparing and dayside, informed by matters that did not likely affect Hölderlin and Jean Paul: rain, lice, insufferable boredom. Mud is an imposing substitute for heroic danger.

Jünger's itinerary began with a train convoy to Bazancourt, just ten miles north of Rheims, close to the trench line. Promise of a merry battle in flowery fields gave way to a phalanx of new realities: the spectral faces of bloody veterans, rheumatism, nights when no sleep was possible, and the distant argument of shells. Routines of the watch and trench cleaning were also challenges, especially to volunteers who wanted hazard, not work. If danger prompted fantasy—after one's first experience of shelling, any sudden sound could jolt the nerves—sweat dissolved it. Jünger and the other volunteers quickly became older men. However, for Jünger all was not unrelieved dreariness. Armed with his school diploma, he was chosen to undergo officers' training. Another advantage of the well-educated that would inform his experience of this war and its sequel was that he was able to greet the natives of occupied towns and hamlets in their own tongue.

On March 24, 1915, the Seventy-third Regiment joined the Seventy-sixth and 164th as part of the 111th Infantry Division, with which it stayed till the war's end.[17] The quarters were now at Herne, southwest of Brussels. Jünger celebrated his twentieth birthday there. The Walloons and Flemish were outwardly friendly as German troops commandeered their beds.

On April 12, the 73rd was taken southeast by train to Paguy, in Lorraine. Ten days later, while in Belgium a yellow green nimbus of chlorine gas began "Second Ypres," the 73rd marched eighteen miles west to Hattan-châtel and the trenches. Engagement was imminent. In a dream Jünger was visited by a death's head.

On the road to Les Éparges, Jünger observed a confused miscellany of the fighting: the wounded calling for water, dead horses swollen on the road, grenades pounding the submissive earth, a comrade dying within minutes from shrapnel in the carotid artery. Peculiar to Jünger's narrative—fictive writers of the late twenties would compete for vividness in depicting the war's capriccios—is his recollection that "amid these great and bloody images reigned a wild, unsuspected cheer," as veterans urged their youngster replacements forward, telling them the French were on the run.[18]

How Jünger could recall this exuberance is hinted in his remarks on his daily record keeping:

> I knew that the things which awaited us were one time and irrecoverable, and I went to them with a kind of supreme curiosity. Also, I had a natural penchant for observation: quite early I entertained a preference for telescopes and microscopes as instruments for seeing the great and the small, and among writers I especially prized those who had, besides a keen eye for all things visible, an instinct for the invisible.[19]

Any photograph and most written records of the combat around Les Éparges that April would have missed not the carnage but the cheer.

To the visible, however, Jünger gives more than its due. Directly after the first day's record he came, wholly unprepared, into immediate sight of the enemy—from the previous year's campaign. Having fallen asleep in grass, he woke up and beheld a troop of French close upon him: "I sprang from the trench in the morning mist and stood before a crumpled French corpse. Fishy, rotted flesh shone greenish from the rent uniform." Nearby against a tree lay another, "his eyesockets empty and a few wisps of hair upon a dark brown skull. . . . Roundabout lay dozens of corpses, decayed, chalkened, dried to mummies, stiffened in an uncanny Totentanz." Looking into the faces of these and other dead gave him "a shudder that I never completely lost during the war."[20]

Despite or by the artful precision of this scene painting, Jünger does not engage himself in its full horror. Recollection in tranquillity secures for him a final distance he might not have enjoyed or had struggled to attain when facing the dead. His remembrance conveys an impression of detachment which the narrative successively reinforces. At Les Éparges, Jünger claims, he had the courage of the inexperienced; he could not believe the firing had him as its target.[21] His freedom from anxiety allowed him to attend what others in their terror would have been deaf to: forest birds counterpointing the shell blasts, their untroubled jubilation emanating from short pauses. Jünger's is a sensitivity that seems never ready to crack. He enjoys not total freedom but adjustable distance. He, too, is vulnerable, and at Les Éparges he is shot for the first time, a graze in the left thigh sending him headlong and reckless to the rear. Along the way he observes others in much greater pain.[22]

After two weeks' convalescence, he was sent to Döberitz for officers' training. In six weeks he became an officer cadet, junior grade (*Fähnrich*). His father urged him to go on to the senior grade (*Fahnenjunker*) and he agreed, even though he was pleased to consider himself a mere rifleman (*Schütze*) answerable to no one else. When he returned to the front in September, he was in charge of a small reserve unit. Having learned something about decisive action under artillery, he recorded what sounds like an instruction book's maxim: "A position's security rests on the fresh and unwearied courage of its defenders, not on the strung-out construction of its approaches or the depth of its fire trenches."[23]

The 73rd Regiment was headquartered with the division at Douchy-les-Ayette, a small town in Picardy, just south of Arras. When Jünger rejoined his regiment there, the sleepy provincial village had been wholly transformed: "The purposeful situation of a military city had grown over it like a mighty parasite."[24] Of another village, Monchy-au-bois, site of desperate fighting the previous autumn, Jünger recalled the ruin with characteristic word painting, neither charitable nor sentimental:

> The destitution and the deep silence, now and again broken by artillery's dull tone, were strengthened by the melancholy impress of devastation. Torn rucksacks, shattered weapons, bits of equipment, among them in grim contrast a child's plaything, shell fuses, deep holes from shell bursts, flasks, harvest tools, shredded books, smashed utensils, holes whose secret darkness betrays a cellar in which perhaps the skeletons of the unfortunate homedwellers have been gnawed by the everywhere busy swarm of rats, a peach tree robbed of its supporting wall and stretching out its arms for help, in the stalls house animals' skeletons still fastened by chains. . . . Sorrowful thoughts steal upon the warrior whose foot rests upon the ruins of such a place when he thinks of those who shortly ago lived here peacefully.[25]

This concatenation of out-of-the-way losses has perhaps no equal in any other record of the time. It qualifies the unreflected assumption that Jünger mongered war and glorified death. He did not, nor did he try to glamorize—how could he?—the life of battle trenches, defenses and tunnels, which extended the time and meaning of combat from hours to an indefinite trajectory of months. Best, Jünger warns, not to paint too romantic a trench world; better to note that "a certain sleepiness and heaviness prevails in bringing you into close contact with the earth."[26]

Although every soldier was, in the Roman way, a laborer at various tasks, having to repair trench walls, for example, when autumn rains disclosed bodies from the previous year's fighting, much of the time was an assault upon boredom: small talking at the night watch, shooting partridges or piles of dud shells, cudgeling rats, recalling life back home as a dreamland that never existed, and then the days of drinking, cards, and tobacco.

When the toll of wounded mounts up from strafing "we curse these common English swine."[27] Yet, over the thirty meters between opposing lines a fellowship of sorts developed. In an exchange of schnapps and tobacco, Jünger's company found itself facing Hindustanis from a Leicestershire regiment. He tells us that he never hated the enemy nor tried to think low of him. He always sought to kill him and expected no less in return, but there was no animus in the attempt.[28]

On November 29, 1915, Jünger was promoted to lieutenant, and in the following spring assigned to further officers' training. He toured the war's industrial landscape, from slaughterhouse to repair shop, from sawmill to landing field. This panorama informed him of the war's greedy compass and shaped his postwar assumptions about the need for total mobilization, an art which both the Allied and Central Powers were learning under the steady impress of necessity and incalculable waste of lives.

This respite occasioned levity. On leave to neighboring Cambrai, he asked directions of a farm girl, living alone, who told him with perhaps studied ambiguity, "I would like to have your future." He called her Jeanne d'Arc, and she called him "mon petit officier Gibraltar." He returned another day and she gave him supper. Whether she gave him something else is not clear.[29]

The British offensive on the Somme began on July 1, 1916. Commanding superior elevations and aware since February of General Haig's preparations, the Germans had planned a counteroffensive but, owing to stunning Austrian defeats at Russian hands, they had been compelled to send troops east. Although undermanned, German troops on the Somme were well equipped to hold back the British.

In anticipation of the offensive, Jünger was sent out on reconnaissance patrols by night to determine whether the English had laid mines. It was a task of singular exhilaration: as tedium was the daily enemy to be fought, the night afforded release through a sharpening of the senses: "One trembles under two mighty feelings, the heightened excitement of the hunter and the anxiety of the wild animal. One is a world to himself, absorbed wholly by the dark, terrible mood that weighs over the desolate terrain."[30] Courage had to become steely. In a war we generally regard as the triumph of mechanism and matériel, the night patrol gave occasion to the hazard of individual play with fortune. Valor, recklessness, fraternity unto death—these attributes of what George Mosse has called "the myth of the war experience" in 1914–1918 are mythic in that most men could not have served on such terms in their full impetus. But the night foray, marginal and almost pointless militarily, required these qualities.[31] Night patrols prompted the will to control, however fleetingly, the war itself and the dirty range of common endeavors. For the effect of shelling was a psychological desolation to match the land's. Jünger likens it to your being tied at a stake while someone constantly menaces you with a hammer: one hit whizzes just past you; the next hits the stake, sending splinters flying. The patrol was a meager triumph of human momentum.

Jünger's initiatives on patrol seem to have won him his fellows' admiration and trust. Once, called to report at Cambrai, he was delighted on return to the trench that younger troops had asked repeatedly whether he was coming back. He gained immeasurably from that solicitude; he knew thereafter that his subordinates followed him because of this "strongly personal credit."[32] Conversely, the responsibility he, at twenty-one, carried for those young men may have given him a resolution and courage he would not likely have known in a lower rank. He noted that the common soldier, preoccupied with his own safety, marvels at his leader's ability to keep his head among countless dangers and distractions: "This marveling spurs one to even greater performance, so that the leader and the led kindle one another to powerful displays of energy."[33]

Jünger is careful not to make battle into overwrought heroics. Rather, it becomes an equipoise of horror and exhilaration. The villages bear witness. At Frégiecourt, the fire is so intense no one can bury the sweetish-stinking dead, yet the place carries a strange, almost brilliant excitement, "such as only death's nearness can engender."[34] At Combles, the shelling becomes so heavy that one loses the sense of gravity. At Guillemont, the forward man misses his way; Jünger and his men tread through grenade pits, knee deep over wounded and dead.[35] At Maurepas, the Germans launch a counterattack during a storm; "as in the Homeric battle of gods and men the earth's uproar competed with heaven's."[36]

The Somme changed the war's imagery by introducing tanks on the British side, and on the Kaiser's side steel helmets. When Jünger first saw a helmeted soldier, the effect was imposing: "The immovable face half-rimmed by the steel and the monotonous voice accompanied by the noise of the front made the impression of an uncanny gravity. One perceived the man had paid out every terror to the point of despair and then had learned contempt. Nothing seemed left but a great and manly indifference."[37] On that day, Jünger found a graphic warrant for a new race of men. Acclimation came quickly. Observing his unit lined up helmet by helmet, weapon by weapon, Jünger admits he was "filled with pride to command a handful of men who might be crushed but not conquered. In such moments the human spirit triumphs over the mighty expressions of matter, the fragile body steeled by will poses itself before the most fearsome tempest."[38]

The Somme became the germinal point of Jünger's altered consciousness of modern warfare. Ferocious employment of artillery, tanks, and gas showed that mobility in battle was as crucial as the intensified competitive firepower, but at the Somme, as at Verdun, men had to stand fast in "an absolute death zone."[39] These battles, static in position yet fiendishly dynamic in their instrumentation, were like millstones that ground up the old field armies. Survival was akin to miracle.

Jünger was wounded three times: grenade shrapnel in the left shank, a bullet through the right calf grazing the left, another grazing him in the head when a comrade idled with a pistol. He was awarded an Iron Medal First Class. The play of happenstance, the daily roles of luck and carelessness measured in little matters of space and time, every soldier learned to appreciate: in the loom of jeopardy these denominators were no less decisive of life and death than were the shrilling, cascaded shells.

Such particulars would unmake any facile celebrant of death. No less effective, Jünger writes, was one's endurance of the wounded. Hospitalized at Valenciennes, he had to bear the groans and cries of the severely wounded and dying. Unlike Remarque, whose fiction dwells upon these wounded (he spent fourteen months of the war in a hospital), Jünger records their effect upon those returned to the front: anyone going back into fire after such an ordeal had passed a kind of supreme test, for it prompted in the mind a fearful, crippling imagination that made the telltale interval between a shell's whiz and its impact even more dire.[40]

Perhaps it was the hospital, a crucible of enforced intimacy, that stirred his affectionate attention toward his fellows on the line, some of whom he describes in cameos: Lieutenant Eisen, who carried all kinds of weaponry on him and was almost exploded when he pulled a grenade pin from his pocket; and Hambrock, a diminutive enthusiast of E. T. A. Hoffmann, whose weak constitution cost him his life after a light wound. (In the trenches, scratches untreated could be fatal if infected by any contact with dung-filled mud or dirty tools.) There was even respectful comradeship with the English, especially those shot on a night patrol as they attempted to cut German wires: "As elsewhere when we met Englishmen, we had the joyful feeling of a bold manliness."[41]

The Somme offensive was stalled by autumn rains, a more potent foe of human resistance, Jünger notes, than any amount of fire. When the Germans withdrew the following March, they were unsparing in their destruction. Everything that could be burned, was. Through villages that now took on the aspect of madhouses, troops went pillaging in "an orgy of annihilation." Dressed in the women's clothes they had rummaged,

> They found with demolishing acuity the main girders of houses, attached ropes and pulled with rhythmic cries of great effort until the whole thing collapsed. Others swung mighty hammers, smashing whatever came in their way, from flower pots at window ledges to the artful glasswork of greenhouses. As far as the Siegfried line every town was a pile of ruins. Every tree was felled, every road mined, every well polluted, every waterway damned, every cellar exploded or made deadly with hidden bombs.[42]

Jünger's distance from the spectacle did not limit but enhanced his attention to the barbarities of fellow soldiers. The record is itself a judgment, perhaps. The Somme retreat showed him how a collectivity closely bonded can proceed to at best dubious ends with ruthless efficiency, unconstrained by any scruples.

His aloofness allowed him to chronicle without demur the double timing of barbarism, a primitivization of consciousness in the troops. On the capture of some wounded Indian infantrymen, for example: "The scene, in which the prisoners' whining commingled with our rejoicing and laughing, had something primitively warriorlike (Urkriegerisches) and barbaric about it."[43]

By the summer of 1917, Jünger's confidence in his leadership was unbounded. Late in May, just below the Siegfried Line, he ignored orders for a withdrawal before greatly superior forces (the First Hariana Lancers), and held out with only twenty men. He killed the enemy's lieutenant. With a Caesarian ability to celebrate his troops' discipline and show that his resolve and example were decisive in their success, he recalled Nietzsche's injunction to be proud of one's enemies.

The western front had by then been stabilized: the Germans had so thoroughly crushed a French offensive (April 16–17) that the French army threatened mutiny. The British dented the Siegfried Line but in concentrating too narrowly at Arras they could not break through the Germans' artillery and machine gun lines. The only victory the Allies could claim that season was the enlistment of the United States. The main event commenced on July 31, when the British Fifth Army opened the battle known as Third Ypres. A barrage of 2,300 British guns had begun ten days earlier.

Two events within this campaign were of personal import. Jünger was given command of the Seventh Company, a rifle unit. With them he learned that human resolve may count over the combination of mechanical forces and superior numbers, for despite such odds, "the work at its determining points was often completed only by a very few soldiers."[44] With the Napoleonic thesis that matter is finally inferior to the human spirit, Jünger holds that human greatness rests on this idea alone, and that the war's awesome matériel served as a theatrical prop made significant only by what was played out before it: "Exactly at the times when the force of things threatened to hammer the soul soft, men were found who unawares danced it away as over a nothingness."[45] The evocation of Nietzschean heroism is patent—the hammer, dance, abyss—but Jünger does not claim his men were somehow immune to the disquieting fears of other soldiers or to a vague dread that even schnaps could not ease. Everyone was a plaything of phantoms against which reason was feeble. Still, the men had *Draufgängertum* within them, that eerie joy in springing ahead toward combat. When Jünger summoned volunteers for a patrol from all the companies of the battalion, he recorded that "nearly three fourths of the men stepped forward. I selected the participants in my tested way, going along the line and seeking out the 'good faces.' Some of those left out nearly wept when they were rejected."[46] More than mud held back the British at Passchendaele.

During the fighting around Langemarck, Jünger learned that his brother Fritz had been badly wounded and lay nearby. Hit by shrapnel bullets in the right shoulder and lung, he had lain for over twelve hours in a shell hole amid heavy fire before he was discovered and carried to a hut where his wounds were dressed. Friedrich-Georg described the scene in his diary:

> The English had already begun to press forward. In leaping fashion they approached and disappeared into the trenches. Cries and calls were resounding outside the hut. Suddenly a young officer stumbled in, covered with mud from boot to helmet. It was my brother Ernst, who, according to staff reports, had been killed the day before. We greeted one another, smiling a little curiously and agitatedly. He looked about and regarded me with anxiety. Tears stood in his eyes. Even though we belonged to the same regiment, this meeting on an immeasurable battlefield had something wondrous and shocking about it.[47]

Feverish and scarcely able to draw breath, Fritz was carried from the field by five survivors of his brother's company.

Late in August, Jünger was transferred to Lorraine, there to battle with the French in the Vallée Rupt southwest of Metz. He was assigned to lead fourteen men into enemy trenches whenever a rout was possible. The equipage they carried was substantial: a dagger, wire shears, a Mauser pistol, two varieties of grenade, a brandy flask, flares, and a white band on each arm so that they could recognize one another instantly within the trench network.

The reassignment was determined by terrain: in Flanders, the clayey soil had become intractable, rendering the storming of trenches pointless from the start, but in Lorraine there was no such glue. The chalky ground readily absorbed even heavy rains, and the trench walls preserved their pristine conformity. The Germans had even set concrete over much of the floor. Jünger delighted in the abundance of fossils he extracted from the yellow-brown rock of the valley, but the situation was otherwise not to his liking: lice were feistier here, and rations meager compared to what his men had in Belgium. Hunger soon bore through the patina of civilized conduct. Jünger claims he sustained this crisis better than his subordinates (officers set the example, of course) and that hunger, like danger, is an infallible test of behavior. Only the superior comport themselves well.

In a cold dawn's assault upon the French, Jünger was wounded in the left hand by a blast, and lost ten of his fourteen men. He makes clear his contempt for the French: they left many of their weapons behind them in the confusing trench network; most had withdrawn to their holes. Jünger relates that of his many adventures in the war, this was the most bizarre, chiefly because the chivalric decorum Hanoverians entertained toward the British could not be shown the French. An oppressive, primitive enmity (*Urfeindschaft*) attended the normal hazard of wandering through the trench maze. Jünger sensed no quarter would be given.

He led his men over the front line, across a barricade of sandbags past the second line, and by way of a communication trench to the third. At their junction he half noticed a saucepan with a spoon in it. Shortly afterwards it saved his life. At a sandbagged dugout there was a brief exchange of grenades (the left hand hit), forcing him and his men to the opposite direction. In the fourth trench line, they lost their orientation completely. As they attempted to dismantle and carry off a machine gun, a grenade sent them scattering. The large number of abandoned weapons argued an equal number of men under cover, likely to emerge at any moment. Jünger now had only two men with him. They were wandering further, certain they would soon be overwhelmed, when he recognized the saucepan, regained his bearings, and took his companions back over the lines to the convincing accompaniment of French bullets.

Jünger's disdain of the French was not helped when a general staff officer castigated him for the failure of the attack and the heavy losses. His patience before this scapegoating was short, but he contained himself with the knowledge that his superior was regarding the deadly terrain he himself had crossed as an abstract grid of rights and lefts. He mordantly noted that when he entered the French lines he did not have a table piled with maps. This disagreeable episode confirmed his prejudice that only those showing merit in combat were fit to lead. No democrat in politics, he became militantly egalitarian about the value of experience over mere patrimony. He did not believe military leadership should be the birthright of a class or caste.

On October 17, 1917, he was sent back to Flanders, posted as an observer (*Spähoffizier*). Although the fighting was far more intense there than in Lorraine, he was glad to return. He enjoyed the Flemish landscape, the names of its streets and byways, and its people: "God grant that this magnificent land in its old essence rise up again from the fearsome wounds of war."[48] By then, he was a veteran of nearly three years of combat, refined yet hardened by the play of innumerable contingencies, each bearing him to the fatalist's view that war is the subliminal dynamic of all human activity. Seconds and millimeters decided who enjoyed an evening's rest. Survivors amid heavy losses found it hard to believe they had escaped death. However much Jünger celebrated the will to battle even in others who sensibly feared, his spare tributes to them subdue exuberance. Happenstance diminished heroics.

On November 20, the British made a surprise assault upon German defenses southwest of Cambrai. Initially, it had been conceived as a raid (no preliminary artillery fire), but ambitious Third Army officers employed nearly four hundred tanks to break through the Siegfried Line, take Cambrai, and push north to Valenciennes. Disaster came within two days: the tanks corps covered five miles and overran the Germans' three defense lines virtually unopposed, but the infantry, no reserves provided, could not hold the gains. On November 29, a German infantry's counteroffensive pushed the British back virtually to the line of ten days previous.

Jünger's Seventh Company, eighty men, was stationed on the far right wing of that assault. Here those men came into their own as storm troops. Under night fire, he writes, the soldier's eye and ear are bewitched by the most unusual deceptions. Within the trench walls, awaiting the dawn's signal for attack, one felt "like a child who has strayed into a dark hedge. . . . Everything's cold and alien, as in an accursed world."[49] But dread did not overcome discipline: in a textbook display of efficiency, with sharpshooters nested to shoot down the enemy's grenade throwers, and machine gunners taking up supporting positions, Jünger's eighty surrounded and took captive British forces nearly three times their number.

Unlike most infantry, the storm troops had more than a few chances to see the men they were fighting, but in a combat of high mobility, casualties depended more upon grenades than rifle fire: "Every time an egg-shaped clump of iron came over the horizon, the eye caught it with that final acuity of which one is capable only before life and death decisions." Jünger likens the combatants' movements to those of a ballet, "a deadly engagement ending only when one of the opponents goes flying into the air."[50] He himself was grazed in the head by a bullet (his fifth wound) that left two yawning holes in the right rear of his helmet. The pitch of tension and exhilaration in this contest inspired Jünger to the warrior's vision par excellence: "Trench fighting is the bloodiest, wildest, most brutal of all. . . . Of all the war's exciting moments none is so powerful as the meeting of two storm troop leaders between narrow trench walls. There's no mercy there, no going back, the blood speaks from a shrill cry of recognition that tears itself from one's breast like a nightmare."[51] For his performance in the battle of Cambrai, Jünger was awarded the Knights Cross of the Hohenzollerns, a sword, a silver cup from three other company commanders, and two weeks Christmas leave.

Cambrai marked, according to Jünger, the first attempt in history to overcome the deadly gravity of positional warfare. The second attempt came in the following March, in Ludendorff's first "Michael" offensive aimed at breaking up British forces in Belgium. The Bolsheviks' armistice with Germany in December 1917 had delivered eastern front forces to the West, a gain the German High Command intended to exploit before American troops arrived. Ludendorff chose to strike at the Allies' feeblest point, between Arras and St. Quentin.

When the offensive began, on March 21 at 4:30 A.M., the Germans had two tactical advantages. Surprise was not one of them: Germans captured shortly before had disclosed the date, but massive artillery (some four thousand guns) had been brought to the front line under scrupulous cover. Also, German gas shells were unexpectedly abetted by a fog that gave an invaluable mask to the infantry.

Storm troops were pivotal to the infantry's success, especially since Ludendorff, misreading Cambrai, continued to undervalue tanks. In effect, the storm troops were the Germans' tactical answer to them. Their leaders were assigned to find and penetrate weak points of the British line. Mobility was primary: they had to carry machine guns and light mortars (in ponderous munitions boxes) moving in front of the main infantry assault and altogether independently around the strongly defended areas. Without foreseeable objectives, their line was essentially improvisatory and continually extended; there was no settling in. The gladiatorial mood of 1914 imposed itself. By the first day's end, Jünger had only 63 of the 150 men he had led out before dawn.

The Somme had posed to the Germans a worthy enemy. The storm troops knew, claims Jünger, that they would be entering a witches' kettle.

The predawn itself was like a Walpurgisnacht: "The wavering movement of the dark masses in the depths of the smoking, glowing cauldron exposed for a second the uttermost abyss of pain, like the vision of a hellish dream."[52] Still, amid the closed columns, monstrously uniform, gray and impersonal, Jünger insists a life affirmation could be found.

He almost failed the test before it started. While his men awaited orders under night rain, a shell made a direct hit in the trenches, and he briefly went berserk. Losing all orientation, he forgot he was company commander and, like his men, strayed off at a good clip. He recovered himself only when he stumbled into a shell hole, then returned and regrouped the few men left to him. One of these was a young recruit who only days before had been derided by others during training because he had been unable to carry a munitions case. He had wept in shame and exhaustion. Now, having survived the shell's hit, he was carrying two cases loaded with missiles. At the sight of him, Jünger fell to the ground in tears. The report of this episode carries a far greater valence than Jünger's many rhetorical ejaculations on the triumphant will to fight because it challenges the assumption that he writes "as though he has observed the war from the loge of a theater."[53] The March 21 record reminds us that Jünger wrote from the war's center.

Nowhere more starkly than in his writing on that spring offensive does Jünger invest the war with a revelatory depth. It is the apotheosis of matériel; the epoch of technological mechanisms shows its bloody cards: the mastery of machine over man, of slave over lord ushers in a new human destiny, one without human accountability. In *Feuer und Blut,* Jünger contends that amid the nightly fireworks provided in the thousandfold hiss of missiles there was no fear because the spectacle was unattainable to human feeling. This view implies that every combatant was indeed, at some moment and angle, a loge spectator. When orders to march forward came, however, one felt like a seaman seeing the saving plank sink under his feet.[54] One of Jünger's favorite images is an Odyssean sea journey, in which the soldier-farer is pulled down to the deepest chasms of terror and up to the highest peak of exaltation.[55] He also admits that "the overpowering wish to kill winged my steps. Fury squeezed bitter tears from me. The horrible urge to annihilate, encumbering the battlefield, concentrated itself in the brain."[56]

In the intoxication of such excesses, when, as Jünger puts it, everyone was drunk without wine, everything became understood as in a dream, as though a higher reality had been attained or another order of nature entered. Three steps over and past a corpse, and Jünger had forgotten it. All that was left to consciousness was "a vertiginous system of power," a kind of foreign will that continuously interposed itself between self and action.[57]

Having presented this deadly momentum of joyous automatons, Jünger reports three times his own backsliding into decency. He entered a declivity in enemy lines and found a wounded English soldier. He was preparing to shoot him when the man showed him a family photograph. "It was a final, dubious appeal—and it succeeded! As though by a miracle I managed to transplant myself into that vanished world whose values in this barbaric landscape had gone to the devil." Jünger gave the man a half-friendly shove, and moved on.[58]

Arriving close under enemy guns, he entered the passageway of a trench and collided with an English officer. So pressed he could not raise his pistol, Jünger seized his adversary by the necktie and hurled him to the ground. "Shoot the dog dead!" ordered a German major from behind, but Jünger simply climbed over him: "Let him see how he's escaped the annihilating will of a hot and raging storm trooper."[59] The will to blood is suddenly rather unconvincing, much to Jünger's credit.

Then, shooting a machine gunner from a distance, he entered the nest to find the dead man's partner loading cartridges unawares. Jünger barked at him in English, "Come here! Hands up!" but the man leapt up and bolted down a corridor. Jünger tossed grenades after him: "I should have shot him immediately instead of making talk."[60] In fact, talk was difficult: Jünger's throat was parched, and he was feverish from tonsilitis.

Compared to the near bombast by which Jünger attempts to depict the psychology of combat, the incidentals continually provide illuminations. The daybooks in all their patchiness rival the narrative derived from them and repeatedly polished. So, too, Jünger's embellishments of his original text (in the 1926 and 1934 versions) strangely subtract by their additions. Some of the most telling passages are wholly free of the exuberance of combat. Jünger writes, for example, of the joy he felt when, seeking cover alone under heavy fire, he came upon a young officer of another company in a ditch. Elated as though they had known each other for years, they soon parted in the certainty they would never see one another again. Another instance: after his three mercies, Jünger observed an orderly shooting captive Englishmen with a repeating pistol, and felt a benumbed attention, a suspense he likens to a spectator's in a theater. From this acquiescent vantage, he could see himself as a killer, and rationalize that a warrior wants only to kill because he is under the sway of a powerful impulse to do so: "Once blood has flowed, the mist clears from his head, and he looks around as though waking from a dream."[61]

On an evening's reconnaissance, Jünger and his adjutant discovered a post where English battery officers had been stationed. Towards night a combat runner gave him an English officer's coat, its thick yellow wool a welcome change from his own thin clothing. During an exchange with some Argyll and Sutherland Highlanders, he thoughtlessly stepped, coat on, from the barricade and was shot across the chest, just below the heart. His adjutant rushed to him and urged him to remove the coat. (Jünger believes it was this man who had shot him.) While being taken to the rear he was hit in the back of the head by shrapnel from a shell blast and knocked unconscious. When recovered, he reported to the brigade general that his men had taken the village (Mory), which the Scotsmen had valiantly defended to the last man.

Jünger resumed command of the 7th Company on June 4, 1918. He was assigned to defend a woodland twenty kilometers south of Arras. The British called it Rossignol Wood; the Germans, Copse 125.

Ludendorff's March offensive had been checked at Arras. Resolved to break the British at this strong point, he failed to follow his own plan to swing north and cut them off in Belgium, but his southern wing had pushed on west to Amiens, and British losses exceeded 300,000, with 80,000 taken prisoner and nearly a thousand pieces of artillery lost. On April 9, he opened another offensive between Ypres and Bethune, but it was halted by month's end. He had been strangely chary of his reserves, and the very success of his divisions in moving the line west by ten miles created insuperable difficulties for supplies. Fortunately for the Germans, the newly appointed Allied commander-in-chief, Maréchal Foch, was not generous in supplying French divisions to support General Haig.

On May 27, a third German offensive began where it was least expected, on the Marne. Within five days, it thrust the forty-mile front over twenty miles southward before it was checked by fresh American troops at Chateau Thierry. Liddell Hart has shown that each of these offensives, abetted by surprise, proved tactical successes (as measured in Allied losses of men, matériel, and land) but strategic disasters because they exposed the Germans to the "sacks" that their own breakthrough had created, and to counterstrokes by an enemy of greatly superior numbers and supplies.[62] The Marne offensive's momentum defeated its own purpose, which was to draw away Allied divisions from the Ypres-Bethune lines and so enable the Germans to press on to Hazebrouck.

Jünger participated briefly in the cutting edge of the first offensive, was convalescent during the second, missed the third, and came closest to death in the last. The narrative of his final engagement in combat almost confounds belief. His company was ordered to storm Sapignies, a town held by elements of the British Third Army. This undertaking reflects in its small way the High Command's wasteful determination, imposed upon and sustained by specialized units, not only to hold the line but to extend it when the regular infantry's forces had already been exhausted, as though the war could be waged by machine guns, artillery, and storm troops. The hardy resistance of such forces accounts for the anomaly of the war's last months: the German lines collapsed but the advancing Allies suffered ghastly casualties. The British lost nearly 200,000 men between August and September 26, the day they reached the Hindenburg Line, but for the storm troops, time was running out.

It was just after 7 P.M., August 24. Advancing upon a sunlit field, Jünger was knocked over by a bullet that had passed through his right lung. Carried to a narrow trench, he rose up, spitting blood, and saw enemy troops approaching through white patches of smoke. He looked back and saw for the first time in the war German troops coming forward with their hands up. Calls for surrender are coming from both sides. The men next to Jünger in the trench throw down their belts. "Now had come the moment to show whether what I had many times told my men about combat while we were at rest was more than empty phrases."[63] He crept out of the trench and was able to lurch past the troops as they exchanged cigarettes. "It was like a nightmare in which you feel your feet are fastened to the ground."[64] When two British officers gathering prisoners blocked his way, he shot one dead. The other missed him with a rifle bullet.

As Jünger with a few subordinates staggered back along the trench line, the mounting blood loss made him giddy. He would have bled to death had not a medical corpsman wrapped him in a tarpaulin. As he was being carried, the rear stretcher bearer was shot through the head. A lance corporal amid a whiz of bullets put him on his back but was killed almost immediately. A medical corps sergeant, saved by near darkness, delivered him to a doctor. On the way "I had to struggle for air, one of the most painful sensations you can have. The scent of a cigarette that a man ten paces ahead was smoking threatened to suffocate me."[65]

Jünger's first edition of *Storms of Steel* ends with a morphine injection and a hospital. After two weeks he was sent back to Hanover to convalesce. In the first revised edition (1926) he passes time enumerating his wounds: six hits from rifle bullets, one from a shrapnel bullet, one from a shell splinter, three from grenade splinters, and two from the splinters of rifle bullets.

Following this admissible vanity is the perorative nationalism that closes this second version. During the train journey to Hanover he had the "sorrowful and proud feeling of being bound to the land more intimately through the blood shed in battle for its greatness." He asserts that the deaths of so many taught him that a nation is no mere gaggle of hollow symbols, that "life has deeper meaning only through sacrifice (*Einsatz*, which denotes military engagement) for an idea, and that there are ideals compared to which an individual's life or even a people's count for nothing."[66] This is the nationalist rhetoric to which Jünger was to pledge his pen in 1925. This second edition ends with the infamous, rather forced exclamation, "Germany lives and shall never go under!"

None of this peroration appears in the 1920 version, which leaves the impression of a not conspicuously patriotic soldier. Jünger deleted the nationalist homily from the next version, published in 1934. By then his fervor had been long spent and nationalism had become the Nazis' defining and exclusive property.

Storms of Steel had three lives, versions that signpost Jünger's character and orientation at portentous moments. Of these, the first remains the best; it is free of the clomping nationalism just glimpsed in the second and free of the literary adornments with which Jünger extensively reworked the third. Like the storm trooper's combat gear, it coheres tightly and without the contrivance of effects. It also goes far to debunk the post-1945 view of Jünger as the purveyor of militaristic violence and masochistic self-indulgence.[67]

Here is a passage that Jünger's post-Hitler critics have not likely ever seen, for they would have grown up with the 1930s editions of *Storms of Steel* from which it was omitted. It comes from late in the war, during the British advances.

> As I greeted [officers] Boje and Kius in our usual pessimistic tone, I
> felt the frightened eyes of one of my recruits, a seminarian, resting

upon me. I penetrated the course of his thoughts and recoiled for the first time from the war's deadening effect. One had come to the point of regarding a human being merely as a thing.[68]

This is not a confession, being too elliptical, but the ambiguity which gives to Jünger's later work a subtle vibrance has an early register here. Recorded by a man who never once wrings his hands over "the pity of war," its valence is high, however brief. It is like an electric charge from a suddenly exposed wire, the current running against Jünger's own psychology of war. For what can Homeric daring amount to if one's eyes, gorgonlike, turn all that is human before them into the inanimate?

Jünger's chronicle of Copse 125 falls between the two Marne offensives (May 27, July 15). As the war's initiative had passed east into Allied hands, he was effectively out of the war, almost. Copse 125 lacked, he admits, the epic proportions of battle; it was like a glowing wound round which two small groups of contestants assembled. Artillery contributed, but it is the fact that a few men held out for a long time that Jünger dwells upon: it showed how the most powerful opposition of means is merely a balance on which at all times the human weight is scaled. *Copse 125* presents the war as a human triumph over the blind despotism of matériel.

A marked inconsistency dogs this book's arguments. On one hand, Jünger valorizes the storm troops as *condottieri* (a name he says they gave themselves), celebrating their manly and reckless lives as proof that the quality of fighting men has always turned the scale. The will knows no impossibilities; thudded by artillery fire, it responds with boiling rage and contempt for death. It is as though Jünger never knew or heard of the phenomenon of shell shock. Near the book's close he describes the impression given as Verey lights caused the Germans' helmets to shine as "of an iron and silent energy and a gladiatorial might."[69] In those words he presumes that the *Morituristimmung* of the war's first weeks had remained intact. *Copse 125* approximates the "undefeated in the field" apologetics of Germany's postwar officer class.

On the other hand, he argues that technology's impress has proven definitive. Tanks, planes, and machine guns have fashioned a "new race of men." Tool weapons have shaped their users. Indeed, Jünger claims it is "the great battle of automata," not infantries, which have tested a nation's fitness. Of what avail, then, the vaunted will of iron if, as he owns, it is fallacious to believe the spirit of fighting men is a match for machines?

Arms or the man? Is war decided by the will or the dynamo? Having set one against the other, Jünger wants to affirm both. In his postwar essays for the Reichswehr we shall see how he did so, but it is noteworthy here that *Copse 125* appeared subsequent to those essays, and Jünger, caught between his own historical record of 1918 and speculations about that year's significance, is unable to resolve the contradictions. His professed aim in *Copse 125* was to reach beyond the episodic to the universal, but this means passage from history to some nonhistorical realm such as metaphysics or poetry.

Appeal to the universal opens the door to the notion of fate and its deeply irrational claims over and against the causalities which we can determine, however imperfectly, in historical action and thought. The Great War's economic and diplomatic causalities may have been manifold but were not inscrutable. In *Copse 125* Jünger ignores causes in this sense and even downplays "cause" in its jingoistic meaning. He does identify the German people as "a great idea" and admits that men can be united only by great feelings (like divine grace in medieval times, he adds!),[70] but in the end causes and their justification do not matter to him. Only the will to power matters, and it is realized in technology: machinery expresses the human will to master nature. Will versus dynamo, then, is a false antinomy. Jünger can fuse them only by a vitalist's suppression of reason, skepticism, and prudence.

Completed in 1925, when Jünger had become an intimate of war veterans banded together in the Stahlhelm, *Copse 125* has a peculiar fervor. *Storms of Steel* had given its author an eminence he had not converted into political coin. Becoming a celebrity in a time of national crisis, years of misfired putsches and precipitous economic chaos, entailed an obligatory voice. Thus the narrative in Jünger's second book is constrained as its predecessor was not. The naive ruggedness of style gives way to an apologia, postulative and critical. Its sobriety we can best appreciate in a glance at where Jünger had stood between 1920 and 1925.

Privileged by rank and merit, he stayed in the army until the fall of 1923, gaining time to consider (postpone) a civilian career, and to write.[71] One fruit of that time is an indispensable ancilla to his war memoirs, a book-length essay, *Battle as Inner Experience,* published in 1922. In it Jünger argues that the war was a massive compensation for all that European society had covered over or held down: the impulsion of profoundly instinctive drives. Whatever the achievements of civilization, the animal still dwells within the human, long dormant, like a house pet on over-stuffed furniture, "but when the curve of life's wave swings back to the red line of the primitive, the mask falls, and the Urmensch, the cave dweller breaks forth in the total release of impulse. . . . In battle, the animal ascends as the secret horror at the soul's base, shooting high as a consuming flame, an irresistible rapture that intoxicates the masses, a godhead enthroned above the hosts."[72] Humanity, situated between the animal and the divine, becomes in war, according to Jünger, divinely animal, something exultantly nonhuman. He had seen it holding sway over crowds in Hanover during the war's first days, but at the Somme and in the last retreat, he witnessed its will to annihilation twofold, in the contest of weapons and in the wanton violence of troops.

This outburst of primordial energy from a kind of dark forest in human consciousness marked the war's begetting of "a new and bolder race," and Jünger was unabashedly proud to be of its pedigree: "We've been harnessed and chiseled, but we are also such as swing the hammer and guide the chisel, we are at once the smith and the flashing steel."[73] This postwar salvo is something other than rodomontade. It derives in part from the vaunting posture of German Expressionism with its cultivation of an internal dynamic that is supposed to discharge itself with stunning energy. The very title of Jünger's essay, like Kandinsky's "inner element" of creative life, suggests an Expressionist inspiration. Jünger's intent, however, went far beyond Expressionism's adolescent urge to scandalize society out of the egotistic confines of the cabaret. The war as a personal struggle for existence, reduced to its barest form in elementary opposition—either you or the man you are aiming at must die—ratified a primeval killing impulse and ennobled the killer. War's desolation, according to *Storms of Steel,* actually inspired a joy in danger. Four years of combat's fire had smelted a warriorhood. While the Expressionists, rejecting the degradation of the human spirit by technology and war, sought a utopist redemption of the individual, Jünger saw his comrades at arms baptized in the horrors of the age.

Imagine all the grave's secrets laid open at the Somme, the dead "dissolved into a greenish fishmeat that glowed at night through their torn uniforms. When stepped upon, they left phosphorous tracks. Others had been withered to chalky, stripped down mummies. . . . In the sultry night swollen cadavers would come to spectral life, as hissing gases escaped from the wounds. Worst of all was the simmering bustle that came from countless worms."[74] Beside these words, the Expressionist's demonic tableaux—Georg Heym's *umbra vitae,* for instance—are pale indeed.

In this landscape, Jünger contends, one often had to tread a fine line between laughter and madness. As *Battle as Inner Experience* is committed to an anthropology of the warrior, Jünger here spends much more attention on the common lot than his egocentric memoirs could afford. The soldiers were in fact cave dwellers, living in rude, subterranean compartments of as many as three strata. The daily toil and tedium they had to put up with subtracts convincingly from the postwar glorifications of battle and of death itself.[75] Jünger says the trench left no room for lyricism; it would grind up and pound down anything that was civilized. But his own account belies the claim: he recalls troops speaking of their former lives, families, and work. He even descends to sentimentality in commenting upon shared intimacies: "So tenderly and unassisted each presented his little world to the others that the wave of his feeling bore them as well high over the trenches. . . . Had a treasure hunter of emotions then stepped over the scarred land, the man-filled hole would have shone forth to him like noble crystal from the depths."[76]

The point of his indulgence is that this depiction of men in their ordinariness makes the more gripping their conversion into what peacetime would hold criminal. He is candidly pointing to the primordial impulses (*Triebregungen*) which Freud had noted in a 1915 essay on war's disillusionment ("Die Enttäuschung des Krieges"), but he carries it to a paradox: life is most gay, even madly so, when death is choking it. It then manages to summon powerful expression, abetted by some self-intoxicant that blurs all sense of danger. Death-dealing becomes a hallucinogen.

We may question the psychology or physiology of this premise, but let us allow that Jünger is attempting to account for the power of compulsions war releases; he is not lionizing the dead nor glorifying death. Indeed, by surveying instincts in war, he threatens to overturn the scale of merit depicted in *Storms of Steel:* if "the true springs of war are deep within us, and all that's atrocious, occasionally flooding the world, is only a mirror image of the human soul," then what is heroism?[77]

Jünger's determinism is an argument for what Freud calls "the plasticity of the soul's life," that "that which is primitive in the soul is in the fullest sense imperishable," however much the hypocrisy of civilization (*Kulturheuchelei*) may seek to cover, tame, or merely denounce it.[78] Thus, sexual urges, which according to Freud civilization constrains into neuroses, were a part of the war's surcharging vim. Jünger recalls that soldiers sought love without veils; health was for those who expected to reach old age, but bloodlust itself was, in its boundless sway, comparable only to sexual love. When Jünger maintains that war is a kind of natural law, he writes of it as a sexual impulse (*Geschlechtstrieb*).[79]

His anthropology of the warrior differs from Freud's in two particulars. Freud argues that an enemy's death allows one to deny his own; it placates a primal hatred, that lust for murder which Freud says is virtually the story of world history. Jünger leaves the killing unmotivated, and thus more direly irrational. Yet, as though loath to leave it totally gratuitous, he exalts fighting itself as something sacred, the effect of courage. "Certainly battle is made sacred by its cause, but still more is a cause made sacred by its battle. How otherwise could one respect his foe? Only the brave can understand that."[80] Jünger's argument rests on deterministic assumptions, but he wants them to sustain a chivalric view of war. It is an ancient paradox: we are puppets of the gods but we can be glorious puppets. In Jünger's terms: war releases incontrovertible wellsprings of violence latent within us, but we can be magnificent even while driven by them.

Honor to the foe is a matter that the noncombatant Freud missed in profiling war and death. Jünger describes a cold rain that flooded the trenches one season so deeply, driving out even the rats, that the English finally climbed out of their holes, and the Germans rose up to meet them:

> Unbelievably we stood between bones and putrefaction, and stared at each other. Thus on Judgment Day the graves and crypts shall burst open in streaming light. Yes, it was a real resurrection. Joy became intoxication. We laughed, shook hands, exchanged wine and whiskey, clapped each other on the shoulder, and toasted. We lapsed into jargon and transformed the churchyard into a marketplace. Soon, it was Tommy here and Fritz there.[81]

The respite does not argue that the war must stop so that all can become friends. Distant machine gun fire drove them all back to their holes. But there is more: if war stirs the blood to joy, as Jünger claims it does, any pleader for a return home would have been whipped out of camp. To quit the field is to quit honor.

This chivalric view of combat presupposes a sensibility higher than crude impulse. It would seem that *Battle as Inner Experience* does not reconcile Jünger's picture of the subliminal brute with the code of martial virtue. Jünger has simply explained warfaring from two extremes, each a reading beyond the apparent measure of conduct. The Great War is a contest of savages and of noblemen, of *Urmenschen* and knights. "In courage this time was richer than any. Many a Hector, many an Achilles tarried in the mists of the battlefield. They, too, shall find their Homer."[82]

Courage complements the impersonality of the killing impulse, but is opposite to pathological enmity. Jünger says it was not soldiers but statesmen, educated, pious, at home, who went "ever deeper into the undergrowth of hatred."[83] True courage, in Jünger's mind, cannot be a mean between rashness and cowardice, because it carries within it an ecstasy or madness (*Raserei*) that knows no boundary. It is a natural force, "the wind that drives to distant coasts, the key to all treasures, the hammer forging great realms, the shield without which no culture stands."[84] Behind this fustian lies what Jünger feels is war's essential antinomy: courage is both unbounded and constrictive, annihilating and procreative. Begetting a "new race," the war also proclaimed the triumph of men over fear and over the material fashioned for their destruction. Courage, finally, is "the assault [*Ansprung*] of thought upon rock and matter, without concern for what may come of it."[85]

This definition is telling: courage amounts to a kind of work. The common soldiers were "patient day-laborers of death" by their daily willingness to move consciously against it. When the whistle for an assault blew, no one hung back. Jünger, middle-class, gazed admiringly at the common infantrymen who fought under him. Amid all of war's confounding, their lives seemed untroubled. Their faces were full of energy, their talk terse and full of catchwords; schnaps was never lacking, and only the moment counted. The feudal, still current term for such a soldier was pointed: *Landsknecht,* one bound slavelike to the soil: "In him the waves of time pounded without dissonance; war was his native element. He carried it in his blood, as the Roman legionary or the medieval soldier before him," while the "bourgeois" soldier "fluttered about like a bird thrown from the nest, keeping his eyes closed because he saw his world sinking away."[86]

Unreflecting, the *Landsknecht* was closest to the resurfaced savage. Observing him return from a night patrol, where the hunter's urge and primal fear had stirred the blood and stretched the nerves, Jünger saw the bloodless haggard face and trembling hands, and wondered whether such a man was not a werewolf. The *Landsknecht* provided no heroic model, however, for, so Jünger claims, only the rare warrior attempting to harmonize his inner and outer worlds could do so. We know where Jünger placed himself.

Their incontestable valor notwithstanding, Jünger and all storm troopers alike were, finally, obedient men. Like the ordinary infantrymen, they received orders unquestioningly. Once away from combat, they were essentially one with the conscript and the "bourgeois" soldier: *Massemenschen*. Those who survived were fated to become consumers. That is why, as though in protest, Jünger must valorize the "inner" experience of battle, as though protecting it from the cloying diminutions of ordinary, postwar living. And the weapon in this rear guard action can only be the pen—heroic excellence in the bardic dimension. "They, too, shall find their Homer." In writing, Jünger could promote himself to commander-in-chief of experience, the impresario of battle as spectacle, the harmonizer of "outer" and "inner." However, the harmonization is not always evident or even convincing. At times Jünger, his share of slaughter done, leaves us wondering about the depth and character of his awareness. On a very young Englishman he had shot straight through the skull, he notes: "It is a remarkable feeling to look into the eyes of someone you yourself have killed."[87] Is this feeling part of the dreamlike impulse? Or is the killing urge now, if only momentarily, sated, so reflective horror may have its due?

It is Jünger's attempt to reconcile savagery and intelligence by hypostasis of a "new race" gifted with "cold understanding and hot blood" that gives *Copse 125* its brooding and fitful menace.[88] It nonetheless rivals *Storms of Steel* in crisp lyricism and pointed observation. Recalling, for instance, a night ride of storm troopers in lorries, with rifles and bayonets clinking, Jünger reflects that though there is a community of experience in war, each man approaches it differently. On the homefront, troops were presumed indifferent to their own life, but no good soldier lacks fear. This qualification to Jünger's own fire-in-the-blood rhetoric suggests that real, fearful courage is the alembic of murderous impulses. It may have figured in his three mercies of March 21.

Jünger gives his remarks inclusive compass. He does not presume, like some memoirists, to justify himself nor to dwell upon confined data about "What I accomplished in the Battle." Free of what John Keegan calls this "bullfrog effect," he also avoids the General Staff view of combat, where everything is rationally explicable. As a fighting soldier, he knew it could not be; his shrewd recollections of the war's impact tell us

so. Under sustained artillery fire at night, for example, it becomes difficult to recall your own name; the most intelligent person cannot count to
three. Only movement suffices to give you a sense that you can still shape
your own destiny. (These notes belie Jünger's earlier assertion that artillery's effect is to stir one's blood to rage.) The spectacle of artillery and
Verey lights he regards as emblems of two cosmic forces before which
men seem wretchedly small and unimportant, but the true marvel for
him is that such titanic resources have been brought against such mere
men. Battle, we might infer, is the greatest inflator of human egotism.
Survival itself is no mean triumph, and the will when responsive to the
threat of annihilation takes on "a panting truculence that rushes head on
into danger."[89] Only in such a condition, when one is contemptuous of
death because unconscious of hazard, has the decisive setting for hand-
to-hand combat been reached. If courage is fearful, it is also angry.

Jünger thus answers the civilian's question, how could anyone continue
to stand, let alone fight, facing imminent death? He gives no due to patriotic duty as a consciously held motive, nor to the communal bonds which
only personal disgrace can sever, nor even to any instinct for survival: he
claims that a mind set upon enduring will wilt and fail. His account is
strictly voluntarist: the very terror which threatens the will energizes it.
That is why the will, surcharged, admits no impossibilities short of death.
Jünger believed the war proved this: "Everything that can be expended in
steel and fiery energies in a night a hundred men can affirm or confound.
There's nothing terrible to which a man cannot show himself superior
in the end. And it's exactly the annihilating intensification of means that
also seems to fetch forth from him the ultimate in boldness and will-
power."[90] Catastrophe, then, is virtually the best ground for resolution
and action, the zero point where deeds alone count. That is why Jünger
could claim proudly, even in the face of apparent defeat, that the storm
troops he led were a match for any opponent in war, and the harbingers
of an iron future. In them and their infantry compeers, all the concepts
furthering war—honor, loyalty, manhood, country—are dissolved: such
notions, cold to reason, have their origin and enduring life only in the
irrational right of the blood, as Jünger calls it, and he proclaims it superior to all other rights, as it is the bond of one generation to those past
and to come. This is the legerdemain by which he would cancel all the
Enlightenment's suasions. The war killed them off, anyway, and the age

needed a new faith. It could not be rooted in any political system, nor in the state because the state is not an absolute, only a means. Volk and Vaterland were the sole worthy vessels.

Jünger laments that the epoch in which he had grown up had no "master spirits" to address youth's enthusiasm, save one: Nietzsche. He was the source of "virtually everything that moves us most strongly."[91] The Nietzschean gospel that life's highest urge is the will to power patently informs Jünger's views of *Draufgängertum,* the savage, the new iron race, and the appeal to primordial rights of blood "to which the lower, bloodless circles of intellectuals will remain forever alien."[92] Only Nietzsche could vanquish what Jünger oxymoronically calls "our atheistical upbringing in protestant surroundings."

In *Battle as Inner Experience* Jünger submits that the war's real lesson was that nothing was any longer clear and purposeful. Fighting had gained its propulsion from an unreflective animal fear, not from discipline or patriotic appeals. Anyone drunk on slogans or bywords was simply the victim of politics or the press. To Jünger the war was explicable not by any causality, only as the expression of an "idea" revealed in the war but for which the war was only a prelude. For coming generations this kinetics would serve as the axle around which life would be whirled ever faster.

Jünger is blurry about details, not to mention logic, concerning the "idea" and its willful realization in the soldier, but he makes a virtue of this shortcoming: the soldier, he asserts, knows little of philosophers, but in him and in his deeds life expresses itself more profoundly than any book can. Jünger's argument thus puts him into the peculiar bind that entraps anyone who makes a plea for the irrational condiments of life on the ground that they form its exclusive diet: he reasons for anti-reason; he articulates for "blood." *Battle as Inner Experience* reads like a tract that would cancel itself.

To anyone of decent instincts, Jünger's pronouncements in this anthropology of war are monstrous. Their author appears to be a standing (or marching) affront to civilized conduct. The impact of *Battle as Inner Experience* is, besides, all the more forceful in the control of its presentation. Given its thesis, we would expect a ballooning rhetoric to match, the slavering excesses of a man too desperate to endure peace. We wonder that Jünger, having discovered combat's adrenaline thrill, is not out on the street assailing passers-by. How can so demonstrably accomplished a war maker sit down with a pen? The baleful message does not jibe with the clinical acuity Jünger imposes on its conveyance. He writes startlingly equably about the prompting to murder on a grand scale.

That is true of *Copse 125* on the small scale, but though he presents it as a miniature of the war's universality and studs it with digressions to sop the wounded pride of a defeated nation, he also admits into it an extraordinary perspicacity. He is coolly aware of how costly the hilltop 125 has been in lives. In the war's last summer he could recall other deadly centrifuges.

> But none seemed to me so horrid as the one here. . . . So perhaps it would be well, as often happens in such instances, to leave it lie without occupation, and if an attack threatens, to compound enemy fire with one's own so that no living being can hold up in it, or after blowing up its defenses, to close it off through a bell jar of deadly and heavy gases, for such places are man traps where continual occupation becomes costly.[93]

For once, topography precludes chivalric play and takes war's annihilating potential to the limit. Jünger views the copse as an officer who learned firsthand how men are squandered without even the subtle gambit of mobility they could exercise in storming a trench. For once, he pleads for life but uniquely, by an arresting, ghastly image. Only he could have summoned the bell jar. War has, after all, its iron mean. This passage is worth pondering by anyone satisfied that Jünger delighted in killing and in death.

Let us remember that *Battle as Inner Experience* and to a degree *Copse 125* are not war memoirs but Weimar tracts. Jünger hoped that as the Great War imposed upon the staid scenery of civilization the unbridled savage, so it showed how the warrior would become the agent of a new world of force. He rejects the possibility that the war's combatants could be reassimilated into the culture from which they had come, for that culture was doomed to the *magnum mysterium* of the "idea." The war had schooled complicit young soldier-servants of the old order into "steel forms, whose eagle gaze seeks out the clouds above the whirling propellers, who are cramped into the apparatus of tanks, who venture Hell's journey through roiling minefields."[94]

These steeled youths were clever but not rational. Jünger mocked officers' wartime lectures on Germany's interests: wars are won by the heart, not by the brain. Besides, reason can demoralize faith. It is part of Jünger's convinced antirationalism that he presents images, not arguments. Rather, the images *are* the arguments. Prophecy had already appeared on the streets in the elitists of the Stahlhelm and other veterans' leagues, and in the rowdy idealists and vengeful thugs of the Freikorps.

For such men and for their humiliated nation, the war had to be more than a proud memory; it became a "spiritual" experience, realizing the human soul's strength of endurance. It is Jünger's prose that informed and conveyed that realization better than any other's. That is why, in his preface to *Copse 125* he says that thousands rightly died for an acre or a village: "for it was a shaping of a world yet hidden in the future that was bound to the possession or the loss of such clods of earth."[95] No matter the devastation, the war was a victory of mortality over the matériel that threatened to crush it. The war proved that men could bear more than was ever believed possible; their power to resist made them winners in the race with their own machinery. So it would always be, Jünger maintained, as long as humanity is the master, not the slave, of its creations.

A horrific gratuity pervades Jünger's narratives of the war's last year, when, as he says, being wearily accustomed to the face of battle, one could see it in a subdued light that revealed a deeper mystery. The battleland bore countless burned out carcasses of planes and tanks. For Jünger and his men there was as well the lethal geometry of the enemy trench, and "frantic straying with its thousand changing stretches through which an individual fate weaves its dark line upon the landscape's fiery tapestry—taken in all, it has the image of a Homeric battle."[96]

The message is not sanguine: the war demonstrated conclusively that homo sapiens is "the most dangerous, bloodthirsty, and goal-conscious creature the earth has to bear."[97] Jünger celebrates this revelation of an elementary power that will always be, "even when finally there are no longer wars nor men."[98] This affirmation culminates the "inner experience" of battle. Those who saw in the war only negation and suffering— the soldiers in Remarque's and Renn's accounts—had merely the outer experience of slaves.[99]

Most striking is Jünger's belief that there were victors and vanquished on both sides of the war. The true victors, English and German, were those who read the war's meaning aright; the losers were all those, regardless of nation or nationalism, unable to comprehend the language of might: might as individual courage, might as revelation of horrendous laws.

It is difficult to know how much personal delight Jünger takes in these sinister tidings. He is certain that to deny them would be foolish. In sum, humanity has prevailed over its tools but has been transformed radically by their use. The revelation of force dooms all rational nostrums: war is not the tool of an age or a culture but "springs from eternal nature upon whose ground every civilization grows and into which it must sink if it is not sufficiently hard before the iron ordeal." [100]

Jünger's language of might and his voluntarist notion of force were born of warfare and given over to a younger generation. We can look back before the war and perceive a special pleading for force from the fantasists of violent urges: futurists, expressionists, doomsday-seekers, the educated who yearned for an aristocratic transformation of self in battle. Nothing short of war's ecstasy, an apocalypse for private redemption, would remedy their boredom. Jünger's difference from them is that, too young to have hated the peace before 1914, he was educated in war. Hence he does not know how to contain the gospel of violence within the occasions of war. He leaves the implications of violence spilling over into peacetime unchallenged. It is that shortcoming which puts him into the dismal company of fascism. Little palliates this fact. The memoirs' appeal to warrior's renown rings anachronistic. Bravery and brotherhood do not carry sufficient valence in a field of wantonness, for courage requires justice, temperance, and wisdom to give it full meaning.

As to the war's outcome, Jünger, confounding the stab-in-the-back myth, stated plainly that Germany's defeat came from defects of leadership. Revolution at home was not the cause of Germany's military collapse. Consequently, defeat must not be blamed on any part of the people; it was a collective failure. From that premise Jünger thought he saw a way out of the turmoil and despondency which had succeeded the armistice: either a vanquished nation no longer has a role in the contest of nations, or, its inner core (a national "inner experience") being sound, it has not been rightly organized. Defeat could be as instructive as victory.

The Seventy-third Hanoverian Fusiliers were decamped in December 1918. Convalescent from his August wound, Jünger had returned to Rehburg, where he was immediately put under house arrest, to remain indoors at his parents' home for six weeks. A week after the armistice, the house was searched by troops of the Scheinwerfer Company. "The remarkable thing was that they didn't seem to know what they were looking for. That's what was unsettling?"[1]

What had happened? Germany, dispirited by defeat, was awash with dissidents, civil and military. They improvised a new government of soldiers' and workers' councils on the new Russian Revolutionary model, and it was under the orders of one such that Jünger became a prisoner in his own home. He was lucky. Many officers returning home had been shot. However, the impetus for revolution was short-lived. The Spartacists' revolt was quickly, brutally crushed by the new republic's seasoned military, though the specter of a leftist upheaval, a second Bolshevik revolution, continued to haunt the republic. Even Hitler, for years after he assumed power, feared the possibility. Jünger, on the other hand, courted the notion of a rightist soldier's revolution and wrote on its behalf during the republic's few years of relative tranquillity and prosperity.

This chapter deals with Jünger's brief career in the postwar army, his desultory attempt to reach professional respectability through university study, and his engagement in the journalism of the rightist veteran cliques which rejected all compromise with the new parliamentary order. Very little of what Jünger wrote between 1925 and 1930 has been reprinted, yet his nationalist essays indicate his proximity to the Nazis and must be weighed. The chiaroscuro of facts warrants a view that Jünger's detractors should consider. Those who execrate him as a John the Baptist of fascism, preparing the way for Hitler, should look to someone else for that role. At the crucial junctures, Jünger rejected Hitler, ridiculed the Nazis, and defended those targeted by their virulent racism, the Jews.

A diffused despondency pervaded the elder Jüngers' home for months after the armistice. Jünger was not fully recovered from the pulmonary wound which had nearly cost him his life. His fretful mother would sit frozen in a stare, lamenting the vanished Second Reich. She would wander in the meadow; Jünger dreaded meeting her on his walks. Even his father's ebullience was daunted by economic uncertainty, especially the possibility that uncontrolled inflation would shrink his wealth. Not one to express emotions, he resorted to a cynical despair. "One morning he came to breakfast, as always in a good mood, and brandished a bundle of freshly minted fifty-mark notes in his hand. 'Now's a good time to commit suicide. Your obituary could read, "He could not survive his country's misfortune." ' "[2]

Jünger himself considered suicide. From his father's library he gathered clinical data on various drugs and pondered an overdose of liquid ether. The motive remains obscure, but Germany's defeat was barely tolerable and the prospect of returning to civilian life was worse. In the event, his experiment with ether proved only comic, as he took to the streets and in an advanced giddiness directly found himself obliged to greet superior officers.

He turned to opium, commended to him in North Africa. It relieved the persistent pain in his right lung. Addiction, however, he resisted, and not only by the sanctions of temperament. He observed in sidewalk cafés the listless, monitory glaze of drugged veterans, "masked faces with nightshade eyes."[3] During the war, a cocaine industry, emanating from Zurich, had enjoyed a brisk trade. Jünger had just enough of his father's puritan censor within to escape the downward way. Besides, feeling sickly prompted a fear that he would be left behind by his generation.

Whether despite or because of his debilities, he enlisted early in 1919 as a platoon leader in Hanover's newly formed 16th Reichswehr Infantry Regiment. (His company commander was Hindenburg's son, Oskar.) At leisure he compiled his war diaries, "the quintessence of four years that I passed not without gain."[4]

Military life reimposed the organizational drive he valued, but the service was ignominious: he led patrols against smugglers in the English occupied zone. As demobilization left stores of weapons at large, he conducted searches for them. In March 1920 he regulated the traffic of Hanover's promenaders, while a machine gun unit intimidated some two thousand men demonstrating in support of the Kapp Putsch. "The whole business had something both annoying and amusing about it, as when dilettantes mix with superior artists."[5]

Shortly after the Putsch collapsed, he was stationed at the Reichswehrministerium in Berlin, where he helped to edit the army's regulations manuals. Jünger was not content with insights gained by his own experience; he was sedulously reading literature of the French military, which he esteemed as "theoretically superior" to the German military.[6] Thus informed, he began to write for the officers' weekly, the *Militärwochenblatt*, published in Berlin by E. S. Mittler.

By staying on in the army, Jünger put himself in the anomalous position of a front-line tactical officer serving a bureaucracy. His war memoirs make clear how little he had in common with the hierarchy of planners and managers. As a front-line officer, Jünger lucidly appreciated the potential and fragility of men interacting with machines. It was for reserve officers like him to articulate what war meant, or would mean, as work.[7] While the staff officers' numbers had only doubled in the course of the war, to 45,923, the reserve officers' had multiplied nearly tenfold, to 226,130. This latter host formed a ready and sympathetic readership for Jünger, not least those who came into the war late, inexperienced, and needy of a seasoned voice to set confusion into order and bitter loss into eloquent scope.

Jünger's essays for the *Militärwochenblatt* are important as his first articulations on modern technology. The initial essay, "A Sketch of Modern Combat Leadership," cautioned that as the war's experiences were becoming blurred to memory, infantry exercises were reverting to prewar patterns. The lessons of 1914–1918 had not yet crystallized, and too many junior officers had had no thorough experience of the front. Although the war's technology had created a fearsome arsenal, Jünger argued that battles would still be decided finally by human qualities. Modern combat would require a combination of "the old Prussian spirit" with "an independent sportslike exploitation of terrain and scientific schooling in the use of technological means."[8] Expressly elitist in his vision of "madkeen daredevils" (*tollkühne Draufgänger*), Jünger was also sustaining the governing paradox of the Prussian army's leaders: they had industrialized the ranks while they themselves remained, in one historian's view, "spiritually true pre-industrial neo-feudalist warriors."[9] In their stead Jünger conceives the new soldier as a reconciliation of antinomies; he must be intelligent *and* reckless, adventurous yet adept.

In subsequent writing, however, he argues that modern war's technology means future wars will admit no men in the field. If "a tank, spiked with machine guns and cannon, is worth a company," where is there a place for infantry?[10] How can human life endure between the grindstones of steel and explosives? Jünger's vantage on war, a business of crafty and daring men, seems outmoded. Not quite. The battle power of the smallest unit (storm troops) must be increased so that a few can perform what many had to do in previous wars. Jünger's models are the tank driver, machine gunner, and pilot—the last a chivalric performer whom Jünger admired and envied. The more refined their weapons, the more technical ability required of them. More than twenty years before El Alamein and Kursk, he predicts there will one day be tank engagements comparable to sea battles.

Most important in this second essay is a sketch of his *condottiere* as one who "can send into action, along with highly developed matériel, a troop of physical, intellectual, moral, and technically imposing excellence."[11] He does not explain what "moral" excellence means in this savage context. Indeed, when reviewing infantry manuals, he has to admit that even the indispensable "driving power of the spirit" cannot be prescribed in instruction books; it depends solely on personal leadership. Jünger casts an elitism within the elite. The storm troops have become a machine of finely coordinated parts, but it is up to their leader to run this machine. As battle is now coordinated by levers, shafts, and cogwheels, battle has become work, and one cannot tell the worker from his toil. Here lies the kernel of Jünger's notorious essay ten years off, *The Worker*.[12]

Jünger resigned from the army on August 31, 1923. Outwardly, conditions in the postwar army had become so agreeable that he might well have stayed on,[13] but his grounds for leaving are not far to seek. As early as November 1921 he confessed to his brother that he felt out of place in the service and continued in it only because it was a haven from "the confused state of things." Although he enjoyed ample leisure to write, he was expected to spend a great deal of time in "social affairs."[14]

These were the years of *Storms of Steel, Battle as Inner Experience,* and a heavy regimen of books. He was reading Goethe, Tacitus, Suetonius, and the *Spiritual Exercises* of Loyola. He discovered Rimbaud, was for a time possessed by him,[15] and tried sharing his enthusiasm with a senior officer, Werner von Fritsch,[16] but this most "old-school" of officers saw in Jünger's literary transports only a sure sign that he did not belong in the army.[17]

Arguably most influential on Jünger's thinking in the early twenties was Oswald Spengler, whose *Decline of the West* convinced him, "I'm not to be shaken in my conviction of the unity of human history. . . . What I mean, of course, is that this unity is hidden like a riddle among people, and in fortunate moments here or there one comes close to its solution." As to Spengler's particular value: "After a second reading, I'm now familiar with his appeal [*Zugriff*], a kind of intellectual pearl-strewing or a melody of analogies repeated in virtually every sentence." The effect upon Jünger was a cultivation of ex cathedra pronouncements that were already "sprouting like seeds" in him.[18] Jünger needed Spengler's prophetic assurance in a period of intellectual and spiritual confusions. He felt himself beset by the relativity of knowledge. "The simplest facts," he told his brother, "opalesce in so many lights, that every uniform color gets lost. We've been botched up [*verpfuscht*] by a liberal education, and must see how we can help ourselves out of it."[19]

Another matter aggravated his intellectual straying. He was getting older. Approaching his twenty-eighth birthday, he spoke of it to his brother as though it was actually the end of his third decade. Time—perhaps energy, too—for overcoming confusion seemed to be running out. "It's a matter of fusing the will to a few formulas from which everything else is drained off."[20] This cold, metallurgic diction is instructive. Jünger might have been thinking of his father, who by twenty-eight had already married, started a family, and begun a career.

Jünger vented his restlessness in a war novella entitled *Sturm,* which appeared in a daily serial from the *Hannoverscher Kurier,* April 11–27, 1923.[21] Sturm is a former zoology student turned soldier, a young "born" leader of men, like Werner in Jünger's Wandervögel troop. With him are three exceptionally articulate men: Lt. Horn, the complete soldier who, if there were no war, would have to cause one; Lt. Döhring, a dandy, artful in coffeehouse affectations; and the painter Hugershoff, who devotes himself to the ecstasy of pure color—all of them pieces of Jünger himself. *Sturm* is a book about writing a book and is set accordingly not on the march but in the trench's close leisure. Sturm attempts to reconcile the polarities tugging within him: the writer's refined contemplation and the inspired bravery of the man of action.[22]

Sturm, aware he is no longer the student, has learned to kill with cold-blooded clarity; the war, "a primeval fog of psychic potential," had opened the door to barbarism.[23] The *Urmensch,* however, has all but disappeared, yielding to a coterie of uniformed aesthetes bound by their literary culture. Beyond the convivial or funereal occasion, *Sturm* affords no sense of a community of ranks. Not only has service to the state paradoxically accentuated class differences (commoners could not be expected to stake their lives for an idea), it has cost everyone his sense of worth. In his diary, Sturm-Jünger complains that the individual "protests against the slave-dealing of the modern state, which nonetheless plods on beyond him like an untroubled idol."[24]

It is an anachronistic lament, because Jünger is manifestly attacking Weimar's postwar state. The bitterness comes from his having to cast away the heroic mold: "All national and heroic ideals that earlier seemed to me driving forces were dissolved [*vergischt*] in passion, like waterdrops on a glowing iron plate."[25] "Passion" means "inner experience" once again, an affirmative participation in war which overcomes any threat of private disillusionment and the state's predacious dupery. Yet the words just quoted come at a second remove, from Sturm's own literary persona, a character he is writing about and names Falk (hawk), as though Jünger by this oblique device could transmit views patently his own but which he did not wish to assert straightforwardly. It is Falk, an artist lost in a mechanized world, who holds a key to *Sturm*'s significance as Jünger's autobiographical record, for he is free, as Sturm is not, to dismiss all the arguments about the war, whether made in sanctification, excuse, or condemnation. Only the experience counted. The last infantryman who fought at the Marne is of greater import for this world than all the books the literati could heap up. Here is the vitalist's brief: "we" in the war occupy life's center, while "they" stand on the mere periphery. Yet it is Falk who affirms the "literary" as experience. Jünger via Falk extravagantly proposes that the writer is a redeemer, "humanity's great conscience, an electric discharge over the wilderness of hearts. In him the age crystallized and the individual found abiding values."[26]

As Jünger's Chinese box of perspectives on the world war, *Sturm* reflects his anxiety and ambition early in 1923: the urge to compact experience and expression, to validate himself as a writer now that the battleground was no longer at his feet. Falk's paean to the writer-redeemer amounts to a challenge or order that Jünger had given himself. Writing attempts its own fulfillment.[27]

Jünger had published a memoir, a lengthy essay, and now a fiction, all centrifuged by war. He also wrote expressionistic poems but later destroyed them. What more could he do? Within three weeks of his departure from the Reichswehr, his first piece of journalism, "Revolution and Idea," appeared in the NSDAP's *Völkischer Beobachter* (September 23/24, 1923). In view of his subsequent distancing from the Nazis, the question looms, why did he choose to speak through them?

The essay goes some way to answer. Jünger reviews the morphology of the world's great revolutions, "storm signals" that require first the incorporation of an idea in prophets and martyrs, then exploitation of the established regime's weaknesses. The leftist revolution of 1918 was misnamed, he asserts, because it was fuelled not by an idea but by greed. The hungry masses trailed after phrases borrowed from 1789, 1848, and "Marxism's long-rotted catchwords." Genuine revolution would herald a birth or rebirth, "the emanation of new ideas." This view sharply reverses Jünger's cynical claim in *Sturm* that expecting ordinary people to subordinate themselves to an idea is like expecting fish to live on land. He resolves the difference here by invoking a "folkish idea," as though that said anything. His sole predication of this idea, that it has now been "polished to a previously unknown acuity," betrays it as no new idea at all. Jünger knew that the Nazis' folkish rhetoric was derived from Wilhelmine ideologues like Langbehn, Lagarde, and Karl Lueger. More to the point comes the promise of a dictatorship that would "substitute deed for word, blood for ink, sacrifice for phrase, and sword for pen." He sees in the NSDAP a mystique of blood that "binds the nation in secret streams and prefers to flow rather than be enslaved." As the begetter of "our new values," this blood would "create the freedom of the whole under the sacrifice of the individual" and "precipitate all substances that are harmful to us."

That laboratorial diction gives this writing away. Jünger saw in the NSDAP a possible release from the intellectual confusions confessed to his brother. The "blood" he invokes is not racist; it is more akin to the alchemist's gold—hence, the "secret streams." The collectivist accent, though, is clear: the alleged "freedom of the whole" is placed under "the individual's sacrifice," that is, dictatorship. Hitler had not yet become Führer, and it is impossible to determine whether he figured in the intent of this essay.[28] In the event, before the November putsch, Jünger had taken a path decidedly away from revolution, if not from ideas.

On October 26, 1923, he enrolled in natural sciences at the University of Leipzig. The register of lectures in his first term shows a wide curricular range: minerology, the physiology of plants, geological formation, the comparative morphology and anatomy of animals. He also attended lectures in philosophy from Hans Driesch, an internationally renowned biologist turned metaphysician. Driesch subscribed to the central tenet of vitalism, that organisms do not owe their empirical existence to spatial or material forces but to "agents coming from outside space and working 'into' it." [29]

Jünger's attention to philosophy was a bad sign.[30] His studies in zoology disappointed him from the start because his orientation to science came from nineteenth-century naturalists. "I expected to gather in a great multitude of images, but instead I was submerged in numbers and figures." [31] As though quantification were not sufficiently repellent, Jünger felt antipathy to "the innate urge of science, to kill life in order to be able to make pronouncements upon it." [32] Coming from a seasoned killer, this remark pleads against the conceptualizer's attempt to demystify nature. "Screwing the world's wondrous, fleeting reality into logical frames" becomes a misadventure, where science "feels out only the mask of life." [33] It is the romantic's brief against the instrumentalist character of science in favor of the contemplative, and it derives from Jünger's childhood forays around the Steinhuder Meer. Content with observation's door to wonder, Jünger could not adjust himself to arranging data, an exercise of the old positivist persuasion Jünger had known in his father.

It seems peculiar that Jünger, long accustomed to military discipline, could not make his peace with academic rigors. The army had challenged him in the full hazard of experience and kept an intellectual tradition (Scharnhorst, Clausewitz, Moltke) that reflected upon it. The university cheated experience and thus impoverished vision. Scientific method availed little if it did not address what Herr Driesch called the "something" of oneself. But Jünger wasted no time protesting. He was using Leipzig as he had Berlin, as a way-station. In fact, he was still carrying the war with him: within his first year at the university he had finished *Copse 125* and in 1924, *Fire and Blood*. Two war books in two years attest the extent of his dedication to academics.

Not that he became indifferent to zoology. Early in 1925 he transferred his studies to the marine biological station in Naples. Founded by Anton Dohrn in 1873, it was the pride of Germans in Italy. Darwin had contributed seventy-five pounds toward its establishment. Jünger, like Winckelmann, Goethe, Nietzsche, and many other Germans before him, felt the allure of the Mediterranean climate and soon rationalized that its zoological riches, particularly insects, afforded a variety of contrasts more intensified than in northern lands. The sea held a special enchantment because it "gives its inhabitants that playful elegance and softness of tones, the iridescent, agitated flow of rare grasses, the harmony of transitions, the wondrous delicacy and intimacy of the imperishable."[34] Jünger's is a keen, if rhapsodic, eye, a mind compelled by nature's inexhaustible provinces.

Every afternoon a lab assistant would gather up slips on which students would request specimens by their Latin nomenclature. Jünger likened these scraps to a child's wish list at Christmas. The comparison is apt, for it was the initial encounter with these specimens which delightingly compelled him: "Astonishment is our best part. It is the sweet confusion that overcomes us above the abyss of love. There is no more serene happiness than that of astonishment over nature's landscapes and objects, than the silent composition which takes nourishment from the image."[35]

Jünger left this terrestrial and aquarial paradise after only three months; perhaps the virtual truancy was too pleasant for him. In August 1925 he surrendered for the only time in his life, marrying a plumply pretty nineteen-year-old, Gretha von Jeinsen (she came from a Hanoverian family of military officers), in Leipzig's St. Thomas Church, home of Bach's sacred cantatas. He had passed his tell-tale thirtieth birthday in Naples, and that could only have pushed him willy nilly to settle himself. Besides, the very contentment he enjoyed in Italy must have enforced upon him how unfit he was, like his father before him, for academic confines. He confessed he had "penetrated like a parasite into the cells of the scientific beehive," an alien from the start.[36]

His few university years might best be called occasional. They did not sharpen his already keen eye nor subdue him to a career's proprieties. The wayward student he had been in so many schools as a child he continued to be as an adult. His real education, in both observation and endurance, had been martial. If, as Anwar Sadat once wrote, only in war or in prison does a man learn his true measure, then Jünger knew himself well, but that knowledge did not help him to accommodate the world into which he had stumbled: an education (although abortive) toward a career, marriage, the army pension, an annuity from his father. The walls of comfort, security, respectability were closing in.

With the fantastic inflationary crisis of 1923 weathered, Germany by mid-decade was becalmed and hopeful of prosperity. The republic had survived assaults from left and right and chose early in 1925 its second president, von Hindenburg, who for five years thereafter gave nonpartisan service to the national good. With the Locarno Treaty later that year, Germany reentered the European community. It joined the League of Nations in 1926. Only nationalists, communists, and Nazis could protest this peace.

The period beginning with Hindenburg's accession and climaxing in the Depression was one of peculiar torment for Jünger. While determining precise motivations may be a dubious business, the circumstantial signposts are there. One we have already remarked. Married in 1925, he became a father the next year, yet nowhere in his published work thereafter does he betray anything of the natural affections one might suppose a young husband and father would enjoy. With a Linnaean urge to neologize, he encoded his wife as Perpetua, and only toward the end of the next war would disaster elicit a deeply felt response from him after it had fallen upon his courageous son, Ernstel. Only during the Second World War does Perpetua come to the fore in Jünger's Paris journals as she reports dreams and horrors from the home front.

Photos of the domestic, if not wholly domesticated, Jünger from the late twenties and early thirties say a great deal: amid a clutch of women or even among children he has the what-am-I-doing-here look of a displaced person, a captive. Such scenes suggest to us how little practiced he was in the art of shared leisure. They present him almost without exception in a bemused frown that carries comic resonance when juxtaposed to the impudent confidence and the puckish smile in photos from his days of military service. In only one photograph, a family gathering with parents, siblings, and nephews in 1934, does Jünger look even vaguely at home, but the dominant presence is the paterfamilias, top center, smiling in triumphant satisfaction. Perhaps Jünger's anti-middle-class sentiments, which surface repeatedly in his Weimar journalism, conceal a deep yet strongly contained attraction to this way of life that his self-image did not allow him to admit.

Who he was and what he had become he had learned from war. In a sense, commotion had been his element from the earliest years: the sub-

liminal resistance to his father, the turbulence of schooling, the breakout
to Africa, the blessed war, the marginal adventures afterward. He cannot
be set down as a disappointed careerist because that way his ambition
did not lie. *Ambition* is a misplaced term in any Jüngerian context. Twice
already, in military service and then at the university he had shown himself immune to the blandishments of advancement. He remained deaf to
the siren calls of success, not least because he was financially well off and
did not need to find employment. Domestic life did not truly threaten to
stifle him, but he still had to find some means to take some air free of it.
The soldierly nationalists' call was opportune.

Jünger was not what we now call a "committed" writer. He neither gave
nor felt fealty to any regime or counter-regime. His egoism, essentially
anarchic, could not have been tethered to any program or manifesto. He
lacked elementary political instincts, the sense of a milieu in which partisanship breeds naturally.

Why, then, did he bother to write on behalf of a militant nationalism?
Without question, the betrayal of the war experience urged him: that betrayal is not to be confused with the stab-in-the-back legend, which Jünger did not accept. He knew and admitted in print (*Storms of Steel,* 1920)
that Germany suffered military defeat in 1918. No; the greater betrayal
came with the restoration of a respectable peace that could affirm the war
only in the strains of sentimental memorializing. Monuments placated
the dead, and Cook's tours of battlefields in Belgium and France sated
the curious and the ghoulish. Jünger resented not only these obscene
intrusions; he resented perhaps most of all the veterans' leagues which
throve upon memories and plaques. The presence of the past had become
hostage to soft, intolerable manipulation. Not that the Nazis' shrill cult
of death suited him any better; as a company commander who had led
and lost many men in combat, he had no taste for this opportunism. He
was interested almost exclusively in the reemergence of a warrior caste—
living, not dead. That was Hitler's desideratum, too, but Jünger wanted
to look past all banners and partisan insignia to a breed of warriors too
errant for party loyalties, as though such creatures could spring up from
the ground as armed men.

When the aged Hindenburg was sworn in as president of the republic
on May 12, 1925, it seemed a time for democrats to rejoice. Germany had
been wedded to republicanism and "Western" notions like popular sov-

ereignty. Harry Graf Kessler, an acute observer in the Reichstag gallery that day, figured monarchists and right wingers were using the old man to co-opt the republicans, but were the republicans to keep together, he wrote, "Hindenburg's election may yet turn out even quite useful for the republic and for peace."[37]

Within a few days, Kessler was not so sure. Hindenburg's election now looked like a triumph of reaction:

> He is the god of all those who long for a return to philistinism and the glorious time when it was only necessary to make money and accompany a decent digestion with a pious upward glance. . . . At long last, until the day the butcher arrives and demands his toll, it is going to be possible once more to live easily as a stuffed sheep or gorged goose.[38]

It was an uncannily accurate perception. The butcher did not arrive for eight years, and for nearly five the republic's sheep and geese fed comfortably enough.

Despising the republican experiment, Jünger had no use for philistinism, either. To him, they were the same phenomenon under two categories, political and psychological: they formed the herd morality which Nietzsche, Gobineau, and Burckhardt had observed in Switzerland two generations before. There, the ascendant petite bourgeoisie had wholly displaced patrician privilege. Democracy, leveling all class distinctions, threatened the authoritarian tradition from which Jünger hoped to secure a warrior's elitism, the warrant of his generation's life and death in the trenches.

Jünger entered the arena of political journalism full-time in September 1925, when he first contributed to the Stahlhelm's newly founded weekly *Die Standarte* (The Standard).[39] The Stahlhelm, a self-proclaimed bund of front soldiers (Jewish veterans were not admissible), was the largest and most enduring veteran's league of the Weimar era. Founded in December 1918 "for the defense of property, morality, and country" against Bolshevism, it had weathered suppression in 1922–23 in the wake of Reichsminister Walter Rathenau's assassination (June 22, 1922), and had by 1925 taken the bitter pill of accommodation to political realities. That means it outwardly eschewed the military coup or putsch as a means of restoring the prewar order. However, by the autumn of 1925, the membership was deeply divided over tactics for gaining a determining influence over the state. Should the Stahlhelm accede to parliamentary processes and work through the conservative parties or crystallize itself for a rightist revolution? The alternatives reflected the league's generational division. The young veteran Friedrich Hielscher saw this bund as "a horde of war-efficient bourgeois" hoping to restore prewar privilege through a constitutional monarchy,[40] but his remark characterizes mostly the older veterans of the war, those who had left behind families, homes, and jobs. It does not speak to those younger veterans, like himself and his friend Jünger, who sought the separatist route of idealism and the purist's ultimate purgative, revolution. Those who were rootless, unassimilated, unemployed, and bored were naturally inclined to extremity.[41] The Stahlhelm's journal was established as a safety valve through which the younger and radical members, the dissidents, could blow off steam. It was not the intent of the young, however, to be kept on a leash, and *Die Standarte* served only to accentuate the Stahlhelm's tactical impasse.

When Jünger began writing for *Die Standarte* he enjoyed unparalleled advantages as a voice for a nationalism centered upon the war's experience. *Storms of Steel* had been twice reissued and, in 1924, revised. *Battle as Inner Experience* was hailed for its "valuable truths about the essence of man and peoples in war."[42] *Copse 125* won praise for portraying the German soldier as "a feeling human being" even while it augured "the restoration of a powerful Germany."[43] Commending Jünger as "not a soldier but a warrior," Helmut Francke pointed to his "masterfully terse and plastic" style.[44] Another reviewer feared that "we might lose this hero to literature."[45] After the Stahlhelm's press in Magdeburg published Jünger's third memoir, *Fire and Blood,* in 1925, he was celebrated as "the preeminent soldier and writer."[46]

With a weekly column he secured an exceptional opportunity to promote to the Stahlhelm's 180,000 members the ideology inchoately formed in his memoirs. Had he entertained political ambitions, he could have used his Stahlhelm association to further them. That he preferred the role of ideologue for nationalism is evident in an article he wrote for the Stahlhelm's yearbook, "The New Type of German: From a Letter to an Old Soldier of the Front." The time's confusion, he claims, lies in the abundance of questions and issues "which have never been so pressing for solutions nor so apparently distant from them."[47] Their "heated contests" would shape what Jünger à la Spengler called "a new life-form." In such a grandiose phrase lay Jünger's all-encompassing "national Idea." If the

Soviet experiment offered "a new world-feeling" (Spengler again), it was, said Jünger, antithetical to Germany's working classes and intelligentsia, but he saw a peculiar bond between the two cultures: in both, nationalism was seeking to traverse national borders. He read these oppositions as auspicious signs of "a great mutual power" at work under diverse surfaces.

The special value of this "Letter" lies in its estimate of National Socialism when the Nazis were at their lowest ebb. Jünger credits the "revolutionary fire" in German nationalist circles to the November 1923 putsch: "We as partisans experienced this party's sudden uprise, we were inspired by it in the November days, and we took its failure as an obscure mistake of history." But the NSDAP's effort had not been in vain. "If now the party sinks into the sea of the past or just remains a party, that only proves to us that it didn't yet have the convincing power which brings great formations."[48]

Jünger felt the Nazis failed because they were a party. Like religions, parties hold something essential but not in itself sufficient. Jünger read this deluded absolutism from the war: every fighting nation presumes itself justified. The contest of parties was basically not one of give and take but of no quarter. It did not occur to Jünger, no student of democracy, that a popular will expresses itself by election through one party and then another. This "Western" premise was entirely alien to his and Germany's authoritarian legacy. The root of his objection was that a state based on partisanship's shifting sands had no lasting character by which to conform itself to a national "folk" identity. In Jünger's mind, the state's sole function was to serve as "the comprehensive means for realizing the national idea." It did not matter to him, or so he claimed, whether that "idea" found articulation in a few voices or in many. Not even the form of government mattered so long as its conception was "sharply nationalistic." Nationalists had to be set at the helm either by the "cold procedure" of working within the state toward a majority or by the "warm procedure of revolutionary hundreds."[49]

Following Spengler, Jünger upheld historical "fate" and the immutability of "blood" in all nations against Versailles' enforcement of internationalist principles: "We want to hope for ourselves that the German will distinguish himself sharply from the rest of the world by his singularity, whether the world marvels at it or hates it. Thus he will best serve both himself and the world. The same is true of every other nation."[50] Jünger rejected any belief in a common humanity that could overcome cultural differences and political antagonisms: what does the Australian aborigine, "barely a bound from the highest ape," have in common with a mandarin of a Chinese culture thousands of years old? To this argument from repugnance he joined another empirical claim: 1914 collapsed the Marxists' internationalist pretensions like a house of cards. "It will collapse again and again, whenever the blood begins to speak."[51] Humanitarian principles, in short, have no lasting, empirical value. With internationalism's sinking ship down goes pacifism. Jünger contends that passion, the irrational and instinctive power, proves indomitable, if only occasionally. Wars and rumors of wars will always be with us. Now he advances a more nuanced case.

First, the Darwinian dressing: all of nature, from the macro- to the microscopic, proclaims struggle. Life is at war not just between but within species. Humanity is no exception, and even in semblances of peace such as economic competition among national markets, strife is latent. What, then, of peace and nonviolent struggle? Jünger draws a distinction overlooked by critics who charge he loved and glorified war. "Every decent person is peace-loving; the front-line soldier does not belong among those who take pleasure in bashing in someone's skull."[52] While for the pacificist peace is an absolute, for the soldier peace is conditioned by values one may have to defend by every means. To the objection that issues for conflict can and should be peacefully mediated, Jünger answers that the pacifist does not understand that you can no more be objective about your nation than about your mother. The pacifist sees only destruction in war, not new birth. The nationalism Jünger proclaimed in 1925 was, in his reckoning, a species unknown before 1914. He cares little that no one entering a war can foretell what sort of "birth" will issue from it. Jünger is advocating the dubious thrill of historical dice-throwing, a fatalism that accepts war as inevitable and adventurous.

His antidote to pacifism, the nationalist "idea" of cultural identity, amounts to a vitalism which, inherently irrational, cannot be logically substantiated or disqualified. "It is the unshakeable life force, the worthy spirit of the German people which manifests itself time and again."[53] Germany's modern cities likewise reveal "a delirious energy" that Jünger declines to recognize as simply mechanical processes; it, too, is part of a seemingly indestructible *Lebenskraft*. His view of the Nazis is also vitalist. When he commends Hitler for having made himself "instantly understandable in working-class circles," thus showing the nationalist's affinity with workers, he says in regret of the November putsch: "Hitler should have been peacefully allowed to cultivate national-socialist trade unions; he knew how to plough up the hardest soil."[54]

The roots, so to speak, of this nationalist metaphor, lay not in Germany but in France. As Jünger has acknowledged in interviews, his nationalism is heavily indebted to the man who coined the very word, Maurice Barrès. It was Barrès who in the generation before 1914 gave nationalism a kind of axiomatic force. Barrès exalted the primordial bonds of family, soil, and nation as the determinants of an individual's worth. His nationalism was a kind of ascetic duty or discipline in service to the chthonic spirits of tradition, a cult of one's land and ancestry. Sometimes called the father of fascism, he cannot be tethered to a system's abstractions; his mind worked from images, not ideas. It was also unabashedly self-centered. The converse to his "tradition" lay in what he called "the cult of self," a pursuit of experience by which merely to garden one's personality.

"I had occupied myself with Barrès' work," writes Jünger, "shortly after the First World War when *Le Génie du Rhin* appeared,"[55] and the grounds of his appeal to Jünger are evident: allegiance to the dead needed no explanation after 1918; the sacrificial yet vague summons to activism beyond specific causes was oddly consonant with a clarion cry for leadership. But the murkiness of Barrès's intent betrays a confusion, not to say evasion, of accountability that can be laid at Jünger's door as well in 1925–1926. Possibly Barrès was attractive to him as an outsider in politics, privately inspired rather than socially committed; first and last, a writer.[56]

Vagaries and inconsistencies in one's life need not invalidate the worth of one's beliefs or thoughts. The challenge Barrès posed was to distinguish nationalism and its blood-and-soil claims from nationhood. Is not chauvinism a part of every culture? Rationalists or universalists — "the world-improvers," Jünger calls them — could argue that nationalism is absurd because virtually no modern nation possesses a homogeneous culture. Nationalism seems rather the necessary dogma of the rootless, of those fearful of losing or of having lost the bonds of earth and the dead. Barrès won prominence in the generation after France's humbling by Germany; he came from a province forfeited to the Germans in 1871. Jünger's nationalism springs similarly from a defeated, dispossessed nation barely fifty years old, its people transplanted into an alien soil of abstractions and forced to till them.

If Barrès looked to the past for tradition, for Jünger tradition meant the ongoing work of the heroic. The roots of a heroic deed "disappear into the past's greyness, its fruits fall into the land of one's heirs which the achiever shall never see, and yet the deed is allotted and nourished from both sides, and precisely there lies its timeless brilliance and highest fortune."[57] Jünger's essay on tradition from which these words come exposes a kind of fault line in his consciousness. He distinguishes the hero-warrior from both the common soldier and the adventurer. The latter's greatness, though possessing the beauty of "a wild penetration into dark landscapes" remains incidental, whereas in the hero "necessity, the fatefully contingent" is consummated: "The hero is the ethical man, significant not only in himself, not only for today, but for all time." The adventurer lacks the communal, historical ties which compel the hero. Jünger fixes this Roman view upon the heroism of 1914–1918. His aprioristic fatalism dictates that heroism entail ruin:

> The hero goes under but his fall is like the sun's blood-red setting which promises a new and more beautiful morning. Thus we must remember even the great war as a glowing sunset in whose colors a magnificent morning is already fixed. Thus we must think of our fallen friends and recognize in their destruction the sign of completion, the keenest affirmation of life itself.

So inspiring is this heroic sense that Jünger complacently presumes forms of government are quite secondary: "We would prefer a republic inspired by nationalist spirit to a liberal monarchy."[58] In fact he believed republicanism too factious by nature to carry out the nationalist will. He expressly hoped the German Communist Party would prepare the way for nationalists by "subverting the parliamentary complex and making it ridiculous."

Jünger did not need to rely on the Communists to achieve this end. Two of the five leading parties, the German National People's Party (DNVP, founded by Gustav Stresemann directly after the war) and the People's Party (DVP, which spoke for industrialists) became increasingly hostile to parliamentary democracy. Only the Social Democrats (SPD) consistently held to the pacifist-internationalist position against the nationalists and the army. As Gordon Craig has noted, between February 1919 and June 1928 "fifteen separate cabinets passed across the political stage, none performing for longer than eighteen months and several disappearing into the wings in less than three. . . . Representation in the Reichstag was shared by so many parties that majorities could be obtained only by coalition and . . . the number of working combinations was severely limited."[59]

Jünger forgot that behind the disarray Germany was being shaped by profound human differences. Weimar had not created the very real contests of interest; it only revealed and brought them to fervid degrees after the constraints of authoritarianism had been removed. Jünger presumed political partisanship incidental and wasteful rather than essentially symptomatic of class struggle. At the same time he saw that even nationalism needed coalition: the military would have to win over the proletariat so as to seize and direct the powerful apparatus of "the mechanical world."

His most important work in his season with *Die Standarte* is an essay on the machine. It shows that all of his polemics on political issues were secondary to the struggle he had perceived during the war between the human will and a burgeoning technology, as though machinery had come to have a life of its own and needed harnessing. "The Machine" stands apart from Jünger's other journalism on another count. Mostly free of tiresome rhetoric about "blood" and "will," it recalls his skill as a lyrically fascinated writer. He describes arrival at a metropolitan station from the perspective of a childhood spent in the countryside:

> Over the great squares and through the hollows of streets speeds an army of machines, thundering, hissing, with warning signals like the cries of dangerous animals. But we go on inattentive and indifferent. . . . And we may well say that this world, in which we are at home, is very much a fairy tale. Everything passes, and perhaps when all this has disappeared, we shall live on in the stories of later times as a race of wicked and powerful magicians. And everyone knows the empty feeling we experience on Sundays when the great machinery rests. It's as though the unoccupied masses in the streets had lost their significance, as though sanctification of the day of rest, inherited from more pious generations, were already for us virtually an offense. We're at the point where life is transforming itself completely into energy.

Even so, he adds, this witch's broom of technological power has cost humanity deeply. With the élan of a materially advanced world has come fear that another deeper world is irretrievably lost. Uplifting statistics cannot hide the fact that "every new mechanical device is a new molestation." Convenience, facility, and efficiency snare the spirit.

The anxiety to which Jünger adverts was hardly new. It had been felt and recorded generations before, and most eloquently by Blake, Dickens, and Ruskin. Jünger's remedy is not refuge in the pastoral nostalgia of Hermann Löns. He believes machinery can confer both material satisfaction and the "higher and deeper satisfaction" it has seemingly threatened. He rejects the view that humanity is intrinsically superior to machinery; it can be so only if it subordinates machinery to human purposes. That is why recruitment of workers to nationalism is so vital to his agenda: the mechanical world must be won "from the ground up."

The conspicuous weakness of Jünger's argument lies in his having junked his own insight. Seeing that mechanization has furtively undermined the spiritual life people enjoyed in bygone ages, he believes that simply controlling the machinery will make sufficient recompense. His faith lacks evidence. How can the most artful wielding of technology restore those desanctified Sundays or the bonds lost between humanity and nature?

In "Metropolis and Countryside," he preaches that the worth of a belief does not lie in its objectivity, rather in the "inner" intensity and "penetrating power" (*Durchschlagskraft*) with which it is held. He means that a nontheistic ideology such as fascism or communism may be superior to conventional religion if it is more vehemently espoused. Content is quite secondary. In mechanical terms, the dynamics of an engine are more important than the uses to which it is put; in military terms, tactical drive is more important than strategic goals. He insists that we put aside romanticism's objections to the city's mechanical culture and make of the metropolis a source of living tradition. The Barrèsian cult of the dead, while honorable, threatens to shortchange the future. Most vital now is the fact that the old dualism of society versus nature has been superseded by the modern dualism of city versus land. Shrewdly aware, as the Nazis were, that fears about the decline of agrarian life were part of a national crisis, Jünger contended *contra* the Nazis that the countryside was now a metropolitan concern. Urban and rural were not antinomies but complements, two realms of fate.

For all that, Jünger subordinates land to city, because nationalism is a metropolitan "feeling." In the Great War, the true battlefields were big-city technologies, not landscapes. Only by their machinery could "our Lebensraum be protected or expanded." In "The Machine," Jünger made workers' participation in nationalism a desideratum; now, he confidently asserted that this participation was a fact; workers were not democrats, parliamentarians, or pacifists but nationalism's "tool and motor." Metropolitan nationalism was, moreover, like the war, a kind of totemic means by which "we can succeed in ranking with our fathers." No matter whether the metropolis was psychologically or aesthetically pleasureable; it had become "the brain by which the elementary will [*Grundwille*] of our time thinks, the arm with which it shapes and hammers, and the mediating consciousness by which the temporal assumes what the eternal has to say to it." [60] Urbanization has become divine design.

Die Standarte's young editors embarrassed the Stahlhelm's old guard and in March 1926 the journal was made independent of the bund. For the next five months it ran simply as *Standarte,* subtitled "Weekly of the New Nationalism," but was still financed by the Stahlhelm so as to avoid open discord. In an opening salvo, Jünger wrote that nationalism would grow by organic necessity and die of its own excess. Spenglerian diction is patent: "Nationalism is the belief in a nation's life-power, in its great community of fate in which one becomes a participant at birth." [61]

An almost piteous, pleading tone sounds behind this pomposity. Jünger's ejaculatory "We long for a faith, for something we may love selflessly" [62] tolls a bell of familial loss: "We greet the dead, whose spirits stand before our conscience admonishing and questioning. No, you must not have fallen in vain." [63] His rejection of the postwar world is all but complete: humanity, democracy, liberalism remain alien notions. Most threatening of all to Germany, "our mother," is internationalism. Life cannot be rooted in abstractions, only in its "maternal soil."

Jünger supposed that only affinity of blood keeps a people from becoming faceless masses. Dissolution of a people's identity under humanitarian nostrums, he argues, would deprive it of its sense of peculiar destiny and its historic symbols. But he also scorned the Nazis' racist anthropology promoted in the name of German identity. Talk of "skull shapes and Aryan profiles" was in his reckoning "nonsense." His notion of blood is not biological; it is a peculiar compound of the historical and metaphysical.

So, too, his voluntarism. If "blood" meant redemption of lost comrades from the political consequences of 1918, Jünger in appealing to "will" attempted to relieve Germany of a far greater, psychological consequence, the imposed stigma of war guilt. The war had shown the merciless indifference of events. "We saw victory fall to the other side, a victory we believed in for years as the certain reward for our will power." Only by submitting willfully to fate's "inner logic of events" would the German people be able to discern some "higher meaning" than the events of 1918 had given. Otherwise, they faced free fall into chaos. "We've got to believe that everything is meaningfully ordered, else we're shipwrecked among the masses of the inwardly oppressed and disheartened or the world-improvers, or we live in an animal-like submission from hand to mouth."[64]

Jünger's iron stoicism presupposes that necessity is not a blind but creative power. (Here he is closer to Nietzsche than to Schopenhauer.) Its pull might well cost a people peace and happiness, but in affirming it, they might discern "the highest unity, a centauric fusion of horse and rider."[65] This nationalism is a kind of metaphysical bet. The will offers a gambit to destiny: by forfeiting reason, scientific deliberation, and programmatic control, it gains hope of something hidden. A total, sacrificial commitment of heart becomes sacramental.

In his would-be mystical pronouncements on "the drama of fate . . . which lets us sense the divine and forces us to our knees," Jünger at thirty was appealing to postwar youth movements. Where better to draw recruits for nationalism's barricades? Restive, eager for direction, and feeling cheated of the war, they seemed ripe for a cause. Besides, claimed Jünger, Germany in 1918 had at last overcome its fear of revolution (he disregards the Spartacists' fate), and it was now revolution that "must be preached incessantly, hatefully, systematically, implacably, even if this preaching has to go on for ten years."[66]

"We must go forward while youth's fire is still in us," he writes in a surcharged editorial, "Close Ranks!"[67] At last he proclaims the goal of revolution: erection of a modern nationalist state. He believes Germany's young men ready to fuse their idealism, "a completely unbourgeois feeling," to "the vital energy of our great cities." He calls for a united front, "soldiers as leaders in the battle for power and workers as leaders in the battle for the economy"—a recall of the concilar structures of 1918. As about 80 percent of the Stahlhelm's veterans were workers, Jünger's summons was not sounded in a void. The strength of nationalism's appeal to the industrial work force lay, to his mind, in its advocates' war experience, a trump card to be played against the middle class and the Marxists. Like the Belgian socialist-turned-fascist Henrik de Man, Jünger saw that revolution could no longer spring from class struggle; it needed a union of left and right which only a cult of the nation could provide.

Jünger wanted to believe his sort of revolutionary was not like the old salon socialists "who build with sharpened pens in heated rooms and debate at aesthetic teas,"[68] but as a *Standarte* correspondent trenchantly noted, there was no nationalist front, nor even enough nationalists to send more than a handful of delegates to parliament. This was a fair estimate. Jünger may have rightly assumed that Weimar's youths preferred passion and battle to republicanism, but how could he assume that boldness of "blood," not parties, would fashion a new state? How could irrational forces, unfettered of all purpose and design, fashion anything? In Jünger's metaphysics the will entrusts itself to fate, which somehow converges with fascism's so-called new value, the Jungdeutschen Orden's cult of heroism, the Nazis' "folkish ideal," and the Stahlhelm's *Frontgeist*. This is Jünger's recipe for nationalism, an amalgam for "the will of a new aristocracy which the war has created, a selection of the bold whose spirit no material can smash and who feel called to mastery."[69]

It is typical of Jünger's political confusion that he conjures "a community of fate" (*Schicksalsgemeinschaft*) and a people's blood-bond on one hand and on the other exalts an elitist voluntarism without defining the relation of "mastery" to community, of storm troops to infantry. His elitism won out when he rejected the call of Hermann Ehrhardt, one-time Freikorps leader and head of the elitist Bund Wiking, for an infusion of nationalism into parliament via elections. Jünger answered that ballots were the only means nationalists could *not* use. To suppose war veterans could give new blood to "a rotten mechanism" would please only democrats, since elections would surely siphon off "the tension of the nationalist will."[70] He urged total abstention from elections, confident that parliament would soon collapse. Then, "powers with clean hands will step forth that have prepared for a state founded not on votes but on the strictest authority."

It was *Standarte* which collapsed. In August 1926 it was banned briefly for publishing an article on "Nationalistic Martyrs" devoted to the assassins of Erzberger and Rathenau. By the time the journal resumed printing, Jünger had left it.[71] Dissident from the start, he admitted impatience with the busyness of Stahlhelm meetings, directives, and executive sessions. Most bothersome was the Stahlhelm leadership's irresolution; it made no effort to win over the working class. This inertia was especially galling to a veteran officer trained to take bold initiatives. It seemed to

Jünger a scandalous absurdity that war veterans could not close ranks for a united front.

Jünger quickly moved to *Arminius,* a journal that had begun publication in January 1926.[72] It seemed an ideal medium, vaunting itself as the only nationalist organ not dependent on a party or bund, but when Jünger and fellow editor Helmut Francke took it over (former editor Wilhelm Weiss went to the Nazis' *Völkischer Beobachter*), they needed money. Ehrhardt, eager to use the journal as a voice for himself, came to the rescue. *Arminius,* to which Hanns Johst, Joseph Goebbels, and Alfred Rosenberg contributed, survived less than two years. Ehrhardt stopped funding when he was thrown out of the Stahlhelm in October 1927.

While editing *Arminius,* Jünger came to believe only a nationalist elite could galvanize the unmoved movement by building bridges across the bunds and parties. It was a natural conclusion for a veteran officer skilled in bounding over trench lines, and with it came the Nietzschean dogma of hardness: "We've learned in a harsh school that life is unfair and must be so to maintain itself. We know there's no lasting right but rights that are fashioned, sustained, or lost. . . . The world is a great battlefield of rights, each of them absolute."[73]

Bundists charged that Jünger, Francke, and their contributors were "fantasists, literati, and firebrands."[74] Jünger countered by summoning them to "the mission of German fascism" via a heroic Weltanschauung of passion, rather than of dogma or class. He said he did not care whether nationalists came from the Communist Party or the Prussian army. The sooner coalesced, "the sooner we can entrust our fate to a leader of men, not of political philistines, rowdies, putschists, and sentimental phrasemongers."[75] Mussolini was one model. Italian fascism's appeal to Jünger was its irrational flare, that one would be "willing to die for a deified man." Germany had bunds aplenty but no one to reconcile them. Nationalism had to promote acceptance of a "leader-personality."[76]

While Jünger denied that *Arminius* had such a leader in its wings, his rhetoric pleaded for an epiphany: "What we must bring to expression is the hidden essence of the great deed—a deed removed from all purpose—and the solitude of the one who performs it."[77] Such clichés of vitalism, with Nietzschean accents on elevation and solitude, would have carried Jünger into political irrelevance had he made them a steady diet. Fortunately, the printed word has left him the better for his disclaimers, as when he denied that nationalism meant war: "No one knows better than a soldier that war is terrible."[78] And: "Because we front soldiers know war from the ground up, we shall do everything to avoid it. . . . There are other battles to be fought now."[79]

Granting that nationalism's enemies were those the Nazis identified—Judaism, freemasonry, high finance, and Catholic "Jesuitism" reaching for temporal power—he insisted the real enemy was the republic. If it could be supplanted by "a purely nationalistic state," all of these "antinational powers" would "feel the iron fist at their throat."[80] Virulent though these words are, Jünger was attacking the isms rather than their upholders, as though Jews, masons, communists, and Catholics could be won over. Thus: "We believe Jesuitism is most harmed when convinced Catholics are allowed to speak of the common work of nationalism and Catholicism." Assuming "antinational" isms were "hostile to the blood," Jünger did not see that their proponents were bound to them by blood and that it would be more effective, as Goebbels knew, to attack people than ideas: not simply Judaism but Jews, not Marxism but reds.

In 1927, Jünger's attitude to national socialism was a guarded enthusiasm. As the bundists remained inert and without direction, Hitler made a preemptive claim upon nationalism by emerging as "perhaps the greatest German orator."[81] Jünger was impressed with Nazism's durability; at the time of the Munich putsch attempt it had no clear mission yet it survived to become "the most modern and progressive of all movements"—sure proof of an indomitable inner strength. But it needed compelling inspiration to go on. Communism's central failure, he noted, was that it lacked inspiration. *Das Kapital* was untenable because it was tedious. The dogma of historical materialism, "the last and dullest consequence of a purely rationalistic worldview," could not answer modern problems.[82] Hitler had grasped the war's essential lesson, that a reawakened belief in the primitive bonds of blood, soil, and fate could and would confound reason.

When, for the second and last time, Jünger contributed an essay to the Nazis' *Völkischer Beobachter* in January 1927, he focused not on the new nationalism's leadership but its work force. Succeeding the old *Arbeiterschaft* (simply, a body of workers) of a capitalistic, class-rigid society would be an *Arbeitertum* (workers with a concept of work), a blood-bonded community with everyone working in and for the state. The triumph of *Arbeitertum*'s "life force" could occur only at the level of nation, not of class.

Jünger maintained that the nationalist state, tightly authoritarian, could be created only by "a new soldierly work force . . . the chosen organ of the nationalist struggle." When he writes of "its striking power [*Stosskraft*] flowing into a single personality," he seems to envision a storm troop unit, but his explicit model was the leftist revolutionary council of 1918:

> I hope I'm not misunderstood in saying that modern nationalism owes the auspicious conception of its work potential largely to the 1918 subversion. This effect was hardly intended by the revolutionaries in whose deconstructive work liberalism celebrated its most noisome and, let us hope, final triumph. But it's a fortunate fact about historical events that effects, not intentions, are decisive.[83]

Although citing the fascists' 1922 march on Rome as a revolutionary symbol commensurate with the storming of the Bastille, Jünger notably omits any reference to Mussolini. Nor is there one word about Hitler. He concludes that the new *Arbeitertum* could be run either by a führer or "a working body of leading personalities."

His equivocation betrays his distance. He had sent Hitler copies of his war memoirs and had received *Mein Kampf* in turn. While Jünger was still resident in Leipzig (August 1925–June 1927), Hitler informed him he would be visiting the city, but the itinerary was changed and they never met. "He would certainly have brought disaster," Jünger mused twenty years later.[84] A meeting could have overcome whatever reservations a lieutenant might have had in following a corporal. When Hitler offered him a party seat in the Reichstag in 1927, he declined.[85]

Jünger underestimated Hitler's ability to supply authority and inspiration over the long term. He accepted Nazism's claim to represent "a pure German will," but he presumed it would have to furnish men "equal to the best German minds of all time." People of mere talent, however many, would fall short unless animated by "that absolute amount of spiritual endeavor which precedes every great revolution."[86] This hyperbolical precondition required the impossible, an elitism broadly diffused among the ranks.

Implicitly, Jünger was backing down from his hopes for one man's leadership. Perhaps history had deceived him: none of the Great Men whom his father had extolled to him in childhood had been exemplary orators. Calling Hitler a great orator placed him with Cicero, not Caesar; with Demosthenes, not Alexander. But Jünger saw well enough that Nazism as a political organization "aimed at winning the actual means of power." He loftily distinguished nationalism as an attempt to realize an idea, as though Hitler, pledging to create a new Germany, had not already found one sufficient by its very vagueness. Nazism's "idea," Jünger complacently assumed, would have to become "wider and deeper" to become a true nationalism. Yet it was his own nationalism that proved shallow in comparison.

He had no taste for what he considered the hysterics of day-to-day propaganda and the rascality of street activism. Goebbels's showy performance as Gauleiter in Berlin was giving many brutish lessons, all unworthy of nationalism's "idea." Jünger, who moved to Berlin in the summer of 1927, believed the hazard in waiting for the storm of revolution to break was that its directors would meanwhile descend to phrase mongering and spectacle, the very scenarios Goebbels enjoyed choreographing. Besides, as nationalism was dictated by necessity, by faith and will, not reason, it needed no articulation, least of all vulgar ones. The true leader would not need to employ popular speech: "He knows that what is timely in the highest sense escapes the masses, and must of necessity draw all the best powers to it." [87]

Already, in 1927, Jünger's constrictive antipolitics had put him in a corner. He presumed his nationalist "idea" did not need Goebbels's coarse media, market-square harangues, and gang fights in theaters, because nationalism's virtue lay in "feelings of certainty, superiority, and great personal dignity," antidotes to the egalitarian reduction of the individual to a quantitative but minuscule part of the masses. The only way to combat this leveling was to summon voluntarism's "fire and blood in convinced hearts," unshakable and remote to shifting partisan allegiances.

Whatever the heroics, the bitter salience of Jünger's politics is manifest in its suicidal urge. We find it in his rejection of the Marxist Kurt Hiller's argument that the sole meaning of politics is humanity. Jünger responded that its sole meaning is "a people's fateful striving for mighty expression." Life does not come down to purpose or morality; its true constitutents are movement and strength. Jünger admits that the logical consequence of this crude notion is imperialism. Every nation wants to be the subject, not the object, of fate. We might presume that Jünger's appeals to a people's right to life are positive, but something sinister obtrudes when he posits that the war's battle of matériel exemplified the highest ethical value. His "moral world of faith" renders materialism void because "the heart depends upon the absolute values" of heroes and saints. [88] He makes an imperative of martyrdom, as though defeat were preordained, even desirable. Death is the final step in the vitalist's procession with fate.

Jünger's would-be revolutionary stance is not political at all, but a kind of metaphysical-historical catastrophism. He speaks of a subjective "time of destiny" irrupting into history like an electric current fastening upon metal.[89] Taking up Hegel's query, Are Germans capable of revolution?, he says that Germany's time of destiny is "larger and deeper" than other peoples' and therefore seems barbarous. Jünger identifies nationalism's coming hour with the incalculable chiming of this clock. He bids nationalism's ephebes keep away from "reactionaries, romantics, utopists, and world-improvers" because "they do not live in our time." For this reason, too, he bids them vanquish (*überwinden*) the example of Mussolini's Italian fascism. Germany must follow its own time.[90] "It may be hard, odious, and wicked—we affirm it, as the sower affirms the field."[91] This assumption of a Cainlike burden was more prophetic than he could have imagined.

When *Arminius* folded in the autumn of 1927, Jünger went to another of Ehrhardt's subsidized presses, *Der Vormarsch,* and co-edited it for five months with Werner Lass.[92] He was turning to a new constituency, that amorphous and fateful entity the German youth movement. *Vormarsch* advertised itself as the journal of "nationalistic youth," meaning for Jünger those who had made up the war's storm troops: "students, cadets with old proud names, mechanics, heirs of prolific manors, saucy urban boys, gymnasium graduates . . . sons of peasants grown up under the lonely straw roofs of Westphalia or the Lüneberger heath." Perhaps the war's dead gave themselves for "something unreal." No matter: "What's essential is not what we fight for but how. . . . We want to show what we've got in us, and then should we fall, we shall have truly lived to the full."[93]

The adolescent reserves Jünger hoped to draw upon were vast. Organized youth groups had burgeoned after the fragmentation of the Wandervögel into various bunds.[94] They gathered themselves into some fifteen hundred student associations, including Catholic and dueling fraternities. Some were adjuncts of parties: the Nazis had *Studentenbünde,* which were destined to swallow up all their competitors by 1938. In the Weimar years the Deutsche Burschenschaft numbered the greatest (11,600 members in 1931), with branches in Austria and the Sudetenland. The large number of periodicals from the youth groups barely hint at their diverse makeup, but suffice to tell us that Jünger was again addressing a potentially enormous audience.

German youth in the 1920s was not singular in its rebelliousness or its craving for leadership, but part of the Weimar catastrophe was that the parental generation was itself unsettled and directionless, its authoritarian moorings having been loosed by war, the threat of revolution, grotesque inflation, and finally depression. The Völkisch ideology, which one historian has characterized as "a spiritual flight from a disappointing present into an ideal future enshrining a greatly glorified version of the past,"[95] formed common ground for restive youth and anxious elders. No wonder that unlike the prewar Wandervögel, Weimar's youth movements became deeply involved in political issues.

Countless numbers of these young had lost fathers and brothers in the Great War. What burdens of honorable grief, vengefulness toward Versailles, or my-turn idealism fired them cannot be reckoned. Germany produced no Sassoon, no Graves, nor Owen to embitter war's sentiments, no Barbusse to proclaim that the war was waged in order to kill war.

Jünger should have been an ideal voice for nationalist appeals to the young. A well-published storm troop leader and too young to pass as a paternal figure, he provided a model of the war's heroism for a myth-hungry new generation. Not constrained by any partisan or religious affiliations, he had not identified himself with capitalist or communist ideology. Yet he did little to tailor his nationalism for youth. He proclaimed that "the battle for belief is the most profound and decisive sign of our time,"[96] but this was no special plea to the young. His exaltation of the selfless hero and saint (a nod to young Catholics) claims only the obvious, that such models give young people a "great and noble feeling." But when he couples his scorn of war reminiscences, parades, and "beer feelings" to the hope that "there are still places in Germany where the temperature can reach the explosive point," he speaks to youth's unreflective, irrepressible energy.[97]

Young Germans, he maintained, wanted an ideal's heat to fire them against the "icy coldness" of liberalism in politics, mechanism in science, skepticism in religion, and egotism in private life. Their foe was a dreadful emptiness and sterility. Accordingly, Jünger draws upon vitalism's heated language, where "blood" is metonymous to "idea." It was up to *Vormarsch* to give its subscribers' "seven thousand young hearts" direction and purpose. His model for an "artful unity" of blood was much on his mind as he wrote. For Weimar's youth Langemarck had become part of the misty myth of battle. Jünger went back to the war's first season and its legend. "We take an oath on the blood of the fallen," but his operative word, *beschwören,* connotes conjuring and entreating, as though like the ghoulish blood-seeking dead in the *Odyssey,* the war's dead had risen calling for the blood of living men.[98]

Even when invoking myth, Jünger does not seem to speak *for* the young. He claims without evidence that the young were beginning to turn away from the military clubs, as though such aversion made them more receptive to his call for a union of soldiers and workers. In fact, few of the young had been in the ranks (save as Freikorp) and, being middle class, most youths were likely as wary as their elders of the working class. To the extent they were völkish, anti-Semitic, and fretful about securing careers, they could hardly care whether veterans and workers were brothers in arms. Conversely, working-class youths might have responded to his summons of a new "bolder, more intelligent and resolute" warriorship, but his refrain that the new order required a highly trained technological professionalism could not have enticed those whose fathers had only within recent decades been able to penetrate the civil service. Many discontented youths might well have been nationalistic, but how many could have been stirred by Jünger's anomalous bid for a totalitarian elitism?

If Jünger entertained any hope of recruiting young people to his nationalism, he dashed it by underestimating the adolescent need for ostensible identity. He ignored badges, uniforms, and carrying cards. Worse, his nationalism was faceless. He likens it to the Counter Reformation and says "every nationalist must possess the virtues of a Jesuit," yet he insists that any attempt to organize this subterranean energy would be doomed to failure. "It is a conspiracy of a very secret and dangerous sort."

In Jünger's metaphoric mystification, nationalism becomes a sort of inhuman force, an arcane power, "the electrical pole in the fluid, itself chemically unassailable and yet precipitating out of all compounds in ever increasing mass the essential, the metallic nucleus. In it lies the essence of our will, and it is up to organizations, groups, and individuals to communicate this essence as much as possible." We might dismiss these formulations as "metapolitical" claptrap, but that would underestimate the fact to which they point, however obliquely: the heavy dynamics of the irrational in the nation's daily, political life. It is no "idea" Jünger articulates in *Vormarsch;* it is the terrible power of resentment which breeds hatred and cruelty, all the more terrible when adorned in the vestments of pride and honor. Here, in the spring of 1929, he opens a small window upon an enormous vista of discontent, fueled in part by an economic recession that had begun in the winter, and now awaiting "precipitation."

On June 28, 1929, Germany observed the tenth anniversary of the Versailles treaty as a day of mourning. Muffled church bells tolled throughout the land. Flags on government buildings were flown at half-mast. The Stahlhelm and the Pan-German League announced huge demonstrations, attendance at which was taken as the requisite measure of one's nationalism. Hindenburg denounced publicly the treaty's effects "in their menace to the existence of our Fatherland. . . . Germany signed the treaty without admitting thereby that the German people were the authors of the war. This reproach is a continued source of disturbance both to the German people and to mutual confidence among nations."[99]

This portentous letter to the world came several months before the onset of a worldwide depression. Unrest was widespread as the coalition government of Chancellor Hermann Müller was being torn apart by the five parties composing it. Two of these, the German People's Party (DVP) and the Center (Catholic) Party, became overtly hostile to the ever-hated Social Democrats and embarrassed their cabinet ministers by defeating a motion in the Reichstag that would have halted construction of warships. Still more divisive was the reparations issue, even though the Young Plan, submitted to and accepted by the League of Nations (August 1929), greatly reduced Germany's burden of annual payments. The Young Plan won a clear majority in the Reichstag but became a bellwether for obstructive nationalist groups: Alfred Hugenberg's Pan-German League, the Stahlhelm, and the Nazi Party.[100]

The nationalists' upsurgent appeals justified Jünger's estimate of the shifting sands in which "the republic without republicans" was sinking. Nationalism needed a much wider popular base than his illusory soldier-worker formations could promise. Open now to the game of politics, he wrote: "The fronts are unstable, and the possibilities of alliances with reactionary *and* liberal powers are so numerous they can't be reckoned but must be decided by instinct."[101] For once, he set aside his own mountain-top posture and with it his elitist presumption about playing the arbiter of nationalism, as though he sensed that at last the nationalist current was gathering to a sweeping force into which, as into a battle's tide, he might enter.

He captures this process in a fabulous image from the fairy-tale contention of a sorcerer with a princess skilled in magic. After a hundred transformations, the princess changes herself into a pomegranate, its seeds scattered over the ground. The sorcerer, turning into a hen, hastily pecks down the seeds. One seed escapes notice, turns into a flame and burns the hen to ashes.

> I'm sometimes asked, what is the true nationalist's distinguishing feature? Well: whoever preserves what is German like such a final, unseen, and magical seed, unaffected by any apparent change, and conceals in himself the deadly flame of the will, whoever safeguards what is German, silently, unassailably, and ready for every assault, he is in my eyes a nationalist.

Jünger had provided a parable of Weimar's ruin.

One of Jünger's critics suggests that compared with his output in the *Standarte* period, the polemics after 1928 lost inspiration.[102] He published only thirteen pieces in that year (twenty-seven in 1927), but more important, he began contributing to journals well removed from the rightist circles he had been moving in. They ranged from the national Bolshevist Ernst Niekisch's *Widerstand* to *Das Tagebuch,* edited by the Jewish liberal Leopold Schwarzschild.

Jünger had to concede the tacit defeat of his elitist nationalism. The "idea" that a revolutionary ascent to power could be achieved with hands clean of the common soot of politics had been unreal from the start. He misread the lessons of the putsch attempts by wanting to believe that in their failure some purity of motive remained, as though the "inner power" of the Nazis was never greater than in the debacle of November 1923. Ehrhardt and Hitler learned to move with the times. Veterans' needs and interests were better met in the economic prosperity Germany began to enjoy in 1925 than in the psychological revolution Jünger was urging. Even those mortally contemptuous of the republic saw, as he did not, the advantages of a truce with parliamentary politics, if only to exploit its inherent weaknesses. Ironically, in calling for a revolution that would not radicalize the economic system, Jünger failed to show how nationalism could emancipate anything but "inner experience." Rhetorically opposed to the existing order, he ended in de facto affirmation of it. His dismissal of the Marxist view of class struggle relegated him to the reactionary middle class whose complacency he loathed.

He purported to despise intellectuals because they were not men of action, but his politics was as immured as their own. As Golo Mann charges, Jünger did not really know what he wanted in a revolution. Certainly, he lacked the ambition to give it shape; his vision of power was hierarchic and static. However, the obverse to this coin of political small change shows Jünger's profile among a very small number of men who did not share a political identity. He was friendly to the national Bolshevist Ernst Niekisch, to the Bohemian anarchist Erich Mühsam, to the putschist Ernst von Salomon, to the national socialist Otto Strasser, to the communists Bertolt Brecht and Ernst Toller. These men could get together in a room and talk in a civil way. It is facile to conclude they were united in opposing the republic. In fact, strong in intelligence, they were political weaklings. They did not attach themselves to the purveyors of power who moved naturally on the political stage. Having loosed his moorings with the bunds, Jünger preferred to associate with these men of ineffectual acuity, loners like himself, leaders of one-man movements and singular visions.

For a while he vastly overrated their importance, presuming even such isolatoes could have a role in international politics. Aristocratic exiles of revolution, underground press publishers, the half-educated poised to mobilize from their stations in cafés and libraries—they would all appear when the desired combat was at its most horrific: "The first artillery shot will find them, too, in their formations, ready for combat." [103] In a review of Trotsky's memoirs, he asked whether such peripheral characters would be the subjects or the objects of revolution. "Perhaps they possess some other significance even more hidden than that which is reflected in their own consciousness."

Observation became Jünger's final, anomalous position. Regularly on Friday evenings throughout 1929 Jünger and brother Fritz met at the home of Friedrich Hielscher on Berlin's Friedrichstrasse. These gatherings usually included von Salomon, the publisher Rowohlt, Otto Strasser, the expressionist writer Arnolt Bronnen, and *Vormarsch* illustrator Paul Weber, soon famous for his prophetic drawings depicting Nazism as a cult of death. The American novelist Thomas Wolfe also attended. Niekisch was present when Goebbels appeared and sought to win him over to national socialism. Failing to convert him, Goebbels admonished the group that those who did not decide for Hitler would be pushed to the periphery when the Nazis took power.

Jünger is sometimes identified with Niekisch and "national Bolshevism" (he contributed to Niekisch's *Widerstand* and remained on good terms with him after 1933), but he did not share Niekisch's Marxist extremism, which took its definition chiefly in resistance to the ascendant Nazis. Effectively the successor of Arthur Moeller van den Bruck, Niekisch had seen in Stalinist Russia the model of a revolutionary socialism based on nationhood, not class. Like Moeller, he championed Russia against Western capitalism and vigorously attacked the Nazis' pseudosocialism as a bourgeois parody of revolution. Jünger lacked Niekisch's combative instincts and remained too reserved to give him allegiance.

Goebbels, who had been making his name by reorganizing and greatly enlarging the Nazi Party's ranks in Berlin, had held Jünger in high esteem after reading *Storms of Steel* in 1926: "A man of the young generation speaks about the war's deep impact on the soul and describes the mind miraculously. A great book. Behind it a real man." But six months later he faulted Jünger for failing to appreciate "the task of the proletariat." [104] That remark came in the midst of Goebbels's short career as a would-be bolshevik.

Goebbels taught Jünger a great deal. Jünger attended Communist and Nazi rallies in Berlin's Sportspalast. It was in these days before 1933, not after, he believed, that Goebbels reached his rhetorical heights. The voice then was not coarsely aggressive but "elegantly distilled, fine-stranded, disciplined." Yet the ideological content of the oratory was platitudinous. Not appreciating the necessity and effectiveness of clichés in public addresses, Jünger left early. To his surprise, when he met Goebbels privately, "the Doctor" continued to speak in platitudes.

Jünger admits that only later did he realize how disastrous the salon meetings were. He had failed to notice carefully the kind of people Goebbels had in his train, that death was somehow present amid all the smoking and phonograph music: "The parquette for dancing was thin." [105] Perhaps Goebbels had beguiled him: the ascetic physiognomy and the concentration of will conformed to Jünger's ideal of a superior society, chivalric and monastic. For his part, Goebbels came to this conclusion in April 1929: "It's too bad about Jünger. But if a political thinker [*Kopf*] no longer draws nourishment from the Volk, from the masses, from an organization, then gradually he is bound to wither up." [106]

Any hope Goebbels had of recruiting Jünger to Nazism was destroyed by an article Jünger wrote for Schwarzschild's *Tagebuch* in September 1929. There, with sarcastic taunts, he derided the Nazis' new-found parliamentarianism and their racism. It was no distinguishing sign of a nationalist that he "eats three Jews for breakfast. Anti-Semitism as far as he's concerned is not an essential issue."[107] Rather, the nationalist seeks "to transform the notion of the proletariat from its economic sense into an heroic one." Genuine nationalism did not involve "taking to the field with lengthy tirades against the decline in morals, against abortion, strikes, lockouts, and the reduction of police and military forces." Nor did it busy itself with "so-called popular referenda" such as the reactionary Reich Committee (Hugenberg and the Nazis) used to oppose the Young Plan.

The Nazis' bid for support from the reactionary middle class he disdained, as even Goebbels did privately. This apostasy from nationalism hardened Jünger's conviction about the exclusivity of his own commitment. Admitting that nationalists of his kind were fewer than he had realized, he went on using the collective first person:

> Because we are the bourgeoisie's genuine, true, and implacable enemies, its putrefaction delights us. We are not bourgeois, we are sons of wars and civil wars, and only when all this spectacle circling in the void is swept away can there unfold that within us that is natural, elementary, truly wild, primitive in speech, and capable of real procreation with blood and seed.

The only reserves he could now hope to secure for revolution were the "prouder, bolder, and nobler youth, an aristocracy of tomorrow and the day after, bound only to spirit and blood." Nationalism, in his vitalist metaphor, was an invisible nerve system, not a programme with banners nor even a rally.

Curiously, his forthright isolation gained him momentarily more attention than he had enjoyed since 1925 or would thereafter. The Nazis' response was swift. Goebbels' organ, *Der Angriff* (Attack), claimed literary ambition induced Jünger "to vilify the national socialist movement, probably so as to make himself popular in his new kosher surroundings." Then the dismissal: "We don't debate with renegades (a misnomer, since Jünger never joined the NSDAP) who abuse us in the smutty press of Jewish traitors."[108]

In fact, Jünger had much earlier dismissed anti-Semitism as misguided negativism, a species of reactionary nationalism,[109] but the vague homogeneity implicit in his "super-bundist" vision had bemused fellow nationalists and threatened Jews as Jews: the new nationalism would require thorough assimilation. Jünger said so in an article for a symposium on "the Jewish question" which included several Jewish contributors: "To the same degree that the German will attains acuity and form, it will become for the Jew even the most delicate, irresolvable folly to become a German in Germany, and he'll find himself facing his final alternative: either to be or not to be a Jew in Germany."[110]

The Jewish community in Germany had long been cognizant of this dilemma: to preserve Judaism, its distinctive life and traditions, or to dissolve it into the gentile "host" culture. Nazism's ascent in the referendum propaganda of 1929 brought this matter to a crisis. As the eminent journalist Carl von Ossietzky suggested, the greatest danger for Jews came from those who, because they were not Nazis, might be too eagerly accepted by Jews as friends. Ossietzky particularly feared nationalist bunds like Der Jungdeutsche Orden (the Young German Order), which, though rightist and revolutionary, did not call for a dictator and did not embrace racism. (Even so, it did not admit Jews.)

Was Jünger a false friend of Jews? As the *Arminius* essays show, neither race nor personality mattered to him. But so far as "liberalism" was alien to Germany and nationalism, its supporters were un-German. He denied that liberalism was a Jewish invention: "The Jew is not liberalism's father but its son, and so he cannot play a creative role, either good or bad, in anything that concerns German life."[111] By the time of that statement, Jünger was staunchly opposed to the Nazis' racism. He had publicly mocked their alarmist propaganda: "Anti-Semites are like a certain sort of bacteria hunter who when they figure they've exterminated a certain spore perceive a thousand new ones. This is a procedure that can only end in madness, to the point that as in delirium tremens one sees at every step Jews swarming like white mice."[112] Thus Jünger caricatures the fear which an eminent historian of National Socialism has identified as salient in Hitler himself.[113]

Having published in Schwarzschild's *Tagebuch,* Jünger was now tarred as a friend of Jews. It did not bother him, since "the Jew is as dangerous to bourgeois values as he is harmless to the values of heroic youth."[114] This enemy-of-my-enemy view could hardly have been palatable to most youth groups and university student organizations, anti-Semitic to begin with, into which the Nazis had already made substantial inroads.

Although liberalism seemed to have provided a home favorable for Europe's Jews, Jünger argued it was a snare because anti-Semitism throve in it as well. It is remarkable that he weighed alternatives for Jews in the military terms of delaying positions (*Aufnahmestellungen*): Zionism and "the increasingly frequent efforts to assimilate the language of German nationalism" were alike "beginning to rush water into the ship" of the liberal state. While leaving open to Jews the assimilationist door to German nationalism, Jünger offered a better course: "For Jews there is only one lasting station, only one temple of Solomon, and that is Jewish orthodoxy, which I hail just as I must hail the genuine and unqualified singularity of every people. Undoubtedly it will recover ground to the same degree that the nationalism of the peoples of Europe gains impetus." [115]

The Nazi blast at Jünger notwithstanding, it stretches facts to consider him a philo-Semite. A thorough philo-Semite would not have submitted articles, as Jünger did six times, to the vigorously anti-Semitic (though anti-Nazi) Wilhelm Stapel, editor of *Deutsches Volkstum*. In a sense, because he was not an anti-Semite he posed a greater danger to Jews than the non-Nazi bunds that worried Ossietzky. "Be a Jew or be a German. You cannot be both." Viewed from beyond the Holocaust, this prescription seems harsher than it was. Jews keenly appreciated the need of a defining identity and allegiance, as Gershom Scholem's family history reveals. Jünger, who had gone to school with Gershom's brother Werner, erred in presuming that a Jew could safely become a German. Scorning Nazi racism, he failed to see the trickery to which assimilation was subject: one's history as a Jew could not be canceled. It was a destiny, if only as a bond to ancestry that one might wish concealed, obscured, forgotten. The Nazis assailed this fact with inimitable savagery. But there were other ways in which Jünger's commendation of Jewish orthodoxy was problematic. A crystallized Judaism meant a community isolated and thus exposed, a ghetto nationalism. Had Jünger been as attentive to the realities of *Boden* as he was to the metaphorical *Blut,* he might have drawn the logical conclusion of his own premise and supported Zionism. In the event, his argument for Orthodox Judaism underscores his opposition to any sort of pluralism within Germany.

Schwarzschild did Jünger lasting service in publishing an essay that made clear once and for all that Jünger did not belong in the Nazi ranks. He performed another soon after in writing one of the few sober and dispassionate critiques of Jünger. He sensibly traced Jünger's worldview back to the trenches, charging that in assuming troop leadership Jünger forgot his initial service as a recruit, forgot the automatization in which millions of other men were obliged to function. Jünger's lieutenancy had fired him with an evangelical faith in battle as a kind of magical opportunity for heroism, but his nationalism, derived from an "aristocratic hero-mystique," was singularly apart from what Schwarzschild called "Hitler's nationalism of plebeian alley scum." Exaltation of the few, though, requires the debasement of many, and modern war admits scant space for heroics. That is why few people, scum or otherwise, could respond to Jünger. Schwarzschild was not bothered by Jünger's revolutionary urges, but he insisted on knowing where Jünger presumed they would lead: "*That*'s what interests us, that's what we want to know, and Jünger too ought to know. But that's precisely what we can't discover." Jünger's mystifying appeal to fate was at fault.[116]

What was the point of Jünger's anarchic nationalism but to show hatred of the bourgeoisie, a term, Schwarzschild aptly observes, that Jünger always uses "not in its socioeconomic sense but as the antithesis to the heroic." All the world is bourgeois in Jünger's sense. Even revolutionaries, their tasks performed, needed jobs. Hence, "the first step from destructive chaos into the nationalistic frontier will be a step into a new middle classness." In short, Jünger's projection of his own *Lebensstil* (Schwarzschild uses Spengler's "lifestyle") onto a nation's millions has no warrant. We might call it a Peter Pan nationalism insistent that a whole people should not grow up, nor old nor fat.

Jünger met Goebbels once more, at Berlin's opening performance of Hanns Johst's *Schlageter,* a play celebrating a terrorist the French occupation forces had executed in 1923 for industrial sabotage in the Ruhr.[117] The year was 1933. When the new Minister of Popular Enlightenment and Propaganda saw Jünger, he triumphantly remarked, "What do you say *now?*" Jünger has not recorded his reply. Twelve years later, only a week after Goebbels took his own life, and the day that Nazi Germany surrendered to its foes, Jünger reflected, "One always answers yes too soon."[118]

Jünger's fervid essays of late Weimar have passed into the dark history of its decline. Over and above them remains the first version of *The Adventurous Heart* (*Das abenteuerliche Herz,* 1929), a series of impressionistic, mostly autobiographical notes and nightmare fictions written in Leipzig, Berlin, and Naples. He also edited three volumes of photographs: one on the war, one on technological transformations of industry and society, and a third on natural and human catastrophes. These collections sound variations on the theme of violence as apocalyptic potential.

It is ironic that Jünger withdrew from activist journalism as the issues he had addressed in Weimar's profitable years came to the critical fore. Only weeks before Hitler assumed the chancellorship, Jünger's vision of a soldier-worker state came to a brief articulation within the government itself, in the two-month administration (December 3, 1932, to January 28, 1933) of General Kurt von Schleicher. This chancellor, fated to die in the Night of Long Knives, hoped to form an authoritarian state based on an antiparliamentary alliance of the army and labor—a program possibly inspired by the utopianism we find in Jünger's *The Worker*.[119]

Much less prominent but a key Jüngerian document is the record of his second visit to the Mediterranean, an evening and a morning in the ravines of Sicily's Cape Gallo in 1929. He called it a letter to the man in the moon. It is his declaration of a critical advance from the optics of distance that shaped his war writing toward what he calls a "higher trigonometry." He opens with an engaging remembrance of childhood when moonlight held him in terror, in that he feared its magnetic power would draw him into space. Sometimes he would dreamily accept this power and see himself being borne "without will like a cork on dark flood waters high over a landscape of nocturnal woods, of village roofs, with castles and churches glimmering like black silver . . . no fear, only a feeling of inescapable aloneness in the midst of a world secretly overwhelmed by deadly silent powers."[120]

Childish fancy gave way to the "northern light" of understanding, but enlightenment, he insists, holds within it both a beam of eternal light and a shade of eternal darkness. Jünger prefers dark riddle to bright resolution because the conundrum mediating between chance and necessity can become resident in language itself. "The language I dream of must to its last letter be comprehensible or wholly incomprehensible as the expression of a most high exclusivity that alone makes one capable of the highest love. Some crystals are transparent in only one direction."[121]

He means that language itself becomes the field of the unknown and wondrous, assuming enticing shades of experiences so valuable they escape the laws of time. In this nocturne, Jünger hails memory as key to what is innermostly human: "What else are we but mirror images of ourselves, and where we sit together as two, there the third, God, is not distant."¹²² If there is a mystical intrusion into the world of chance and necessity, it comes in this grace of perceiving identity between the wondrous and the real. The lunar landscape provides work for astronomical topography but also for a magical trigonometry, and so the moon is simultaneously a province of science and spirits: "the imagination, which has conferred a face upon it, has understood with the depth of a child's view the primeval script of runes and the daimon's language." Here Jünger reaches back over his restive adolescence and reclaims the awestruck child of a moonlit room.

After Africa and the war, he had learned to see mystery in proximity; it no longer needed situation in the exotica of a jungle or the battle-front's havoc. Romantic desire for the remote, ideal, and fantastic could only bring disillusionment in the attaining. For Jünger, distancing became more desirable than the distant. He had moved from the boyish adventurer's need to assert and overbear to the more subtly appropriative position of withdrawal. The romantic perspective upon an idealized, distant object yields to a perspective that is itself distanced so as to encompass everything, yoking opposites. It is like the moon, which sees "the pale masks of lovers" and once saw the tobacco smoke of young enlistees "who would soon have to break the secret seal of death, as its message had already been prepared for them."

As the child is father to the man, Jünger identifies himself retrospectively as the juvenile victim of "a tormenting dichotomy" that made the real and the wondrous into contraries. Unable to escape this dualism, he, "the great grandson of an idealist generation, the grandson of a romantic, and the son of a positivist," had presumed resolution of the either-or impossible. One had either exalted wonder into transcendence, making it the end of impossible yearning, or had denied it altogether. Jünger believed he broke the ancestral bonds in discovering the real is as magical as the magical is real.

That message had lain hidden all along in his childhood's stereopticon. With the double images of that magical instrument fused into one, "the new dimension of depth emerged in them." Concrete particulars could become ciphers of hidden meanings. The wondrous is simply what secretly waits for a perspective to unconceal it. Jünger's "higher trigonometry" reads depth into and behind the seeming flatness of immediate objects.

Had he satisfied himself wholly with enchantment, he would have remained sequestered in romantic rebellion against his father's positivism, that totem of scientific rationality. The final stage of revolt would have been a baleful anti-intellectualism. His attacks upon intellectuals in the Weimar essays suggest he came close enough to this zero-point. Such isolation would also have impoverished his writing. The yoking of the empirical to the mythic and oneiric allowed him to penetrate recondite strata of reality and showed him that the mission of language is to determine those revelatory points where the physical and metaphysical conjoin. "Magical realism" could as well be denominated metaphysical realism.[123] As Spengler, following Hegel, had tracked a hidden unity in history, Jünger scouted a hidden unity in sensibility. Mediation of experience and dream, the discovery of their interpenetration, ratified his withdrawal from political activism, where only the nimble opportunism of a Goebbels had demonstrable success.

4 · Beehives in a Botany of Steel:

The Worker, 1932

he Worker: Mastery and Form (Der Arbeiter: Herrschaft und Gestalt)
appeared in 1932. It stands, after *Stahlgewitter,* as unquestionably
the most important of Jünger's works in the crystallization of his
reputation as a fascist. It is his answer to Marx's paradox that technological advances endow material forces with intelligent life and stupefy
human life into a material force. Jünger's publisher grandly proclaimed it
as an exposition of the twentieth century's "meaning and will," the answer
to Spengler's "cultural pessimism," posed with a hardness and coldness
bound, so the press hoped, to frighten liberals, parliamentarians, democrats, and all who still gave credence to Weimar's republic.

The book was virtually stillborn, as it identified nationalism and socialism alike as part of the nineteenth century's detritus, to be swept away in
anticipation of a new, "planetary style." The Nazis had no use for it—
Hitler himself allegedly dismissed it—but Jünger was let be, and the book
was never censured. It was even advertised as late as 1939 with the incongruous assumption that it attested "our faith in the national future."[1]

Jünger never revised *The Worker.* When in the late 1950s his publisher,
Klett, planned a series of his collected works, only Martin Heidegger's
urging induced Jünger to include it. It is a work he would perhaps sooner
have forgotten.

A brief overview of this book, never translated into English, may be
helpful. The future state Jünger projects is manned by a technocracy of
soldier-workers. These faceless units achieve a Hegelian synthesis of freedom, derived from affirmation of technology, and obedience, a submission to the mystified spirit at work in their machines and themselves. They
are the totalitarian agents of an impersonal destiny. Technology has conveniently swept away the old contests of ideology, capitalist and commu-

nist. Nationalism, too, has become anachronistic. One hallmark of this new state is its universal character; every society will become an ensemble of industrial and technological tasks. Another is that, with comfort and security outmoded, work has become the only goal. Performance is itself mastery and achievement. History has at last advanced humankind to a unitary completion, with all the instinctive and task-mastering drive of a bee colony.

Because *The Worker* entertains a totalitarian future, we presume Jünger's projections were fascist. *The Worker's* own evidence, however, justifies an estimate weighted with careful nuances. The question, then: why did he propound a Nietzschean "barbarism from on high"? Why did he presume that amoral technology would supersede apparently futile contests of political ideologies and resolve crises of industrial capitalism?

So-called technocracy enjoyed high esteem among European intellectuals and other people in the 1920s. Technology's productive potential became prestigious in the postwar years as a way out of class conflict and wearisome partisan strife. All social and economic differences, it was believed, could be resolved by engineering. Automated rationalization of industry and scientific organization of work processes augured a new social harmony that political partisanship and gross economic disparities had never achieved. Although working-class leftists suspected that technology would only refine capitalist exploitation of labor, Lenin himself in *State and Revolution* foresaw that a government stripped of bureaucracy might serve as a mechanism of high-technical perfection. Ideologues of mechanical progress such as Eugen Diesel, Graf Coudenhove-Kalergi, and Heinrich Hauser urged peace with technology's power on the ground that it complemented ethics and nature itself.[2] The planned economy promised as much to capitalism as to socialism. It is, of course, easy to overestimate the appeal (or threat) of technology in the consciousness of most people. Testimony on its virtues comes from a well-educated, articulate, and cultishly inspired minority.

The war's ruin of the German economy had prepared the way for "the new objectivity" (*die neue Sachlichkeit*), a phrase denominating the intellectuals' embrace of an oncoming host of technological devices. Inspiration came mostly from abroad: taylorization or clock-calculated factory production in America and the constructivist ideology of revolutionary Russia pointed the militant way. As Futurism before the war had celebrated speed and violence for overcoming the old order, so after the war, as that order tottered amid civil strife and then inflation, Dadaism and the Bauhaus celebrated industrial efficiency. Artistic creativity itself became stylized as a workshop effort. Writers and painters proudly presumed themselves laborers or laboratory technicians of their own talent. Brecht and Moholy-Nagy dressed like mechanics. Intellectuals and artists who had long felt marginal to society now seized with a convert's fervor upon a new world of gigantic apparatus in which they believed they could play central, determining roles. "Cultural bolsheviks" and "asphalt literati" marveled at standardization, Fordism's conveyor-belt culture, and the centrifugal dynamism of big cities.

Perhaps film best exemplifies the élan of new processes and the intellectual excitement over them. Virtually from inception, it enjoyed enormous public reception. Germany's film industry throve in the early Weimar years because the economic and political turmoil kept out foreign (French and American) competitors. Of later Weimar films, Walter Ruttmann's plotless *Berlin, die Symphonie einer Grosstadt* (1927) holds special import, for within its silent restiveness the film's audience observes itself as commuters throng herdlike in the metropolitan subways. The "new objectivity" was showing humanity entangled in its own processes, caught on film. In the most famous image of the time, in Fritz Lang's *Metropolis* (1926), a man is affixed cruciform to a huge clocklike disc, his arms and legs stiffly jerking (or jerked) like hour- or minute-hands set to some recondite tempo.

Where the Nazis entertained the sinister ethic of a false god, the State, the cultists of technology entertained another, efficiency. Jünger's *Worker* conjoined these idols. The contestant workshop states he envisages, states ever poised for war, will still be nations, but he does not infuse into them the sloganeering claims of racial or cultural supremacy. The nostalgic *Blut und Boden* ideology of Hermann Löns has no place here. Whatever nationalist fervor Jünger once felt now disappeared completely, his aristocratic instinct of autonomy emerging like some marine mammal at last seeking air.

The Worker is indebted to the Hobbesian philosophy of the jurisprudential theorist Carl Schmitt. Jünger accepts uncritically Schmitt's case for warfare's inevitability based upon ever shifting friend-and-foe relations among states. He also owes much to Heinrich Treitschke, Wilhelmine Germany's court historiographer, who articulated a nationalist mission for the new federal state. Unlike Treitschke, however, Jünger did not presume that Germany was bound for supremacy in the contest of nations. In fact, it is Treitschke's Prussian world that Jünger explodes in *The Worker*. Jünger attacks the once worthy German middle class because it has become, to his vision, anachronistic. The compromising low-order values it cherishes, security and comfort, have been proven inadequate to the needs of a violent age.

The Worker issues no romantic summons to revolt on behalf of individual freedoms. To the contrary: the "individual" is only "that wonderfully abstract figure of man, the precious discovery of middle-class sensibility, the inexhaustible subject of its artistic imagination."[3] With that other sacred entity, the masses, the individual forms a double image of the nineteenth century's anarchy, the political vessel of which was parliamentary democracy. Here Jünger stands with Spengler, who saw individualism as the last expression of humankind's predatory soul seeking a release from the spiritual and intellectual leveling effected by great numbers of people: "The idea of personality," Spengler wrote in the year of *The Worker*, "darkly inchoate, is a protest against mass man. The tension between the two is waxing to a tragic end."[4]

Since the old order is crumbling and the new must succeed it, why, we may wonder, Jünger's peculiar hostility to the bourgeois? We have noted that he rejected the stab-in-the-back legend, but Jünger's version of a national betrayal is far more radical and encompassing. He points not to a particular party nor to any minority (Jews or communists) but to the very heart of the social order, the German middle class. His "November criminals" number into the respectable millions. The troops in the trenches, he alleges, were betrayed not by "Western" parliamentarians at Versailles, nor in some cabal of so-called international Jewish conspirators, but in their own homes. Jünger's attack on the bourgeoisie seems a scarcely veiled totemic assault upon his father's hearth, a counterattack, though tardy as a delayed-action bomb, carried into the truly domestic front.

By "bourgeois" he understands people as both masses and individuals. Although modern industrialism and the growth of cities have shaped them, neither the collective nor the singular is an economic unit, nor does Jünger give either a substantial profile. He does not heed vintage Marxist-Leninist issues like ownership of production, finance capitalism, the mass strike, nor even Rosa Luxemburg's revisionism. The masses are indiscriminate aggregates guided by political and economic forces over which they have no control. Within but against them are individuals who seek yet cannot attain differentiation or dominance.

Jünger's masses are not Gustave Le Bon's *foule,* the crowd or mob fickle, impulsive, intolerant, and susceptible. Neither does he admit the notion of an articulate mass such as trade unions. Nietzsche had recoiled with loathing from "the herd" (a term Jünger eschews) and sought refuge in a mountain-top psychology suitable to "aristocratic" sensibilities,[5] but Jünger remained imperturbable (a more convincing aristocratic posture), because he, unlike most intellectuals, had been a leader of men. He knew "the masses" can bleed. A man who for years regularly led many men to death or disfigurement knows them as more than numbers.

The bourgeoisie before the Great War had enjoyed the luxuries of progressive science and art for its own sake; it had also tamed workers through benefits, but war mobilization had exposed all the façades. War required asceticism—poverty, work, courage, or what in another time would be called blood, tears, sweat, and toil—as a visible sign of a concept much deeper than anything before it.

The task of reading and interpreting these signs clearly could not fall to the masses or their dialectical partner, the individual. Jünger conveniently posits a third group, "the few." Only these seers could show the way by surmounting the force and speed of processes in which everyone was caught. Whatever else *The Worker* may be, it can be construed as a kind of adventure, a campaign through a cosmic marsh vivid with danger. Taken that way, rather than as a crypto-Nazi tract, it invites less repugnance.

Jünger's principal weapon in this campaign was *Gestalt,* a word so polyvalent that it threatens to become meaningless, or, like Humpty Dumpty's words, to go on any number of errands. The Grimm brothers, in their mammoth dictionary, tried to exhaust it within twelve pages of small print.[6] Jünger's *Gestalt* is a predestined form of the self which one must reach. Rather than seek an English equivalent for it, we shall see how Jünger works from it.

If he has committed the fatal German error of conceiving will as a metaphysical rather than a psychological entity, the same kind of error lies in *Gestalt.* It is an hypostasis all its own and cannot be subjected to rational formulation. Since Jünger's whole impetus in *The Worker* is directed against the conceptual, it is consistent that he eschews a precise definition. Instead, he offers mystifying analogical characterizations. *Ge-*

stalt is a whole greater than the sum of its parts, as a man is more than the sum of his atoms, a marriage more than a man and a wife, a people more than data of population.[7] Humanity as *Gestalt* belongs to eternity, the proper province of one's highest existence and deepest affirmations. One may claim "a right to *Gestalt*," to self-realization carried to some irrational limit.[8] The worst possible despair, says Jünger, is not to have fulfilled oneself, not to have become a semblance of *Gestalt*. It might be called the sum of all one's powers in action. The middle class cosmos of calculable, convenient interests shows itself antithetical to *Gestalt* by hedging in the potential for a unifying fullness of life. Hence, the way to *Gestalt* requires that one discard every valuative category, aesthetic, moral, even scientific—and that of the elder Jünger's positivism (a sort of evangelical mixture of ethics, aesthetics, and science) perhaps most of all.

Jünger's brave new world begins with total negation of inherited norms. *The Worker*'s most notorious boutade says that the best answer to the mind's betrayal of life (the bourgeois enterprise) is the mind's betrayal of mind: "One of the high and horrid pleasures of our time is to have a share in this demolition."[9] We note that it is the mind itself which betrays.

Jünger's aggressive language was not novel to the age, nor was his desire to sweep away paternity. He stands in rhetorical succession to Strindberg ("wreck everything for the sake of air"), to Nietzsche the *Feuerwerker,* and to those prophetic zainies, the Futurists. Concluding his famous manifesto, Marinetti had exhorted, "So let them come, the cheerful incendiaries with charred fingers." There is, however, a chasmic difference between Jünger's and all the earlier bombast. The Futurists' call to revolt, for instance, their cult of danger and mechanical energy, their longing to destroy every museum and academy, their superpatriotic celebration of war—"the world's only hygiene" Marinetti called it—all of that preceded the Great War. The exuberant anger before 1914 was substantially theatrical, a summons to youth to shake off the mortmain of the middle class and its cult of the past. Avant-garde aesthetics, the vehicle of young bourgeois intelligentsia throughout Europe, offered no new order, only emphatic disorder. No one knew how very soon it was to come.

Although seeming to revive these titanic impulses of the prewar, Jünger could not escape history. All who wrote before 1914 had lived in a world of innocence. He wrote from a world exhausted by experience, but in 1932 he was writing not so much after the war as within it; the scope of his prophecy is not merely prospective.

The worldwide Depression initiated an epoch that promised to make all things new. Perhaps 1929 would prove, like 1914, a harbinger of cataclysm. It had gone far to overthrow the assumption that fate is reducible to probability, and that human consciousness means all-sufficient mastery. This crisis fired no artillery, but it heralded danger, and the human heart, Jünger argues, seeking the adventures of love and hate, of defeat and triumph, feels a need for danger as for security.[10] His expectation that civilization was reaching the zero point from which a wholly new order would come seemed well-founded.

He was caught, though, in the fatal illusion that the Great War had been a protest of his generation against old and long-uncontested values. He did not wish to see it as the effect of empires jockeying for prestige, sending their youth to the presumed glory of battle in order to defend inglorious material interests; he did not recognize that he and his fellows, friends and foes alike, fought a war for the sake of the middle class and privileged everywhere. An apocalypse should not be vulgar, and so Jünger persuaded himself that the war's effect—in Germany, a congeries of resentments—was also its cause.

In *Battle as Inner Experience* he had conceived the war as the expression of primitive impulses brooking no restraint. To this psychological fatalism he adds in *The Worker* a singular voluntarism from the trenches. The war empowered youthful romanticism by forcing it to be heroic and not fugitive; hardy, not valetudinarian. Jünger says the war realized a congruence of the elementary and the romantic; no longer was romanticism a mere dialectical protest or bourgeois negation of the bourgeois. Suddenly, it had been exalted into the heady dynamics of peril. The hazardous, unknown, and exceptional became for four years the ordinary. Now, in the early 1930s, Jünger, comfortably passing into middle age, seeks to reclaim that time's high tensions: the Depression signaled the reemergence of danger, "as though it had broken in from primitive times and great distances. Spirits have arisen from the fire-torn, blood-drunk earth who will not depart with the cannon's silence. They flow weirdly over all values, and give them a transformed sense."[11]

Jünger did not wish to give the dead an elegiac uplift or morbid pomp. Memorializing, easily tinged with sentimentality or vulgarity, was alien to his hauteur. He knew just what differences stand between heroism and its public face, but in *The Worker*'s new order death holds a covalent integrity with life. Freedom, manifested as a particular expression of ne-

cessity, meets fate on a knife's edge. This new world of intensified means
and powers requires "a percussive spectacle of attacks," a condition like
a dream's confusion but from which the mind supposedly arises with
new power.[12] Jünger holds that living at the convergence of necessity and
freedom begets "heroic realism."[13] It is heroic as it admits, affirms, and
endures anarchy; it is realism, as it embraces the elementary forces of life,
not least the most violent and destructive, as complements of a cosmic
whole. He intends this heroic realism to signify an unambiguously splendid state of affairs, open-ended like one of his boyhood's adventures in
the marsh. No marsh nor jungle, however, held the world's present lawlessness; that you would find in the big cities, those "burning points of
all conceivable contraries," of production and consumption, of apparent
order and recondite crime.[14] A telescopic view of these contraries would
dissolve their differences and reveal a cellular unity.

The key word in that cellular unity is *work*. It is an odd term for Jünger to employ, in that he had never been obliged to earn his own living.
Perhaps that is why he ignores the class struggle. Jünger does not understand work as grim, grinding toil or clock-set tedium in factory or office,
or even the sometime adventure of a laboratory. It is exactly the worka-
day realm and its punchcard realities that he disdains. He argues that "the
shopkeepers of freedom, the buffoons of power," the bourgeoisie *grande
et petite,* understand work only according to the confining, punitive moral-
ism of a corrupted Christianity, which takes work as evil or as penance
for evil, and freedom as delivery from work.[15] Jünger sees the claims of
work as identical to those of freedom. Work is the pursuit of one's own
laws, the calling of one's *Gestalt,* an autonomous expression of self and of
mastery. It is also service, the dues of necessity. The dynamism of Jünger's notion of work is nothing other than Nietzsche's Will to Power.

Jünger sketches a landscape where all prerogatives of comfort begin
to vanish. In the new age, everything is to be conceivable as work: not
only the performances of brain and heart, but all manifestations of love,
art, science, faith, war—everything. Warrant for this all-embracing momentum Jünger secured from prewar ideologies: from the centrifuge of
expressionism, cubism, quantum theory, and the "energetisches Impera-
tiv" of Wilhelm Ostwald, father of physical chemistry. Indeed, the turn-
of-the-century conversion of sciences from classical to modern models
might be conceived as Jünger's sort of mystification of work.[16]

Jünger characterizes a pure work-world not by its products (it is not certain there are any) but by its processes, which he sets at a Prussian army's tempo: "a fusion of elements, rhythmic marches, heroic battles." Not quite Henry Ford's assembly line, this "new school of anarchy" promised to increase the burdens of labor but concomitantly the power needed to overcome them.[17]

Jünger wants to impose upon the notion of work an energetic compass that first de-coins its standard value as toil and then identifies it as an elementary process more fundamental than life itself. He needs this primitive universalization of work to establish that his worker has risen above conventional notions of labor, especially those of partisan ideologies, but in this process he demeans work as anyone's creative expression.

Who is the worker? Not, certainly, the Marxist's proletarian laboring under capitalist oppression. Following Schmitt, Jünger equated Marxism with liberalism; it misconceived the proletarian struggle, which was in fact a self-negation of the bourgeoisie. The worker in the Marxist conception could be no more than a successor to the reasonable and virtuous individual: international, democratic, and pacifist. "Proletariat" means for Jünger the masses of yesterday; it is an economic or humanitarian concept, not a symbol of the worker's *Gestalt*. He predicts that the masses will be replaced with new quantities, much as the representations of matter had been changed by the advent of physical chemistry.

Jünger's worker is, or so he believes, an emerging power. He submits that those who toil in factories will remain puppets of the old order so long as they fail to see that, relative to modern society, they stand not in a condition of opposition but of total "otherness" (*Andersartigkeit*). Opposites can be tamed, bought, made respectable, as Rome's plebeian tribunes were when insinuated into patrician ranks. Industrial workers will be the true enemies of the bourgeoisie only when they cease to feel, think, and exist according to its molds, when they stop desiring what the bourgeoisie says is desirable. Jünger's desideratum is not a society where workers would be "elevated" into the bourgeoisie, but a new state, where legal ties give way to military, contracts to commands.

As Jünger does not concern himself with economic realities, his bourgeois is only a straw man that lacks any social or economic profile save as a disposition of mind.[18] The working person, the proletarian in Jünger's vision, is similarly insubstantial. We may ask whether, given his slighting of economics, even of the Marxist categories of production and property relations under capitalism, his new-world view admits tangible alteration of the old. Anticipating this objection, he insists no economic transformation is possible without stirring the mud of interests and claims—what the working class really wants is to become bourgeois—and no breakthrough from them can succeed; no transformation will occur, only more detestable contracts.

He is confident that economic contests for material freedom and power are secondary to "a higher law of battle," one in which his own metaphysical rebelliousness finds no check.[19] Chiefly, he does not want his worker to be tinged with the Marxist *ressentiment* which blights the suffering and dispossessed, nor to be won over by so-called benefits. He does not share Spengler's fear that tensions between owners and workers have become dangerous or that workers have grown ignorant of and hateful toward their work.[20] No; the worker's means shall be those of a warrior "holding sway over provinces and great cities, all the more securely as he knows how to despise them."[21] Getting past this Zarathustran fustian, we see that Jünger's worker is the Great War's frontline soldier returned, one who by a fiery baptism sustains "the unknown, the extraordinary, the dangerous" as welcome constants of the new age.[22] Jünger barely hides his desire for dark provinces where the anthropology of war can be renewed. In a new world of unremitting hazard, there comes, Jünger pledges, a new kind of human relationship, one bearing "a hotter love and a more terrible mercilessness," and with the most strenuous field order possible ensues "the possibility of a joyous anarchy." It is the spectacle in which his generation immersed itself on the plains of Belgium and northern France, and which anyone could now behold in any large, metastasizing city.[23]

The urban landscape of the early 1930s had become a revelation greater than the martial field half a generation before. It carried the dynamic ambivalence of the times to an extreme pitch: economic catastrophe and political crisis were being played out vividly in the large city, that most fertile ground for the restive and angry, the unemployed, the dispossessed and anomic. But there, too, one could see the titanic anarchy of productive processes: capitalism's voracious need for growth and mass consumption, its uncontrollable creation of comforts. Jünger delighted in its Janus-faced centrifuge of luxury and misery, in both the desperate downward turns of the unemployed, and the frantic "progress" of industrial output. He did not even disparage the passivity of consumerism because he saw in the dependency upon industrial and technological goods a tacit subservience useful to the worker's totalitarian tomorrow.

Seeing this double aspect in the metallic wizardry of modern times, he invoked Nietzsche's Will to Power as technology's concomitant. Only some exaltation of the will could match the daunting prestige of modern industrial sciences, and so he recast Nietzsche's Will into a mastery of means for regulating the world's economy. His belief that the new world order would induce a succession of wars was more than a concession to the hardheaded antiutopism of "the new objectivity": because, in his ethic, the new humanity wants commands, not promises, and the deepest joy lies in sacrifice, not convenience, the iteration of conflict is virtual necessity, the indispensable condition for stringent virtues.

The sinister converse of this strange uplift is plain: the human being becomes a means, not an end, a bearer of power but in service to the *Gestalt*. Jünger says that this new humankind is the *Gestalt*'s "sharpest weapon."[24] Against what, he does not say.

Jünger writes as if the Will to Power is struggling to keep up with Being, Being as both an elementary and historical power. The world's anguish, he says, lies in the fact that the will's mastery of Being has not yet been realized: technological means continue to seem more significant to us than we seem to ourselves. If his worker admits an image, it is Rimbaud's *ouvrier* (in "Le forgeron"), someone holding fast to the mane of a fleet horse, struggling along its windy side to gain the commanding position on its back. It is human destiny, our *Gestalt,* to ride the horse and to be carried by it, to sit as master and to comply with the unruly, dangerous, and magnificent power of both matter (nature) and of means (technology). The aim of that power is indeterminable and finally pointless; power is not some entity floating about and waiting to be seized. It is, says Jünger, an inseparable part of a resolute unity of life (*Lebenseinheit*).

Jünger's view of this struggle to mastery is redolent of the Faustian enterprise: an affirmation of a metaphysical despotism that plays itself out in our commerce with nature. Spengler had already portrayed the modern epoch as Faustian in its essential impulses. Jünger says that the hidden meaning of all our discoveries in, say, geographical or astronomical exploration is a raging will to total power, to omnipresence and omnipotence.[25] You shall be as gods, promises technology's siren voice.

Nature or matter, in Jünger's reckoning, seems to long for order. The means by which the mind can impose order includes the very chaos of human events. Chaos subsumes the means of power: technology, with a destructive potential as mighty as its constructive, and mass movements such as political parties, which busily seek domicile in governments. Whether these are cloaked as nationalisms, cults, or even as the concepts of intellectual coteries, Jünger foretells that some new and decisive kind of power will emerge from their struggles. It is as though human commerce could produce, like some undiscovered chemical combination, an explosive reaction.

The catalyst lies in technology's transformation of work. It has collapsed the quasi-feudal class differences which nineteenth-century industrialization had perpetuated. The new language of work is its pervasive movement: differences between mechanical and organic labor are increasingly obscured, so that work operations take on the character of cellular or planetary movement.[26] Moreover, Jünger contends that in this century it has become virtually impossible to observe one man. In an epoch of the masses, people move in antlike columns of discipline, not just in factories and businesses, but in their politics and leisure: the political rally, the sports stadium, the industrial firm all manifest the same primitive motion, like a magic lantern casting off a variety of images from its light. How might one distinguish an industrial plant's operations from the mobilization of men and resources on a battlefield? Even the laboratories of science are anonymous; discoveries and inventions are shrouded at their source.[27]

As life's possibilities seem to narrow, it may be that everything and everyone will be moving to a single point, that "a will to race-formation is coming alive," consuming all in preparation for a steel order.[28] That will be the chemical reaction bringing final order out of present chaos. Because Jünger sees this joyless prospect as all encompassing, he does not subscribe to the class war long desiderated by Germany's national revolutionaries (including Joseph Goebbels) nor to the Nazis' racist triumphalism. The steel order will come from the smelting of everything and everybody that has gone before it.

In *The Worker*'s landscape-to-come, race has no biological significance. The worker's *Gestalt,* a center of calm hidden within all processes, will mobilize without differentiations. Technology, the language of work, will provide both a grammar and a metaphysics of universal symbols foreign to all previous forms of representation, including the nationalist.

The Great War showed the way. Rather than conceding that the Allies won and the Central Powers lost, Jünger says there were victors and vanquished on both sides. The true victors, implicitly only the young and the

junior officers, although unable to understand fully the realm into which
they and sacrifice had moved, felt empowered by the grip of the war's
technology as "a fiery source of a new life-feeling." [29] They could observe
the war as an all-embracing work process of national efforts stamped with
a new image, what Jünger pompously terms the "organic construction" of
the world. Their elders meanwhile continued to bluster over boundaries
and treaties. Unifying the young of both sides against the elders was a
realization of deep brotherhood across the enmity, a bond forever closed
to humanitarians eager to abolish struggle, sacrifice, and destruction.

From there, Jünger presumes that a new breed, the nameless soldier,
shall attain a magical perspective upon the wholeness behind all apparent contraries of nations, classes, and ideologies. It will master society by
accommodating technology (Jünger does not expressly say the veterans
will become technocrats), passing through the present dreamlike anarchy
into a new order. The movement toward that order, a dynamic without
the support of parties, Jünger denominates a "wordless revolution." This
mystification is convenient because through it he can escape the obvious
objection to all he has said about his anonymous soldier-turned-worker,
that he has given nothing but argument by assertion. Where is the evidence that the youth in trenches on either side were uplifted by a con-
flagrant new "life-feeling"; that the shibboleths of nations and of political
parties had lost their efficacy; that the cults of individualism and of the
masses would soon yield to the militarizing organicism of technology?

Prognosticating a collectivity in masterful service to technology and
endowed with the antibourgeois "otherness" of "the simultaneous, uniform, and unequivocal," Jünger allows his prophetic vantage too great
a distance from the realities in which his polemics had been immersed
only a few years before. He forgets that economic, social, and political
forces in contest, blind armies of the night though they be, may not direct the course of events but do shape and reshape its contents. He forces
concrete relations and historical causalities to yield to his fixation upon
the irreversible destruction of the age, a fatefully necessary decline and
fall. He needs this metaphysical imperative—another argument by assertion—in order to validate his new and "other" anthropology. The almost
chthonic hiddenness of power is one of Jünger's favorite motifs, but as
an observer he scorns the din of partisan differences and underestimates
their virulent persistence. It is as though human plays of power, being
overt, are somehow not genuine to his eye.

Even the chivalric notes of individual worth which resounded in *Stahl-gewitter* and the other memoirs have reached a diminuendo. The attributes of martial individuality—the will made free, the inspiration of camaraderie, the inebriant scorn of death profiled in *Battle as Inner Experience*—none of these is applicable any longer. Fate seems to have abandoned humanity to a new unexplored world whose steel laws appear meaningless. The steel this time comes not from the episodic thunder of battle, but as a kind of metaphysical climate. The Great War's terrain necessitated maximal action and minimal concern over why and for what, so any attempt to reconcile the war, positively or negatively, with individualism, with romantic or idealistic desiderata, faced futility. Jünger in effect dismisses the vast store of fiction on the war, not only plangent and pacifist but apologist as well, which was published in Germany during the late twenties and early thirties. To him, the true face of the war was fixed, like the Worker, in a redemptive "otherness" manifested by storm troops and air squadrons. The warrior's face had changed into a semblance of his weaponry; it had become metallic and galvanized. Storm troops and air fighters now embodied a new pedigree for the work front's specialized labor. Jünger thus conjures up the anomaly of an anonymous elite, conjoining in their work the new means and the new humanity.

At no point in *The Worker* does Jünger admit that technological advances can or will further civilization's material gains. The strenuous work of an elite seems to eliminate it. Jünger's witness to the new imperium of mechanics had been violent, and he wants to carry over the brutish aspect of war technology into civil life. Humanity and machinery can make only a loveless marriage, albeit an exciting and even (to recall Faust) demonic one. Jünger realizes that the consequences of taking technological wizardry into one's consciousness may be dangerous, all the more so as they are not apparent. Indeed, because the bourgeois could only accept technology within the eudaimonism of progress, Jünger underscores technology's bleakness and hazard.

The demonic element lies in means before which humanity seems insignificant, threatened as a plaything of objects. This grotesque and comic state of affairs Jünger believes is best captured in films. Having come of age with Futurism and Expressionism, the cinema mirrors their violence, particularly well in comedy. Cinematic technique makes up its own reality by devices such as accelerated motion, fade in and fade out, montage, yet the audience accepts that reality, affirming it through the terrible, primitive enmity of laughter. (We might reckon Charlie Chaplin technology's first internationally popular figure.) More important is film itself, as it exemplifies a total otherness of reality akin to the worker's. It has a greater claim to "otherness" than does theater because it offers a completed reality, internally consistent and self-determined. Its mechanical distortions of our daily life are manifestly arbitrary yet understood by people (in masses) as a kind of language. The mass audience's acceptance of film and its language exemplifies the consumers' passivity and tacit dependence upon technology that Jünger sees in the new order.

Film interprets the age better than do books. Jünger finds that in film's inimitable vitality we rediscover the union of life and cult, a wholeness bourgeois liberalism had long left fragmented or submerged within specious claims of security and property. People, he adds, show a far deeper piety at the movies (he mentions racetracks too) than they do in churches. In fact, technology's Janus face—film can represent our world or distort it—indicates it is a content system wholly other than the Christian.

Jünger's futurism precludes religious faith because the church's very attempts to speak technology's language only facilitate secularization. As the *Gestalt* is now manifesting itself in non-, if not anti-, Christian terms, the church will have to make the peace of the inferior, even as it did in Galileo's time after failing to destroy heliocentrism. Likewise, bourgeois postulates of "humanity" and "morality" will be compromised since the bourgeois cannot subordinate technology to them: trains carry troops as well as citizens, motors serve tanks as well as cars. (Hitler brilliantly employed the airplane and automobile in his Weimar campaigns.) Technology reflects disorder and menace in the age no less than promise, and does so with amoral abandon.

Jünger welcomed the political, social, and economic anarchy of the early 1930s. He welcomed the impending ruin of large cities—he said they carried the scent of death—and the apparent nihilism of technology atomizing life's wholeness. His sardonic affirmations came from his conviction that all visible signs of degeneration and dissolution signified transition to order. Of course, terms such as "transitional period" are otiose: every time passes in some tempo of flux. War or economic crisis merely provide a more exigent transit than peace and stability. But Jünger in *The Worker* proclaims an end time: the flow of history was about to be dammed.

The chaos ensuing upon the worldwide Depression seemed to call for dictatorship, economic and political. Even in democratic America, Franklin Roosevelt upon his inaugural told the nation, "We must move as a trained and loyal army," and both the Soviet and Italian styles of state control (the latter admired in American business circles), took on a timely allure among the desperate parliamentary states. In Jünger's vision, though, dictatorship is an office of temporary emergency, as in Rome's republic, because the worker's eventually total "otherness" requires no dictatorship. As Spengler had argued, freedom and obedience would be identical.[30]

This culmination of a "wordless revolution" would come with the ability to read technology's inner logic: "In technology we recognize the effective, incontestable tool of total revolution."[31] But "totality" in Jünger's lexicon carries a daunting ambivalence. It signals closure: Jünger maintains that our heady pride in boundless progress, an ideology in which ever advancing knowledge has displaced Christianity in redemptive promises, has rested in fear and an instinct for self-preservation that requires the unending. Now, he preaches, we must conceive the world as a closed and limited totality; development cannot derive more from Being than Being has. Technology is not unlimited; it is enclosed in the moment it serves as a tool for the actual, immediate needs which the Worker's *Gestalt* determines for it.

In affirming technology's dynamic unrest, Jünger the marshland adventurer and onetime soldier makes his peace with a society that had apparently sealed off its borders to wanderlust and the longing for hazard. Technology offered him a symbolic warfront, and the sole medium of the Will to Power. Were not political and economic issues at best secondary to technological questions and soon to be wholly eclipsed by them?

In one critic's estimation, Jünger's model of totality "anticipates in its details the later totalitarian reality of the Third Reich."[32] Jünger, it is alleged, foresaw the use of film for indoctrination of the masses, even though the Soviet film industry had already been exploiting that potential in the works of Pudovkin and Eisenstein. Precluding the argument of a proto-Nazi construct in *The Worker* is Jünger's expectation that war-veterans-turned-revolutionaries would form a new aristocracy at the peak of a technologically determined social pyramid. He naturally presumed that men of his own visionary stamp (Schauwecker, von Salomon, Niekisch, and brother Fritz) would emerge on top, but these were men hardly compatible with the mediocre and for the most part intellectually negligible sorts who formed Hitler's hierarchy.

The problem with Jünger's paradox of freedom in obedience is that it was fixed upon the galvanic years 1914–1918. His model of totality lay back in the Great War's mobilization, and the elitist image of Jünger's "new aristocracy" was shaped by the singular autonomy which junior officers in the German army had exercised. They had served an authoritarian system by improvisations that combat foisted upon them. Many, like Jünger, were educated, upper-middle-class graduates of gymnasia or the Realschule. Only such people would have felt themselves qualified and entitled as a "new aristocracy." They were city dwellers who had seen history pass by the Junker fiefdoms, but they had not noticed, as Goebbels had, that power was now determined in the streets. They wanted violent overthrow of the republic and presumed they were moving toward it from the salon. Jünger's elitism reflects this near-sightedness. He cannot reckon the daily life and needs of any group or class beyond his own, narrow ambit.

Even so, his diagnosis of contemporary ills makes an eloquent, shrewd pathology and gives *The Worker* its continued value. He describes an age feverish in its transformations and attended by confusion and anxiety. Life is like a deadly competition requiring every possible energy, a savage thaumaturgy. Those not within the rhythms of the age must think it mad. It is instructive that Jünger notes a Christian would judge this time satanic. Although not a professed Christian, Jünger argues precisely this satanism: the capitalist landscape has turned into an inferno of frustrated efforts. Just as on the battlefield, no one wins; neither work nor property pays. As living standards worsen, one becomes more dependent upon comforts believed necessary yet always changing. Expenditure exceeds income; inflation destroys the last vestiges of security, while improvements in the technological arsenal mean that bread must cost more.

However dated some of Jünger's assumptions—nothing is so dated as a failed apocalypse—much that he remarks on technology still carries a point. He maintains that the twentieth century has felt technological power without learning its responsible use. Anxiety will attend use until we achieve the will to master danger. The problem is that an increased facility of means begets a naive trust that averts the eye from facts, but some means are so terrible that we close them away like poisons in a cabinet: "The highest advance of technological efforts may attain nothing more than death, which is bitter alike to all ages."[33] Yet, he adds, it is as wrong to believe that technology is a weapon for deeper enmities as to presume that in trade it will guarantee peace. Its mission is service to power, pacific or martial. Jünger tells us it matters little whether war can or cannot be justified by reason and morality. Books on this question he deems futile as far as praxis is concerned, for any war's justification can always be contrived before, during, or after the fact. The real issue is whether might and right are truly identical; the accent must fall upon both words. (Would a Nazi have argued that?) By 1932, the question reached "planetary significance" because it was bound closely to technology as the decisive means of war.

In this perilous new era, when war machinery had reached an annihilating potential (Jünger read 1918 as the next generation read 1945), nothing could be gained either from liberal "Western" models or from the reactionary chauvinism in Germany itself. Jünger rejected both parliamentary-democratic and fascist states because he saw that no nation can long monopolize technological changes nor even hope to control their terrifying tempo. The reason, he moralizes, is that we can no longer assume, as the Enlightenment's eudaimonism assumed, that we are basically good: we may be potentially good and evil at the same time and capable of anything, as the Great War demonstrated. Like many of his works, *The Worker* records Jünger's pietistic fascination with evil, a force the stronger in his reckoning because it is so furtive, hidden, and too often denied. That is why for him no meliorist argument that life or humanity is improving wins final credence. No optimism can hide the ever deadlier conflicts among peoples. The only solution is a supranational unity, one too profound to be left to treaties and alliances. Jünger contends that only the worker's technological *Gestalt* can insure that unity because only it has planetary sway.

German critics identified *The Worker* as bolshevist prophecy.[34] Its mystification of technology, patently at odds with the Conservative Revolution's regression to folkish nationalism, drew fire. In the *Deutsche Rundschau,* for instance, his supposed "attempts at planning and mechanization" were denounced as contrary to the "Urgestalt of the People." Jünger's analysis of the world crisis was elsewhere attacked as "thoroughly bolshevist."[35] As it seemed just that to Ernst Niekisch, he hailed *The Worker* as a "transfiguration of the Russians' experimental world."[36]

These assessments, positive and negative alike, overshoot their mark: Jünger nowhere claims the Soviet experience is the paradigm of his projected *Gestalt* or even its approximation. That globally the age is one of transitional "necessary anarchy"[37] means any number of organizational types *might* serve to create a new order. Because this service would, in Jünger's view, require a willing, sacrificially disposed youth, he entertained a number of models: civilization's arsenal can best be served by a martial or monkish personnel like the Society of Jesus, the German Order of Knights, and the Prussian army since Frederick the Great.

For all his keen perception into contemporary maladies, Jünger remains oddly indifferent to the fateful role of political power. Whether the new order comes from a military coup or a government minister (Schleicher?) is all one to him. The new order's final severity of discipline and sacrifice alone matter.[38] His failure to ground analysis in historical data takes an odd turn: he cannot demonstrate that the Soviet model of economic development, for all its discipline and sacrifice (we can think of other words), would more likely realize the workers' *Gestalt* than would the supposedly doomed leisure societies of the West. To this criticism he would answer that even in the West, particularly in the United States, the dynamics of technological industry were transforming the national culture. Stalin himself allegedly admired the "taylorization" of American labor. In short, the new dynamics provided the denominator common to East and West, transcending all political differences. That is why in the worldwide movement toward "organic construction," mobilization through technology, it did not matter to Jünger who won or who lost.

His contention that the state was becoming the indispensable arbiter of all activity seemed to his critics a cryptic endorsement of the Soviet system. In 1932 Germany was still a constitutional republic, and the threat of totalitarian statism appeared to many to come more likely from communism than from National Socialism.

Ironically, bolshevism itself took inspiration from the German war machine which had served Jünger as a prototype of total mobilization. Lenin expressly modeled his state planning committee upon the Kaiser's central office for armaments production, the *Waffen- und Munitionsbeschaffungsamt* ("Wumba"). His *State and Revolution* took the state-monopolized "war capitalism" of General Ludendorff as the model for disciplining workers: everyone, whether in a bureau or a factory, would become an employee of the all-encompassing state syndicate. This totalitarianism barely differs from Jünger's workshop landscape that harnesses everyone's energy in peace and in war. Lenin believed statism was a necessary step toward socialism, even as Jünger accepted it as a transit to "organic construction." Apparent congruence of vision and the prototype of the "Wumba" do not, however, obscure Jünger's fundamental difference from Lenin: he believed technology was displacing every political ideology. Its worker would be neither fascist nor republican but a titan achieving a "unity of mastery" long resident "in the cosmopolite's dreams and the teachings of [Nietzsche's] Superman."[39]

This new uniformity, suprapartisan and extranational, Jünger called a "type" (*Typus*). Drawing upon biology, he likens it to a natural force that reproduces forms but not differences within them. Nature's "stern law seeks to preserve an unbroken constancy of every form."[40] Therein lies its aesthetic appeal, the rule more wonderful than any exceptions. Nature, claims Jünger, resists mixing; the proof is that in all species there is a stamp (*Prägung,* the impress of *Gestalt*) superior to cause and effect. Science explains incident and contingency but not the necessity that furnishes the natural and human world with definite, unequivocal images, what Jünger calls "a festive monotony of symbols."[41] The acanthus leaf, the phallus, the lingam, the scarab, the cobra, Buddha in repose, the pyramid, Segesta's temple—these are his cherished instances, evocative rather than rational choices.

A Darwinian motif lurks in Jünger's grim wedding of nature to metaphysics. Human life, he says, presents itself historically as intention but not yet fully as expression; anxiety, restlessness, aggression are the anarchic signs of failure to pass from one to the other, yet in all of nature's creatures completion inheres. The *Typus* will signify that completion by reconciling the organic and instrumental within the human, so people may attain "that naive certainty with which the animal uses its organs."[42] The "wordless revolution" will achieve this animal-like totality.

Because of its planetary significance, this human beehive will not be the same as any national state. The antievolutionary aspect of this development is that the *Typus* once achieved will be unalterable; stamped by the *Gestalt,* it will pass from the planned landscape into "the terminal world of forms."

That termination is peculiar because, although Jünger carries the legacy of earlier revolutionary writers' utopist accents—Rousseau's antinomian dismissal of civilization, Marx's presumption of a eudaimonistic process in history, Nietzsche's vitalist gospel of self-overcoming, the Futurists' embrace of steel and speed—he rejects utopism as an illusory attempt to master history. His own worker state seems to close history off. The human will, more obedient than free, is shortchanged. Implicitly, Jünger rejects Hitler and the Great Man notion of historical development.

Jünger's suprahistorical worker state is both more and less than the modern totalitarian state: more, as it reaches global expression; less, as within it the individual wins "real mastery." Jünger the bourgeois has insured a safe corner for his own sensibility. The very notion of completion in order implies the security he despised in the elder generation, but his micro- and macroscopic views make of the worker himself at once a bee and a titan. Jünger precludes ordinary dimensions of human endeavor. He does, though, allow what he calls a "workers' democracy" — one equipped with the magical means of the age: zeppelins, turbines, mechanized cities, motorized armies, gigantic arenas — a democracy of processes, not views. Like technology, it is dynamically symbolic, not programmatic.

What would the worker's world look like? We might suppose the totally planned technological landscape with its flashy dynamics would afford all the metallic lovelessness in the futuristic fantasies of H. G. Wells or Aldous Huxley. In one of his photographic anthologies, Jünger captioned an aerial photo of Manhattan's Chrysler Building "the cosmopolis." The skyscrapers of America's city profiles, a fascinating anomaly to the most urbane of Europeans in the 1920s, served as emblems of the titans' cybernetic hubris. Jünger believed that, with a new sense of space, the worker's society, even while building upward with skyscrapers (the titanic gesture par excellence), would extend horizontally and cancel all differences between town and country. Gone, the ancient containment of city walls.

Planning this urban landscape would be an artist's task. Jünger cites with high esteem historical models of a conceptual power he wants to see translated into the new order's architecture: the Aztec capital of pre-Columbian Mexico, the lofty rock-walled towns of Tibet, the Moorish gardens of Grenada, the castles of Palermo, the earthly paradise of the Taj Mahal. In each of these splendid sites he read the identity of art with a space-filling life force, yet nearly all the models he holds up occupy a small scale; his megalopolis would dwarf them and their exotic charm beyond comparison. The new scale of things may be the inevitable dimension of a world revolution, but is there an aesthetic of the gigantesque? The monstrous man-dwindling plans projected in Third Reich architecture are monitory.

Those menacing scenes alert us to other questions: would a "mastering race" admit differentiation into classes of workers? Would the longest-running contest in history, the class struggle, be transposed into higher and lower orders? Is Jünger's cherished scheme of command and obedience only a militarization of bourgeois consciousness (with private property secure) over those who by historical fiat truly deserve to be called workers? Jünger's prophetic tact keeps him free of precise images, but what he wants is a biological aesthetic, that human society organize itself like a beehive—an exquisite image of motion amid stasis—and that the city, too, realize an exfoliation that reconciles it to nature's environment. His landscape, planned as a titanic apiary, would be a botany of steel.

In retrospect he has said: "What counts in *The Worker* is the vision. It concerns a grandeur that is neither economic nor political, but quasi-mythic: the epoch of the gods has passed and we are entering the age of the titans. That's obvious everywhere. People act exactly as I have analyzed them, but it irritates them if you say so. They want to pass themselves off as philanthropists or Marxists, but in fact they are simply power wielders."[43] In conflating the metaphysical and the mythical Jünger, like Plato, realizes that a mythic image is far more eloquent than any philosophical argument because it reaches us at an elementary, irrational level of consciousness. *The Worker* is, among much else, an encomium to the "elementary." If its word images are few, its heralding of a total "otherness" in the worker, of a "mastering race" guiding a technological juggernaut that sweeps away all the old values while reconciling humankind to nature in a kind of biologized Hegelianism—all that is vivid enough.

In his projection, Jünger still keeps company with the rightists by entertaining that deterministic incubus, Nietzsche's Will to Power, by siding with a supposed destiny against the processes of reason and responsibility, by salvaging within that fatalism the solace of elitism and its privileged visions. If immune to the truculent revenge fantasies of other rightists, he could no more escape than they could memories of the Great War's curtain-raising on an order at once hugely cohesive and immeasurably violent. What more imposing argument for the Will to Power was there than that war, what more convincing semblance of human capacities dormant or perhaps rotting in peace: courage and self-sacrifice but also the primitive, intoxicant summoning of all one's energies. The war's technological spectacles argued that the human species had taken irreversible new direction, forever modified by the mechanical dramaturgy of its own vices.

Jünger recognizes that no criticism of an age can escape its bounds to some superior vantage of judgment, a concession that subverts the seer-like elevation of his predominant tone, but he insists upon the singularity of the 1914 generation and what he calls its fate-time. Even though *The*

Worker eschews a historical exposition that might have informed its many insights into the disjunctive rhythms and frets of its age, the notion of fate-time is fetching. Jünger felt the Great War's cosmic jolting of human sensibility had superannuated the youths of his generation. Their fate-time, their "rendezvous with destiny," was violently, inextricably bound to technology, a phenomenon that had imposed upon high and popular cultures alike a sense of inevitability and incalculable power.[44] Yoked to its wide-open dynamism, the war's survivors could make a truly titanic claim upon history. The coming planetary revolution, Jünger announces grandiosely, would reveal a new and unknown world "both richer and more annihilating" than the discovery of America.[45] If technology, the open sesame of this new world, has enriched the amoral Will to Power with satellites, missiles, and computers, while setting their efficiency as an absolute value against the old virtues—justice, temperance, wisdom, not to mention Christian charity—then Jünger's *Worker* has proven a sound prophecy.

We miss this point if we construe totalitarianism only as a political ideology from which everything is derived. Jünger's totalitarianism unifies the mechanical and organic; it enfolds sleek armies and factories, agriculture, architecture, travel, and communications. Oddly, conceived as a kind of magic, technology makes the worker and the worker state passive. Perhaps Jünger's preoccupation with "mastery" betrays anxiety over an implicit recumbence, that the vaunted Will to Power amounts only to some "higher" receptivity. Such is the not so cryptic lesson of any fatalism, Jünger's included: the *Gestalt* happens to us, we are stamped, and we must ride Rimbaud's horse.

Is that why wars are always likely? Only a few nations in 1932 were capable of technological supremacy, and others of the second rank, such as Soviet Russia, were struggling under the disproportionate burdens of transition to a "worker's democracy." And yet the feverish preparation of war machinery in that time proved that the attempts of disarmament treaties to reduce the danger of war were pointless; they merely rechanneled the energy of "the total work-character" to other creative purposes which could serve in the event of war.

It is noteworthy that while *The Worker* initially assumes that wars are inevitable, by its end Jünger wants to believe that *military* conflicts are not. The real warfare, transformation of the old world of security, class strife, and unemployment, is internal to every modern nation-state. Meanwhile, subordination of smaller, weaker peoples to imperial states will continue. Jünger does not distinguish this process from old-style colonialism. He does not show how the old economics and politics would necessarily fail to adopt the new technologies and thus fail to perpetuate the values he considered outmoded. Indeed, his own proprietary concern about security comes through at the book's end: preparation of the planned landscape should include efforts to avoid foreign conflicts that would disturb new deployments. Jünger even suggests that construction of new empires, while tantamount to an attack upon the divisive nation-state, would make possible "wars without gunpowder": "The gravitational pull of the total work-character makes the use of special battle equipment superfluous."[46] The modern community of interests and the possibility of global federation could preclude military engagement among competing empires. About the progress of technological competition Jünger remained indifferent, unlike old-guardsman Spengler who, in the year *The Worker* appeared, lectured on his fear that with revolutionary threats sapping once dominant nations, once "backward" states like Japan, having acquired the Promethean fires of technology, would turn the trick upon the debilitated Western states and gain predominance. Jünger contentedly believed all plan-landscapes would become one.

For all the starkness of his vision, he is an optimist. While Spengler's is a doom-saying tone, Jünger's in *The Worker* sounds a cosmic harmony; all the old divisions within people and between them and nature would at last be overcome. Spengler concluded that all history is evanescent, but Jünger looks to abiding unities and hidden harmonies: the entrenchment of Christian Europe only hastens revolutionary socialism. Hence, his insouciance, the mountaintop calm of Zarathustra.

The Worker's defects are clear, chiefly in the semantic confusions of its operant terms. We presume that Jünger's *Gestalt* is virtually Plato's world of forms or Schopenhauer's Will, a spiritualized yet impersonal metaphysics. Like other transcendent realms, Jünger's does not move out of its own murky void. The worker experiences the Will to Power to the fullest, but the delineations of its exercise remain opaque. Like Nietzsche's prophetic "revaluation of all values," Jünger's projection lacks final focus.

A stubborn amorality gives *The Worker* its chilly, inhuman cast. The coming worker state is, despite (or because of) its technological "mastery," a dystopia. Sweeping away old illusions of well-being, Jünger neglects to salvage simple human affections that are no less elementary—

let us hope they are more so—than the unruly and presumptuous Will to Power. Work itself, after all, is, whatever its manifestations, not only energy expended but a caring at some level. Jünger dismisses, possibly fears, anything that might bring personal consolation or satisfaction. Human affections would shortchange his war-nostalgic asceticism. Like Gide, he has a protestant's horror of comfort.

The Worker remains open to scorn because of its proximity in time and temper to Nazism. Jünger's dissembling remarks in his Paris journals, that this book showed him swung most powerfully toward the pole of collectivism, that it was his dialogue with technology, do not count for much against the book's fateful position in 1932.[47] Although Jünger rejected the Nazis, both when they were outside of total power and when they were manipulating it, he did go far to proclaim a somber and daimonic totalitarianism such as engulfed Germany within months of *The Worker*'s publication. Hitler did not need Jünger's prophetics in order to achieve power. Der Führer even dismissed Jünger's notion of the worker state as a hindrance to Nazism.[48] But Jünger's worker state is cousin to the Third Reich because of what it seeks to destroy: not the blurry bourgeois but the prime constituent of human life, which is family.

I submit that Jünger's essential impetus is totemic: he is attacking his father's rational-progressive values and his hearth. We recall his models for a future society of barracks. He hails cadets of old army schools and those "on whose faces the influence of seminaries is to be read," and evokes lastly "the oriental gardens in which no one has memory of father and mother."[49] That is perhaps the most ghastly pronouncement of all. Jünger rejects the family as the state's bedrock. This dogged turning away from intimacy is the preface to all that follows.

The Worker's most telling weakness is that, lacking the progression of a historical causality and the cohesion of a philosophical system, it obdurately overwhelms its own insights and subdues the tempo of its own expectations. Having no professional training, Jünger goes the random gentlemanly route of Spengler's sort of *Kulturphilosophie,* making pronouncements that too easily elude facts. Like Spengler, he is propelled by a vatic amateurism that shows itself to advantage only in brief, aphoristic passages. *The Worker* tests our ability to accept a patchwork of intuitive discourse that admits no demonstrative reasoning. Despite differences of tone and assumption between Jünger's optics and Spengler's, *The Worker* shares too well a defiance of logical sequence that characterizes *The De-*

cline of the West. The form of both works mirrors the clear disdain of reason which makes up much of their content. A work that purports to be a vision of things to come cannot be held to logic, but neither need it be tethered to the bulk of three hundred small-printed pages.[50]

Prophecy's accents betray a restive hand. Like his contemporaries Theodor Adorno and Walter Benjamin, Jünger seems eager, if not desperate, to proclaim and embrace a horrific future just over the horizon, to show that by heroic exertion humankind can live on the dreadful terms technology shall dictate. An odd genre of discourse, this resilient alarmism can be traced back to Nietzsche and on through Heidegger and his structuralist successors. In its lineage, Jünger occupies a central post. In war he saw how technology, begetting an utmost violence, assumes rhetorical force. Marxists preached that technological advances entail ideological changes. For Jünger technology is its own ideology, superseding all others. Fuzzy as to details, he leaves little doubt that our accommodation to the furtive despotism of machinery will find only a few on top: cybernetic storm troops.

Projections of fearsome things to come in a technocratic age have long been commonplace in literature. Jünger makes other contributions after the Second World War, in *Heliopolis* and *The Glass Bees.* Such works enjoy a timeless insularity; they continue to engage on their own terms and need not depend upon the historical contexts that produced them in order to sustain interest. But *The Worker,* lacking fictive adornment, has fared otherwise. History discredits it. Like Spengler's *Decline,* it can be facilely dismissed as pseudoprophecy. Republican democracy has twice within this century triumphed, apparently, over its totalitarian foes.

Historical process, however, admits no closure. We know that fascism has an ongoing and tenacious life: rooted in despair of morals and reason, it is the abiding incubus of nationalism. Jünger looks beneath political categories, pressing on to the dark underside, to our ambivalence about technological magic, to our intuitive unease that what outwardly liberates inwardly shackles. *The Worker* is a Spartan's text: in it the human will, lean and sinewy, makes grim peace with the machinery it has wrought. It accepts the shackles, as though doing so makes them more bearable.

5 · The "Internal Emigration": 1933–1939

Although Jünger withdrew to his garden after the Nazis took power in 1933, his name kept a high profile throughout the thirties.[1] Literary and cultural journals such as *Deutsche Rundschau, Deutsches Adelblatt,* and *Literarisches Centrallblatt* serialized excerpts from his war memoirs. One might say he became a canonical writer, his war books serviceable to the National Socialist rearing of a new generation. Boys could expect to find a revised edition (1934, 1935) of *Stahlgewitter* in the Christmas stocking. It was recommended reading for upper grades of the gymnasia, and schoolbook publishers included passages from the war memoirs for German and history classes.[2] Jünger was inevitably a subject of critical discussions of Great War literature.

Attention to war literature became more pronounced after Hitler reintroduced universal military service in March 1935. At that time even Germans averse to Hitler saw his action as a move to restore Germany's status as a nation among equals.[3] But Jünger's prominence in the schools and presses cannot simply be ascribed to the Nazi push for *Gleichschaltung* or conformism. Unlike the Soviet government, the German state did not attempt to achieve monolithic cultural authority: "An all-encompassing conversion to National Socialist conceptions could not have succeeded and would not have been politically expedient."[4] As Nazi ideology did not change property relations, it tolerated an apparent pluralism that appealed to the middle class because it was nonpolitical. Even the Party's weekly magazine, the *Illustrierter Beobachter,* had the innocuous semblance of middle-class vulgarity. As one scholar of Third Reich popular culture observes, "until the war's outbreak and in a very restricted way even into the forties there were open channels for non–National Socialist literature in newspapers and journals."[5]

Jünger's popularity in the thirties was not the effect of Nazi propaganda; his early works had long appealed to anti-Nazi conservatives intent upon awakening consciousness of national honor and power. His war service had been exceptional, not typical, yet convenient to a warrior idealism the Party sought to make normative. Jünger was the latest exemplar in a long literary tradition of *Heldendichtung* ready for appropriation. Not that he was without critics. Granting that the war produced Jünger's "heroic sort of man," one argued the war's chief significance was "the attainment of a new value of nationhood" to which Jünger's "manly conduct in war" should be subordinated.[6] Jünger had mistakenly made heroism into something unto itself and had failed to idealize the role of the Volk. However valuable as war documents, his books failed to "fulfill the requirements of genuine *Kriegsdichtung*."[7]

Even so, the Wehrmacht made use of Jünger's war books. They and his 1930 essay on total mobilization (a sketch for *The Worker*), were reviewed in military science journals. With preparation for another war built into the 1936 Four Year Plan, the military found Jünger's books valuable in combat training. The flowery 1934 revision of *Stahlgewitter* did not detract from regard for the book's war psychology and its concrete view of tactics. "In short," wrote one military reviewer, it was "a profoundly experiential but also cunning, scientifically interpretive book."[8] Still more useful was *Battle as Inner Experience,* where the atavistic instincts that beget war are so coolly profiled.

Jünger kept his distance from the Nazis, and, because Göring was atop the military, did not reenlist. When Hitler became chancellor in January 1933, Jünger was still living in Berlin, where he witnessed the closing of Jewish businesses and with his brother attended the Reichstag Fire trial of van der Lubbe. When elected in November to the newly reconstituted Academy of Poetry he refused the position:

> The singularity of my work lies in its essentially soldierly character, which I do not wish to prejudice through academic ties. In particular I feel obliged to express even in my personal conduct my views on the relation between armament and culture set down in my book *The Worker,* ch. 59. So I ask you to understand my rejection as a sacrifice imposed on me by my participation in the German mobilization, in service of which I've been active since 1914.[9]

This statement is disingenuous. Like old Stefan George, who had repeatedly refused invitations to join the Academy, Jünger wanted to go his own way. Joining a military rank and file might have been admissible; joining an academic society, intolerable. Besides, the Third Reich's literary lineup was staggeringly mediocre. Only Rudolf Binding, whose four-years' diary account of the war, *Aus dem Kriege,* rivals *Stahlgewitter* in poise and lucidity, could have kept Jünger company. And Binding, nearly thirty years his senior, learned the sorry cost of conformism. He initially rationalized Nazi racism and the April 1933 book burnings as "peripheral matters [*Randerscheinungen*] which do not affect at all the actual sovereignty, essence, and truth" of the "movement."[10] Binding's life companion was Jewish, and as racial persecution became more than "peripheral," he wrote hopeless letters of protest.

In December 1933 Jünger moved to Goslar, in Lower Saxony, allegedly the oldest town east of the Rhine and famed for its architectural vestiges of medieval life. This was the first in a series of provincial residences which insured him some freedom for his writing. Having proclaimed big cities the tool of fate and the Zeitgeist, he turned his back on both present and future.

In May 1934, the Party organ, the *Völkischer Beobachter,* published without his authorization a portion of *The Adventurous Heart.* Jünger protested that this printing "gives the impression that I am a contributor to your journal. That is absolutely not the case." He stressed that it was "inadmissible" that "on one hand the official press accords me the role of contributor while on the other it thwarted the printing of my letter to the Academy of Poetry on November 18, 1933."[11]

Jünger was going against the time, not with it. During the republic he wrote of war and urged revolution; during the thirties he wrote exactly what the Nazis suspected, despised, and denounced as "psychologizing, aestheticizing" literature. He even transformed the taut chronicles of *Stahlgewitter* into a "literary" product, thus setting himself apart from the hack nationalists who wrote war fictions and memoirs contra Remarque. Three of his best works, his account of his breakaway to Africa, the surreal version of *The Adventurous Heart,* and his parable against totalitarianism date from the peacetime Reich.

His war writings did not make Jünger a best-selling author or *Renner* (racehorse), as the Germans say. The prevalent mediocrity of literary productivity under Hitler encouraged the already conservative reading public to favor Weimar era writers and some from preceding generations such as Hermann Löns. The most popular war book during the Third Reich came from this older vintage, Manfred von Richthofen's *Der rote Kampf-flieger,* 1917. In twenty years it sold 420,000 copies, a huge sum in that generation.[12]

Jünger joined what the novelist Frank Thiess called "the internal emigration." Why didn't Jünger, indisposed to the Nazis, leave Germany? This is a common, anachronistic question. Jünger had no crystal ball in which to foresee the disasters to come. Was it certain that Hitler would last longer than Von Papen had? Was the Empowerment Act of March 1933 perceptibly worse than the parliamentary chaos of early Weimar or the possibility of civil war in late Weimar? Yet, these questions are pale extenuations, for nothing was so convincing a portent of Hitler's ruthlessness and opportunism as the Röhm "purge" of June 30, 1934, when the SA's would-be revolutionaries were rounded up and shot without trial. Röhm's too vocal desire to sweep aside the old Prussian generals and establish a new military order was not entirely at odds with Jünger's own desire to enfranchise the generation of 1914–1918. Jünger destroyed his journals of this time after the Gestapo came to his home searching for papers of Ernst Niekisch.

His war writings of the twenties made Jünger in the thirties willy-nilly an ideological prompter for a war that Hitler had by 1937 resolved to prosecute, but the object of Hitler's intent, annihilation of the Bolshevik (allegedly Jewish) menace to Europe, was a desideratum wholly contrary to Jünger's hopes. Jünger's identification with revolution in his Weimar polemics, his proximity to national bolshevism in *The Worker,* and his contributions to Niekisch's anti-Nazi *Widerstand* (Resistance) were not overlooked by Nazi ideologues who, as late as 1936, identified him as "a communist socialist."[13] But Jünger the alleged bolshevik was mostly ignored or forgotten.

Jünger's independence from institutional professions insulated him from the brute realities of the Party's *Gleichschaltung.* Had he occupied a university chair or research post at a scientific institute he would have witnessed the expulsion of Jewish teachers and scholars, a demoralization that had immediate and incalculable cultural consequences. But his withdrawal to Goslar could not entirely insulate him. Although, like Spengler, he disdained Nazism's appeal to herd instincts, its exercises in mass oratory, and its racism, he could not become a Robinson Crusoe. In fact, he traveled abroad and travel gave him a critical perspective upon the Third Reich that most Germans were not permitted to attain.

Being able to afford and being permitted travel abroad under Hitler's regime constituted an extraordinary privilege. Economic recovery made vacationing expensive if not impossible for most working Germans. Roads were primitive and car ownership exceptional. In 1934, the ratio of people to cars in Germany was 96:1; in the United States, 5:1. The Third Reich early projected the Volkswagen as "the car for millions" that would show "how true socialism looks: that the good things of this world are not for one class of people alone but for the whole productive Volk."[14] Construction of the seven-thousand-kilometer Autobahn, the Führer's showpiece—"Coming centuries will say, 'These are the roads Adolf Hitler built'"[15]—progressed at an average of 1 km a day in the spring of 1935. By June 1936 three hundred kilometers were completed, and one thousand by that October. Well-publicized engineering advances notwithstanding—Hitler's engineers invented clover-leaf intersections[16]—the auto industry was constrained by Germany's dependence upon imported rubber and by the furtive priority of military rearmament.

There were few admissibly advertisable places for travel abroad: tiny Lichtenstein; Iceland, where "Nordic features predominate"; and Finland, with its "culture-people of Nordic stamp."[17] The dirigible Graf Zeppelin carried the wealthier to Rio de Janeiro, the Hindenburg to America. By ship, one could visit Madeira, the Greek isles, or Morocco on three-week cruises. Norway, Portugal, and Brazil were havens. It is a substantial measure of Jünger's financial security in the thirties that he was able to afford three of these approved routes of tourism abroad. His wife, burdened with two small children (a second son, Alexander, was born in 1934), remained at home.

"Innermost within me I have maintained, so I hope, an untouchable portion of elementary freedom wherein I know how to prize the value of all good, natural things,"[18] Jünger wrote to his brother, Fritz, from Norway in the summer of 1935. He spent the late autumn and early winter of 1936 in Brazil with stops at the Azores and Morocco; April and May of 1938 on Rhodes. He kept careful journals on each tour, anticipating that he might not see such places again for a long while. He took no camera; it mechanizes remembrance, he complained.

Visiting Norway, he felt he had stepped away from historical time, back to a world where one needed no names and dates; even heroic deeds impinged no more upon memory than did the northern lights. The Norwegians occupied a realm of elementary powers, where "the pure anarchy" of enchanted isolation opened onto "the blue depths of metaphysical space [and] the mind refreshes itself in unseen chambers."[19] Entering a land unmarked by war and ponderous industries he likened to going into a park's hedges for refuge from a storm.

Jünger resisted his own romantic indulgence by accompanying a paramedic fisherman on his rounds among melancholics. He also visited an old woman sequestered by leprosy. He took woodland walks with fellow traveler Hugo Fischer, an old friend from Leipzig. They could stroll the whole day and see no one, absorbing the land's hidden beauty which, Jünger remarks, at once saddens and cheers the heart. Here "the elementary" of a culture's lore was literally at one's feet, in the moor's down (in Norwegian *myrdun*, his journal's title). From its tiny blossoms, said legend, fairies would spin and make clothing for their Erl prince.

Fischer was exceptional among Jünger's friends because he influenced him, as Jünger acknowledged in calling him "der Magister." A naturalist, Fischer encouraged Jünger's antipathy to academic science and his attention to nature's secret correspondences, particularly those between people and animals. Nature is a series of picture puzzles opening the certain path to amazement, joy, and occasional terror. Fischer eschewed experiment in favor of the metaphysical, meaning he conscripted observation into the service of mystification. The dark side to his fondness for the hidden was his fascination with the ultimately hidden. "He called death the most wondrous journey a man can take, a genuine bit of magic, the invisible cloak [*Tarnkappe*] of all invisible cloaks . . . the last unassailable fortress of all who are free and brave—in discussing this matter he was wholly inexhaustible in similes and eulogies."[20]

But Fischer's strange company did not keep Jünger from the peace and rest he enjoyed amid Norway's "wholly unformed chaos."[21] Particularly illuminating are a few elliptical remarks on the world from which both men had come: "We often first realize we have suffered when an outbreak of joy grants us a higher awareness. Time has beaten down its traces in us like the snow of many years, in which debris, boulders, and the bitterness of wars and civil strife have accumulated. But when light falls on the clefts, the avalanches go into the valley."[22] An elitist's image par excellence: it is the mountaintop that is made pure, clean, and free. The not so hidden theme within *Myrdun* is release, "for with each wall that man erects, he adds a piece to the primeval fortresses of constraint in which the world spirit's cunning holds him prisoner."[23] Far more pointed is the admission that Jünger's generation had obtained "a wicked lot in which old and new evils are intertwined, and who knows whether a full wind will once more get behind our sails."[24] Within a month of Jünger's return to Germany, the "Nuremberg laws" against Jewish citizens were promulgated. Within five years, the German army would invade and occupy the Erl prince's land.[25]

A full wind was behind Germany's sails the following year, 1936. Hitler's gambler-throw reoccupying the Rhineland (March 7) paid off handsomely in overwhelming support by referendum. German prestige rose further with the hosting of the Olympic Games in Berlin. These festivities obscured the fact that Germany was about to embark on its Four Year Plan of economic independence and war preparation. The announcement came on September 9. In November, Mussolini made public the "Axis." By then Jünger had put a full wind behind his own sails, bound by steamer for South America.

So-called travel literature is easy to overlook; it seems occasional and impressionistic, but Jünger's *Atlantische Fahrt* (Atlantic Journey) ranks among his most important works. It could not have been published during the Third Reich.[26]

Jünger wanted to observe a jungle's vitality firsthand, having been cheated of the deadly chance twenty-five years before. On an expedition inland from the Brazilian coast he remarked the jungle's "secret architecture," that "the pure power of growth uplifts and presses down every individuated representation; in its violent tendency it expresses the extraordinary power of the life impulse so that the observer feels it directed even against himself." Some plants' narcotic attractions terrify him, and enormous "islands" of vegetation fret his consciousness by their "glaring chaos of light and darkness." Here the "elementary power" which invited leisurely metaphysics in Norway turns menacing. It invites the mind's excessive imagination to wed itself to a phantasmagoria of shine and shade, to become lost in its own propensity for rendering images into magic.

Jünger, keen-eyed, enjoys giving danger its Linnean nomenclature and dramatizes himself by locating deadliness in a luxuriant foliage, not in a serpent's venom. Stepping back, he regains equipoise. When he discovers a rare Amazonian water lily (Victoria regia) he notes that it represents a warmer time on earth, has now withdrawn to the equator, and will pass thence to the transcendent realm, a perfect "form" of rose.

Reminded of death latent in life, he visits a snake farm near São Paulo where serums are produced. He delights to find snakes restored to their ancient Greek service as healers. Science, no less than the occult, now gives them their due. "The common horror of snakes would be unthinkable if people would only relate themselves to what is strange and unknown."[27] Three years later, Jünger will carry his enchantment with reptiles onto the Marble Cliffs, where the serpents' venom alone defeats a barbarous foe.

It is clear in these pages that Jünger is not, as the conformist phrase went, "working toward the Führer."[28] He distances himself from other Germans, who as tourists prefer photography to observation. Jünger enjoys immersion in a foreign culture's total otherness, securing "the Sinbad feeling of being alien," especially where the native language is wholly unknown.[29] He resists the European's colonial vantage. At Pernambuco he wonders at "mighty realms in the making," evidence for which comes from the "tangle" of several races. He reckons that mulattoes will predominate because they seem best to accommodate themselves to the climate. "The image of future worlds" lies here, he notes dispassionately.[30] Racial and cultural diversity make Rio de Janeiro "a residence of the Weltgeist." One "longs for" such a city where the *genius loci* or daimon is so splendidly manifest.[31] He pays Rio the highest compliment: not since the Great War has his sensibility been so bedazzled at every step.

Jünger does not ignore vestiges of colonial slavery among Brazilian laborers. Observing that hierarchy among slaves is a function of color, the darkest at bottom, he concludes that what counts in life is not happiness but freedom of the will. Only self-determination insures dignity. In authoritarian Germany this thought was not a commonplace.

He meets German monks, mostly Westphalians and Swabians, in a Benedictine cloister. Eating, they face him four-square on elevated stools; their guest sits below them, embarrassed, in the center. The talk turns to the Spanish war, now four months on. Jünger prophetically likens Spain's position to Iberia's in the Roman civil wars, the provincial beginning of a much greater conflict. The cloister's atmosphere uplifts him: "The monks' hospitality was especially gratifying to me when I realized it is a part of their cheerfulness. In those short hours I had an impression of the powers one can develop in living according to old and trusted prescriptions. There are indeed athletic schools for the mind." His longtime enthusiasm for Jesuits and medieval monastic orders as ascetic models had been abstract and bookish. It seems to have surprised him happily that one can be rigorous yet cheerful. He had not given his Worker a cheerful face.

His pleasure in the trip to Brazil was the greater as the return recalled him to "ever more clearly threatening times." (The steamer had passed near Spain's smoking Bay of Biscay.) How blindly presumptuous seems his hope that, withdrawn to Fritz's home on the Bodensee, he might continue his work "free, cheerful, active—despite all the baseness that surrounds us."[32] But he was prepared for the dismal reentry to Germany by the enforced company of ship's passengers, their bourgeois idleness as intolerable as his own. He felt invisible, like Poe's Arthur Gordon Pym. Such, he concluded, is the individual's fate in modern society. Jünger's only antidote is the vanguard elitism he fetched in his Weimar essays. The individual, not "the masses," must somehow become the arbiter and dispenser of social values. Jünger fancies a Roman republican order of the educated under a Sulla pledged to maintaining ancient privilege. If not a new Athens, then a new Alexandria: philosophers, theologians, and artists would regain the rank usurped from them by technicians. He offers not the faintest idea how this turnabout might be effected. What matters is not the remedy but his source of grievance, Hitler's vulgar Caesarism. Jünger blames the masses for begetting "demagogues of the purest water who seek to debase and exterminate all that does not suit them. To show oneself religious, intellectual, or artistic risks the greatest danger."[33]

The fruit of the following year, 1937, was a new edition of *The Adventurous Heart*. So thoroughly did Jünger recast it, cutting nearly 220 of its 263 pages and adding many entries, that the second edition is virtually another work. The autobiographical entries have vanished. In their stead come naturalist's sketches, metaphysical *topoi,* and reflections on literature. Some pieces come from the Norwegian and Brazilian notes. This book remains the best introduction to the diversity of Jünger's lifelong pursuits.

Not least of these are his unsettling fictions, in which, as in Goya's capriccios, we cannot discern where the quotidian has become nightmarishly fantastic. More than dream passages, they record what a subliminal or nocturnal consciousness produces from the pit of a totalitarian arena. In Hitler's state only dreams could not be censored, nor the dreamer arrested for traversing them, and yet, as Jünger tells us in *On the Marble Cliffs,* a gangster regime invades even the oneiric recesses of seemingly private life. A most instructive book that we shall never read would be *What People Dreamt in the Third Reich.* In lieu of that, we have bizarre miniatures in what Jünger might have entitled "The Disquieted Heart." Retention of an old title helped him to pass censorship, but it would have taken a keen official eye to catch the refractory images of a terrorist state on the page. They are there.

A charming picaresque tale like *African Games* was escapist, a fond reminiscence of late Wilhelmine adolescence, but it also carried a muted, needlesome despair; in its apparent major-key resolution a minor-key's chord is heard. It shuts the door on adventure: one can never escape for good. The second *Adventurous Heart* imposes this closed-in feeling on its reader. Claustral horror such as one finds in Kafka pervades the fourteen fantasies. Here is a sample, "Violet Endives":

> I stepped into a luxurious gourmet shop because I had noticed in the display window a quite uniquely violet sort of endive. I wasn't surprised when the salesman explained to me that the only kind of meat with which this dish could be served is human flesh—I had already rather dimly suspected that.
>
> We had a long talk about the manner of preparation, then we went down into the cold-storage chamber where I saw people hanging on the wall like rabbits in front of a meat merchant's shop. The salesman made it a special point that here and without exception I got my prey and did not even consider the pieces crammed in rows at the breeding establishments: "leaner, but—I'm not saying it to boast—far more aromatic." Hands, feet, and heads were set out in particular dishes and planted with little price labels.
>
> As we were going back up the stairs, I remarked: "I didn't realize the civilization in this city has already advanced so far," whereupon the salesman seemed to hesitate for a moment, so as then to give me a receipt with a very obliging smile.

The matter-of-fact tone makes revulsion more acute. Save for the sardonic irony in the narrator's only remark, there is no rhetorical dressing. The narrative's master stroke comes in depicting an enclosure or entrapment, the descent to the chamber, to which the narrator has been an accomplice. Lengthy talk about preparing the dish furthers his collusion, and in the storage room we learn that he is a regular customer. Dream logic obtrudes as the narrator's response suggests he has learned all this for the first time. The story even has a self-satiric bite: as a gourmet, the narrator reflects Jünger's own fastidious taste, elitism on a culinary scale. Only the specialty shop will do.

For Jünger, cannibalism, whether presented in choice cuts or in the assembly-line products of breeding houses, is a figurative signpost of modern technological society. Individual human worth has been made flesh. Butchery is not, of course, the invention of "advanced civilization." It is the timeless hallmark of despotism. In the Third Reich, proprieties could be stripped down at any moment; the consumer, consumed. Jünger, the *spectateur,* had had his home searched. Even so, the terror he writes of in *The Adventurous Heart* is not absolute: pleasure hides out, and in the fantasy we have just read there is implicit accountability. One cannot observe and not become an accomplice. Jünger indicates that inaction, too, has its hazard: "Here is the province of capriccios, of nocturnal jests which the mind unstirred enjoys as in a solitary loge, and not without peril."[34]

Is Jünger's dream narrative a deception? He has merged consciousness with dreaming in order to create an aesthetic distance from the content, and that content is nothing but barbarism. Writing becomes a self-protective device.[35] Yet, the stories in *The Adventurous Heart* are prickly with irony, black humor, and no little sense of moral queasiness. They unsettle, as dreams do, but with a vivid density of accusatory images.

Jünger argues in his book for dream's revelatory power, but he is not concerned with dream as a Freudian message about the self and its putative disorders; rather, dream offers an illimitable showcase upon the world. The mind works with a magically encompassing sensuousness. In dreams, we may all be geniuses: "We're like the electric current that rushes now through human bodies, now through animals or even inanimate things, right down to atoms. Our visual power, too, is not limited to our eyes—the dream world is like a plant that we're in a position to examine at every point of its form."[36] The dramatic progression in "Violet Endives" serves as a linear metaphor for dream-knowledge; it gathers into a wholeness seen finally even in its secret parts.

Jünger makes the dreamscape into a collective destiny: first, the writing becomes the reader's own dream record, an initiation into horror. Second, the writing makes it the same dream for each reader, just as in an age of mass communication a film is a kind of dream that countless numbers of people have. Technology, as Goebbels, a genie of modern culture, realized, insures programmatic dreams for millions. The Jüngerian dream is about this kind of shared destiny. What has been called "Planet Auschwitz" is adumbrated as unimaginable savagery becomes processed, commonplace as the mechanical world put into its service. A scribe of the horrific, Jünger is a successor to Kleist and E. T. A. Hoffmann.

Minds of the first order, he remarks, possess the master key; they penetrate the house's every room. They can see both the forms given to light and the generative powers which remain in the dark. *The Adventurous Heart* beats at one level in celebration of the natural world in these complementary aspects. It urges that we preserve our immediate sense of natural phenomena; the eye must sustain its power "to see the earth's works as on the first day, that is, in their divine splendor,"[37] and attend to "the recondite harmony which informs all the properties of an organism."[38] Here again sounds Fischer's accent upon the hidden, that abiding source of enthrallment. Jünger describes a Stanhope orchid and a tigerlily conjoining beauty and danger; a caterpillar observed as in motions of perfect symmetry it devours a leaf; the "telluric mathematics" of cliffside birds flying to and from their nests; and, in a botanical hothouse, the singular tactile attention a group of blind schoolchildren pay to the lancepoint leafage of a rare New Zealand specimen. Jünger followed the children silently through the garden that day, a double watch.

In such passages he is at his lyric best, his descriptive wit undiminished by his ready penchant for the elusive harmony or the alluring color. Virtually every entry on flora or fauna he presents with a votary's fascination. In the dullest landscape Jünger would find wonders, deploying his sensibility, his metaphoric skills and jaunts into abstraction—what Hamann called "the energies of our freedom"[39]—all to the service of nature. He enters into happy bondage to it, like the lad in *1001 Nights* who lived with and was loved by Peri Banou.

No less wondrous, his writings on naturalia take the reader far from the unenchanting human world in which they were set down. They remain in starkest contrast to the somberly vicious world of informer and jackboot. As though addressing the Four Year Plan, Jünger moralizes that we cannot banish need; utopic efforts to do so will only beget worse, even as technology, designed to reduce work, only seems to intensify it. At a time when the government issued certificates of merit to women bearing many children, Jünger called for a "theological understanding" of excess.

He asked his readers to remember with Hesiod that the gods have hidden our sources of nurture. The road of excess leads to war. "Mars is the insatiable devourer in this world." [40] That is what the Führer reckoned upon.

Against the juggernaut of industry and technology that Göring was supposed to set at full tilt, Jünger believed he found "an artful counterweight" in what he calls "the museum impulse . . . an inclination to imbed life in that which is at rest and inviolable." Churches had become museums, a kind of surety for "civilization" that might "leave behind a faithful likeness of our life and its most remote stirrings." As if this "impulse" were a foil to the will to power, Jünger calls it "the will to permanence" (*der Wille zur Dauer*) and ascribes to it a "mighty force." [41]

Having no Christian faith, Jünger lacked the impetus essential not simply to preserving the past but to making it vividly present. He entertained like many humanists an aesthetic regard for the outward works of a spiritual tradition. Any nonbeliever could respond to the magnificence of Romanesque architecture or to the sublimity of chant, but such "museum" experiences would remain only that. "Generally we divide people into two large classes, such as Christian and non-Christian, plunderers and plundered. Everyone does it because of all divisions the twofold is nearest to hand, but it is noteworthy that bifurcation is not a harmonic division; it is of a logical or moral nature." [42] What "harmonic" divisions could Jünger have determined when, as he confesses, one encounters "the sort of people in our cities who could *feed* upon the torments of others"? [43] The dreamscapes he sketched were close enough to the Third Reich's street realities. How, then, could he have avoided the central moral dichotomy of the time, which set one with the Nazis or against them? The imposing fact is that like countless others who lived irresolutely, indolently, or even see-no-evil-complacently, Jünger remained immobile. He expended the "energies of freedom" in the only way he knew, by writing.

The Adventurous Heart cannot be called "resistance literature," but it registers the divided consciousness many people carried through the Third Reich: a submerged awareness of official cruelties accepted easily because one's own security was not hazarded. The masses Jünger scorned took refuge in books and films, as he in his metaphysical lens upon plants and animals.

It is as though he had been set down in Octave Mirbeau's *Jardins des Supplices* (a favorite book), where natural splendor and refined tortures codwell. The effect is not horror, fright, or even anxiety, but displacement

(*Entsetzen*). Jünger makes himself an accomplice to this process by imagining enormous layers of sheet metal such as theatrical producers employ to simulate thunder. They are arranged horizontally like pages of a book yet spaced widely above one another:

> I raise you up over the topmost sheet of this mighty pile, and as your body's weight touches it, it breaks crashingly in two. You fall upon the second sheet, which likewise splits and with a more powerful bang. The fall goes on to the third, fourth, fifth sheet and so forth, and the fall's intensity causes the blows to succeed one another in an acceleration that's like a drumroll growing in tempo and vehemence. The falling and rolling become ever more frantic, changing into a huge rumbling thunder that finally bursts the limits of consciousness.[44]

In fact, Jünger wrote this dire scenario before Hitler came to power. It is one of the few passages from the first *Adventurous Heart* he included in the second. There it achieves a prophetic aptness, a Poe fantasy that anticipates the crescendo of war which in early 1938 was believed impending: "Do you sense what occurs in that space through which perhaps one day we shall fall, the space stretching between awareness of destruction and destruction?"

Jünger joked to himself that every quarter year he picked up fifteen new readers. He felt no need of more. He was enjoying "the godlike superiority of *désinvolture*," a confident cheer in private power he presumed innocent because it came not from exertion but as though by grace, "and as such it is much more closely related to fortune or magic than to the will." Francis Bacon had written that in the possessor of *désinvolture* the wheels of the mind keep step with the wheels of his fate.[45] "One believes nothing more certain," Jünger writes, "than that he is leading a life predestined beyond all chronological orderings."[46] A capacity for psychological remoteness was his safeguard. He wanted to believe it had saved him from destruction in four years of war; kept him finally aloof from the turmoil of late Weimar; kept him free from the clutches, appropriative or otherwise, of the Third Reich. He must have believed he led a charmed life. We suppose that were Jünger to be dropped through the cacophonous sheet metal, he would somehow survive the crossing of that border of consciousness, like Odysseus returned from the dead. Before every desolation, "the *Odyssey* is the great canto of lucidity, the song of the human spirit, whose course leads to its own goal, through a world full of elementary terrors and dreadful monsters, even in the face of divine opposition."[47]

As he characterized it, the opposition Jünger faced in the thirties was monstrous, howsoever oblique. It becomes direct in a tale called "The Head Ranger." Summoned by the sinister Ranger, the narrator learns that one of the preserve's staff is supposed to be exterminated for having hunted a blue viper. (In Jünger's color symbolism, blue signifies the wings of the spirit.) When the Ranger tells him that the blue viper attracts the best game, he rejoins that the slopes where it lives are never visited by men. He is sent on the way and encounters a crone digging a grave. Asked what she is doing, she titters, "Sorry, don't let it bother you—you'll find out soon enough!" He then realizes that he is the hunted. "And I began to curse my cleverness and my solitary presumption, that had ensnared me into such company, for I saw too late that all the refinement of my activities had only served to make invisible the threads with which he entangled me." It is once more the theme of complicity but with a new variation: entrapment. "The Head Ranger" reads transparently as a fable of Jünger's trackless relations with Hitler: adroitly going his own way in the "solitary presumption" of a search for freedom, he is caught. Here he provides a fearsome answer to the idle hope which closed his Brazilian diary in December 1936, that he might find free and cheerful days "despite all the baseness that surrounds us."

In the spring of 1938, as *The Adventurous Heart* went to press, Jünger left Germany for Greece. Brother Fritz, well acquainted with Greek mythic culture, accompanied him. Greek antiquity had long exerted a magnetic attraction upon educated Germans. Winckelmann and Goethe set the course of enthusiasm. Schliemann's amateur excavations of the Peloponnese, then Dörpfeld's rigorous work at Olympia and Furtwängler's at Aegina, made these unaging spaces into spas of Teutonic pride. Jünger, not one for standard itinerary, ignored most of the mainland sites. He rushed on to Rhodes, a crossway of Hellenic and Turkish cultures, with glimpses into Oriental depths of wonder. If Rio offered compacted images of the future, so did Rhodes of the past. If Brazil becharmed Jünger with life's relentless fecundity, Greece offered him death.

It meets him at every turn: in birds tormented by hunters; in medieval graveyards; in a funeral procession of wildly keening Greek women, and in another of Turkish; in the melancholy desolation of ancient ruins. At the Lindos acropolis, the brothers conclude that restorations—Sir Arthur Evans's work at Knossos was the model—were not such a good idea. Better the Turkish indifference, for in it antiquity remains neutralized. "One feels best and saddest amid ruins that are untouched and virtually forgotten: like Emir Musa in the city of brass." [48]

Counterpointing these gloomy occasions are the ever stimulating discoveries of plant and animal life, but even in magnificent exfoliations there is menace. Under an enormous, blossoming Aaron's rod, an overpowering scent of carrion is exuded, "as though a corpse were hidden within it." [49] Jünger's *Naturphilosophie* seems never to admit a simple pleasure; he is as ready to recoil as to rejoice.

Homeward along the Adriatic coast on one last excursion, he enjoys amid countless black and green lizards the freedom of microscopic views. "That works as a counterweight to technology, which daily and more powerfully consumes space." [50]

Hitler, too, was consuming space. Jünger had left Germany only a month after the annexation of Austria (March 12) and by the time of his return German troops were maneuvering near the Czech border. One night during his time away, Jünger noticed that the Führer was accompanying him. What transpired in this dream Jünger did not record. Was the Head Ranger about to summon him once more?

In Greece, freedom's home, Jünger's most eloquent hours were Jewish, including a visit to a large Jewish cemetery in Rhodes:

> There was not one standing monument to be found, only recumbent tombs, often with an ancient scent, occasionally with round niches about the size of a halved apple [bearing] a cultic significance unknown to us. Even here the slabs had been piled up; a housing shortage exists in necropolises. Going through was effortful primarily because of the Hebrew lettering, whose effect I remarked in my childhood. It differs from all other scripts in its highly condensed substance, and is thus among alphabets what radium is among the elements. [51]

In the city of Rhodes, he walked through the ancient Jewish quarter, his interest quickened because such grounds had become forbidden zones in his native land. Before the door frames stood the Torah scrolls, one of glass, others revealing their curvature through veils. Tablets in the tabernacle were out of view.

In his time Goethe was bemused and irritated by the Jews of Frankfurt, so alien and incomprehensible were they that he could not understand how "the most remarkable book in the world" had come from such people.[52] He, too, once stood helpless before Jewish inscriptions. Distance informed his ignorant outbursts—he felt Jews were loveless and without honor—but his was an age presumptive of light; Jünger's, one of dimness. The Kristallnacht fell within six months of his return. He has left no writing on it, but for nearly two years, in the midst of war, he read the Jewish scriptures, historical and prophetic, daily.

The Third Reich's twelve years produced a scant literature of enduring merit and little in opposition to the regime. Jan Petersen's *Unsere Strasse* (1934, published 1947), Werner Bergengruen's *Der Grosstyrann und das Gericht* (1935), and Frank Thiess's *Das Reich der Dämonen* (1941) stand as prose testimonies.[53] Foremost in the select band is Jünger's *Auf den Marmorklippen*. Hailed by his friends and accepted by his foes as evidence of his opposition, albeit tardy, to Nazism, this work is better known to the English-reading public than his other books. *On the Marble Cliffs* was published in 1947 and has been widely available since.

It was noticed in England during the war. In December 1942 F. A. Voigt, editor of *The Nineteenth Century and After,* took *Marmorklippen* as proof that Germany "has begun to find itself at the approach of catastrophe." He called Jünger "a German of genius who has passed prophetically, as it were, through the catastrophe," achieving thus "some of the calm, profound vision that lies beyond." Here was irresistible grist for propaganda's mill:

> It is astonishing by reason of its audacious and trenchant attack on modern tyrannies and on the cold intellectualism that makes them possible. The nightmare figure of the tyrant and the catastrophe which he brings upon himself and upon his fellow men, the liberating power of the inspired word, and the final triumph of the spirit, are drawn with a daring and an intensity of vision that makes Jünger's book one of the masterpieces of the world's literature.

Even with allowance that wartime's fervor hinders critical acuity, that was heady praise, and almost completely misplaced.

The narrative's first sentence: "All of you know the wild grief that seizes us in the remembrance of happy times." To the attentive, these

words recall Francesca da Rimini's to Dante, but Jünger hints at an earlier
expression, in the *Consolatio Philosophiae:* the most unhappy misfortune is
to have once been happy.[54] Are we in Dante's hell or with Boethius in
prison? Who are "all of you" if not the Reich's Jünger readers made initiates into the magical circle from which the story is told? Theirs is tacitly
the Vergilian hope of exiles (*Aeneid* 1.203) that the time of woes, now endured, can be recalled from the survivors' higher ground. Within his first
words, Jünger hides three immortal references, and what censor would
have found Vergil, Boethius, and Dante in a sentence?

To the story. The Marina, a lakeside community, is gradually threatened by a forest-dwelling warlord, the Head Ranger. Its protection lies
in a fraternal order of knights errant and their stolid rustic friends. Complementing the danger from without is the menace of opportunistic vigilantes within the Marina. Two knights, the narrator and his brother-friend
Otho, gauge the Ranger's looming power, as the Marina is subverted by
spies, informers, and evil dreams. The brothers are also self-suspended in
a contemplative devotion to botany. Withdrawn to a hermitage library,
they enjoy the talismans of a mirror and a lamp, both of rock crystal. The
mirror composes the sun's rays to a higher-powered fire; things kindled
in its glow attain the pure distillation of the immutable. The lamp pre-
serves the fire's power in darkness and emergency. These instruments
give the brothers magical assurance of rescue in the blackest hour. That
hour comes suddenly, the Ranger's savage dogs in the lead. The Marina
is conflagrated, but the brothers after a brief misty battle manage to survive and withdraw by boat to a distant land.

On the Marble Cliffs defies the linear contiguity of plot. It is a series
of images, passed briefly before the reader like the floral specimens that
captivate the brothers. It also defies the coherence of space and time.
Jünger admitted to his journal that he composed the marmoreal setting
from seasides he treasured in his travels: from Rhodes and Corfu, Rio de
Janeiro, and the Bodensee.[55] Lest precise geography provide too clear a
reference, Jünger imports Greek mythological elements. The isles of the
Marina are known as the Hesperides. Cypresses shading the coast recall
Calypso's island in the *Odyssey* and Böcklin's famous painting, *The Isle of
the Dead;* as arboreal emblems of death, they belong to the cult of the
dead which the Marina's people have long tended. The campagna's abundant harvests—winter brings no snow—suggest Odysseus's enchanted
way-station, the never-never land of Phaeacia.

Jünger commingles historical periods. The brothers' spiritual advisor, Father Lampros, modeled on Fischer, is a Christian monk but the world around him is alive with pagan cult deities. The Ranger's surveying of Marina's fields with runic poles invokes a Norse world: his memento mori, a human head and many hands impaled on a forest hut's gate, recalls the fate of Varus's legions in the Teutoburg Forest. And yet the botanizing brothers pay homage to the eighteenth-century Linnaeus. Battles are waged with chivalric gear (swords, daggers, spears), but at a festival the knights toast machines which have put down a rebellion in Iberia—this, an aside on the Legion Condor's thorough work in the Spanish Civil War.

Integral to Jünger's technique, this historical and cultural zigzagging may challenge patience.[56] By confounding any continuity of reference he steers free of historical fiction, yet the almost pointillist precision of his images reinforces the subjective character of his narrative vantage. He does the same with diction; he defies the linguistic fetishism of the age, the push toward a supposed purification of German, a *Verdeutscherei* that would remove all foreign-based words. (This chauvinism, so blind to the history and use of borrowed words, became so obtuse that Hitler himself put an end to it in November 1940.)[57] *On the Marble Cliffs* is a trove of borrowings (Latinisms and Grecisms in particular), Teutonic archaisms, and striking linguistic compounds.

Jünger's persona observes two disparate realms: the dark commotions of the Ranger transform the human scenery into a vortex, while the natural order provides a kind of metaphysical relief against which calamity attains nearly overwhelming force. Only in the narrator's very private experience do these two worlds conjoin. On an expedition with Otho to discover a rare flower known as the Waldvögelchen (the helleborine orchid, *Cephalenthera rubra*),[58] he discovers the Ranger's torture hut, tended by a sinister gnome. Horrified by this unexpected reconnaissance, the brothers flee the site but soon return because they have found the precious flower nearby and wish to transplant it to their herbarium. A seeming rescue, this wrenching of the flower may not finally be so distant from the Ranger's dismemberment of his foes. *On the Marble Cliffs* counterposes two hunters, the bandit seeking to plunder all visible order, and the narrator seeking to arrest secrets within that order. As foil to piratical disruptions, a transcendent harmony awaits contemplative grasp. The story sustains its tension in this contest: will aesthetics win out over brutish violence?

The question is awkward because its terms are incommensurable: the

Ranger imposes evil upon humanity, not just ugliness. The opposite of barbarous cruelty is an armed compassion, but the brothers, dutifully called to battle and participant briefly in its chaos, have no charitable ties with anyone. At the moral level, this work depicts a world of everyone for himself, and the brothers finally triumph not by affirming any good over evil but by recourse to their talisman. Their escape through this magic amounts to evasion. As conjuration is feeble ethics, Jünger's fable provides a shattered lens upon the limbo of morals within the Third Reich.

Let us turn to the story's portraiture. Although *On the Marble Cliffs* is often read *à clef*, Jünger has rejected comparisons of its characters to personalities of his time, but he has also taken pride in his book's prescience of events. He began the writing in February 1939 and completed the final draft on August 12. In some vivid particulars the book was prophetic and has been locked into its time, an exposé of Nazi totalitarianism. This says too much and too little. Half of this work belongs to Linnaeus.

Consider the central villain, the Ranger. Never once does he appear within the story's action; he is present by his absence, by the aura of despotic power emanating from him. The narrator recalls him as a great, slightly ridiculous lord. Enjoying inestimable wealth, he keeps his marauders in grip by his "terrifying joviality" at drinking tables. This is not the abstinent, humorless Hitler. Göring, who held the titles of Reichsforstmeister and Reichsjägermeister, who cultivated an oriental self-indulgence and mediated his brutality with bonhomie (accessible "Uncle Hermann" to the German public), clearly conforms to Jünger's warlord. So does Stalin, whom Jünger himself has mentioned in discussing this figure. In the period of the purges, Soviet music by injunction expressed a kind of insistent official joy, precisely a "terrifying joviality." The headhunting Stalin enjoyed, among the Kremlin's grotesquely incongruous appellations, the title of Great Gardener.

The Ranger is no enthroned dictator presiding over an iron peace. He is a force of disorder, an agèd mafioso. The narrator calls him "der grosse Boss," whose power extends wherever slaves have refused service, wherever there has been mutiny or desertion of a king in battle. The crimes of his retinue are a world apart from the Prussian orbit of discipline and service Jünger esteemed. The brothers at their botany resolve "to keep ourselves at Linnaeus's wonderwork" and to ignore the Ranger's men as one would avoid wild beasts. "Thus we did not accord the lemurs a freedom of will. Never may such powers prescribe the law to us to the degree that we lose sight of the truth" (p. 85). *Die Lemuren,* "evil spirits," became Jünger's code name for the SS in his war diaries.

What, then, of active resistance? On this point, two characters merit highlighting as they visit the brothers on a reconnaissance mission. First of these is Prince Sunmyra, remote in temperament as in name, young but prematurely aging under the weight of now useless traditions. "Thus decadence was deeply stamped in his being; one noticed in him the feature of an old ancestral greatness, and also the counterfeature which the soil works upon all heredity—for heredity is the wealth of the dead" (p. 104). This is a caricature of all nobility in the face of discord when, enfeebled by the joint forces of history and nature, its claims become delinquent. Traces of nobility are oddly discernible in Sunmyra: "In this weak body lived a strong inclination to suffering, and as in a dream he kept on his course, almost without reflection and yet with sureness" (p. 108). Sunmyra's attempt to resist the Ranger's upsurgent evil could only be futile, and he forfeits his head. Five years, almost to the day, after Jünger finished his first draft of *Marmorklippen,* Claus Schenk, Count von Stauffenburg, the Hamlet of the German aristocracy, paid with his life after failing to assassinate Hitler.

With Sunmyra comes the unprincely Braquemart, a seeker of power who holds to a master-slave view of humankind. Belonging to "the dangerous sort, those who dream concretely" (p. 103), he is both a utopist by his cold reason and a nihilist: "Like all his kind he conceived of life as a watchwork, and so he saw in force and terror the driving wheels of life's clock" (p. 106). In his cold cunning, Braquemart seems worse than the bestial Ranger, but the narrator finds a palliative in his character that links him to Sunmyra: suffering. It is not the wistful suffering of the decadent but "the bitterness of a man who has lost his salvation. He sought to avenge himself on the world because of it, just as a child in pointless anger destroys a many-colored show of flowers" (p. 107). Whatever his utopism, Braquemart is as much an enemy of order and beauty as the Ranger. Even the apparent foe of chaos carries within him the malaise of the age, that confusion of right and wrong which makes an age "ripe for terrible things" (p. 62).

Braquemart's physiognomy is a giveaway: "a small, dark, haggard fellow yet not without wit" (pp. 101–2). This, with the profile of a cynical despair, points forcefully to Jünger's acquaintance from the Friedrichstrasse days who now directed the Ministry of Propaganda. According to Jünger, Goebbels protested to Hitler that *Marmorklippen* should be banned.[59] Although possibly delighted to find his rival, Göring, transparent in the chief villain, Goebbels, if he recognized himself, must have felt slighted since he had once "laid bridges of gold before Jünger, but he didn't want to cross."[60]

Within two weeks of its publication, *Marmorklippen* sold fourteen thousand copies, but Jünger's editor, Benno Ziegler, was nervous: reviews in Swiss newspapers were identifying characters in the book with Nazi hierarchs. Jünger imperturbably wagered that the regime would show its hand by banning the book. In the event, the book owed its survival to Hitler who, when the governor of Niedersachsen complained, answered that Jünger should be left alone. If Hitler ever read this book (it seems unlikely), he would not have found himself in it. Nor should we. Even in virtual mirror resemblances like Braquemart-Goebbels, Jünger was creating a type. There are no fast-fixed correspondences: the Ranger could be found in the Kremlin or in Cicero, Illinois. Braquemart is the cunning man of instinct who gains unsteady prominence in times of upheaval: every great social convulsion has its Danton.

Goebbels's corrosive spirit is perhaps better situated in the decay of the Marina's literary culture. Poets once enjoyed honor there because their songs praising the dead secured divine favor. But now hirelings at funeral celebrations stumbled into the metrics of hate and revenge. It was a scenario familiar to Jünger and Berliners late in the twenties. A cynical corruption of the past became Goebbels's speciality in his early days as Berlin's Gauleiter. His extravaganzas staged over Nazi "martyrs" like Herbert Norkus and Horst Wessel were merely occasions for vilifying the Party's foes.[61] When Jünger's narrator observes that history is a contest between idolatrous images and the mind's capacity for thought, the remark's pertinence to those Berlin days is transparent, yet this observation stands outside of the narrative. No cultism centers upon the Ranger. Like Hitler, he mysteriously disappears from the havoc he has wrought.

Jünger's characters pass by like sketched portraits in a gallery. His composites of one and many prove to be bloodless constructs; they lack the full dimensions of a novel's personae, such as we find them in, for example, Malraux's *Condition humaine,* another fiction about murderous social upheaval, and a work Jünger esteemed highly. *On the Marble Cliffs,* by its author's reckoning, is not so much a "literary" work as a dream vision. Its scope justifies the incongruities of time and the curious perspective of a narrator incapable of resistance to impending evil yet empowered miraculously to escape it. The dream sanctions his passivity, so he remains basically a spectator throughout; he and his brother manage only to transplant the rare orchid, retrieve Sunmyra's severed head for cult worship, and withdraw to a distant land. Only through the dream's permissive circuit can this story function as "magical realism." It satisfies what Jünger identifies as the human need to approach two borders: where the divine appears, and where we become one with animals.

No *deus ex machina* resolves the tensions in this story, and the self-immolation of Father Lampros (Fischer getting his way with death) toward the story's end is a one-man show. Jünger settles for his own ancestral pietism: despite the Ranger's devastation, sacrificial smoke wreathes upward from the Marina's templar ruins, and from the chapel comes a communal hymn calling for God's help. Sunmyra's head becomes a foundation stone for a new Christian cathedral. If, as Jünger believes, the historical continuum must pass through a refining fire, to be reborn phoenixlike, then it will reemerge in some ecclesiastical guise. This point does not impose itself, however, because the narrator does not share in the communal rebirth. He has been vouchsafed his own alchemical way out of history and fire.

So much for gods, what of animals? They provide the only real action. The Ranger's most ferocious agents are his dogs, chiefly a monstrous hound named Chiffon Rouge, or Red Rag. While this name evokes the bloodthirstiness of all political subversion, nazi and bolshevik, the dog is integral, in cat-loving Jünger's view, to much more: "The North, the active world, melancholy, dogs, beer all go together, even as do the South, dreams, wine, cats, and Dionysian cheer. We can find such chains and extend them at our pleasure, like molecules of organic chemistry."[62] It is no coincidence that the Marina is a composite of southern climates and that the Ranger's habitat is a primeval Nordic forest, whose only clearing holds the ghastly torture hut.

Superior to both these realms looms the chthonic or subterranean world, whose zoological emblem is the snake. In ancient Greek folk religion, the serpent served as a household guardian and is such here, but Jünger also draws on its symbolic power as "a creature in whom poison unites both deadly and salvific power."[63] The Marina's land abounds in deadly vipers with whom the narrator's young son, Erio (an Old High German name for cultivator), enjoys exclusive bonds. This Kipling figure, significantly motherless, feeds them like pets. Foremost of these is the female, Griffin. (Jünger initially titled his story "The Snake Goddess.") In the climactic struggle, when Chiffon Rouge leads the barbarians to the narrator's garden, the Griffin and her fellow snakes dispatch them all. Only the primordial powers of the Earth (Mother) can prevail against male-driven anarchy.

Jünger's recourse to the earth's primitive energies on one hand and to divine magic for initiates on the other mark a private despair over any human redress of evils the Ranger has brought. He has taken refuge once more in the German haven called fate; the cosmography mirrored in *On the Marble Cliffs* is the amoral *amor fati* of flint-hearted stoicism. The charge weighs more forcefully as this love of fate is the passive ethic of the contemplative, the posture Jünger's narrator assumes most of the time. Private vision admits public catastrophe. The "internal emigration" of literati who sat out the Third Reich may have been all too internal.

Before assessing the fairness of this charge, let us review one notorious passage, the community's destruction as the narrator observes it from atop the marble cliffs:

> Now the depth of ruin had become manifest in lofty flames, and far off shone the old, fair cities in destruction along the Marina's shores. They sparkled in fire like a chain of rubies, and from the water's dark depths their crimped image rose. The villages, too, were burning, and the hamlets in the broadlands, and from the proud castles and cloisters in the valley the fire's ardor strove high. The flames raged like golden palms smokeless in the still air, while from out their crowns a fire-rain fell. High over this whirl of sparks hovered red-beamed swarms of doves and herons which had risen in the night from the rushes. They circled till their plumage wrapped itself in flames, then sank like burning Chinese lanterns into the conflagration. As though space were wholly without air, not a sound made its way up to me; the spectacle extended into dreadful stillness. I did not hear the children weeping nor their mothers wailing down below, nor the battle-cry of the clans nor the bawling of cattle in their stalls. From all the terror of destruction there ascended to the marble cliffs only the golden shimmer. So distant worlds burn up to the eyes' delight in ruin's beauty. (pp. 142–43)

There is more here than the telescopic distancing which facilitates Jünger's aesthetic of destruction. Initially, it seems his narrator enjoys a seat in the loge of the morally deaf: the spectacle performs itself like a silent movie. But he has supplied what is unheard yet sensed: the people's lamentations, the cows' bellowing. The stillness is the more awesome by the magnitude of what is seen. The rub is that the narrator finds not only beauty in this horrific scenario but, because there is beauty, pleasure. With ruthless candor, Jünger admits that this apocalyptic violence charms the eye: the cities become glowing gems, the flames become golden palms. The narrator is arrested in a dreamlike immobility. His situation on the marble cliffs provides physical, but also psychological, distance: the beauty of this ruin sets the narrator apart from himself: "I did not even hear the cry which arose from my mouth. Only deep within my innermost being as though I myself were standing in the flames did I hear the crackling of this fiery world" (p. 143). "As though," but the narrator does *not* stand, as Lampros did, in the fire. The interiorization of sound is part of the jumbling one experiences in dreams, where normative causality is suspended and moral accountability all but dissolved. In a dreamy trance the narrator, supplying from within himself "the crackling of this fiery world," becomes a kind of mystic, initiate to a violent revelation and not overwhelmed by it.

The moral question grazes aesthetic fascination: is the beauty of ruin in fact a beautification? or can destruction admit a compelling charm we would prefer to deny? If the modern sensibility has grown numb to issues of moral urgency, too inured to terror by distancing, cinematic representations of it, surely Nazism's cult of hardness prepared the way. Concomitant to that hardening which devalued human life went a cult of fire— Bertolt Brecht called the Third Reich a pyrocracy—the intent of which was not only annihiliation but transcendence. The Kristallnacht, smoking chimneys at Auschwitz, Hitler's instructions to Albert Speer for the incineration of Germany's industries near the war's end—all form the dire concatenation of a bogus mystique. With *On the Marble Cliffs* Jünger stands close to the Nazi cult of fire and death, to what has been called "the opposing needs" for submission to harmony and apocalyptic destruction.[64]

As though noctural pyrotechnics were not enough, the narrator is an active accomplice; he uses the magic mirror to kindle a fire that consumes his precious library. The rationale is eerie: "There is no house built nor plan laid in which downfall is not the foundation stone, and that which lives eternally in us does not rest in our works. This shone out to us in the flame, yet there was joy in its brightness" (p. 150). Such consolation through acceptance finds reinforcement presently when the brothers observe Father Lampros smiling weirdly in the fires consuming his altar as he consecrates a final host. The brothers merely witness this transfiguration, but in catastrophe's wake lies a lesson with obvious metaphoric weight, that by morning "we saw dire scenes in the cold smoke, and yet a new confidence was alive in us. Thus the morning brings counsel; and already the return of light after this long night seemed to us wondrous" (p. 152).

This aftermath holds no cheap grace, no heaven-sent transfiguration or even purgation: the vigilantes remain in charge, a sinister bureaucracy that weathers every turmoil. Pledged to beer and contemptuous of humane letters, they seem to harbor later menace. No final good triumphs, nor any evil. Jünger's narrator does not affirm the destruction: he has not willed it, only seen its inevitability and a countervailing beauty arising from it. *On the Marble Cliffs* follows the themes closing Wagner's *Götterdämmerung:* curse, ruin, rapture.

During the Second World War Jünger had occasion to talk with soldiers who had read *On the Marble Cliffs*. Some said they found consolation in it, but it is chiefly Jünger's consolation.[65] Like *Stahlgewitter,* it records a personal uplift from a vast disaster. The perspective has shifted from the active to the passive, from lucky *Draufgängertum* to circumspect stoicism. Yet, plumbing deeper than its apparent political "message" and even deeper than its metaphysical moorings in Heraclitus, we find it a confession.

Let us recall the story's first sentence. This retrospective—it must have seized many a reader's attention in the autumn of 1939—intimates that a journey into hell or prison is about to commence. It is a penitential journey. Jünger's narrator early admits he once enjoyed the Ranger's rowdyness: "Then his company was pleasant to us—we lived in haughtiness and at the tables of the world's mighty" (p. 29). What follows reads like a recantation of the nationalist essays and *The Worker:* "A mistake becomes a defect if one persists in it. . . . So we drift into past times or distant utopias, while the moment slips by. . . . As always when despair comes with maturity, we turned to power" (pp. 29–30). Although the narrator's spiritual guide is a Christian, the talk is of mistakes, not sins. Jünger's moral universe is Greek: not that the heart has transgressed; the mind has strayed. There is also renunciation. The narrator has given up the games of power and domination, and when summoned to combat the Ranger's men, he puts aside the chivalric claims of honor. He now feels, with great bitterness, the nullity of renown.

A much deeper despair concerns language faltering in the face of experience. The pen's inadequacy becomes a torment analogous to one's attempt to fly. With a rapturous gaze upon the still peaceful Marina, the narrator, trying to catch it in a description, finds that "In the same moment, almost painfully, I felt the word loosing itself from the phenomena, just like a string that snaps from a bow when too tightly drawn" (p. 26). Conversely, language becomes a mystery or hunt when the brothers by metrical exercises seek "to lay hold of a fragment of the world's mosaic" (p. 27). They pass from the micro- to the macrocosmic, describing grains of sand and the marble cliffs, and metamorphoses that occur over seconds and over centuries. Two weighty facts frame this linguistic chase: first, the attempt is recognized as a threat to balance and measure. The interior journey toward meaning may be as perilous as the outward one of youthful hubristic adventure. Second, no sooner do the brothers complete their exercises than they burn them, but not as failures. Quite the reverse: they have drawn inspiration from their efforts, and discover "The word is monarch and magician alike . . . and more wonderful than all realms which the sword contests" (p. 27). The word is politically not mightier than the sword, but its true province is infinitely greater: it imitates God by re-creating order. All the story's nominal miscellanies of history and geography are intended to cohere in the narrative itself as fragments of a cosmographical mosaic. They all contribute to the narrator's intimation of an elementary order. Hidden, like the red helleborine, from day's random commerce, "imbedded," says the narrator, "in the chance and confusions of this earth," it can be approached (p. 27).

The narrative challenges us to find its coherence. The problem lies not in the plot, which is straightforward, but in finding an integument for the arbitrary fragmentations of episode where characters and meditations are discretely stationed. *On the Marble Cliffs* reads as a series of diary entries.[66] Jünger saw the discontinuity and fussed about "spading over every sentence": "The rough passages furnish me a double chore because I'm laying them upon the already perfected ones. That contradicts the rules of economy." He likens the elusive wholeness of composition to sewing, when light is concentrated only where the needle is stitching. His fastidious honing is apparent in carefully wrought, almost poetic syntax and probed diction. Proclaiming the word's at once royal and magical power, this book comments upon itself.

Oddly, the herbarium, locus of refined musings, has something in common with despotism's cellars, those "stinkholes of a gruesome kind in which an eternally depraved rabble revels horridly in the profanation of human dignity and freedom" (p. 96). Both are subjected to the narrator's meticulous verbal scrutinies. The ordering word creates violent juxtapositions: the lovely helleborine grows by the Ranger's torture hut; ruthless Braquemart accompanies lofty Sunmyra. Enchantment and terror occupy the same world. From Goethe's garden to Buchenwald it is a walk. When Jünger wrote, the same radio carried Furtwängler and Goebbels.

Through his narrator Jünger shows his indignation at human cruelty. The passage just cited attests courage, but nowhere does he presume nor give hope that evil can be eradicated from its human position. Only nature's beneficent poison overcomes the Ranger's gangsters. Jünger's piety presents, finally, an ineffectual humanity: "He is to be esteemed fortunate whose will lives not all too anguished in its strivings" (p. 150). The brothers burn their exercises — so much for the Will to Power, but we are left with a stoic resignation, *amor fati*, accepting both good and evil.

Jünger has not scuttled or even qualified his elitism. *On the Marble Cliffs* abounds with subjective assignments of the high and low, the noble and base. Lampros, the Prince, and the brothers at their botany are the poised arbiters of all that's lofty and worthy of transcendence. Their superiority of *Geist*, both spiritual and intellectual, seems incontestable before the incorrigibly vicious "forest rabble" (*Waldgelichter*) whom, in true aristocratic fashion, they hardly deign to notice and cannot recognize as condign adversaries. Here, Jünger's equanimity takes refuge in the irrelevance of the all too private. In the vivid face of barbarism, a studied insouciance, while undoubtedly courageous in its way, carries the burden of futility. It is not the Marina's community that requires rescue but the narrator's own scrupulously hedged-in sensibility, its carefully exercised and detached curiosity. *Amor fati* reflects Jünger's predisposition to images, types, and structures, and his aversion to the linear course of human motivation and intention. The acuity of his perception depends upon a specimen-jar verticality of design even at the risk of language itself and its contextual, horizontal flow. It is as though he would check the inherently discursive, on-going nature of language by compacting it into semantic and syntactic perfections: sentence symbols. If the inadequacy of language mirrors an imperfect world, what but a symbolic language would suffice to parallel the hidden order glimpsed in the helleborine?

For all the story's lurid violence, it is recollected in the narrator's remote tranquility. Whatever the brothers' response to the horror, nothing can change their inner lives. Not these events but the narrator's temperament has shaped observation.

The key to *On the Marble Cliffs* lies in Jünger's journal entry of August 19, 1939, only days after the manuscript's completion. He had returned from a two-day visit to Hamburg, and noted how with the city's industrial growth the population had become visibly lethargic. Technology's increasing momentum, read in the rhythm of roads and the iterations of propaganda, carried "the mighty cradlesong of monotony." This lesson completely controverts the *Worker*'s gospel of a new race, informed and masterful:

> One finds the best view of the completely automated condition in E. A. Poe's story "Descent into the Maelstrom." The Goncourts in their diaries early and rightly designated him the twentieth-century's first author. The conduct of the two brothers is well differentiated: the one, blinded by the fearsome sight of the mechanism, moves in unreflecting reflexes, while the other continues to ponder and perceive — and survives. Also at work in this figure is the responsibility that is starting to fall to an increasingly diminishing elite.[67]

On the Marble Cliffs might be called Jünger's descent into the maelstrom, a record of terror seen and survived. It is for the few to observe and assess terror from an exalted position.

The analogy, even so, exposes a critical difference. However veiled an attack upon totalitarianism's savagery, Jünger's account cannot render that savagery into an amoral natural force like Poe's maelstrom. The narrator acknowledges an *evil* force, feebly resists it, then wins aesthetic but not moral disengagement from it and its baleful effects. *On the Marble Cliffs* stands a target of Cocteau's boutade that there are those who have clean hands but have no hands. Jünger's vision cannot be handed over. An allegory that does not moralize, its hermeticism is inviolable and inimitable.

Jünger's vision is at its best intuitive and leaves the fragmentary mosaic in a chiaroscuro. The only real light in his narrative's human darkness is the magical lamp's tiny jagged fire passed among the chosen few, an obvious emblem of the mind's fragile yet enduring potence. The narrator's outcry for "human freedom and dignity" is real enough, and coming *de profundis* it is undeniably valiant, but it serves first and last the preserve of few. It is not in service to the indistinguishable many, who remain faceless occupants of the Marina's towns and the campagna's hamlets. They are left with consolatory hymns. What Voigt, praising Jünger, called "the liberating power of the inspired word" holds only for those who actively cherish the word, who tend its rich recesses and avoid Braquemart's snare of "dreaming concretely."

Jünger has said that when he wrote *On the Marble Cliffs* "the political situation had attained its point of poetic concentration, and because of that the book has taken on a political significance,"[68] but, as he insists, the story is not dependent upon a historical encoding. It merits emphasis that Nazism as a racist ideology is not even implicitly condemned in these pages. The hearty, vicious Ranger is a figure of indiscriminate evil and destruction for its own sake.

The "political situation" in the summer of 1939 had long been signposted. Why, then, does the book not portray racist virulence? Jünger's answer is that "all political facts are ephemeral, but that which conceals itself behind the demonic, the titanic, the mythic, remains constant and keeps an immutable value . . . [It] is absolutely necessary to entrust oneself to the reality of behavior and not content oneself with political orientations or tendencies."[69] Is it more important to steady one's eye upon the face common to hatred than upon its particular expressions? Is our probing of racist fury and cruelty shortchanged if these base passions are subsumed under some generic profile of psychopathology? In such a profile a specific kind of evil may be obfuscated or relativized. There are hierarchies of malice: Nazi persecution of Jews was not on the same order as its persecution of political dissidents, and it is a sophistry that Hitler's first victims were the Germans. Jünger's remarks unsettle those who abhor him:

> For the writer, the important thing is to depict what is fundamentally bad, be it anti-Semitism or a systematic anti-German mentality. It's possible to make general judgments but only starting from a dense and concrete description of persons and events, not directly to do with political reality. As Novalis says, "That alone is true which has never occured at any time or place." So I can imagine a situation relevant to numerous actual situations, one that fashions from them an image as it attains strata common to various historical conflicts.[70]

A final look at the doomed prince, Sunmyra. His severed head betrays to the brothers when they find it "a smile's shadow of loftiest sweetness and joy," a triumph over fear. "Then what I had often doubted became certain to me: there were still noble men among us in whose hearts the knowledge of the great order lived and affirmed itself. And as a lofty example leads us into its service, so I swore by this head that henceforth it is better to fall alone with the free than to go in triumph with slaves" (p. 136). Jünger hazarded all the constricted nobility of his elitism, and possibly his life, in writing those words. But the catastrophe which ensued he could not have foreseen. Within ten months he would be riding a horse, that chivalric anachronism, down the streets of subdued Paris, leading a uniformed train of triumphant slaves.[71]

Not a beam was left standing when German troops demolished buildings during the Somme retreat of March 1917. Published with permission of the Imperial War Museum, London (IWM Q.45347).

Jünger called Germany's soldiers of the Great War "the patient day-laborers of death." Storm troops manning a trench behind a smoke screen, near Sedan, May 1917. Published with permission of the Imperial War Museum, London (IWM Q.45340).

Jünger in 1919 wearing the Pour le mérite, Germany's highest military
award, conferred by the Kaiser a few weeks before the war ended.
Photo inscribed to the author.

Christ without the Cross. "The calm after the storm" was Jünger's title for this photo in *The Face of the World War: Front-line Experiences of German Soldiers (Das Antlitz des Weltkrieges)*, ed. Ernst Jünger, 1930.

The Führer in 1935. *Illustrierter Beobachter*, 9 January 1936.

The Jünger family at Christmas 1934. Jünger, top right, stands behind his wife, Greta, and their sons, Ernstel and Alexander. To his right, his brother Friedrich-Georg. Their mother is seated in the center. Top center, Jünger's triumphant father. Published with permission of Ernst Klett Verlag, Stuttgart.

Confounding the Nazis' hopes for Franco-German "understanding," Parisian women queue up for rations during the Occupation. Published with permission of the Imperial War Museum, London (IWM MH.11120 R.465).

Jünger in 1942, out of uniform and at home in his terrestrial paradise, Paris. Photo by Florence Henri. Published with permission of Ernst Klett Verlag, Stuttgart.

(left) German troops and tanks under fire before Notre Dame in August 1944. Published with permission of the Imperial War Museum, London (IWM MH.11151 R.700).

(below) The center of Jünger's home city, Hanover, April 1945. Hanover's Nazi district leader threatened to shoot anyone displaying a white flag to the advancing Ninth U.S. Army. Published with permission of the Imperial War Museum, London (IWM EA 63010).

6 · In the Golden Cage of Suffering:

Paris, 1940–1944

Jünger had been now writing deep within the world Goebbels had helped to produce by "dreaming concretely." In his own image, inspired by Nietzsche's fragmentary *Will to Power,* he was on a sea journey with a logbook, recording the pull of a maelstrom sighted long before by Hölderlin, Poe, Dostoevsky, Rimbaud, Melville, and Conrad. They had cast beacon lights over nihilism's increasingly rough, inclement waters, but "their texts were often hieroglyphic—and so there are works for which we today have just become mature as readers. They're like transparencies whose inscriptions are revealed by the glow of the fire-world."[1] In this image Jünger establishes the continuity between *On the Marble Cliffs* and the diaries he wrote throughout the Second World War known as *Strahlungen*. As that word denotes emanations of light, we might say that Jünger fancied he was carrying the Marina's magic lamp into a darkness more ominous than the Ranger's copse.

Jünger argues that, like painting, a diary sustains the perception and multiplicity of tones in an ever increasing measure. He concludes that it is the best medium for such a task, and "in the totalitarian state it remains the last possible conversation."[2] As diarist he had long been conversing with himself. He kept a diary during his picaresque excursion to North Africa in 1913. *In Stahlgewittern* bears the subscript "From the Diary of a Storm Troop Leader." His 1929 studies of Sicilian flora and fauna, *Aus der goldenen Muschel,* is a logbook. Succeeding those came the three journals of peacetime travels beyond Hitler's Germany.

Jünger's Parisian diaries record the force of happenstance, the vice-tightening exigencies of war, timely visits to galleries, parks, and society women—all impressed upon an acutely perceptive sensibility. Four years and nearly seven hundred pages furnish a manifold litmus. The topical range forbids summary, but two motifs emerge in a compelling grip and persistence: the criminalization of the war and the biblical portent of ruin. I discuss the Parisian books under broad thematic headings: political, covering the observed course of the war and Jünger's compromised service in Paris as well as on the eastern front; aesthetic, marking his continued preoccupations as a naturalist; and spiritual, denoting the ascendant influences of the Bible and the Catholic fanatic Léon Bloy on his Protestantism.

Jünger's first recorded intimations of war date from the spring of 1939, when Hitler's Legion Condor returned from Spain, and German troops marched into Bohemia and Moravia. The political tensions of that season reminded him of the last weeks before the Great War, but he noted a now different public mood, one of "keen sensitivity which stands in growing contrast to the fearsome accumulation of matériel" (April 16, 1939). His insouciance remained. War meant an end to writing at leisure, but he could go on with his diary. "There will be no lack of spectacle" (April 19, 1939). For him the theater of war would be precisely that.

An inner catastrophe was obtruding, too. At forty-four, he noted for an essay on suffering the bitterness of aging with its attendant disillusionments and irreparable mistakes, the more keen in women: "Bitterness first presents itself in life's second half when with facial wrinkles the lines of fate appear in their inalterable way. It shows as well a kind of lost innocence" (May 6, 1939). Before the mirror on August 30, 1939, he was once more in uniform, "like many men in Europe today who never thought they would again be in service." No sooner had he observed this mischance than a telegram came from the army's commander-in-chief, General von Brauchitsch, informing him of his promotion to captain of the second company of the 287th Regiment. Jünger took his advancement as a sign "that Ares has not meanwhile become disinclined toward me."

His regiment moving toward the Rhine, Jünger perceived "the stuff of tragedy since Agamemnon's time," and like Mycenae's king he eyed the fair women of other cities "floating by like dream apparitions" (September 6 and 17, 1939). Departure quickened his sense of hidden depths in human affections, so that "in the seemingly transient populations of great cities we discover treasures as in the unknown mines of Peru" (November 3, 1939). This image, hinting plunder, recalls his sentimental musing on story-swapping among troops in the previous war's trenches. Leaving his family, he gives us no sense of what he felt or they, his wife, brother, and sons. Only as spectator could he record his perceptions on the universality of loss,[3] but his aperçu on bitterness in middle-aging women hints at a domestic source.

Once more he was stationed on the western front, now fixed in an edgy standoff known as the *drôle de guerre*. The ramshackle housing of 1914–1918 had given way to bunkers of iron and concrete:

> Here I first recognized the place as the dwelling of iron-clad cyclopes who lacked the inner eye—quite as one often in a museum perceives objects with a sharper sense than those who long ago prepared and employed them. As though in a pyramid's interior or a catacomb's depths I confronted the Zeitgeist, saw it as an idol wholly without the agitated shimmer of technological finesse, and grasped its horrid might. (January 5, 1940)

Ever detached and cosmopolitan, he enjoyed wary botanical excursions into the countryside, and lively readings: Hesiod, Hebbel's letters, an 1831 tract on tropical diseases, Boethius. The *Consolation of Philosophy* reminded him that all human action is rooted in divine dispensation. Our deeds we do freely yet they are in every particular predetermined. "Eternity," Jünger notes on February 13, 1940, "abides like a condiment wonderfully in all things." From there he took up Boethius's message on the ineradicability of suffering in this life. We cannot diminish it; we must "experience it to the full" (*auskosten*) by transposing it to a higher order: "While it possesses chaotic power in life's lower ambiance, it wins *Gestalt* by contact with exalted and noble Being. Consolation puts suffering into a golden cage, or better, upon an altar that holds greater value than all the harm a short human existence can endure."

This says much in what it does not say. Jünger has found escape from the cyclops's cavern. He feels confident that *he* can situate suffering (his own?) on the high altar of nobility. Tacitly the message as he construes it remains elitist, heedless of pain's broad, lower reaches. The very predication of rescue into "high and noble Being" seems to leave a great deal to ignoble chaos, and "all the harm." Effectively, the high-low dualism on the marble cliffs recurs in Jünger's reading of Boethius. It opens a window upon Jünger's conduct and perceptions during his time, shortly to begin, in Paris. At some crucial junctures he seemed blind to the chaos, to its source and issue.

Limited though action was along the Rhine in the early spring of 1940, Jünger distinguished himself by recovering under sustained French fire the dead body of a lance-corporal. That engagement fell on his forty-fifth birthday. He was awarded an Iron Cross three months later, the only medal he was to win in this war.

On the night of May 9–10 he dreamt that bomber squadrons were flying overhead. It was no dream. Hitler had launched Plan Yellow for the conquest of the Low Countries and the invasion of France. In a week Jünger was recording his concern that, just as in the autumn of 1914, he might not reach the fighting before it was over.

In carrying out Plan Yellow the German army's staff brought along the local maps used a generation before. Veteran officers expected prolonged sieges. The conventionally minded military had not reckoned with Hitler's endorsement of von Manstein's brilliant stratagem, which dumped the old Schlieffen fixation and directed the offensive through the Ardennes. The Germans were no less amazed than the French when defensive lines collapsed within weeks. The Third Reich was doomed by that success, for Hitler was now unshakeably assured of his own military genius.

Immediately before Plan Yellow became operative Jünger was assigned to train storm troop squads in his regiment's companies. Tanks and planes quickly made that effort anachronistic. He did miss the war in the west, but he observed its effects at close hand and as vividly as he had twenty-five years before. In Rimbaud's Charleville-Mezières, Jünger noted the bombed-out façades of houses with interiors exposed as in an architect's sketch. In villages he looked into windows of homes where tables had been set; on church altars, gold and silver plates lay—everywhere an eerie emptiness,

> a horrendous foyer of death that shook me powerfully as I passed through. In an earlier part of my mental development I often became absorbed in visions of a world completely died out and void of humanity, and I won't deny that these dark fancies gave me pleasure. Here I see the idea realized, and might believe that, even were there no soldiers, the mind would soon be troubled—already in the last two days I have noticed how the appearance of destruction pivots on its axis. (May 27, 1940)

The pace of devastation was like a cataclysm of nature.

Jünger concluded that these scenes which so depressed him "lie in the nature of things and are not attributable to us alone." Now no participant in laying waste, he was at least an accomplice, yet could not admit it. He stood far distant from the restless, adventurous youth who had joined the Hannoverian Fusiliers. Long well-settled, he could read calamity from within the domestic life it was now visiting: "Things are so constituted that the *nomos* disappears from an abandoned home; the *lares* and *penates* do not stay behind. At all events one learns to esteem from such sights the enormous, almost invisible work that a family carries on" (May 27, 1940). Tardy reckoning from a middle-aged man, but the inner dynamics go deeper: Jünger could not align himself with the forces of destruction. Logistically he had become more tourist than soldier—and a circumspect tourist, at that.

His diary records conversations with home-shattered civilians. His fluent French having set them at some ease, they confided their losses to him. On a seventy-year-old woman whose children and grandchildren had fled by car: "The old woman ailed like a plant that had been shaken at its roots. I consoled her and commanded the orderlies, who were very understanding, to relieve her of all her chores, including the cooking" (June 2, 1940). The matter-of-fact tone recording such exchanges tells us that Jünger was as incapable of sentimentality as of full sympathy toward the war's victims. "All our truly significant deeds are removed from sharing," he noted.[4] All the same, his out-of-the-way attention to the French and his scrupulous awareness of their suffering did not ingratiate him with the German government: his first volume of diaries, published as *Gärten und Strassen* (Gardens and Avenues; April 3, 1939, to July 24, 1940), appeared only once in Germany, in 1942.[5]

Amid others' misery and displacement, Jünger's aesthetic proclivities enjoyed a feast during the second week of June. His company was stationed eighty miles northeast of Paris at Laon, site of one of France's most magnificent late romanesque cathedrals. Here Jünger was charged with some seven hundred POWs. So dispirited were they, eager only for food and the war's quick end, that the few men under his command had no trouble managing them. Meanwhile, exercising "the museum impulse," he took a cordial interest in the cathedral and the treasures of the civic vaults. From the church tower overlooking a bustle of rails, airways and roads,

> I grasped the unity of that earlier time and our own. I felt that, above all, this unity must not escape me, and I swore hereafter never to forget that I am responsible to the ancestors. . . . Today a presentiment

took hold of me that these cathedrals are works, living compositions far from the dead heaps of the bourgeois world. With that came the thought that this church stood under my protection. I pressed it to my heart as though it had become quite small." (June 10, 1940)

It seems a strange propriety, naive and egotistic, faintly impious. Protestants may feel an outsider's awe before monumental Catholicism, but we have observed Jünger at this studious point before, in the fantasy whose title suggested beauty and danger in a unifying perspective. The correspondence deepens when we follow him to the civic library, where, like the Marina's botanist among the dead leaves, he hovered over invaluable manuscript collections bound in Carolingian parchment, some as early as the tenth century. "I rooted in this silent place like a bee amid withered clover until the twilight shadows invaded. An hour of first-rate observation on renown and ruin in the laurel's dust" (June 12, 1940). Reckoning himself alone in appreciating this archive—the papers were fastened together with long-rusted pins "in the wicked fashion of French librarians"—he considered putting it under guard, but the responsibility weighed too heavily, so he left it to silence. Consider the plundering of art treasures by coarse men like Göring and Frank, and Jünger's discretion is the more admirable.

It was soon clear to Jünger that the invasion had passed him by: "If as a soldier I'm sorry about that, I am glad of it nonetheless for those who are suffering." Overwhelmed with the importunities of the bereft, noted precisely in his diary, he concluded that keeping civil order was nearly hopeless: "One must keep the eye limited to the area for which one is responsible. As regards practical help, the individual is constrained, just as a lifeboat has only a certain number of places" (June 21, 1940). This odd remark from someone in a conquering army argues a singular dissociation from both conquerors and conquered: "the individual" is in no way a cause of present disaster but neither can he fully address it. Precisely by that dissociation Jünger could, after the French surrender, sympathetically assess the return of refugees to their homes as a kind of sacred rite, a remembrance of some primeval settlement: "In this circumstance, all work, all enterprise becomes a source of joy . . . and behind the sufferings life shines forth in a new propitious depth" (July 5, 1940).

Most French felt not so much joy as sheer relief in being spared from their own fears of German barbarism cultivated in the Great War. That relief may account for the unctuous subservience Jünger experienced from some peasant homes, and which he mistook for hospitality: "One is constantly coming upon houses that are filled with a generous commotion (*spendende Erregung*) at a soldier's approach, as though the insatiable Herakles himself had come to table" (July 7, 1940).

Skepticism is in order. German occupational forces depended from the first upon two unreal and contradictory assumptions: first, that with France out of the war life would go back to normal. For their own peace of mind needing to avoid unpleasant realities, many in France hoped this would happen. The middle class even took some comfort in the Germans' iron presence because it rescued their property and anxiety from the syndicalist labor movement. As Jean Guéhenno's eloquent diary, *Journal des années noires,* relates, some French politicians and intellectuals were quick to promote the new *pax germanica*—and themselves. These men pandered for the second assumption, that a new era of Franco-German friendship had dawned. Hitler had united Europe. In fact, the German program for things-back-to-normal and for "understanding" was a bootless delusion from the start. Jünger shared it.

What was life like for a German soldier in occupied France during the first year? To Guéhenno's judicious eye, "He's forced to feel more a stranger every day. He doesn't know how to get along on the streets of Paris nor whom to look to. He is sad and exiled. The jailer has become the prisoner. If he were sincere, if he could speak, he would excuse himself for being there."[6]

Turning from this indulgent view to the daybooks of the German quartermaster general in Paris, Major General Jaenecke, we gain a different impression. Many German soldiers lost no time in going the ancient way of conquerors. They became dissipated, sybaritic, and delinquent. As Mars yielded to Bacchus, Jaenecke groaned to report: "The seed of almost all blunders lies in alcoholic abuse."[7] Indeed, Paris did not lack spirits. A November 1940 inventory records 42,400,000 liters of Midi wines; 880,000 liters of Bourdeaux; 5,000,000 of cognac, and 3,800,000 of rum.[8]

Venus attended Bacchus. Guéhenno grumbled upon seeing at a Versailles restaurant "three big, potbellied, unbuttoned, nostalgic [Germans] with their hands on three dreadful whores, who were caressing them, pecking them on the cheek, curling their hair. They were all stretched out, growling together with pleasure. Oh German virtue! Oh Siegfried!"[9] The quartermaster issued a notice on how to obtain the ever popular American condom. No use sending any more checks via Lisbon to New York, for the British were now controlling the mails. However, "another way of payment is negotiable with representatives of American firms doing business via the American Express Company. If no difficulties arise in border traffic, the wares can be in Paris in two weeks."[10]

German soldiers became so lax about sanitation that a plague of vermin came mid-winter that first year: rats, cats, and savage dogs were thriving on the garbage piling up around the billets.[11]

The Germans' real problem was not alcoholism, venereal disease, or garbage. It was success. As Jaenecke boasted: "Our enemies conceded we have well-trained and courageous soldiers, superior weapons, adequate munitions, and the boldest resolves, but they didn't figure it possible for us to make provision for vast areas. Its brilliant organization, even over the greatest distances, . . . has been for our enemies the real surprise of this war."[12]

Departing Laon, Jünger concurred in "an awareness of indomitable supremacy" (June 16, 1940) as endless columns of panzers and infantry took two hours to pass. Asked by fellow officers to account for the Blitzkrieg's success, he answered that it was the triumph of the Worker. The sight of ten thousand French POWs huddled by a few bayonets added another dimension: "the suffering of such great numbers in a narrow space was strange to see; one feels the individual is no longer recognizable, and notes the kind of mechanical dragging which characterizes catastrophe" (June 18, 1940). He concluded portentously that "the experiences of this campaign will probably effect significant transformations in the world's armies" (June 23, 1940). Between the monstrous Worker and the abject nonindividual, Jünger drew up these commonplaces: "It is *we* who form the world, and *what* we experience is not dependent upon chance. Things are chosen and cultivated through our condition; the world is as *we* are constituted; everyone of us is therefore able to change the world—that is the terrible significance given to humanity. And that is why it's important that we work on ourselves" (June 23, 1940).[13] However banal in formulation, this plumping for a voluntarism at least implicitly ethical shows Jünger remote from his wonted fatalism and from the anti-ethics of the Nazi behemoth.

His Paris notebooks date from the spring of 1941. General Otto von Stülpnagel had been serving as the military governor (*Befehlshaber*) of the

city for six months. Scion of a Prussian military family, he was, in Jünger's eye, "a mixture of softness, charm, and flexibility, like a courtly
dance leader, with wooden and melancholy features. He uses Spanish expressions of courtesy, wears high, polished boots, and golden buttons on
his uniform." Jünger reckoned him weak, but that is a comparative judgment and came late, in February 1942, as Stülpnagel yielded his post to
his cousin, Karl Heinrich. "In these generals the impotence common to
the bourgeoisie and the aristocracy is manifest. They have sight enough
to perceive the course of affairs but lack power and means in the face of
minds that know no other motive than force" (February 23, 1942).

Stülpnagel's first surveys of the disastrous political and psychological
landscape are invaluably shrewd and, in their way, tragic. The first winter
revealed to the Germans what they were up against. Black marketeer-
ing had become too efficient to be fought. Although the "Aryanization"
of French society was deemed successful (French law dispossessed Jews
of their jobs and industries in October 1940), the Germans were finding it hard to work with an indifferent, sluggish French bureaucracy.
The far deeper problem was a renewed French patriotism. "At the cost
of mutual understanding," wrote Stülpnagel in January 1941, "a national
self-consciousness is gradually returning. A unified political resolution
and objective haven't yet become evident. . . . Until now internal political
interests seem to stay confined to only a small part of the people, the intelligentsia above all. The masses will always follow whoever undertakes
to relieve their economic distress." [14]

For all his cynicism, Stülpnagel was interested in winning over men of
ideas. It was they, he felt, who determined France's internal *Machtkampf*.
Pétain's dismal regime had not replaced Third Republican ideology with
anything new. The Catholic Church, although officially behind Pétain, remained suspect for its here-and-there renegade priests and its young labor
movement, the *Jeunesse ouvrière chrétienne*. Stülpnagel, noting increased hostility to the German Occupation, ascribed "the decline of opinion" to
"above all, reverses in the politics of understanding," but it was in part
collaborationist jackdaws like Marcel Déat and Drieu la Rochelle who
turned the sullen lethargy of their compatriots into shame for France and
loathing for Germany.

Difficulties of coordination with the French bureaucracy were bad;
worse, the military government became divided within its own iron
house. As military governor, Stülpnagel had the Parisian deputies of

Himmler's security police under his authority. The SD was to report to him monthly on the registration and surveillance of Jews, communists, and emigrants, and on the church's political activities. But in a fateful relaxation of his command, Stülpnagel left the door open for virtually autonomous operations by the SD: "In urgent cases the Einsatzcommandos of the Security Police can independently carry out arrests, house searches, and confiscations. What cases are to be considered urgent it is up to the conscientious judgment and responsibility of the Security Police Chief's agents to determine."[15] The contest for power proceeded furtively from that moment in March 1941.

Such was the lay of the occupied land when Jünger took up his post in Paris the following month. His assignment during his first term of service (April 1941–October 1942) included "historiographical exercises, but with time and opportunity for his own work."[16] During his second term (February 1943–August 1944) he was assigned to Abteilung IC of the military governor's staff. His group, IC/I, was charged with censorship, translations, and interception of foreign radio transmissions. Most of the staff worked at the Majestic Hotel (rated "de grand luxe") at 19, Avenue Kléber, but was billeted elsewhere. Jünger lived at the Hotel Raphael, opposite the Majestic, on the Avenue des Portugais.[17]

We first join him on a Sunday evening, April 6, 1941, at a girly show where "the henlike aspect of the Gallic race is powerfully manifested." With his eye for women, such indulgence was inevitable: we can expect love from women, but not justice, he generalized, yet he found relations with them more negotiable when eros was not in the works.[18] Throughout the Occupation he had friendly company in several sophisticated women, most notably Florence Gould, who had married into a family of American millionaires and regularly hosted members of the military staff at her home, the Palais Rose, Avenue Foch. Jünger's hobnobbing with the idle and cultivated of Paris is held against him by righteous critics: he wined and dined while most Parisians slowly starved. The charge is captious. Jünger did not batten. He did seek out the company of fellow writers and artists: Cocteau, Jouhandeau, Braque, Picasso. Two men of letters he found particularly engaging: Henri de Montherlant, self-absorbed, aristocratic, ranked by Guéhenno with Gide as "maîtres comédiens,"[19] and Paul Léautaud, who, famous for his love of cats and contempt for his fellow French (especially Jews), had no trouble with the German presence.

Jünger kept mostly his own company. The circles of French intelligentsia he moved in would have naturally been his orbit in peacetime, and that fact more than any other distinguished him from most German officers. Like Laon, Paris was a treasure he tended like a curator. He was especially fond of less conspicuous sites like the elegant little Parc Monceau with its ruined colonnades. He was enchanted by the Musée de l'Homme (in the Palais du Trocadéro) and its collection of ethnography. He preferred Ste. Sulpice to Notre Dame and the botanical garden in Auteuil to its racetrack, and the residence of the noble dead at Père Lachaise to the Tour Eiffel. And he cultivated a now nearly vanished species, the bookman, eye-keen for the antiquarian and exotic. He read mostly French and English (translated) literature.

This leisure suggests how lightly his tasks at the Majestic weighed upon him, but his daily life was not all galleries and reflection. He was assigned to censorship of the civilian mail coming from Germany. Every morning a sergeant placed a pile of letters before him which had been passed through the army's control board. Reading was "an unpleasant and difficult task with unexpected insights into the human comedy and tragedy. There's nothing people won't set down in letters. Melville characterized such a situation in his beautiful story 'Bartleby.'"[20]

The first letter he read was from a woman informing her soldier-husband that his furlough had left her pregnant and that she had found a doctor to abort. In another, a woman complaining about curtains burned in a bombing raid wrote to her husband, "Now all I can think about is revenge on Hitler." Jünger took a risk and shuffled such random notes into a metal locker. A more conscientious censor would have cost lives. After a while Jünger could depend upon a troop of subordinates to run operations without his constant presence.[21] He played chess with staff officers.

Among them, Lt. Gerhard Heller, a student of romance languages, now censor for the propaganda bureau, decided which French books the Germans could let out. In effect, he determined who among the literati would be "collabos." He was indulgent, and the book industry in France throve throughout the Occupation. Averse to the Nazis, he agreed with Jünger as a "point of honor" not to greet one another with the obligatory Hitler salute.[22]

Most important among those in the Paris offices who felt scant loyalty to Hitler was Stülpnagel's chief of staff, Col. Hans Speidel. He had arrived amid the triumph of June 1940—he performed as Hitler's guide during the famous hurried tour of Paris—and served till his call to the eastern front in March 1942. (He returned to Paris in April 1944.) Speidel recognized in Jünger a fellow of erudition and taste. At a soirée in Sacha Guitry's home, they fastened upon a portfolio of letters from Debussy and Flaubert's manuscript of *L'éducation sentimentale*.

Speidel, trained as a historian, had a sharp awareness of human motivations. His 1941 staff reports on "The Political Situation in France" argue a mind candid, insightful, and sometimes blind. Early on (January 25, 1941) he saw collaboration failing because Germany "has done *nothing* so far that could enlist the French in a common effort." Only a few were following Pierre Laval's "politics of understanding," while most others hoped for a "white peace," meaning that, by waiting, France would not suffer further in its relations with Germany and England.[23] Winter darkened the French mood. Germans were blamed for tightened living standards and lack of coal. Realizing that would-be leaders of French public opinion had no real following, Speidel assigned their failure to "traditional Franco-German enmity."[24]

Hitler's attack upon the Soviet Union, June 22, 1941, doomed all collaboration efforts. Speidel reported a month later that the French public was indifferent to German propaganda about imminent victory in the East. The French communist party, driven underground by the reactionary government before the war, had become dominant in the French labor movement and now, released from the unreal constraints of the 1939 Nazi-Soviet Pact, served as the vanguard for active resistance. "If communism succeeds only in resisting Hitler," wrote Guéhenno, "it has a good chance of winning all of Europe. One will be a communist out of gratitude."[25]

Industrial sabotage and work slowdowns were hard to detect and to punish, but not so the random killings of German soldiers. Stülpnagel authorized severe reprisals, round-ups of communists and Jews, and executions. The execution site, la Vallée-aux-Loups, became a field of martyrs and then a terminus for pilgrimages that so embarrassed Stülpnagel he had it dynamited and suspects shot elsewhere. When those responsible for attacks on German soldiers were not exposed, he ordered a curfew for sunset. Pétain on the radio denounced the attacks but said nothing of German reprisals. After a field commander was killed on October 20, 1941, Stülpnagel ordered fifty hostages shot, and a hundred after another assassination. Bounties were offered to no avail.

While shortages were suffered in bitter privacy, nothing so quickly unified the French people as this gratuitous barbarism. Speidel's October 1941 report identified the historical lesson:

> The Frenchman, educated for the past century and a half to an emphatically formal notion of justice and deeply shaken by recent shootings of hostages and death sentences daily carried out over the last weeks for possession of weapons, stands at the moment in shock at the fact that people are being shot who are not directly responsible for these attacks.[26]

Speidel returned to Germany to secure from Hitler a more tactful policy on hostages. Stülpnagel, never having Hitler's confidence, was replaced by his cousin, who had been on the eastern front.

Men like Speidel and Heller took no pains to show their French "hosts" they were not barbarians. They reasonably believed they were not. Of Speidel, Jünger noted, "Under his aegis we have built here within the military machine a kind of cell, a spiritual knighthood that meets in the Leviathan's belly and yet seeks to maintain the eye and heart for the weak and defenseless" (November 13, 1941). The chivalric fantasy of the marble cliffs had come to life, but fantasy it remained, as Jünger had to learn. Surrounded by French literati and German "knights," he had unwittingly run the hazard of isolation from the hard, pressing facts of Parisian life. Whatever the sincerity of refined and educated Germans in gardening good relations with the French, the SD had no such scruples. After the invasion of Russia, its furtive business became openly brutal. Stülpnagel's increasingly harsh desperation had played into the hands of Himmler's agents.

A reading of Speidel's Christmas Day report of 1941 can only amaze. Now able to credit failure in French cooperation to the frustration of German prospects for victory in the east—"so long as the war's outcome is uncertain" was brave phrasing in a report to Berlin—he still supposed that "through decisive German steps toward a positive collaboration in the sense of a new Europe," France could yet be brought round.[27] But the retribution for *résistance* which the military government meted out that month confounded Speidel's dim hopes: one hundred Jews and communists had been shot, a thousand Jews deported, and a fine of one million francs was levied on Jews in the Occupied Zone. As Speidel dryly observed, "mass shooting without judicial process will always be regarded as an abandonment of 'right.'" France's 1789 mentality was not up to such policy. The significance of German reprisals that December is that Hitler, not Stülpnagel, had ordered them.

Incredibly, confronted with the Führer's algebra of terror, Speidel concluded his December report with the singularly upbeat note that "the best propagandist is still as before the German soldier—at the end of 1941 this must be expressly emphasized—not least the three active eastern divisions transferred to France."[28] Here a thoroughly professional officer labors to distance the dutiful German *Soldat* from Hitler's murderous countermeasures, as though the German military's ancient honor kept it from complicity. Speidel did not see that the collective German presence had become abominable to most French people. Dinner parties put him among insensitively privileged coteries that helped to perpetuate the fatuities of Franco-German friendship.

Jünger, moving in this tiny orbit, gave the pathology of collaboration his clinically detached eye. Among the sycophants and backstairs crawlers, Dr. Louis-Ferdinand Céline, a splenetic actor who enjoyed provoking people, forthrightly argued for harsher measures than even Hitler had yet resorted to. When he met Jünger at the German Institute (on the day Pearl Harbor was attacked), "he remarked his astonishment that we soldiers are not shooting, hanging, exterminating Jews, his astonishment that someone with bayonets fixed isn't making constant use of them. 'If the Bolsheviks were in Paris, they would show you how to do it, how you comb through the population, district by district, house by house. If I had a bayonet, I'd know what to do.'" Jünger listened for two hours to Céline "rage on," surcharged by "the monstrous powers of nihilism."[29] A subsequent meeting (April 22, 1943) at the home of novelist Paul Morand revealed Céline's morbidity. The war had decisively turned against Germany and reprisals were now commonplace. Céline "is soon to visit the mass grave at Katyn, about which so much propaganda is being made. It's clear such places attract him."[30]

Jünger met Céline one more time, at the German Institute, on November 16, 1943. The eminent sculptor Arno Breker was there, and an unseemly crew of "hired scribblers, people that one wouldn't touch with fire-tongs. The whole lot of them is stewing in a mixture of self-interest, hate, and fear, and many already carry the stigma of horrible death on their brow. Céline with his dirty fingernails—I'm now entering a phase in which the sight of nihilism is becoming physically intolerable." Had

Jünger known Céline's writings, he would have glimpsed the mainspring of Céline's temper, his contempt for humanity's sorry imperfections and sordid distance from the redemptive poise he found only in ballet. But Jünger was right: Vichy brought human shabbiness to a kind of acme, and Céline rode it to its ascent and beyond. Jünger discerned the spiritual squalor long before it huddled at Sigmaringen, where the Vichy lackeys of fate and of the Germans settled toward the war's end. "I'm frequently meeting men and even women these days," reads the entry of April 23, 1943,

> who brag that the terrors and especially the mass killings of our time do not disturb them, and that they see in them something understandable, natural, even aspirable [anzustrebendes] and familiar. One feels this confession gives them pleasure as though they were casting off a secret long borne with boredom. . . . Thus, too, the naive, absolutely shameless smile in such confessions; it's like looking into the eyes of young girls who boast of the pleasures of masturbation and similar procedures. At such times one sees the company one has kept, as though at the end of a masked ball.[31]

About the barbarities committed in France and abroad Jünger learned chiefly by oblique remarks, but his recording of them carries an eerie vividness. As early as May 1, 1941, before Stülpnagel's heavy-handed vengeance was at work, Jünger set himself the task of studying how propaganda first passes into terror, how might "goes on cat's feet, subtly and cunningly." *On the Marble Cliffs* depicts this phenomenon well, but now its author was situated in a gigantic laboratory equipped for terroristic experiment. Intrigued with historical absolutism, Jünger saw the absence of aristocracy in modern absolutism as a catastrophe. Hitler held no court, and in Jünger's estimate he had reduced the military to tools of power without conscience. Almost. In the autumn of the first reprisals, Speidel secretly assigned Jünger to chronicle the contest between the army and the Party.

Unfortunately, when Jünger's life was on the line, he destroyed the notes for what would have proved an invaluable history. As noted, the seed of contention lay in Otto von Stülpnagel's directive giving the SD discretionary powers which Himmler had no discretion about abusing. The first contest came over control of hostages. Ten days after becoming military governor, Karl Heinrich von Stülpnagel himself summoned Jünger, asking him for "a precise description of the hostage question for later times" (February 23, 1942).[32]

In his diaries Jünger encoded the agents of Himmler's State Security Bureau (RSHA) as "Lemuren" or nocturnal spooks: the SD and SS had offices and informers all over Paris. Jünger had been under the Gestapo's eyes for years, and he knew as a renowned writer and Wehrmacht loyalist that he had no friend in Himmler. Although sheltered by the military governor, he was still suspect. He kept his journals under lock and key.

He reviews the Nazi state's crimes equanimously. Hitler's programs of extermination he prejudges a failure: "It's said that the sterilization and murder of the insane has increased the number of children born mentally ill. Just so, the suppression of beggars has made poverty common, and the decimation of Jews has led to the propagation of Jewish Old Testament qualities in the world. One doesn't extinguish archetypes by extermination; rather, one liberates them." Jünger, amateur botanist, sees humanity subject to the organic law of pruning, but he knows better than to palliate killing: "Lemur festivals, with the murder of men, children, women. The gruesome spoil is buried. Then other lemurs come and dig it up. With ghastly pleasure they film the dismembered and half-wasted remains, then show each other this film. What a bizarre urge for carrion is developing" (March 12, 1942). When Speidel shared some of Hitler's orders with him, Jünger noted that "the transition from the diabolical to the satanic is now becoming clearer" (March 16, 1942).[33] Rumors of Einsatzkommando murders and mass graves in Lithuania came through officers returning from Berlin.

These horrors, filtered as rumors, informed Jünger's awareness of how the Second World War differed psychologically from the First. The war of 1914–1918 had posed the question of technology's predominance over humanity. In 1932 Jünger had attempted to integrate them by construing the Worker's *Gestalt* as the twentieth century's Will to Power: man and machine in a steady dynamic of coherence. New crimes of war, the lemurs' programmatic slaughter of civilians, signaled a sinister internalization of the mechanical into human consciousness. The present question was, will people or automatons inherit the earth? "Some universal depravity must be at the bottom of the general transformation to automatism that threatens us—ascertaining it would be the task of theologians, just the people we're lacking." For his part, Jünger pleaded privately that "we must above all fight in our breasts whatever wants to harden, become metal or stone" (June 6, 1942).

The day he wrote those words, Jews in France were obliged to wear the star of David. "In the Rue Royale I met the yellow star for the first time in my life, worn by three young girls who passed by arm in arm. . . . Such a sight is not without repercussions—I was immediately embarrassed to be in uniform" (June 7, 1942). Six weeks later he witnessed the mass arrest of Jews, the first stage in their deportations:

> Parents were first separated from their children, so there was wailing to be heard in the streets. At no moment may I forget that I am surrounded by the unfortunate, by those suffering to the very depths, else what sort of person, what sort of officer would I be? The uniform obliges one to grant protection wherever it goes. Of course one has the impression that one must also, like Don Quixote, take on millions. (July 18, 1942)

A sense of noble futility offered him a dodge. He was *not* surrounded by "those suffering to the very depths," nor could he have defended them. The mission he assigned himself was negotiably egotistic: to avoid the hardening of his own heart.

> When I close my eyes, I now and then look upon a dark landscape with stones, cliffs, and mountains on the brink of eternity. In the background, on the shore of a black sea, I recognize myself, a tiny little figure drawn as though with chalk. That is my forepost, straight up against nothingness—there below on the abyss I'm fighting for myself. (July 9, 1942)

In this inhuman landscape, the spectator becomes the sole human spectacle in a fight, not a Nietzschean dance, with total meaninglessness. Jünger took consolation in death itself, as a visit to Père Lachaise told him that "life lies in death like a small green island on a dark sea. Examining it, if only along its margins and breakers, constitutes true science, next to which all physics and technology remain trivial" (July 19, 1942). By then, as the possibility that Germany would lose the war was becoming more forceful, even party conversation took on a macabre cast. When Jünger recalled his 1929 tour of Palermo's catacombs, the Marquise de Polignac suggested the sight of all those shriveled corpses would inspire their visitor to embrace the first person on the street. "Perhaps in ancient times," Jünger rejoined, "mummies served as aphrodisiacs" (August 17, 1942).

Dwelling on death and the dead could not isolate him from the specter of death-dealing and the despair in its train. When the Jewish wife of a Parisian chemist he knew was dragged off, he deplored the defenselessness of the innocent. Not even suicide availed. "Even when they kill themselves, they choose it not as the lot of the free withdrawing into their last refuge but seek the night as frightened children seek their mother." Yet more appalling to him was the tormentors' blindness in the face of defenseless people's suffering. He refers to young Germans "too weak for the chivalric life; yes, they've even lost the simple decency which forbids striking the weak. On the contrary, they even see in it their repute." In these men Jünger saw his youth's valor betrayed. Their coarseness worked the more unseemly in his eyes since some of them knew him as the author of *Stahlgewitter*. As though to distance himself from them he reiterated to himself the moral injunction he recognized two weeks before: "Never may I forget that I'm surrounded by the suffering. That's much more important than all the renown of weapons and wit or the hollow approbation of youth who take pleasure in them" (July 28, 1942).

While he had little comfort in moral outrage, he knew that thanks to Heller and Speidel he was not isolated. He did not know that chivalry was not a denominator sufficient to set him and them finally apart from the SS. The lesson came home to him from an unexpected source, in a stationery shop on August 18, 1942. A young woman was waiting on him (he was in uniform), and the expression on her face struck him:

> I realized she was looking at me with astonishing hatred. Her bright blue eyes, in which the pupils were contracted to a point, dove openly with a kind of lust into mine—with the lust, perhaps, of a scorpion boring its stinger into its prey. I felt she was of a sort that mankind had not experienced for a long time. Over such trajectories nothing but annihilation and death can come to us.

He concluded that this hatred could pass like the germ of a disease or a spark into oneself. Jünger had well observed the Hitlerian hatred that must "answer for the blood of millions," the nihilism of "the satanic will, a cold pleasure in the destruction of people, perhaps of humankind," and he saw that "many of the French value such schemes and are eager to perform the hangman's service" (February 8, 1942). But the shopgirl's hatred was of another species altogether, primitive and without banners, perhaps all the more effective in someone so defenseless.

Acquainted with many clever, attractive women, he met the foil of them all on that August day. Here was no society hostess, no *belle dame* of tattered aristocracy chatty over porcelain and tea at the Ritz or recumbent in some fashionable garden. In this speechlessly eloquent young woman's hatred Jünger might have read the soul of a degraded France. This minor but revelatory drama, heightened by anonymity, forms a definitive contrast to a tableau from the earlier war, when a farm girl welcomed and fed him, "mon petit officier," near Croisilles in April 1916. It is as though she had now been reborn in a wholly different guise, transformed by a bold, completely helpless, wrath. The earlier scene: a pastorale where gallantry could play, even under war's nimbus. Now in Paris, most feminine of capitals, gallantry was an obscene impertinence.

On the day he visited the stationery shop, Jünger destroyed the initial sketch of his essay on a postwar Europe begun eight months before. It is not certain from his diary's entry for August 18 whether he did so before or after the visit. It is tempting to suppose the latter. That the shop girl had unsettled him profoundly is clear and may account for the refuge taking he admits to himself in the following weeks: he writes of the appeal of dream life (August 26), of the "active solipsism" which provides a tempting escape from misanthropy (September 10), of the cosmopolitan consciousness traversed in hallucinogens (September 17). Concomitant with these musings goes a more vigorous denial of hatred's gravity. Paris has become his second home, "an even more potent image of the old *Kultur* that is dear and precious to me" (September 18, 1942). In the park at Vincennes he regards boule players as worthy philosophers who would scarcely notice the decline of empires and the failure of campaigns. As Léautaud was disgusted by the Parisians' life-as-usual ways, Jünger felt relief in observing them. Above all, there remained that "oasis in the world of destruction," the book. A visit to the Bibliothèque Nationale consoles him with its elephantine cataloging: "We stand here before a new *chinoiserie,* a mandarin realm that surely lacks creative power and yet knows how to deal tidily with its impressed ideograms" (September 30, 1942).[34] These movements were tactical reassurance that the young woman's "trajectories" could not reach him.

Such evasions collided with obstinate facts. Paris had to prepare for another winter of scarcities. Preparation of food, Jünger realized at a friend's home, had become an artwork because shops were already empty at the beginning of October. Always slender, he was now losing weight, but no dietary stringency was responsible: he began to suffer bouts of melancholy. Dissatisfied with what he vaguely called his "situation," he felt inclined to treat his body mutinously: "One has the impression the body wants to say something, speak with us, yet in the artful life we lead we scarcely understand its words better than those of an old farmer who talks with us in our city residence about a church festival, a harvest, or bad crops" (October 7, 1942). He was sleeping badly.

The real source of unrest lay not in Paris, even amid shortages. Since June 1940 the city had been the optimal holiday site for every German soldier, and Jünger himself had found its largesse the connoisseur's "second home." In 1942 it had become a haven to cling to as assignment to the eastern front inspired dread. On March 25 Speidel became the Fifth Army's chief of staff in Russia. On leave Jünger visited him and his family in Mannheim before he went east. When would his own turn come?

Fortunately, in the new military governor of France, Karl Heinrich von Stülpnagel, Jünger had found a man far more like Speidel, accessible and cultivated, than cousin Otto. He shared Jünger's botanical interests and something of Jünger's antiquarian penchant in his knowledge of Byzantine history. In temperament, too, he proved refreshing, possessing "an unmistakable *désinvolture* and besides that a princely bearing" (March 10, 1942).

The tension which mounted between the army and the SS during the fall of 1941 was relaxed when the SS got its own chief in Paris on June 1. That meant reprisals for resistance activities were taken out of the military governor's overburdened hands and delivered to Hitler's army of police. The change suited the second Stülpnagel perfectly; he had the professional soldier's disdain of politics and was happy to leave terrorism to Hitler's appointee, General Karl Oberg, a suitably brutal fellow who looked like an inflated Himmler.

The directive for the appointment of an SS chief contains intriguing cosmetics. All of the military governor's personnel were called upon to assist the SS chief and his staff "upon request." Although Oberg was nominally subordinate to Stülpnagel, the SS gained the upper hand. In case of military emergencies or "internal unrest," it was stipulated, the military governor could supersede the SS and police authorities, but that was Heydrich's sop to military pride. Stülpnagel fully appreciated Oberg's capacity to handle "unrest" without military assistance. (They had served in the same regiment during the Great War.) Besides: "It is to be observed herewith that precisely in connection with military efforts, police measures attain special importance under their own responsibility."[35] With a virtual declaration of independence, the honorable military could now look the other way.

Jünger was assigned to the eastern front in October 1942. Troubled by insomnia and "wicked melancholy," he knew that pleading illness was not an acceptable excuse. That autumn he planned to write an essay on death as consolation for the chanciness which dogs everyone's life:

> From here it could be concluded that as individuals we are imperfect: eternity is neither suitable nor bearable as far as we are concerned. On the contrary, we must transmute ourselves back to the absolute, and it is precisely death that affords us this possibility. . . . Death has its mysterium, exceeding even love's. We become initiates, mystics, at its hands. (October 14, 1942)

Nothing morbid obtrudes in these notes. Jünger had been a familiar of death; he knew its many faces. Now he gives it the voluntarist's accent of nearly eager acceptance.

Going east to join the recently formed Army Group A, he had good reason to be reconciled to death, for the group's commander was resolved upon no retreat. This was the Führer himself. He personally assumed leadership of the drive into the Caucasus aimed at the Baku oil fields. Paulus was pressing upon Stalingrad with the Sixth Army; Manstein led Army Group Don, centered in Rostov. When Jünger arrived in Rostov on November 22, 1942, Hitler had only hours before relinquished command of Army Group A to Colonel-General Ewald von Kleist. Jünger met him at dinner three days later. By then, the eastern campaign was doomed, though neither knew it: the Russians' counteroffensive, launched November 19, had encircled Paulus and 200,000 men.[36] Jünger came to the Caucasus just as the battle's tide was turning against the Germans.

He served under a man cut from the venerable military cloth. Loyal though he was to the oath Hitler imposed on the army in 1934, deep-bred allegiances kept Kleist indisposed to Nazism. He did not share Hitler's racist scorn of Slavs; he had served through most of the Great War in the

eastern campaigns. He sensibly exploited the hostility toward Stalin and
Russia among peoples of the Caucasus; he recruited over 800,000 genu-
ine volunteers; he performed a brilliant counteroffensive in the battle of
Kharkov (May, 1942). But arguably his greatest achievement was a tactical
retreat at the year's end: he saved the nearly 400,000 men of Army Group
A from the Russians' vigorous attempt at engulfment.[37]

Jünger's eight-weeks' diary, *Kaukasische Aufzeichnungen* (Caucasian
Sketches), bids comparison with *Gardens and Avenues:* there, whirlwind triumph he could barely keep up with; here, retreat with doom in the air.
As usual, he was taken with the women, their Slavic voices "not exactly
melodious, yet pleasant. There's power and cheerfulness hidden within;
you think you're hearing a deep life chord vibrating." They reminded him
of Brazilian Negresses in their "profound, unbroken gaiety after generations of slavery" (November 25, 1942). These women presumed that the
Germans had come to liberate them.

While Kleist sighed before the illimitable steppes and their innumerable
tribes, Jünger probed deeper. Slavs had "a feminine but also dark, amoral
character" (December 1, 1942). The sight of peasant women bearing wood
from the forests around Woroschilowsk (Stavropol) suggested an ancient
abundance: "You sense what has been lost to this land through abstraction (meaning Stalinist totalitarianism), and how it would flourish under
the sun of a benevolent, paternal power" (December 6, 1942). But whose?

The Caucasus late in 1942 was a seedbed of epidemics: typhus, diph-
theria, dysentery. From a visit to a disease institute at Woroschilowsk,
Jünger learned that pestilence came regularly every ten years, borne in
caravans from Astrachan on the Volga. The syndrome's tell-tale was that
rodents died first. In the Jüngerian optic, immunization against typhus
became a sacrament:

> Earlier I compared it to baptism but perhaps communion is the
> more precise equivalent in the spiritual realm: we use the living
> experience others have gathered for us through sacrifice, sickness,
> snakebite, the lymph of a lamb that has suffered for us. The miracles
> are prefigured and contained within matter—they are its highest
> realization. (November 26, 1942)

This life-giving, however, carried with it a crying futility. The encirclement of the Sixth Army Jünger likened to the siege of a doomed city
in antiquity: "One sees death approaching from afar, over weeks and

months." He pitied troops wasting away from exhaustion and fearful of annihilation, pale lives "on the borders of being." Their deadly debilitation was easy to read: they had no healing power for even minor wounds.

The fit fared worse. Propaganda intensified the eastern fighting's mercilessness, but the partisans, in Jünger's reckoning, "stand outside the rights of war, if such can be spoken of. They're like wolf packs in their woods when surrounded for extermination. I've heard things here that cut into the zoological" (December 11, 1942). The heightened grotesquerie of war technology complemented this barbarism. Jünger paints a bleak, almost comic horror toward Christmas Eve. He stood upon the narrow planking of a funicular high above the river Pschisch. Clutching the cable, he could see nearby a ruptured tower from whose hollows an officer was calling for artillery support. Down below, cannoniers were gathered about "a gray monstrosity," withdrawing as a red stream of fire pierced the air. Puffs of artillery smoke halted in the air, unmoving, "like a snake's scales brightly edged." Long trails of wounded were being ferried; everywhere, men and metal fixed in unreal conjunction. A Bosch painting heard might sound like this: "With a superhuman voice melodies of Christmas carols fill the monstrous cauldron: the Propaganda Company's loud-speaker system plays 'Silent Night, Holy Night.' And with it, incessantly, the pounding of mortars echoing through the valley" (December 22, 1942).[38]

He realized the ruthless absurdity of The Worker's technologized humanity was playing itself out. He now saw the war as a contest between the mechanical power of "automatons" and the chthonic power of the earth and its capacity for suffering. Masculine violence opposed feminine endurance. This dualism blurs ideological differences: Hitler's tanks were in character not distinct from Stalin's; both wore the metallic face of totalitarianism. Stalin, however, had shrewdly perceived that the war could only be fought for "Mother Russia," not for communism. Even so, the maternity Jünger discerns lies deeper than the nationalism to which Stalin was giving effective, if cynical, concession. It was on the faces of those indomitable Cossack women, anti-Soviet and anti-Russian. At the same time, and incongruously, Jünger assessed the war as a crossroads of freedom: "In terms of the history of ideas, this Second World War is completely different from the First; it is probably the greatest altercation over the will's freedom since the Persian Wars" (December 21, 1942). The Russian adversary threated enslavement, as Darius and Xerxes had twenty-five hundred years before: "The Germans lost the First World War together with the Russians; maybe the Germans are losing the Second together with the French."

This yoking of Germany and France is startlingly amiss. It suggests that Jünger subscribed to the Nazi feint about a "United Europe" against bolshevism. So Hitler had proclaimed in a speech at the Sportpalast on October 3, 1941. But "German" never meant "Nazi" to Jünger. His Parisian time nourished in him the illusion that Franco-German amity was possible in spite of Hitler. "Freedom of the will" required safekeeping for Europe and men of Jünger's sensibility: connoisseurs, not conquerors.

Jünger's capacity for total dissociation, as though he was not a participant in Hitler's war of subjugation, is astounding: in the Bosch landscape of terror and misery he rejoiced to find time for entomological pursuits: "This sort of thing serves to preserve dignity, an emblem of my free-will world" (December 24, 1942). He was living out the botanist's marginal life on the marble cliffs.

Even so, facts cold as the Caucasus spoke. On New Year's Eve, Jünger recorded for the first time, in tandem with reports of the SS's "horrible deeds of shame" on taking Kiev, rumors of the mass gassing of Jews. "These are rumors, and I note them as such, yet undoubtedly slaughters (*Ausmordungen*) are taking place in a great compass." He remembered the Parisian pharmacist's Jewish wife. In that small, ominous corner of grief he read a fatalist's lesson:

> When you have looked upon such individual fates and then imagine the figures tolled in the slaughterhouses, you attain a view of suffering's involution before which you drop your arms. I am seized with loathing for the uniforms, epaulettes, medals, and weapons whose splendor I have loved so.

Ashamed to admit that he stands among the Ranger's rabble, he summons a caveat from *Crime and Punishment*. Raskolnikov looked upon his fellows as vermin. "That is precisely what we must guard against if we're not to pass into the sphere of insects." His chivalric code now a relic, Jünger took refuge in the cosmic order. Under a starry night that New Year's Eve he asked himself, "What are we human beings and our earthly years before this magnificence? What is our fleeting torment? At midnight, with the noise of drunkards near, I think vividly of my loved ones and feel how penetrating are their greetings."

If *On the Marble Cliffs* obliquely condemns despotism's unspeakable crimes, the Caucasus diary brings them into a higher lucidity. It affords no talisman for escape. Jünger is cornered with only his conscience, finds it inadequate, yet struggles to keep it alive, a single match in an enormous cave. The only surety lies in the fragile strength of loving. As the new year began, he resolved to keep his eyes upon the unfortunate. "One is naturally inclined not to apprehend genuine misfortune; indeed, one averts the eye. Compassion hobbles after." Also, he would banish the temptation to rescue himself "in the maelstrom of possible catastrophes. It's more important to preserve one's dignity" (January 1, 1943).

These were formidable challenges as the meaning of Stalingrad literally came home to the Germans. Inchoate panic gripped many before the specter of Russian advances. Legends of Bolshevik terrorism in 1917 fed the alarm. Soldiers on the eastern front, learning of these domestic apprehensions, knew them well founded. Jünger saw in the growing dread yet another proof of how technology had penetrated moral consciousness: "One feels he's in an enormous machine from which there's no escaping."

On February 18, Goebbels, in the most infamous speech of his career, sealed all possible exits from the machine. Answering British propaganda that the Germans had grown weary of the war, as surely the sane among them must have, he called for an affirmation of total war. He masterfully trumped any inclination to despair or defeatism by making the disaster at Stalingrad into a spectacle of heroic sacrifice. It dictated the marshaling of every effort to defend "the two thousand years' legacy of our civilization and everything that makes life worth living."[39]

Jünger's diaries do not indicate that he heard Goebbels's address; he was en route to Paris on the day of the broadcast, but it was repeated. There was talk of Hitler resorting to gas warfare. Jünger responded: "Propaganda counts before all else. In this case it would depend upon his creating a chasm between peoples such as even the best will cannot bridge. That befits his genius, which rests upon division, disunity, hatred. We've come to know his tribunes" (February 19, 1943).

His few weeks in the Caucasus gave Jünger a close window upon the realities of Goebbels's "total war." Once more secure in Parisian ease, he might have turned away from the war altogether to cultivate his garden of aesthetic delights. Heavy Allied bombings in western Germany precluded such dalliance, and he notes regularly their effect through his wife's apocalyptic letters and other reports, "many taking on an unholy eschatological complexion, like calls from the maelstrom's lowest ring" (July 3, 1943).

Phosphorus bombs — true fire from heaven — took sixty thousand lives in a single night. Mothers were seen throwing children into rivers. Asphalt in Hamburg and Hannover became so hot that those fleeing the phosphorus sank into it. "This dreadful intensification of crime has called up a kind of nightmare; one expects unheard of retaliations, the employment of still more powerful devilry that is standing ready" (June 25, 1943). In August, so many lives were lost in Hamburg that city officials could not count bodies: "The victims," writes Jünger, "died like fish or locusts, beyond history, in the elementary zone that knows no record" (August 17, 1943).

Refined technological terror and reduction of life to the primitive: these long familiar processes were taking bizarre variations in the east and now at home. Jünger saw them for himself during a furlough in November 1943. The swirling and scurrying of Hannover's populace recalled scenes from Ukrainian and Georgian cities he had toured. With the fatalistic reckoning he had used in *The Worker*'s cosmography he demoralized the devastation and made it into an impersonal historical force to which humanity had become partner:

> The catastrophe had to come; it chose the war as its best instrument. But even without the war, civil war would have done the work, as happened in Spain, or quite simply a comet, a fire from heaven, an earthquake. Cities had become ripe and brittle like tinder — and man was eager for conflagration. What had to come could be read when he set fire to churches in Russia and synagogues in Germany, and put his own kind into compulsory camps without trial. (November 27, 1943)

We note that Jünger's conjunction of natural and man-made ruinations carries force only as to their effects: citizens of Hamburg perished as horribly as those of Pompeii. Such similarities cannot obscure the fundamental difference in cause. Vesuvius did not intend destruction; Allied bombers did. By yielding intent to some ineluctable force, Jünger again slips into the trap of resigning everything to fate. His doing so here is odd, as he claims that humanity, or some fatal portion of it, craved destruction. Nazis (and communists) were stooges of destiny; so, too, their adversaries, those men on bombing missions over Germany.

All of this we found in Jünger's ascription of the 1914–1918 war to a demiurge as blind and purposeless as Schopenhauer's cosmic Will, revealing itself in history, a force to which humanity has been tethered by its own impulses. Jünger states that in the First World War he had dreamt of the Second, "even as during the advance through France in 1940 the scenes current at that time terrified me less than the preview of coming worlds of annihilation that I sensed in areas where no one was to be found" (October 24, 1943).

Jünger knew the urgent distinction between the world wars. The First was a jockeying of empires; the Second, the work of one man. In his first Parisian journal, that is, before his departure to the east, Jünger refers to Hitler (coded as "Kniébolo") only six times, two of them in accounts of dreams; in the second, there are over twenty references. The Führer (never so named in any of Jünger's writings) held his moral and psychological attention only when the evil star was at last in decline.

Without question, the mass murders of Jews imposed that attention. By April 1943 rumors had won confirmation. Jünger confessed to himself in that month "the apprehension of a dreadful danger. I mean that in a wholly general sense and would not be amazed if the earth flew into pieces whether from a comet or an explosion" (April 21, 1943). Devoting himself to apocalyptic literature, Jünger meant the comet this time would be an instrument of divine wrath. Only "demonic impulses" could account for the selection of Jews as victims and their murderers' irruption of the earth with mass graves. Hitler, "the world's enemy" (February 28, 1943), gave this devilry its impetus.

Jünger was clear sighted enough to put final blame for Hitler and Nazism's "demoniacal powers" upon a common indulgence. He says that although never suspected before, these powers were always potentially present. "The singular fact lies in their manifestation, in the permission given them to harm people. Our common guilt lies in this permission. While we divested ourselves of obligation, we released the infernal. So we cannot complain if evil strikes us individually as well" (April 16, 1943).

He contrasted "the elementary, subterranean" aspect of Hitler's greatness with Napoleon's personal majesty and Hindenburg's historical power. "Sometimes I have the impression the Weltgeist chose him in a cunning way" (December 6, 1943). It is noteworthy, however, that Jünger, often charged with paving the way for Hitler, did not content himself with the self-excusing hidden within the Hitler-as-demon view. By "obligation" he did not mean parliamentary vigilance, but rather the old code of authoritarian order he esteemed in the Prussian army. Hitler was begotten by a negative freedom, the absence of order's compulsions.

Jünger's genie-out-of-the-bottle explanation for Hitler's rise sounds strange against the conventional predominance of political and economic accounts, but it complements Jünger's fascination with psychological arcana and the hiddenness of evil. Further, it accords with his historical determinism, his long-held view that technology's nihilistic advances made chivalry anachronistic. In the old knighthood of generals steeped in Prussian military traditions there was close talk of removing Hitler. As is now well known, during the Munich crisis of 1938, a cabal of generals had considered deposing Hitler if he resolved upon war with Czechoslovakia. They—Karl von Stülpnagel among them—believed the German army was not prepared for war. Hitler's diplomatic triumph, ironically frustrating his desire for war, stymied their plotting. Another plot, with Col. Gen. Franz Halder carrying a pistol to shoot Hitler, grew after the invasion of Poland: it was intended to stop Hitler's plan for a winter offensive against France. Bad weather, Halder's shaky nerves, and wrangling among the generals over invasion strategies saved the Führer.

Jünger's first reference to a new conspiracy is dated March 31, 1943. Suitably obliquely, over a chessboard that evening, someone mentioned to him that "among the more significant generals there's a movement that recalls a passage in Matthew's Gospel: 'Are you the one who is to come or are we to await another?'" Whether Jünger knew in 1943 about the previous moves against Hitler is not certain. He did learn later from Stülpnagel "details which every historian hereafter will consider unbelievable" (March 29, 1944). By the fall of 1943 he had grounds for skepticism about the prospects for a successful coup. That September, as Allied forces were penetrating Italy and bomber squadrons were leveling German cities, he wrote of Hitler as an astrological portent, with

> aspects of Mars descending, yet still another constellation is at work in him in its unholy glow, thus Jupiter. He has all the properties that initiate an epoch of discord, such as the instrument of wrath which Pandora's box revealed. When I compare the Fatherland's legitimate claims with what has developed under such hands, an unending sorrow seizes me. (September 23, 1943)

On October 16, in conversation with a well-traveled fellow officer called "Bogo" in his journal, Jünger learned details of the ghetto industries at

Lodz, the vehicular gassing of Jews (at Chelmno), and crematoria in which masses of Jews, under the ruse of resettlement, were being incinerated. "Bogo" told Jünger he would be willing to assassinate Hitler. The obvious problem was to gain access to him. Jünger that day wrote down his perception of a more elementary problem. "Elitists" like Bogo and the generals were "rushing into the metaphysical realm with the élan of reason," a totally insufficient weapon. They were hanging on to a nineteenth-century disposition in a cultic century. "That is why Kniébolo is still alive, and hence the complete incapacity of the liberal intelligentsia even to see the position in which he is standing." An impenetrable mystique guarded Hitler. In effect, this peculiar rationale took the Führer at his own estimate (fate's unassailable instrument) save that what Jünger viewed as Hitler's talismanic nihilism Hitler regarded as a predestinarian force.

Jünger's mystification of Hitler is ahistorical, even while reminding us how powerful the Führer's charismatic authority was as late as 1944. Absolutism did not protect Julius Caesar from assassination, but Jünger was more attentive to the brilliant records of failure, shipwrecked conspiracies like the Stoic republicans' against Nero, and the Fronde in seventeenth-century France. In those histories the sorry skill of courtly intelligence lost to apparent fate or the *Weltgeist*. Besides, Hitler was hallowed by a supremely irrational dynamo, the dream. One night in April 1943, Jünger learned of Hitler's visit to his father's house,

> for what reason I did not know. All kinds of precautions were taken while I hid myself in a remote room so as not to meet him. When I came out, he had already been there. I heard details about his visit, in particular that my father had embraced him. On awaking it was this fact that especially struck me. (April 16, 1943)

In this oneiric realm nineteenth-century positivism gave weird sanction to twentieth-century barbarism. The totemic powers of paternal authority made a sinister compact against the son. The dream argues a displacement, with Hitler now attaining ultimate power, the domestic seat. Jünger's father had died three months before, a week prior to his son's return from the east.

Given his susceptibility to the seeming dictates of fate, the zodiacal sign, and dream's message, it is surprising that Jünger marshaled any stamina to counter them. He was keeping the constant company of resolute conspirators, men he honored and trusted. Late in March 1944 he received a telephone call from one of them, Cäsar von Hofacker, Stülpnagel's aide-de-camp and cousin of Stauffenberg. As the phones and rooms were likely tapped by the SS, they went for a walk up and down the Avenue Kléber, from Trocadero to l'Etoile. Hofacker indicated that the SS regarded Stülpnagel with distrust and Jünger himself with suspicion. It was an obvious ploy to enlist Jünger, most helpful at his communications post, in the conspiracy Stülpnagel was heading. Hofacker argued that catastrophe for Germany could no longer be avoided but might be mitigated: if some settlement could be made with the Western powers before they invaded France, the much more dire threat from the Russians might be staved. All of this presupposed an end to Hitler. Jünger stated his reservations about a coup, but Hofacker remonstrated. If communications could be taken over, arresting Hitler would suffice. Von Rundstedt, the western commander-in-chief, would throw in with Stülpnagel. "Then all the western transmissions will be in your hands."

Jünger remarks of this meeting that nothing better indicated the extraordinary significance Hitler knew how to give himself than the degree to which even his strongest opponents, the western generals, depended upon him. At the same time he gave himself a new rationale for reticence in joining the conspirators. Even should Hitler fall, "the great match is playing out between the plebiscitarian Demos and the remnants of the aristocracy. . . . The hydra will fashion a new head" (March 27, 1944).

The "Demos" had wandered before him in a brief February visit he made to Berlin and Hanover. Amid nearly total debris, the streets were full of people. To these scenes Jünger conjoined those of urban chaos during the Kristallnacht. The vulgarity and potential violence of the masses belonged to despotism. Even or especially in ruin, the demos would find some new desperate tribune. Like Plato, Jünger believed that the masses, without the constraints of a guardian class, inevitably turn to tyranny. That America had not produced a dictator of Hitlerian proportions did not concern him; it had shown how technology, the machine's democracy, is cohort to nihilism's negation of value. The destruction of old Berlin and old Hanover was mass produced.

He saw, too, that the old warrior caste, defending ancestral claims of military honor, was up against a new caste of power wielders, "the technicians." What he calls Hitler's "will to the destruction of values" had found expression in the infernal potential of device: Goebbels's radio, Himmler's poison gas factories, Panzer divisions staffed by murderers, the "higher cannibalism" of police interrogation methods (February 16, 1944). Jünger judged the contest lost: old Germany against a technologized world of the masses, with Hitler on the other side. The Nazis might as well have been Americans.

Jünger's historical fatalism could deny the conspirators acuity of vision, even deny them the future, but not a profoundly courageous patriotism. His own son, Ernstel, showed the way. While in marine service, he and some fellow students were arrested and imprisoned at Wilhelmshaven. A spy charged Ernstel had said that if the Germans wanted peace, they would have to hang Hitler. In a letter to his parents, Ernstel denied making any such statement, shrewdly adding that so portentous a remark would not have come even by a slip of the tongue. He tried to assure them he was being well treated and felt no bitterness or anger, "rather an inner calm that sometimes even has something cheerful about it. In my situation you must above all not reflect, else you too easily fall into a brooding that degenerates into melancholy." [40]

Jünger wrote urging him to keep his head up. The father need not have worried. He was pleased with the report that under interrogation his son had displayed no regret. That would have been tantamount to a confession of guilt. It was Ernstel's arrest that took his father to Berlin. He attempted to see Admiral Dönitz but then realized a visit might compromise his son and lead to a heavier sentence. After several months in prison Ernstel was released on condition of "voluntary" service in northern Italy.

Jünger's diary codes for the officers' plot were "the situation" and "the summons," the latter being his essay on a post-Hitler peace for Europe. How did he evaluate himself? He confessed his views on war had changed:

> Yet one at work in these old tunnels never knows whether or when he is hitting a mine. One also has to note the bore-hole, which is comparable to a sandglass. While the granules of sand are moving to the point of greatest compaction and friction their inclination is other than when they have passed through it. The first phase stands under the law of concentration, of narrow passage and total mobilization; the second, under the law of final arrangement and extension. In the cycle which the image affords, the particles remain the same. (March 27, 1944)

Perhaps no other image in Jünger's writings so well captures his fatalism while maintaining his privileged position as spectator. One has not chosen his situation and is not responsible for it. To employ another figure, de Tocqueville's "historical theater" (February 29, 1944) casts us all in certain parts on a narrow stage. Fate plays the impresario, assigning the same actor different roles. Jünger's sandglass metaphor says more: history has no final internal effect; it achieves only a logistical rearrangement. In observing that the sand particles remain identical throughout, he adroitly implies rescue of the will's integrity which the sandglass image and the "laws" seem to deny altogether. His diction shows its usual studied ambivalence: the "*Tendenz*" of particles may be "inclination" or "intention." While the image of tunnel-boring carries an evident voluntarism ("*Tendenz*" as the intentional work of an army's pioneers), the particles neither make nor choose to go through the narrow passage. But a particle named Jünger had once *intended* total mobilization, and had descried in *The Worker* an imminent narrow passage, the zero point where decadence would reach conversion to the new order of workshop landscapes, "the final arrangement and extension" of humankind.

The truly narrow passage had been not Fate's creation but Hitler's. He, only he, forced Jünger to final awareness that chivalric standards of war had been made forfeit. Perceiving the peculiar dependence of Hitler's adversaries upon him, Jünger neglected to include himself among them. If historical "laws" could be likened to a sandglass's process, Germany could only be likened to a cauldron, and "that was already clear to me before this war began, as the exemplary fate of Judaism showed." Jünger compared his own situation to a bridge over dark waters, precarious and near collapse; on the far shore, a thick mist whence dim lights or sounds issued only intermittently. "That is the theological, psychological, and political situation" (April 22, 1944).

Speidel, now a lieutenant general, honorably forced him to cross the bridge. On May 1, 1944, he had Jünger's "summons" delivered to his superior, General Rommel, whose prestige the conspirators considered invaluable in establishing their authority immediately after Hitler's removal. "I gave it up reluctantly," noted Jünger. Speidel has said that Rommel was "deeply impressed" by the "Christian" ideals Jünger had set down.[41]

Jünger for his part perhaps saw in Rommel a Sulla, "a simple general of the people," who could give the conspiracy's "moral substance" a necessary political gravity (April 29, 1944), but he estimated that Speidel, not Rommel, would prove the decisive player in the conspiracy's acting out. This was an assessment of temper, not of shrewdness or courage: "In his midst calm prevails, a stilled wind suitable to the wheel's axle, to the hurricane's center" (May 13, 1944). Indeed, as we review the superior ranks late that spring, the impression of irresolution among the leaders grows. Stülpnagel, for example, no matter his "princely bearing," was becoming unnerved. Jünger saw him worn out, habitually rubbing his back with the left hand as though seeking to support himself. He talked of the stoic's virtue in suicide when circumstances so dictated. What could be expected from so troubled a man?

The field marshals fared little better. After the Allied invasion confounded their months-long preparation of a counteroffensive, Rundstedt and Rommel dithered about telling Hitler that it was time to make peace. The Führer bullied them into mute acquiescence to his down-to-the-last-man intentions to hold Normandy. Speidel, as Rommel's adjutant, had been with him and Rundstedt when they met Hitler at Soissons, June 17. The next week he passed to Jünger his impressions of the Führer: "Kniébolo has apparently become old and bent, making increasingly careless digressions in conversation. . . . He seems to hope and perhaps even to believe that the favorable fate which so often has gotten him out of doubtful situations is going to rescue him here" (June 24, 1944).

Jünger learned from Stülpnagel some details of the July 20 assassination attempt the next day. They had a luncheon appointment for the twenty-second to discuss philosophy. Fate prevented their meeting. "It gripped me," Jünger noted, "that amid the confusion he remembered to cancel our engagement. That was a significant feature of his character" (July 22, 1944).[42] Summoned to Berlin, Stülpnagel tried to shoot himself near Verdun. When Hofacker informed Jünger that the young Stauffenberg had served as the would-be assassin, Jünger realized how prescient *On the Marble Cliffs* had been: Sunmyra, last vestige of ancient aristocracy, and failure.[43] Hearing the attempt denounced in the Paris offices, he found full confirmation of his view that nothing could be changed, surely not improved. Having unsuccessfully urged Field Marshal von Kluge to arrange an immediate surrender to the Allies in the west, Stülpnagel had had the SS and security services in Paris arrested, only to have Kluge release them when final news of the plot's failure came from Berlin. Behind closed doors, Stülpnagel remarked to Jünger, "The dragon was in the bag only to be let out" (July 21, 1944). Jünger traced the disaster to an elementary failure: the news of Hitler's death had not been confirmed before the arrests were made. He blamed not the precipitous Stülpnagel, who had acted immediately upon receiving the code word "Launched," but "the wholly incompetent and sickly Colonel von Linstow," the chief of staff. Hofacker also bore substantial blame because as go-between for the Berlin and Paris wings of the plot he had not apprised Stülpnagel or Speidel that July 20 was the chosen date.

Stülpnagel, Linstow, and Hofacker were hanged. Rommel and Kluge died by their own hands. Speidel, at the western front on that fateful day, was arrested September 7 and imprisoned but could not be charged with an active role in the plot during its crucial hours. (General Guderian and two other officers defended him against Keitel's recommendation that he be sent to the People's Court, a virtual death sentence.) Speidel narrowly escaped Himmler's order of April 14, 1945, that no political prisoners should fall into enemy hands. Trucked by prison guards through southern Germany, he witnessed a grotesque celebration of Hitler's birthday in a small Bavarian town (banners hoisted one last time, a children's choir), and was rescued from the Gestapo by General Béthouart's First French Army Corps on April 29.[44] With Stülpnagel's botch of his stoic suicide, Jünger knew the game was up with the knightly order he had presumed to find in the Paris offices, that "small circle of the last chivalric men, free spirits, feeling and thinking beyond dull passions." In the Great War, his friends had died by bullets. Now, that was a privilege. "And yet these sacrifices are important because they create and safeguard inner space, so that the nation falls into the terrible depths of fate as one whole" (July 22, 1944).

That Jünger himself did not fall victim to "the terrible depths" which awaited his superiors nor was even arrested for complicity seems astonishing. Hofacker, long subjected to torture, or even Speidel might have named him. For the while, beloved Paris saved him. July 20 unleashed Hitler's suspicious fury against the Wehrmacht's Prussians but it also renewed his superstitious confidence in his destiny. To secure withdrawal from France, he had to spare the Wehrmacht and he could make peace with it now that, as in 1934, the SS had gained ascendance.

In early August Jünger made his private round of farewells: a last visit to the German Institute, to Mrs. Gould's salon, to his barber of four years who hoped "things will work out." On the steps of Sacré-Coeur he cast a final glance over Paris: "I saw the stones trembling in the hot sun as though in expectation of new historical embraces. Cities are womanly and only to victors are they beautiful" (August 8, 1944). He departed Paris toward nightfall on Monday, August 14, having set his room at the

Raphael in final order: a bouquet on the table, and a tip. "Unfortunately I forgot some irreplaceable letters in a cabinet drawer." Ten days later, General Leclerc's Second Panzer Division embraced the city.

Jünger spent the last two weeks of August stationed at Saint-Dié in Alsace, not far from the concentration camp Le Struthof and from the site of his first fighting in the previous war. The barracks at Saint-Dié had once been named after Witzleben, one of the doomed inner circle of July 20 conspirators.

Having observed desolated France en route, Jünger resorted to historical reflection. Over a book on Louis XVI, he mused,

> The old world's destruction, made visible with the French Revolution and even before, with the Renaissance, is like the atrophy of organic ties, nerves, and arteries. When the process ends, men of force appear; they sew artful threads and wires into the corpse and prompt it to more violent but also more grotesque political play. They themselves carry the aspect of puppets in their strident, gruesome, charlatan's way. The new states have a devouring tendency. They can flourish only where there is still an inheritance. When that's used up, the hunger becomes unbearable. Like Saturn, they consume their own children." (August 18, 1944)

Sinister technology does not for once perform in Jünger's somber reckoning. Contra Spengler, he gives center stage to his father's Great Men, *die Gewaltmenschen*. We think of those whom fortune, that supreme impresario, exalted mightily and then forsook: Cesare Borgia, Robespierre, and Napoleon, and the foremost charlatan in modern history, whose tanks were now burning across Europe. The condottieri, committees of public safety or "security" forces behind such figures make up the life-ravaging apparatus of modern government. Although, like Spengler, Jünger sees an incontestable atrophy of society into chaos, it is that final mythic reference to Saturn which arrests our attention and gives the passage a palpable human gravity. Jünger, like true conservatives, cherishes a past that the present is ruthlessly consuming. Hitler's demolition order for the Seine's bridges stands as an example. *The Worker* presented the modern technological state as a ready-for-war machine, but Jünger in 1932 had not drawn the full conclusions of its logic. Hitler, a latter-day Saturn, had done so with his Hitlerjugend, whom he was now using up as his final defense.

In the Caucasus, we saw Jünger celebrating Cossack women and the maternal power of the earth to endure suffering. Now he saw this endurance in children, including his own. Calamity had come to his doorstep. The state had robbed him of the woman named Paris whom he loved, and now it called for his son. He arrived in Kirchhorst on September 4, and found it and his house overrun with refugees from the east. Within two weeks he was put into the reserves, suspended in anticipation of the lemurs' "prophylactic vengeance." "If they were more intelligent, one could say to them with Seneca, 'No matter how many you kill, your successors will not be among them'" (September 16, 1944). He found Ernstel, now in a Panzer division, still uncomplaining but exhausted by imprisonment; he feared his son was not yet up to the exertions of training. On October 25, he saw the boy off on a train to northern Italy. Ernstel died under fire within a week.

Germany had become the likeness of a pauper "whose lawful possessions a villainous lawyer has reclaimed" (September 18, 1944), but the unmistakable signs of its complicity remained. The Germans "after long fasting had been led to the mountain top and shown the world's might. It had not taken long before they were worshipping the tempter" (October 6, 1944). Hitler's radio call on October 18 for national defense (*Volkssturmbataillone*) was to Jünger's ears patently "directed against the people as a whole," yet artfully couched so they were given the opportunity to consent to their own destruction. The public's "frenetic applause" of the Führer's summons Jünger termed an act of high nihilism. "My horror comes from the fact that I heard through it from the start, the dreadful exultation in ratcatcher's music."

Jünger had heard nihilism's dissonance "from the start," but did not recognize it as such in 1933. Had he done so, he would not have needed to proclaim his horror amid conflagration nearly twelve years later. Yet, this objection is not altogether fair. Jünger's distance from the regime had been unequivocal all along. He did not need to make excuses for his conduct in the thirties. Aristocratic detachment and contempt for the vulgarities of Nazism did not amount to resistance, but they kept a residue of dignity. Jünger's elitist disposition, not his judgment or clairvoyance, had kept him free of Hitler. The beguiling Führer had led the people to the mountain's top; Jünger had already been there on his own in *The Worker* and had learned to descend. *On the Marble Cliffs* and *The Peace* furnish lasting, honorable proof.

On October 20, Jünger learned of the order for his dishonorable discharge from the Wehrmacht. (He was formally discharged on October 27 in Bothfeld.) Having read of Speidel's arrest (by a letter from his wife), Jünger knew he could now be subjected to civil court proceedings. He attempted to concentrate upon reading and writing. With publishing industries virtually gone to ruin, he found his writing "more meaningful and aimless" (October 20, 1944).[45]

Preliminary proceedings against Jünger may have begun soon after his dismissal. If they did, nothing came of them. When we weigh his proximity to Stülpnagel, his aversion to the Nazis, and the writing of *On the Marble Cliffs,* it is amazing that he was never brought to court. When his book appeared in autumn 1939, some of Hitler's henchmen urged that Jünger be put in a concentration camp. "Nothing's to happen to Jünger" (Dem Jünger geschieht nichts!), the Führer had said.[46] Now, once again, Jünger was spared. Had his "case" appeared adventitiously, when Hitler was too preoccupied with far greater matters: in the summer of 1939, preparation for war with Poland; in December 1944, with the Ardennes offensive? That seems unlikely. When roused to suspicion or vengeance, Hitler's power of concentration did not fail him. Was he scrupulous about celebrities? Rolf Hochhuth has suggested, in regard to the July 20 plot, that Jünger's literary prestige was too high for him to be prosecuted. Next to Gerhard Hauptmann, Ricarda Huch, and Ernst Wiechert, says Hochhuth, Jünger was "the most highly esteemed writer in the Reich."[47] Hitler did have a deferential regard for creative personalities. Jünger was also a Pour le Mérite veteran. But the assumption that this twofold prestige guarded him is deceptive. Consider the fate of other Great War bearers of the Pour le Mérite: Martin Niemöller, the evangelical pastor, was sent to Dachau (but he was allowed to officiate services there). Rommel was given the option of suicide so as to avoid trial and possible harm to his family. Dubious allowances apart, both men were Hitler's victims. It cannot be claimed that Jünger's medal protected him. All we know is that Hitler was not susceptible to protests against Jünger.

I submit that Hitler had made up and closed his mind about Jünger long before 1939. Neither Jünger's rejection of nomination to the Prussian Academy in 1934, nor even his rejection of Hitler's invitation to serve as a party deputy in the Reichstag in 1927 had altered Hitler's estimate of him. After the war, Jünger noted that like many political leaders the Führer had a memory with sealed compartments. "He didn't like to change his views of people after he had settled them" (April 2, 1946). His views on Jünger would have crystallized around 1925, when Jünger had sent him copies of *Stahlgewitter, Wäldchen 125,* and *Feuer und Blut,* one inscribed to Hitler as Führer. Hitler's esteem for him rested on more than strokes to his vanity. He knew that in the Great War, the life expectancy of storm troops, not to mention their leader, was about as dim as that of courier, his own rank. And that Jünger had been the exemplary leader can hardly be doubted from *Stahlgewitter*'s final chapter, when Jünger, his small band of survivors surrounded by English (and by Germans who had already yielded their weapons), ordered them to resist down to knives. This was the sort of man, lean and "hard as the steel of Krupp," whom Hitler wanted for his own war. That such a man was not a Nazi ideologue scarcely mattered to him. Jünger's two contributions to the Nazi journal *Der Völkische Beobachter* indicate only that his nationalism was centered but upon what one critic has aptly called "a convulsion of the soul, a glowing fantastic vision requiring submission." [48] For a brief while, Jünger and Hitler could presume that each shared the other's worldview. Hitler then went the way of parliamentary partisanship, and Jünger toward an ever refractory quixotism. Jünger never opposed Hitler politically.

We should look again to the Great War. The soldier's soldier, Jünger performed well above the common infantryman in daring, skill, and luck, yet was never so high in command as to share blame for the final defeat. Most important was his triumphant writing of the war he experienced. "The German war book," was Goebbels's verdict on *Stahlgewitter.* If Hitler read this book (there is no reason to suppose he did not), he found in it the accomplished man of arms he probably could never have been and certainly did not become. An analogy may be in place here with Albert Speer, the "artist" such as Hitler, under the aegis of destiny, was not permitted to be. Hitler, I believe, had a blind spot, almost deferential, toward both of these surrogates.

Speer himself may be helpful here. In his Spandau prison diaries he mentions talking with fellow inmate Baldur von Schirach about Hitler's indifference to literature: "Hitler took everything as an instrument, and of all the arts literature lends itself least to the uses of power politics. Its effects are always unpredictable, and the mere fact that books are meant for private consumption must have made him suspicious. The audience for every other art could be swayed by showmanship but not the solitary reader within four walls." [49] This argument may be too neat, but it suggests a compelling symmetry. Hitler's blindness to literature complemented Jünger's to politics, for Jünger's Weimar polemics had been from first to last "within four walls," a politics of readership, not power. How apt that Jünger, having looked past the man who came to realize the *Führerprinzip* with a vengeance, should have been spared by him; that Hitler in turn looked past the writer who has left the one enduring literary masterwork of the Third Reich, a depiction of its horror at the root.

Of the hundreds of entries making up Jünger's Paris journals, some few have attained notoriety. They are quoted again and again against him, as though by iteration to establish that his years in Paris amounted to one prolonged indulgence of aestheticism, a romp in high decadence, something akin to the chic of Nazi sado-masochism. Complementing the image of the ardent war lover comes the image of the dandy, the habitué of *tout Paris*—mind, heart, and soul ice-dead to all humane feeling.

The first much-cited occasion fell on May 29, 1941, only a few weeks after Jünger had been appointed to the military governor's staff in Paris. Listless for months, he likened himself to someone in a wilderness, housed between a demon urging him to action, and a corpse to sympathy: "Added to the flood of unpleasant things weighing on me, it happens I've been ordered to oversee the execution of a soldier condemned to death for desertion. At first I intended to report sick but that seemed a cheap way out. I also thought: perhaps it's better that you are there rather than someone else." A "higher curiosity" seized him. In the previous war he had not observed a deserter shot nor anyone prepared for the precise moment of death. Here was a situation "daily threatening each of us, shadowing our lives."

The condemned man had deserted the army shortly after the surrender and had hid out with a French mistress in Paris. When he abused her, she turned him in. Jünger arrives at the execution site (likely la Vallée-aux-Loups) toward dawn. On sight of the prisoner he is overcome with a feeling of oppression, as though breathing itself has become difficult. The man's face has features attractive to women. While his death sentence is read he seems to attend with keen awareness,

> yet I have the impression the text is passing him by. His eyes are wide open, motionless, absorbing, large, as though the body were hanging onto them. His whole mouth moves as though he were spelling.

His glance falls on me and tarries a second over my face with a penetrating, searching tension. I note that the excitement confers upon
him the look of something intricate, blooming, indeed childlike.

The minute's reading seems interminable. The blindfolded man kisses
a small silver cross, and a doctor places a piece of red cardboard over
the heart.

I would like to glance past [Jünger coins the word *fortblicken*] but
force myself to look straight on [*hinsehen*], and seize the moment
when with the salvo fire dark little holes appear in the cardboard,
as though dewdrops had fallen on it. The man shot is still standing
by the tree; his features express a dreadful surprise. I see his mouth
opening and closing as though it wanted to shape vowels and still,
with great effort, to express something. The situation is perplexing,
and again the time stretches out. It even seems the man has become
dangerous. Finally, his knees give in.

The man's face looks "as though a bucket of lime-water was poured over
it." The physician explains that the dying man's gestures were only empty
reflexes. Jünger is not persuaded. "He hasn't seen what became evident
to me in a ghastly way."

A by-way incident in a war, but Jünger invests its account with more
than even his usual fastidious care. He admixes casual observation (the
woman-pleasing face) with screw-twisting details that build the tension
(the incredulous eyes, the childlike piteous glance) and carries that tension beyond the expected moment of release. The fear preceding the
shooting yields to a strange terror after it. The seeming protraction of
time which Jünger felt goes on in the dying man's "reflexive" response to
his own death. He freezes the second and imposes it on his readers. We
must traverse five sentences between the salvo and the buckled knees. To
the condemned man's puzzlement Jünger counterposes his own sense of
an overwhelming gravity. The observer observes himself, but not once
do we glimpse an emotive response. Without trace of fear, revulsion, or
pity—why the wish, though, to glance away?—he serves as a barometer.
His inner disorientation confounds the straightforward cohesion of narrative, and renders the whole into a kind of dream episode. The irrational
dynamics of dreaming threaten to disrupt this tableau of military justice.

Taken superficially, this passage ratifies a central objection to Jünger, that he achieves aesthetic concentration at the cost of moral sensitivity, as though he had uncannily followed to the letter John Ruskin's famous advice for "the great painter": "Always cool yourself as you either look on, or take any necessary part in the play. Cool, and strong willed— moveless in observant soul. Does a man die at your feet—your business is not to help him, but to note the colour of his lips. . . . Not a specially religious or spiritual business this, it might appear."[50] Jünger's rationale, that he might observe the very moment of death's stroke, seems a morbid, not "higher," curiosity. It is his narrative that is "higher," higher than any film record could be, because he is humanly susceptible, yet it escapes the merely clinical estimate which the physician provides at the close. "Empty reflexes." Jünger rejects this convenience because he has read "dreadful surprise" in the soldier, perplexity in himself, and danger in the air. Framed by "a new, more powerful onset of depression," this narrative hardly fits the charge that Jünger's aestheticism is morally insensitive. To say that he shows no compassion does not prove he does not feel it or is incapable of it. More important, his narrative gives the reader grounds for pity and terror.

The same may not be said of another outrageous passage a year later, May 17, 1942:

> After the repulse of a Russian patrol, Grüninger's men found among the dead a seventeen-year-old girl who had fought fanatically. No one could say how it happened but the next morning her corpse lay naked in the snow, and as winter is a brilliant sculptor who keeps his figures stiff and fresh, the garrison had lots of opportunity to wonder at her beautiful body. When the advance point was later pulled back, volunteers frequently reported for a patrol so as in this way to feast their eyes once more on the sight of her splendid form.

Jünger's critics do not always acknowledge that in this instance he did not experience what he records. Yet, he was sufficiently engaged by Grüninger's report to include it among the war's "usual capriccios," a sight Goya had missed. Necrophilia, a clinical term, seems out of place here. The strange compulsion in this story, a pull Jünger obliquely feels and accepts, is beauty disclosed within death. On the eastern front the messy barbarity of death-dealing had become commonplace. The troops would have no urge to look upon one more corpse, even a nude one. But the ineffable conjunction of beauty, youth, woman, and death—the mystery that possessed Poe—enchanted even the coarsest sensibility. The last sentence tells all: men were willing to risk their own deaths to see the winter's fair sculpture. Like the story of the deserter's execution, this miniature tells of life grotesquely enhanced by death. The chivalric accent (knights come to pay the lady homage) is askew: this *belle dame sans merci* would gladly have killed each and every one. How her angry ghost must have despised them all! Jünger borrows the common soldier's rapture and gives to the savage history of Operation Barbarossa a fleeting, bizarre moment of the sublime.

Out of the war's grimy commotion, such moments of beauty-in-terror were not infrequent. A certain opportunism may lie in Jünger's observations, but imagination is opportunistic and mercilessly gratuitous. Let us take the entry most often cited against him, his observation of a bombing raid over Paris, May 27, 1944. From the Raphael's sunset roof Jünger observed a host of Allied planes passing in an attack on the Seine's bridges. Explosive clouds arose from the area of Saint-Germain. When a second fleet came by "I held a glass of burgundy in my hand, with strawberries swimming in it. The city with its red towers and cupolas lay in prodigious beauty, like a calyx which is skimmed over to deadly fertilization." (The 1949 edition's entry ends here. In the Klett edition Jünger added to it: "Everything was spectacle, it was pure might, consented to and elevated by suffering.")

The apiarist's imagery is superbly wrought: planes like bees, towers the stamina of a calyx-city, bombs a mortal pollen, the whole a process of fatal *Befruchtung*. It is the burgundy in the hand, of course, which provokes indignation. It strikes a jarring note of callousness and cruelest indifference, evidence to one critic of "something Neronian about Jünger." [51] Another, claiming this entry "surely belongs to the most macabre passages in German literary history," may be typical of some who know it only by hearsay: he presumes Jünger was actually toasting the planes and that they were on their way to bomb Berlin, Hamburg, and Dresden. [52] Nothing helps like an accurate reading, except citation of another bombing observed, not by Jünger but by Guéhenno, a man of letters and no friend of the Germans. Of a raid over Paris, April 20, 1944: "We stayed in our fragile house, with all windows open, and had no other recourse than to watch the spectacle. Magnificent, but rather frightening. Man is astonishingly powerful and bestial." One man sees a beast, the other a bee.

Our three examples concern death but their vital denomination lies in the beholder's astonishment at what death reveals. Each momentarily exposes what would otherwise remain hidden, as though a natural law allows a flash into itself. Jünger mystifies the moment by not articulating what its meaning may be, thus calling into question the very imputation of meaning. One could argue that the deserter's witness to his own death, the orderly chaos of bombing—"a terrible beauty is born"—are finally experiences without meaning. That would be true horror. Yet Jünger is so convinced that beauty and horror are conjoined in this life that he can scarcely admit one without the other. The forest walks and marsh tramp-ings of childhood and the brutish trenches of young manhood have one integrating factor, an extraordinary sensibility. We suspect Jünger takes almost impish pride in it.

Nowhere, however, is he more engaging and intimate than in his at-tention to a realm overlooked in every history of the Occupation, and where he was most at home: among plants and animals. A review of his "adventurous heart" and astonished eye requires attention to this out-of-the-way corner of the warring world. In the Occupation's treacherous peace, he cultivated his naturalist interests assiduously. They were a kind of therapy for him; a purgation, even. He once likened them to bathing after a dusty trip, but they afforded much more: a sense of freedom and dignity preserved. A salamander reminds him that "on countless occa-sions the sight of animals, like a life source, has endowed me with new strength" (March 1, 1941). The teeming of bees suggests an erotic force in nature: "Perhaps all our theories about communal zoology are the wrong way round, and what we observe to be work is, after all, pleasure" (June 4, 1940).

Jünger maintains that the primary intellectual appeal in zoological studies is aesthetic apprehension of the unending diversity within a species, particularly the entomological. It affords delight in what he calls "prismatic variations," those arabesques of detail which his father's learned inspiration had taught his childhood to appreciate. At the core of this aesthetic is the belief in a supernal source or demiurge from which all nature takes variety, as from a Platonic form. On visiting a zoo shortly before the war Jünger mentions his melancholy fear that all the earth's animals might one day be extinct, but then he consoles himself that "they rest in their creator and only their appearance will be wiped out. Every destruction takes away only the shadow of their forms" (July 23, 1939).

In a rare, elevated moment he spoke with an old French Jesuit who had spent his life in China building churches. The priest tried to assure the captain that distant travel was profitless since everything is derived from a few elementary patterns. Such a religious person, Jünger concluded, "loves life beyond the prism," and so sees little value in the spectrum's many colors:

> Our talk reminded me of my earlier uncertainty, about whether upon our entrance into Oneness we lose a pleasure which only time and its variety can sustain, and whether the purpose of our existence lies hidden in the fact that God needs individuation. I've had that feeling so often in observing insects and marine animals and all the untold wonder of life's flow. It's profoundly painful to think that one day there must be a leavetaking of it all. (March 21, 1943)

Pleasure in the wondrous, by this testimony, amounts to an emotion of almost religious force. Not incidentally, this passage has a theistic context. How odd of Jünger to suppose (blasphemously?) that God requires the variety of creation. Logically, that variety is presupposed by "entry into Oneness," but Jünger is inclined to what Thomists call love of the secondary good (creation) even over love of the primary (creator). He does not care that if it is dangerous to conjoin aesthetic value and moral value (as Plato did in disparaging Homer), it is all the more dangerous to give aesthetics a divine sanction. An aestheticism indifferent to all else may result. Ruskin gave warning.

Jünger moves toward a divine aesthetic in a famously derided passage, dated September 16, 1942. He was walking through the Jardin d'Acclimation in the Bois de Boulogne. It had been created in 1854 to acclimatize exotic birds and plants but had been degraded to an amusement park where children could ride elephants and camels. Keeping shy of these torments, he found among the cranes, peacocks, and pheasants a pair of Sumatran hens and was immediately enchanted by their splendid shimmer, "a cascade of metallic green."

> Why is enchantment especially vivid when something we've known from the first, like our barnyard cock, appears in unexpected form, shaped on an island beyond the long-traversed sea? It affects me so powerfully I'm almost moved to tears. . . . It is the One, the primal image, that becomes visible to us in these magic shows. Seeing them brings on the feeling of vertigo: we fall downward as in a spring's

jet from the iris-colored aura of qualities onto their essence. The rainbow's hierarchy—to think that even the world as a whole was fashioned after a primal image which modified itself into a myriad of solar systems.

If in this aesthetic everything in creation has an archetype which transcends yet determines it, Jünger occupies a Platonic universe, yet he remains too predisposed to the vertigo of amazement to embrace a metaphysical system. While entertaining the possibility of archetypes, he prefers not to relinquish the observable world of mutation. He has none of the Platonist's disdain of passing nature. He practices a sharp eye upon biology, but never shuts the garden door on mystery.

His botanical enthusiasms show as much. He says that the kingdom of plants is a showcase for "the whole of metaphysics; and there's no better course of instruction on invisible things *that become visible* than the garden's year" (April 5, 1944).[53] At the botanical garden in Auteuil he dotes on umbels and wisteria but dismisses azaleas for not being metaphysical; their colors are one-dimensional. There lies their popularity, he adds, for they speak only to the eye, lacking "the beads of arcanum arcanorum supercoeleste" in their tincture. For this man, sensuous pleasure in flora is not a sufficient aesthetic criterion. One must read nature's unwritten order in them, hear their unspoken language.

This is the prejudice of an inspired amateur, like Goethe. Indeed, Jünger's rapture over the Sumatran hens stands as a plea for the "primal phenomenon" which Goethe considered the source of aesthetic amazement.[54] Goethe insisted it was a manifestation of the contingent world, not a Platonic form.[55] He urged that we should not tamper with its "divine simplicity" by "useless experiment" but rather entrust it to our "discernment and faith."[56] The point is relevant to Jünger because he, too, advocates a meditative, noninstrumental, yet empirical practice of science, one that uses natural variations to argue an all-subsuming Oneness. The twofold source of aesthetic wonder for Jünger as for Goethe is that the ever-renewed discovery of variety reconfirms its unity.

For Jünger nature is a magician performing shows for our wonder. He claims there is a language of plants, even speaks of "befriending" jasmine for its fragrance, but such spectacles of nature's magic, though objects of delight and surprise, be they chrysomelids or salamanders, count less than his and our perceiving them as partakers of archetypes. In Kant's terms, to feel that something is beautiful leads to a conceptual grasp of an order the perceiver imposes; Jünger does so by the pleasurable intimation of unity in variety, Goethe's "discernment and faith." We might object that the archetype or any other metaphysical brick intellectualizes the experience of beauty from the start and so does not admit aesthetic feeling. How can we truly feel wonder if we have primed ourselves for it? The answer is that the notion of variety in unity does not necessarily indicate how that variety will manifest itself. We continue to depend upon what Goethe called "the eternal play of the empirical." [57]

We have come a long way from the war. The botanical gardens of Paris, a heavenly island in the midst of an infernal sea, gave Jünger brief refuge from "this slave ship" (September 29, 1943) and its darkening world of schemes. No escapist, he knew that orchids and SS agents were occupying the same world. His aesthetic was no private exit into prettiness; it was an attempt to read an order that includes things ugly and horrendous. Must not aesthetics account for what is repellent, too? Yes, but there is still one thing lacking. We need not agree with Kant that beauty is a symbol of morality in order to admit that aesthetic experience finds its true completion in religious vision. Into this realm of consciousness Jünger made his most hazardous sojourn during the Second World War.

Jünger's father, an atheist, made sure his children did not receive a "religious" upbringing. Sundays were never boring. School instruction in religion had been mandatory, but Protestantism, at least in this scholastic guise, was flaccid, dull, and embarrassed. Jünger went his own way. In adulthood it took him, during his post-1918 term in the army, to the *Spiritual Exercises* of Loyola. He had no intention of becoming a Roman Catholic, let alone a Jesuit. He was attracted to the forms of a rigorous psychological discipline. If the content of the *Exercises* informed him, he never admitted it. It is impossible to imagine Jünger practicing Loyola's injunction to meditate prayerfully upon Christ's agony and crucifixion.

It would be amiss to suppose he ever suffered from some sort of spiritual void. Had that been so, the fanaticism of conversion would have filled it. Jünger was too much of an individual to cave in. The Great War, a laboratory of chaos, taught him that one can create meaning and that doing so may be preferable to receiving it secondhand. Jünger was by temperament a pagan, keenly receptive to the abiding mysteries of our life in nature; he could not have accepted the pull of any conventional religious faith toward some other world than this one with its bounteous, all-sufficient marvels. As he felt no need of formal religious dogma, he responded with alert detachment to religious sensibility in others.

He was engaged only by minds militantly convinced of their faith or mightily at odds with it. Jünger in his Weimar years believed the Great War's generation won a new spirituality that left inherited values in total discredit. That belief informed his enthusiasm for the French Catholic novelist Georges Bernanos, whose *Soleil de Satan* he reviewed in 1928.

Bernanos, a royalist and one-time supporter of l'Action Française, served four years in the trenches. He showed Jünger's sort of contempt for intellectuals by speaking "a language made possible only after and through the war."[58] He, too, was fired by a will to believe. Bernanos's depiction of the soul in isolation as, in Jünger's view, "a perpetually endangered sentinel of God before Satan's contestant powers" sounds more Protestant than Catholic, but that only says that "religious fiction" is by its very nature heterodox. Jünger sees Bernanos's persona "fortified by glowing love" (of God, presumably) and "a proud, innate hatred of all that's common: rest, peace, and cheap happiness." This character finally reaches "the last territory, where the powers of good and evil are manifest." Bernanos's knight of faith according to Jünger's in-reading is indistinguishable from the soldierly worker animated by love of a revolutionary "idea."

Bernanos's Catholicism is entirely secondary here, but Jünger is fascinated by the Catholic Church's resilience in an age when most established authorities have lost their hold. In the twenties, many thoughtful people in Europe lost faith but exalted personal freedom. Inner unrest had cast the self-vaunting individual upon a treadmill of doubt. Jünger admits that the will to believe cannot create belief nor stand in for it. This is a remarkable concession to the claim and force of content, yet he remains suspicious of how substantial the content of a formal faith can prove. Doubt can be hedged by dogmas but its source is much harder to master. Hence, according to Jünger, the appeal of cultish catchwords and fanatical personalities. Catholicism's strength lay in its refusal to forfeit its "Gothic powers," the carrot of security and the stick of submission. In an age of intense mobility, the Church was "the most dangerous soul catcher and most successful fisher" of weary individuals. To Jünger nothing could be more deadly than Catholicism's proffered peace of mind and security of soul. So he rejoiced to see in Bernanos, an outward believer, an uncompromising questioning of faith to the point of despondency.

A presence far more forceful upon Jünger than Bernanos was another French Catholic, Léon Bloy (1846–1917). An extraordinary personality such as the French call a *monstre,* Bloy could be called an anti-Jünger. With the countenance of a bulldog, bulging eyes, and a Nietzschean mustache, he presented a calling card identifying him as a demolition expert. He wrote prolifically, invented "the Catholic novel," and led a life of embittering poverty. He gave frequent vent to a cruel spleen, concentrating his animus upon the *haute bourgeoisie.* His pleasureful notes on the Opéra Comique fire of 1887 and the *Titanic* suggest psychopathy. He had the wounded soul's longing for an apocalypse to give cosmic release to his fastidious parochialism. With thoroughgoing chauvinism he abominated Germany and England, the great political, military, and spiritual enemies of France. He idolized Napoleon. He was intrigued by mystical experiences of the faithful but received no visitations. No angel would have dared approach him.

On Carl Schmitt's recommendation, Jünger began to read Bloy before the Second World War. What would an elitist of cosmopolitan and pagan disposition find attractive in this self-styled "ungrateful beggar"? Jünger answers: "I believe I've learned to recognize men in their mind even though they differ from me in will, and to see them in their Gestalt, which lies beyond borders and oppositions" (October 4, 1942). His earliest remarks on Bloy, when reading the novel *La Femme Pauvre,* indicate an almost clinical interest in the book's lively dynamics: "Bloy is a twin crystal of diamond and dung. His most recurrent word is 'shit.' His hero Marchenoir proclaims that he shall enter heaven with a crown wrought from human excrement" (July 7, 1939). Citing other coprophilic passages, Jünger finds only one gem among many "perfect and accurate sentences": "It is the festival of man to see die that which did not seem mortal."

Jünger, cosseted by ease most of his life, could not go far in sympathy for Bloy in his grinding poverty. To Bloy's journal entry that time is a dog who bites only the poor, he answered that time bites everyone. "It is the democratic principle, in contrast to space, which is aristocratic" (June 22, 1942). But even Bloy's "maniacal and indiscriminate outbursts against everything German" did not keep Jünger from feeling "continually contented" with his books. Bloy offered an antidote to Jünger's psychological unease during the Occupation precisely because he spoke to it. On reading Bloy's fin-de-siècle journal, for instance, he commends his "complete immunity to the illusions of technology." This "anti-modern eremite" regarded the automobile as an engine of destruction. Acknowledging a demonic beauty in the catacombs of the new Paris metro, Bloy intuited the death of the human soul there, too. His sort of dread makes technology God's oblique instrument for accelerating the contest of good and evil.

If Bloy showed a luddite indisposition to machinery, his attitude toward scientific advances was positively antediluvian. We shudder at his clapping of hands upon the accidental death of Pierre Curie, "the diabolical inventor of radium [whose] precious brains made contact with a bit of shit [*une moindre ordure*]." [59] His glee suggests that death became his ally, his means of revenge against the world. As Jünger saw, it was also Bloy's rescuer. On his *Meditations d'un Solitaire* Jünger comments:

> It reflects all of its author's virtues and vices—even his terrible strength in hatred, where he rivals Kniébolo. And yet I find reading him not only refreshing but even decidedly invigorating. There is a genuine arcanum there against the times and its debilities. Raising himself to such heights from a mired plain, this Christian offers a rare spectacle. His tower's battlements soar into the lofty air. A longing for death must be a part of it, and he often gives it powerful expression: a longing for the wise man's stone to appear from lowly scum and dark sediment; longing for a great distillation. (July 14, 1944)

How, though, did Bloy's longing for death, his ghoulish delight in disaster, his persistence in hatred of classes and whole nations differ from the nihilism of the SS lemurs? For all his admiration, Jünger could see the Führer in this Christian, and read the calling card's message as nihilistic. The key to Bloy's exceptional appeal for him lies in an unshakable egotism and its conviction about private access to the supernatural world. Deaths of enemies and cherished disasters were like signs of divine favor for him to read. To Jünger, like many Protestants a cosmic loner, Bloy's metaphysical egotism was wondrous, like one of nature's magic shows, and all the better that the resilient absolutism of his medieval spirituality was set so completely against an age of flux and slippery self-consciousness.

It was Bloy's home-grown passion that built his battlements. "His mind has something compact and scalded about it, like a soup made of extinct fish and crustaceans that has stood through lengthy cooking. Very good to read when one has lost the appetite for all too lukewarm dishes." The taste Bloy cultivates is for death, but with a condiment Hugo Fischer had never remarked: "Twice he mentions that dead people awakened him; they knocked on his door or he heard their name. Then he arose and prayed for their salvation. Thus perhaps even today we live not only through the power of past but also of future prayers that will be made after our death" (July 7, 1942).

It is substantially thanks to Bloy that Jünger won distance from his own nontheistic fatalism in which the world seems a puppet theater governed by cold and immutable laws, with past and future played out like a senseless card game.[60] "It is humanity's privilege not to know the future," he writes. "That is one of the diamonds in the diadem of the will's freedom. Were man to lose it, he would become an automaton in an automatic world" (August 9, 1942). Bloy's *amor fati* engaged Jünger because it had a fervor far deeper than anything humanism could achieve, and a more elevating freedom than mere voluntarism could afford. By the summer of 1943 Jünger was using his own freedom of will in a new way, prayer.

It is as though the aristocratic confidence and aloofness had been fissured, the need of something beyond the self at last acknowledged. Was it Bloy who led Jünger to a Catholic service on August 15, 1943? Jünger called it "a lucky accident, since in this way I enjoyed a good, brief sermon on Mary as the Eternal Mother." He must have visited the crypt of Notre Dame des Champs on the Rue Montparnasse, where services were held exclusively for Catholics in the Wehrmacht. (Under military staff orders, German soldiers were strictly forbidden to attend any French masses or other public services.)[61] Pastoral care for German officers was "exclusively the task of the military chaplain," but Jünger did not seek it, even in melancholy, nor, it appears, did he attend Protestant services for the Wehrmacht held on the Avenue George V, no. 23.

Conversion would have been anathema to Jünger's Olympian distancing from collective urge and institutional suasions. It would have exposed a personal inadequacy he would never have sensed or admitted. Even modern aesthetic and nationalist cults centered on figures such as Gide, Stefan George, Charles Maurras, and Maurice Barrès, all transparent surrogates for conventional religious faith, were in his reckoning fruitless, the shallow intoxicants of "pure emotion" (April 27, 1943). Jünger lacked formal religious conviction but also lacked religiosity and any inclination to fakery or autosuggestive enthusiasms. If his hauteur kept him from the humility of self necessary to a genuine religious life, it also kept him from self-debasement required by the supreme pseudospirituality of Nazism.

Prayer, then, to the unknown God? Jünger observes a virtually Hebraic restriction upon the very word *God.* He avoids *religious,* consistently preferring to write of "theological" issues. It is "theology" that must combat the nihilistic "transformation into automatism which is threatening us" (June 8, 1942). Faced with the oppressive sense of contingency, he commends "the theological release from this labyrinth" via Boethius (March 7, 1944). He never gives the written appearance of a spiritual struggle, but it requires little historical imagination to see that his taking up the challenge of prayer was not leisurely. "We begin to believe when things get worse for us," he recognized early in the war, when they had not yet (January 4, 1940).

As they became so in the first year of Operation Barbarossa, Jünger withdrew even more into himself. "In every life," he rationalizes, "there are certain things that one does not confide even to the dearest person. . . . It is the most wicked and the best within that one most anxiously guards. And if by confession he disburdens himself of the evil, he still carries the best for God alone. The noble, the good, the holy lies far from the social sphere; it cannot be shared" (October 2, 1942). He says that even in the confessional there can be no sharing, such is his Protestant recalcitrance before the priest who might judge him in God's stead. That left only the pietist's iron-clad privacy, deep resident in "the terrible, yet saving meaning of prayer, that for a moment it unfolds the heart and gives it access to the light. It affords a man, especially someone in our northern stretches, the sole gateway to truth, to a final and determined honesty." These are stringent words, startling even in Jünger.

Seeking not salvation nor even intimacy with God, he claimed he came nearest to the absolute in his love for truth:

> I can violate moral laws and be treacherous to my neighbor, but I cannot swerve from what I recognize as genuine and true. . . . Truth for me is like a woman whose embrace condemns me to impotence toward all else. In her alone lies freedom and happiness, too. Thus it happens that my approach to theology comes through knowledge. I have to prove God to myself before I can believe in him. That means I have to go back along the same way on which I abandoned Him. (July 18, 1943)

To reach the other shore he would have to cast up his own bridges, do his own "subtle pioneering."

Jünger's is an athletic Protestantism, making as well as going its own way. It rejects the all-sufficiency of Lutheran faith and even the stern grace of Calvinism. "Surely grace would be more beautiful, but it doesn't fit the situation I am in." (We wonder, why not?) He positively requires the counterplay of doubt to strengthen his effort. It is the modern note of the solitary's struggle. "We can redeem one who is ever striving" was the celestial pledge in Goethe's gospel. In Jünger's, one must arrive on one's own at the farthest point in an epistemological patrol.

The Bible provided way stations. According to his entry of May 28, 1944, he began to read it in sequence on September 3, 1941, but he had read brief passages from it during the *drôle de guerre*. He began his forty-fifth birthday, March 29, 1940, with a reading of the seventy-third psalm. He passes it by with a lengthy account of a day on the then still listless western front. The psalm was prophetic and its mention allegedly offended Goebbels when *Gardens and Avenues* was printed in 1942: "Truly God is good to Israel, even to such as are of a clean heart." Then comes scorn of the godless who prosper: "Pride compasseth them about as a chain, violence covereth them as a garment." When the psalmist enters God's sanctuary he foresees their ruin: "For lo, they that are far from Thee shall perish." Why this psalm on that day? Nowhere in the neighborhood of this entry does Jünger mention any other nor any biblical reading.

During the Occupation, Bible study classes were held among Wehrmacht officers every Tuesday evening at St. Joseph's church on the Avenue Hoche.[62] Jünger never mentions attending them, but only when he started a progressive reading of the Bible did its pertinence to the war begin to work upon him. After the first Russian winter beset Hitler's armies, the divine curses of *Deuteronomy* seemed dreadfully apt. The *Book of Esther* Jünger interpreted as the bronze serpent for Jews, their surety from an ancient and magical world into his own time. "I once saw a Polish Jew at Berlin's Silesian railway station, and thought, 'That's probably how you stood once under Babylon's Ishtar Gate.'" This entry came on July 23, 1942, three days after thousands of Jews were deported from Paris. Two weeks later, Jünger saw in *Job* "the terrible distance that keeps humankind from wisdom" (August 2, 1942).

He read the prophetic literature as kaleidoscopic windows upon "the substance" of laws both natural and metaphysical. To construe the prophetic books as projections into history, he maintains, debases them. *Isaiah*'s imagery of destruction, for instance, heralds no new epoch in history but "the new and indestructible synthesis in the divine spirit" (October 15, 1942). He finds the same cosmological structure in *Ezekiel*'s initial visions, their insight "surpassing the boldest thoughts and the highest works of art." And *Jeremiah*: "In [historical] decline he sees not the cosmic catastrophe which stirs pleasure as well as horror, but political collapse, the shipwreck of the state which departure from the divine order brings on." Jünger attributes Jeremiah's unshakable boldness, the certainty of his vision, to his "divine nexus." The distinctive appeal of these prophets to Jünger is that the dreamlike egotism of their mystical experience makes a poetic claim upon the cosmos. It grasps artfully a divine justice.

When Jünger read *Jeremiah* he was serving in the Caucasus, observing firsthand the incipient shipwreck of the godless, but biblical apocalypse as the sanction of elementary laws was not only destructive. It proclaimed restoration. Knowing this, he was taken aback when a German pastor in Paris welcomed Goebbels's propaganda about new weapons for annihilating the population of England: "That a man of the cloth should not only be gripped by such madness but see our only salvation in destruction shows the level at which refuge has been taken" (September 24, 1943).

Long before the war, Jünger had read the great drama of fall and rebirth as processes. *The Worker* unfolded a triptych of decline, disorder, and renewal: the Spenglerian decline of the West to a zero-point of calamity would initiate a new global technology of worker states, but that welding of humanity and machinery was gloomily secular. God was not even an absentee landlord in 1932. Now, Bloy and the Bible's prophets had educated Jünger on the incompleteness of his metaphysics. He was learning to read upward.

On September 9, 1943, he completed the Jewish apocryphal literature and took up the New Testament with the original Greek in hand. The biblical account of man first as God's creature, then as God's son, begged, he felt, a third testament: after resurrection, transfiguration. Did not *Revelation* foretell as much? "Yet one might say that each of us is the Third Testament's author, and from it the higher reality of the text shapes itself into the invisible, into the realm after death" (September 9, 1943). This blurry consolation suggests that Jünger's notion of transfiguration is the latest recourse to German Romanticism's gospel of a freedom ulterior to death.

Following Boethius, he expected to find in the New Testament a treasure house and did, but, as so often, seeing brilliantly he does not see whole. On *Matthew* 25, for instance, the parable of the ten virgins' lamps:

"The chapter's great theme is that man within his life's span can win worth beyond time, can gather oil for the eternally burning lamp, can with his inheritance gain an imperishable kingdom." Jünger omits the parable's definitive symbolism: Christ coming as bridegroom to the ready virgins. His own conclusion is therapeutic: "We live in order to realize ourselves; thereby death becomes insignificant" (October 10, 1943). This could be Goethe speaking, but it strays far from Christ's koan-like injunction to *lose* life in order to find it. Jünger could read only so far.

In the same entry he remarks that though surrounded in the war's midst by comfortable scenery (he uses the theatrical term *Kulisse*), he was now at much greater hazard than during the days of Flanders and the Somme. "I have already noted in *On the Marble Cliffs* that even the bravest begins to become fearful when the lemurs have fastened upon the commanding bastions."[63] Warfaring had passed from "the heroic sphere" into the demonic. With grim aptness Jünger read *Luke* 22, on Christmas Day, 1943: "Satan hath desired to have you, that he may sift you as wheat." Christ's concession to his adversaries in the garden, "This is your hour and the power of darkness" (22:53) could be "the motto as well for the atrocities of our time which are carried out in ghastly darkness and behind façades set up for popular taste."

Jünger takes Christ at his Johannine word, the eternal man, divine, outlasting even the cosmos. The fourth gospel complements the Hebraic "optics of mortality" even as baptism complements circumcision (January 16, 1944). In sum, the biblical testaments à la Jünger form metaphysical balances or antinomies: they are not ethical guideposts nor redemptive histories. He seized upon the message of a supernatural succession (*I Corinthians* 15:22), and compared Paul's "putting on immortality" to "the discovery of a higher chemistry." (How would his father have answered that?) Christ the Johannine mediator facilitated a metaphysical uplift inherent in humankind from its beginning. Redemption was nothing more than the "higher" activation of a material potence (March 7, 1944). This laboratorial reading (Christ the catalyst) shows how distant Jünger stood from a sacramental acceptation of Christianity. Like Goethe, he interprets idiosyncratically, not communally; the Christian *logos* is construed, not received. Goethe, declining to admit Christ's historical role, insisted that his singular life was instructive only for individuals as such. Christ's teachings would enable one "to feel great and free as a human being."[64]

Jünger's perspective is virtually identical to Goethean egotism, a humanism that is not Christian because it accepts no cross.

Jünger finished *Revelation* and his first complete reading of the Bible on Pentecost, May 1944. His retrospection looks not to the testaments but to his childhood's education away from them: his father's "ecstatic realism and positivism," tediously compulsory biblical studies in school, and the "higher criticism" of the late nineteenth century which had informed them. All this had fatally blocked access to a world he now saw suffused like the Arabian tales with the supernatural.[65] Even in his adult mind there remained a residue of need for some kind of foundation:

> I'm thinking here less of provability than of the intellect's witnessing, its proximity, which ought always to figure even in illumination [*mitleuchten*]. That's where I part from the Romantics; it's what gives light to my excursions through the upper and lower worlds: in my spaceship, in which I dive, swim, fly, and course through fiery worlds and dream realms, a navigational instrument always accompanies me that has taken its shape through science. (May 28, 1944)

His father's instruction had proved as irreversible as osmosis. Jünger's problem was the sufficiency of his perspective. He registers no despair, no wretched "Help thou my unbelief!" The oddity is that his aesthetic criterion, the desire for wonder and amazement, does not carry over into a comparable spiritual desire. He could readily intuit a Platonic form behind natural phenomena—what he called "hidden science"—and this wonder showed him the world suddenly transformed and elevated.[66] He had also diagnosed in his generation a need to believe that lay disquieted beneath the surface certainties of the day, submerged by "idolaters of reason and charlatans of science" who were incapable of "genuine faith" because they were incapable of doubt.[67] A thorough protestant, he knew that to banish doubt would entail the loss of possible grace, a condition of "icy death." With homiletic urgency he had addressed the "color blindness" of an age that "confuses crime with sickness, value with numbers, and progress with redemption"—all symptoms of an evil no longer considered virulent.[68] Bernanos and Bloy won his rare esteem by dwelling so vividly in a world of Good and Evil, with all its attendant heights and abysses. Jünger's own travel through that world, as his spaceship image betrays, was an adventure, not a pilgrimage. He could never relinquish the voluntarist's failsafe of final detachment. He does not so much "witness" to biblical apocalypse as visit its fantastic folds. In an epoch of so-called committed writers, this kind of independence can only be suspect. It smacks of tourism, a dilettante's metaphysics. The wonder, however, is not that Jünger did not formally accept Christianity but that in his secret tract, *The Peace,* he promoted the churches of Europe as bulwarks for the postwar reconstruction.

Postlude: Hitler's War, Jünger's *Peace*

None of Jünger's writing may be more important to a lasting estimate of him than a lengthy essay he wrote in the fall of 1941, burned the following summer, rewrote largely in 1943, and completed, with revisions, in the spring of 1944. Entitled *Der Friede* (The Peace), it began as a "purely personal" work, "an exercise in justice," but its subtitle, "A Word to the Youth of Europe" gave it proclamatory breadth.[1] It is braced by Spinoza's statement that hate wholly overcome by love passes into a love stronger than one that has never been hatred. Such proves the excess of conversion, but Jünger, in whose diction "love" seldom appears, does not indicate whose hatred is to be transformed nor how. Is this scenario of grace and penance meant for Germany or the individual's conscience?

In *The Adventurous Heart,* he had addressed moral accountability, noting that doubt in its role as father of light and darkness safeguards ambiguity. To banish doubt would be to lose grace and enter "a condition of icy death." For him the opposite of dubitation is not certainty, the illusion of order which schools, parties, and dogmas promote, but neutrality. Modern civilization suffers from "the confusion of crime with sickness, of value with numbers, of progress with redemption"—symptoms of an evil no longer recognized as virulent. Their cumulative effect was "moral castration, a total excision of moral awareness that produces a peculiar condition in which one is changed from evil's servant into its machine." Jünger calls the collective impulse of this mechanization "satanic."[2]

The Paris diaries fitfully record Jünger's struggle with neutrality in the stark face of evil. Reading the farewell letters of men shot in reprisal, Jünger reminded himself that "human dignity must be more sacred than life to us," that "in the face of crimes, one must devote oneself not to beauty but to freedom." He reckoned that it meant fighting alone, cheered only by the example of those "who know freedom by instinct."[3] Writing was his sole weaponry. When he began *The Peace* he found himself in "a search for order between cliffsides and sharks," but his confidence was unshaken. The writer composes as "Great Man, that is, as a man who guides his pen for man."[4] Only by this Carlylean notion of authorship could Jünger have believed his writing would have effect. The man who had prided himself on gaining fifteen new readers a season now presumed to address the youth of all Europe.

Jünger claims that, as the Second World War is humankind's first collective work, the ensuing peace requires a common foundation. The war must bring fruit for all, seeded not by hate, persecution, and injustice but by the sacrificial impulses deadly conflict has summoned from all contestants. He seeks a chivalric measure for this "civil war of the planet." That phrasing palliates essential differences between the contestants; only one side can be charged with the crimes of an offensive war. Jünger insists, however, upon distinguishing the perpetrators from those of their German participants who might also be reckoned their victims.

He had seen how the war exacted "pure suffering" from the German people: armies had died of hunger and exhaustion, civilians had been incinerated in the ruins of their homes. What of the complicity these war victims had once borne with their sinister compatriots? Worse than the war, says Jünger, was "the mass impulse that pushed on in an uncertain course, in hateful, vengeful eagerness, ending in fire."[5] This Thucydidean view of Nazism makes it a pathological mysterium; like Thucydides, Jünger points to an epidemic inversion of values: labor and science devoted to death, the sword protecting crime, courts made tribunals, teachers destroying God's image in their students. Jünger does not forget the true innocents: "The guilt alleged to the misfortunate was the crime of existence, the stigma of birth. They fell as sons of their people, their fathers, their race, as hostages, witnesses of inherited belief or bearers of convictions which overnight laws stamped defective."[6] He avoids mentioning Hitler, his henchmen, or Jews and others who suffered and died, yet his gift for precision has eloquent moments. The singular monuments of this war are the camps, "the great lodgings of death where the iron tyranny in bond with technology celebrated endless blood-weddings. . . . Into these swamps the all too clever age of discovery discharged itself." If ever a new arrogance should overtake the Germans, Jünger foresees as its cure "a look back to those multitudes who like animals for slaughter were driven to the pits and the crematoria."[7]

Jünger's indictment of the war has a slippery feel. He says that in the Great War people sustained suffering with pride, but that in this war there has been only sorrow and shame, "for the disgrace has been such that it affects the human race and no one can be freed of complicity."[8] This is a curious argument from ontology or original sin: humanity itself is responsible for Hitler, as though he exemplifies an evil everyone is capable of and must recognize. A Christian might grant the point; Jünger's problem is that a Wehrmacht officer is making it. He does not see that *vae victis* means arguments now had validity only according to who made them. The inclusive stigmatizing of Germans who survived Hitler became a moralist's Versailles. Jünger is impervious to this rude fact.

He deftly recalls the hubris with which Hitler's triumphs infected the German people until 1942. Mothers, he writes, became Niobes as all the pain of war found final expression in them. Now, as the Great War had its Unknown Soldiers as treasured emblems of suffering, the second must have a transnational offering (*Erdopfer,* untranslatable), the creation of a new order "for which the interplay of passions, pain, and fire were needed."[9] Were they? Was the war's show of immeasurable courage truly necessary to the peace? It is an odd, unprovable claim, like the guiding premise of *Battle as Inner Experience,* that war is an abiding condition of humanity that oscillates with, in fact hides within, peace. Jünger submits that in this "civil war" the fronts concealed from agents and victims alike "the unity of the great work in whose circuit [*Bann,* connoting a magic spell or curse] they performed." The language is clear: the war was a cataclysm of those national work landscapes Jünger had sketched in 1932, and the peace, too, will manifest the Worker in yet another succession.

The essay's second part, "The Fruit," carries an epigraph from the Sturm und Drang poet Christian Schubart: "Religions will be reborn not in conformity to the bourgeois world but in apocalyptic thunder." (Whither Spinoza's love?) Having proclaimed an end to the old world in *The Worker,* Jünger now says it has survived. As monarchy gave way to democracy in 1918, nation states will give way to synthetic empires, Russian and American, and Europe, their ancestor, will itself become an empire of states. Treaties, says the essay's sole fetching metaphor, must be marriages, with member nations bringing themselves as dowry to the new house. Jünger had hoped for this kind of fealty in Germany's shotgun wedding to France, but in unifying Europe Hitler failed to see that conquest is ephemeral. Jünger rather fantastically suggests a way might have been found to change unity by force into a unity of free will, but conceding that freedom never came, he admits that all the horrors in its place require atonement; wickedness cannot be excused on the ground that it was compulsory or that the times required it. Jünger anticipates and deflates the most familiar evasion of the incriminated, that they were following orders. The distinction between criminal and noncriminal acts (*Untat* and *Tat*) must be drawn; the latter he describes as resistance to cruelty even at the cost of personal danger.

No peace, Jünger urges, will last unless the historically restless problem of space is settled: European unification must admit and preserve diversity. Unity may be economic, technological, and political, but must support an organic variety of cultures, singular in their languages, history, and art. "There cannot be too many colors on the palette here."[10]

Another issue, rights, would be unexceptionable save that the advocacy of human freedom and dignity comes from a veteran of a militantly authoritarian culture who had given more than his share of abuse to Weimar's parliamentary democracy. Jünger's view that the war forged upon all contestants the same work processes and rhythms shows he could not escape his own history. He wants to believe peace will rechannel the totalitarian impetus and realize if not the moral equivalent of war, an aesthetic one.

That may be why the diction of penance is absent here. It would be gratuitous to raise this point if Jünger did not commit his vision to a Christian revival as the spiritual bulwark of the new order. Indeed, his vocabulary for peace—education (*Bildung*), purification (*Reinigung*), and healing (*Heilung*)—implies a kind of religious conversion. He wishes to find in the churches a countervailing power to nihilism's totalitarian legacy. Nihilism, he preaches, has struck so deep it must be fought in the human heart. It cannot be overcome by a restoration of liberalism but only by Christendom. New life for Europe must reach back to the old sources of faith, and Christianity, he asserts, has held out against nihilism on behalf of millions. It does not trouble him that German Christendom, with deep-rooted Catholic and Protestant traditions, was unable, apart from incidental resistance and martyrdom, to stir from the incubus of Nazism, not to mention the virulence of its own anti-Semitism.[11] For Jünger, Christendom, however compromised, had served as repository of aesthetic and theological traditions. Theology, as mediator of the highest values, must, he says, inform all other intellectual pursuits. This covert plea for neoscholasticism is no bid for an established church or national religion. Jünger is too Protestant for that. The integer of faith for him is the Bible, where the pattern of human history is laid out in truths far superior to "the base laws of terrorism's world." [12] The biblical "pattern" is Jewish but, like T. S. Eliot's "Christian Europe," Jünger's has no Judaism nor Jews.

His perspective, as its diction shows, is more humanist than Christian. He says we have reached a point where we must require, if not faith, then piety. Trust must be given to what is higher than human reason, but Jünger names neither God nor Christ. Nominally deferring to the churches, he recognizes no creeds. He confines expectation to ecclesiastical politics: the Reformation and the Church must be reconciled, for the Christian schism led to nationalism, even though both churches fought nihilism. Jünger would give back to them the authority wrested by Hitler. Institutional power is more vital than belief—logistically, since only "piety" can be expected of the individual, and psychologically, since only the churches can combat nihilism. To the individual is left vague trust in something above reason. Jünger leaves open the possibility that once again the church could be suborned to the sheer power of the state. [13] As technology can become a ruthless force for a political establishment, one must be "metaphysically strengthened," but his terms—piety and trust in the "higher-than-reason"—are too blurry to carry much strength or appeal.

Plainly, Jünger seeks an authoritarian state that will unify Europe. He cites as visionaries of this union Richelieu, Cromwell, and Bismarck, champions of statism but not certain friends of individual conscience. Suggesting that a democracy can be both authoritarian and liberal, he likens the state's security and the individual's prosperity to a mussel: hard outside so the pearl within may grow. History, however, tells us the hardness is likely to crush the pearl, and the very models of union Jünger adduces, the USA and USSR, should have told him that dictatorship and racism can thrive in federated polities. Indeed, unified Europe's entry into the constellation of these two empires, a course Carl Schmitt prophesied during the war, would only recast to a higher exponence the contest of vast inhospitable forces sketched in *The Worker*.

Where can there be peace? If this Wehrmacht captain has found a way through despotism's thorny wood, it points not to the state nor church but to the seemingly least promising denomination of power, the individual. Fascism and war had made it too easy to underestimate the individual. Jünger admits that giving way to fear and demons makes one their instrument, not responsible yet helpless. Even then, the individual must be the final judge of just and unjust deeds. Jünger leads from this moralist's commonplace to the urgent argument that true peace requires a courage exceeding that of war, a courage manifest when people know how to deliver themselves from evil. Spinoza has the last word, after all.

It is the strength and weakness of Jünger's peace that he essentially recasts within it his own life's experience, from the Kaiser to the Führer. He envisages an imperial state in tandem with a virtually established church, a tableau that conjures authoritarian Prussia. Under the putative shelter of these monstrous structures he presumes to find pearls of regional vigor and individuality. Whatever his concessions to democracy, Jünger is more Roman than Athenian: willing compliance to authority is the surety of order. Weimar's chaos was too close to memory. The keystone of the new order may be theological, but Jünger is no theist: he is less interested in the object of faith than in the humble submissiveness it enjoins. The churches must vouchsafe that submission. Again, the Roman orientation: religion keeps the people compliant; it is indispensable to social cohesion.

Was this work, begun in 1941, destroyed, rewritten, then circulated in 1944, a statement in good faith or a sophisticated piece of political manuevering tailored to survival? According to Speidel, "Jünger forcibly spoke in October 1941 for the first time about the necessity of preparing a creative peace. The sketch [*Entwurf*] of a 'Call to European Youth with the Aim of a Just Peace for All and the Punishment of the War's Guilty' can be taken as a predecessor of the *Peace* essay."[14] Jünger's diary entry of January 5, 1942, speaks of an outline (*Grundriss*) but does not mention a "Call" to youth.

In the first (1949) edition of *Strahlungen,* he vigorously denies that *The Peace* was the fruit of Germany's defeat:

> Today that's always the cheapest explanation one must reckon with, and often too the most hateful. Yet, here as always in my writing, I never directed myself to an outward event and never stood in accord with any of the ruling powers.[15] The planning of this writing coincided rather with the expansion of the German front. Its purpose

was purely personal; it was to assist my education as, one might say, "an exercise in justice."[16]

In this apologia, Jünger says he did not share the July 20 inspiration, believing rather that a Sulla would be needed for an assault on "the plebescitarian democracy."[17] Even so,

> I considered it an honor to contribute with my means, and in this connection the writing took form as a summons to European youth. . . . Its advice is not political but pedagogic, in the highest sense autodidactic: the author lets the reader participate in his development. May I also add that at the time I was already tired of the political-historical kaleidoscope and did not expect an improvement of its turning. Not in systems but in people, thus in the seed, must new fruit grow.[18]

When and why was the first version destroyed? Jünger's journal for August 19, 1942, opens offhandedly: "In the morning papers destroyed, among which the constructive peace scheme that I set down this winter." Jünger was anticipating transfer to the east and may have wished to secure himself against investigation. In fact, the Gestapo searched his home in Kirchhorst prior to his departure for the Caucasus. Much in his journal, too, might have brought him into trouble, but he did not destroy it.

The second draft he completed in October 1943.[19] Revisions, including expurgation of the first person, began on March 25, 1944.[20] A few weeks later he sent the manuscript—whether in a preliminary or finished version remains unclear—to Speidel, newly appointed chief of staff of Group B, Rommel's army on the western front. On April 30, Jünger visited Speidel for the first time after his promotion, at army headquarters, La Roche-Guyon, a chateau of the Rochefoucaulds. Speidel wanted Jünger's essay to be available "at a given time," when, the coup having succeeded, a manifesto could immediately be published. He lost no time. On May 1 Speidel sent "the manuscript of the summons" to Rommel.[21]

Was the second version substantially identical to the first? The answer is mixed: no, as much of the content of Part 1, such as references to death camps, Jünger could supply only after Barbarossa began to collapse. It is uncertain when Jünger became aware of wartime resistance to Hitler. There were two bungled attempts on Hitler's life in March 1943. The plot speared by Stauffenberg began early in 1944 after Jünger had already begun his second draft. The late revisions were demonstrably made in knowledge of the plot.²²

Jünger felt the essential contest was between the old Prussian aristocracy and Hitler's "Demos."²³ As *The Peace* vaguely entertains two kinds of democracy, authoritarian and libertarian, we can infer that the old guard would be reestablished in the former, the "Demos" tamed into the latter. Jünger's program for a theologized state is germane to this division because the "higher" theology presupposes an elite of interpreters to reconcile the classes and even the war's victors and vanquished. The authenticity of this new theology he presumed to derive from his daily Bible readings during the war, in particular apocalyptic passages on retribution for wickedness. His own position he had read (October 11, 1943) in the story of Sodom. "This is also a symbol of the individual's terrible responsibility at present. For untolled millions, *one* can be surety." Coming when Jünger was completing the second draft of *The Peace,* these remarks closely inform its prophetic tone. Like an Old Testament seer, he claims a redemptive vision for Germany and the world, but his words are mantled in the private sensibility of a Protestant conscience. The heritage of evangelical pietism complements Jünger's inveterate Olympian distance. He writes under a Kantian sort of imperative, the supreme "as if," as though he, the beloved son of chaos, were now legislating for universal peace.

Inconclusions: Jünger and German Guilt

For anyone who was born a German does have something
in common with German destiny and German guilt.
—Thomas Mann at the Library of Congress, May 29, 1945

To condemn Ernst Jünger for his service under despotism, for his writings, above all, for his survival, is too easy. It may be more important to ask, would he have been the accomplished writer he was if he had not held a politics which remains distasteful to many, at least among the learned and academic in and beyond Germany? Is there not evident a link between his fastidious, wood-carved prose, its careful, often brilliant and sometimes elusive imagery and the rightist penchant for elitism and the revered past?

Jünger is hated by some for his alleged glorification of war, yet the themes of his most important writing have retreat as their common denomination. He sounds that note again and again. His memoirs of the Great War, for example, attempt to buttress individual valor in an age of fierce and whelming mechanization. Then, confronted with the steel-faced standardization of life which communism and Nazism alike ensured in the twenties, Jünger turns to the dreamworld of a very private bourgeois sensibility. In such times of general upheaval there is something Proustian about Jünger's self-important carryings on. In the Nazi era, his near-resistant fictions might be read as a self-satiric programme of escape-hatching. Finally, the Paris journals epitomize this withdrawal to the point of caricature. It is to Paris, to the Hotel Majestic and those strawberries in the burgundy that people who contemn Jünger usually turn.

One might also accuse him of romantic loitering: in a century of mass-produced tastes and processed values, he persists in anachronistic assumptions about the self. The *Autor,* the anarch, is a Rousseauist construct, safeguard of an egotism that takes itself as the only possible society. To a degree, however, Jünger's extraordinary personality, his dazzling acuity of perception, the range of his life's experience as a soldier, world traveler, and (not least) as a reader, seem to warrant the Olympian self-removal.

It is unnecessary to determine when he set out upon this Goethean enterprise of self-creation or self-stylization—possibly as early as 1913, when he started to write a journal and staged his revolt against the totemic authority of his father and the Kaiser's schools. It is instructive that this egotism can be discerned where we might least expect to find it, within the dismal folds of his totalitarian polemics. Jünger's presumption to speak above yet on behalf of the factious militarist leagues of late Weimar, to articulate a nationalist "idea" of soldierly elitism, is the sort of private enterprise typical of writers and intellectuals who have no sense of politics as a shared dirtying of hands. Events quickly pushed Jünger and other salon nationalists to the inconsequent periphery. Yet on that periphery he wrote *The Worker,* a tract of vatic scope that presumes to drop a cataclysmic curtain upon the bourgeois world scenery and to furnish introduction and allegro for a supernational technocracy of militarized workshops. We are reminded of Rousseau, again: even as Jean-Jacques admitted he could not mediate between everything and nothing, so Jünger is unable to mediate between the subjective and the cosmic, between a fussily tended garden disposition and the force of destiny with all its leaden laws. He admits no in-between of human endeavors, no community of faces.

Here too, then, retreat has been sounded. That is true not least in *The Worker.* In the *Contrat social,* Rousseau's "general will" is not the so-called popular will but a kind of metaphysical force supposedly guiding the people in its own best interest; so, too, Jünger's *Gestalt,* to which the worker brings a conformable historical expression, is only the vaguest hypostasis. It is a light year's distance from the world of daily work it is alleged to subsume and determine. In succession to Hegel, this sleight of hand exemplifies what Jünger has identified as a peculiarly German weakness of the mind, the reduction of reality to the elementary.

Jünger is a skillful accomplice in that reduction. His psychology of war reduces courage to a savage voluntarism, a tautness of will that scarcely admits, because it scarcely notices, the commonplaces of fraternity even in combat. The warrior, jealously possessive of a ruthless valor, reaches the acme of a terrible fury that transforms him into something like an elementary power of nature, alien to gods and to human beings. Perhaps the iron-clad virtues of the Prussian military—obedience, duty, fidelity—explain this self-insularity better than Achilles does by example. They are vertical sorts of virtue, obliging one to something higher than self and others. Conversely, absent from Jünger's war profile are the horizontal virtues, the warm tenacity of love, the humbling equity of brotherhood. Isolated as a leader of men, he writes even of his batmen as curios; not so much compeers, they seem faithful dogs.

Jünger's verticality does not, however, bind him to the state, to the Kaiser, to Hitler, or even to Germany. His point of higher reference, as we have noted, is nothing short of cosmic. The warrior belongs to fate, not to the homeland. Jünger is the least chauvinistic of war chroniclers. However much we may personally recoil from the icy-handed fatalism to which he clutches, it kept him immune to the superpatriotic tunnel sickness of those who so readily transferred their allegiances from Kaiser to Führer. Jünger seems to have suspected shows of warmth of any kind, not least the ardor of fanatics. It is as though an imp from one of the oriental tales he loved had rescued and kept him distant from baleful enticements. One may throw charges at Jünger's feet, but opportunism, the need for a savior, and all the craven conveniences upon which Nazism throve are not among them.

Let us consider Jünger's urge to reduction from another vantage, his naturalism. For all his keen attention to the varieties of botanical and entomological life, he is ever drawn to their unities in symbol. They form concentric occasions leading to some single source, to a symmetry hidden so that it may be discovered. Everything manifold, incidental, chaotic holds in fact a recondite order. Jünger approaches this order in romantic fashion, by intuitive accord and by the private recesses of intimation granted his ever-receptive and venturesome *Geist*. Although he leaves the reader with the impression of cocksureness (the initiate's exclusivity), the moments of its expression are small-scale and unpretentious. The garden serves time and again as Jünger's assured treasure house of the secret order, and gardening is his adventurous medium. The domestic soil's resurgent vitality in the shattering spring of 1945, when the human order seemed to be disintegrating, offered Jünger once more the consolation of nature. It prompted in him an almost flinty indifference to close catastrophe and the ravaging of his native land. This private rescue sounds one more echo from the eerily prophetic *On the Marble Cliffs* when, at the end, the narrator escapes communal ruin and finds a refuge akin to the safe-dwelling of his father's house. Not incidentally, Jünger's garden in those awful April days was also a paternal haven, for the order renewed and reclaimed there affirms, by at least half, the positivism of the father: the garden is the terrain of compromise between father and son, between the chessboard within the house and the haunt within the marsh. Nature teems within the confident fencing of observation and control. Mystery has been domesticated. Jünger's insouciant *amor fati* is not finally so distant from his father's positivism. An almost forward air of triumph wafts through both of these mental realms.

It is that sovereignty of spirit which can so readily unsettle the reader of Jünger's Paris diaries. Only infrequently, in alcove admissions of melancholy or moral disquiet, does Jünger make vivid his awareness of being an accomplice to the outrage of a fallen nation's dignity. Most of the while—that while lasting four years—he moves about with a tourist's ease as though he were not among the helpless and the despicable. When hazard comes very close to home late in the spring of 1944, he retreats to his old fantasy of a modern *Rittersorden,* a chivalric company closing itself off from the Gestapo's barbarity. By then, any whom these valiant men could have rescued are gone. Knights errant, indeed.

It is pointless to moralize about Jünger and his extraordinary record of aloofness and control. Just as an absurd causality can be constructed to fashion him into a pathfinder for Hitler in late Weimar or even a fellow traveler of Nazism before 1933 (absurd because he rejected that ideology at its racist root), so it gets us nowhere to inveigh against him for not leaving his country after 1933, for not refusing military service in 1939 under a man he knew to be a consummate despot. These are issues worthy of a Tacitus, and one is left wondering how to pose rightly the questions of justice, some of which are perhaps unanswerable. On behalf of Jünger and many of those who stayed and to one fateful degree or other served (served by staying in) the Reich—accomplished people like Gottfried Benn, who shamed himself on radio, Werner Heisenberg, Martin Heidegger, the courageous Ricarda Huch, Wilhelm Furtwängler, and many others—the last-pitch argument says to every would-be plaintiff, how do you know that you would have comported yourself better than those you accuse? Such a question summons the ancient proverb that you do not know a man until you have walked a mile of his path with him. Any caveat against ahistorical righteousness carries this weight, but it may also bear a demeaning force against the very people in whose defense it is summoned. Squabbling over someone's dignity does not tend to preserve it. What shall finally matter is our capacity to read a dark history on Spinoza's terms, with neither contempt nor hatred but with understanding. Granted, that is a very tall order.

The cardinal issue for that understanding is guilt. As Karl Jaspers argued shortly after the war, there are differences between criminal and political guilt on one hand and, on the other, moral and metaphysical guilt. A tribunal addresses, as at Nürnberg, the first kind, the visibly accountable crimes against humanity. A furtive sort is the second, in which, Jaspers insists, only one's conscience can speak and before only a divine tribunal: one must penitently condemn oneself for turpitude or evasion, for lemming loyalty and false enthusiasms, for the delusion of resistance or wait-and-see. The varieties of compliance seem as innumerable as Milton's friends.

Jünger, it cannot be denied, straddled the Third Reich: refusing its blandishments, he received royalties thanks to its adulant promotion of his war writings. Of impeccable military honor, he knew he was a tacit accomplice in official barbarism. We must balance historical weights in our hands. Jünger, who refused to submit himself to Allied de-Nazification proceedings in 1945, knew that in publicly admitting to any guilt, he would implicitly bring within the range of his own penance all the austere nationalism of pre-Hitler Germany, all the soldierly ethos of the Great War's veterans, the codes which he embodied and now carried as survivor. Guilt may have an infinite regress within it: penance over Hitlerism or one's dim corner of it could be construed backwardly to a culpable nationalism in the kaisers and even in Frederick the Great (whose image the Nazis summoned like a shade from Sheol)—all of this because of 1945. The imposition of guilt upon Germany by the Versailles accords had carried a bitter and indelible lesson, and one from which Hitler profited immeasurably. It is not to be wondered that even the perspicacious Jaspers shuddered at the implications of *vae victis*. Jünger refused to make any show of surrender to the new victors.

That obstinacy has to this day kept him august within the circles of Germany's conservatives: he embodies a German past that refused to become Westernized, Americanized, or otherwise transformed. He is a kind of Teutonic Farinata, proud and immoveable and alone. Champion of an irretrievable past, Jünger is too often tagged a rightist, for he is

18   *PT*, January 27, 1942.

19   *PT*, January 29, 1942. The story of Pari-Banou does not occur in any of the English translations of *A Thousand and One Nights* I have consulted. I have used a French translation.

20   See *Annäherungen*, pp. 254–55: "No matter which woman we sleep with—in her we want to return to the mother. To her, and not to Aphrodite, belongs the altar to which we bring our sacrifices."

21   *AHI*, p. 44.

22   *Der abenteuerliche Simplicissimus* (Stuttgart: Reclam, 1990), p. 178.

23   *AHI*, p. 49.

24   Ibid.

25   *Don Quixote* (Penguin Classics), part 2, chap. 59, p. 852.

26   See *AHI*, pp. 179–80.

27   Löns's reputation survived both world wars. In the 1960s a multivolume edition of his works appeared, a remarkable tribute to a minor writer of presumably only regional interest.

28   *Das Wäldchen 125* (Berlin: Mittler, 1926), pp. 151, 152.

29   Ibid., p. 156.

30   Ibid., pp. 157, 158. These should be imposing words for those who are convinced that Jünger is a celebrant of death.

31   "Um die Ulenflucht," in *Mein braunes Buch* (Hanover: Adolf Sponholtz, 1910), p. 19.

32   *Das Wäldchen 125*, p. 158.

33   *PT*, December 20, 1943.

34   To Julien Hervier, *Entretiens*, p. 159.

35   *The German Classics of the Nineteenth and Twentieth Centuries*, ed. Kuno Francke (New York: German Publication Society, 1913–14), 15:466: "This horde of near-sighted fellows is often useless; for how can a man do much in life when he cannot use his eyes? In the upper classes of the Gymnasia the number of near-sighted is about 74 per cent."

36   To Hervier, *Entretiens*, pp. 48–49.

37   Ibid., p. 40.

38   Quoted in Heimo Schwilk, *Ernst Jünger*, p. 29. These schools find crystallized images in Jünger's 1973 novel *Die Zwille* (The Slingshot) where the young non-hero is subject to the inscrutable hatred of his mathematics instructor, Doktor Hilpert. This sadist's impenetrable lecture on geometry "came on like the locomotive of an endlessly long train loaded with iron. It ran on shiny rails—Herr Hilpert's parallel lines, which laid tangents on the heavy wheels that rolled along over them. And then the lights—these were Herr Hilpert's eyes. They annihilated" (p. 151).

39   *AHI*, pp. 20, 22.

40   *AHI*, pp. 22, 23.

41   *Annäherungen*, p. 93.

42   Ibid., pp. 109–10.

43   *AHi*, p. 26.

44   William K. Pfeiler, *War and the German Mind* (New York: Columbia University Press, 1941), p. 83.

45   To Hervier, *Entretiens*, p. 25. His grandmother had given him *Im dunkelsten Africa*, published by Brockhaus of Leipzig in 1890.

46   *AHi*, p. 34.

47   "A tramway," wrote Henry Stanley, in *Through the Dark Continent* (1899; rpt. New York: Dover, 1988), 1:34, "is one thing that is needed for Africa. All other benefits that can be conferred by contact with civilisation will follow in the wake of the tramway, which will be an iron bond, never to be again broken, between Africa and the more favored continent."

48   *AHi*, pp. 35–36. Disdain of stone barracks is retrojected here, something Jünger felt after the Great War, not before it.

49   *AHi*, pp. 36–37.

50   *AHi*, p. 37.

51   *AHi*, p. 38.

52   Stanley, *Through the Dark Continent*, 1:181.

53   *Strahlungen*, October 17, 1945.

54   Jünger told Hervier, p. 40: "The events are precise but transcribed into a more elaborated language."

55   *Afrikanische Spiele* (Hamburg: Hanseatische Verlagsanstalt, 1936), p. 12. Hereafter *AS*. In the revised Klett edition, "freilich" ("of course") is omitted.

56   *AS*, p. 93.

57   *AS*, p. 132.

58   From this vantage, *Afrikanische Spiele* bids comparison with T. E. Lawrence's depiction of barracks life in *The Mint*.

59   *AS*, p. 146.

60   *AS*, pp. 155–56.

61   *AS*, p. 166.

62   *AS*, p. 177.

63   *AS*, p. 188.

64   All of the papers from and to the elder Jünger on this incident can be found in the archives of the Foreign Office in Paris.

65   *AS*, p. 212.

66   *AS*, p. 219. In revising this work after the Third Reich, Jünger changed "I felt abandoned in my pride" to "I felt abandoned in my freedom."

67   J. E. Russell, *German Higher Schools* (New York: Longmans, Green, 1905), p. 172: "Until a student has attained a profession of his own, the Stand (social status) of his father follows him everywhere he goes."

68   *Jahresbericht des Städischen Gymnasiums und des Ober-Realschule zu Hameln für das Schuljahr von Osten 1912 bis 1913* (Hameln: C. W. Niemeyer, 1913), pp. 8, 9.

69   *Jahresbericht des königlicher Goethe-Gymnasiums (Lyceum II) zu Hannover für das Schuljahr*

von Osten 1909–1910 (Hanover: August Grimpe, 1910), p. 6, and ibid., *1913–1914,* p. 6.

70 *Hameln, 1912 bis 1913,* p. 9.

71 *Bericht über das Schuljahr 1910–1911, Königliches Gymnasium zu Duderstadt* (Duderstadt: Fr. Wagner, 1911), p. 6.

72 Joseph Riehemann, *Schulreden* (Meppen: Wegener, 1910), pp. 25–27.

73 In *Mein Kampf* Hitler decries Germany's failure to match the Allies' degradation of Germans into bestial images of "Huns."

74 So Jünger told me in an interview, July 25, 1992.

2. The Quill of Ares

1 As a young man, Jorge Luis Borges read it in a Spanish translation made for the Argentinian army around 1922. Visiting Jünger sixty years later, Borges recalled the book's impact: "For me it was like a volcanic explosion." Quoted in Julien Hervier, *Entretiens avec Ernst Jünger* (Paris: Gallimard, 1986), p. 28.

2 See his review, "Junger or Junker?" *Sunday Referee* (London), April 20, 1930, p. 6, and my essay, "Whipping Thersites out of Camp: Richard Aldington vs. Ernst Jünger on the Great War," in *Richard Aldington: Essays in Honour of the Centenary of His Birth,* ed. Alain Blayac and Caroline Zilboorg (Montpellier: Université Paul Valéry, 1993), pp. 29–40.

3 For the history of the storm troop units' evolution see my essay "Ernst Jünger: German Stormtrooper Chronicler," in *Facing Armageddon: 1914–1918, The War Experienced,* ed. Hugh Cecil and Peter Liddle (London: Leo Cooper, 1996), pp. 269–77.

4 *Autor und Autorschaft* (Stuttgart: Klett, 1984), p. 90.

5 Rachel Bespaloff, *On the Iliad,* trans. Mary McCarthy (1947; rpt. New York: Harper, 1962), pp. 44–45.

6 John Keegan, *The Face of Battle* (New York: Viking, 1977), p. 63.

7 Karl Marx, *Texte zu Methode und Praxis,* ed. G. Hillman (Hamburg: Rowohlt, 1967), 3:35.

8 *Autor und Autorshaft,* p. 258.

9 *In Stahlgewittern* (Leisnig: Robert Meier, 1920), p. 106. Hereafter *SG.* In my discussion, two versions, published in 1920 and 1934, share a kind of parity. Another version, published in 1924 and in 1926, is far less important but is also noted. Ulrich Böhme, *Fassungen bei Ernst Jünger* (Meisenheim am Glan: Anton Hain, 1972), offers a scrupulous discussion of differences in style and content among these versions, as well as analyses of Jünger's *Kampf als Inneres Erlebnis, Feuer und Blut,* and *Das Wäldchen 125.* A book-length study of the lives of *In Stahlgewittern* is in progress.

10 Quoted in *Die Schleife: Dokumente zum Weg von Ernst Jünger,* ed. Armin Mohler (Zurich: Arche, 1955), p. 53.

11 Ibid., p. 54.

12 *SG,* p. 1.

13 For contrast, see the sober view of Walter Bloem, *The Advance from Mons, 1914,* trans. G. C. Wynne (London: Peter Davies, Ltd., 1930), p. 8: "Those in power must surely see what a mighty flood of misery and suffering they were letting loose on humanity, and find some other solution than this impossible and incredible war."

14 Walter Rehm, *Der Todesgedanke in der deutschen Dichtung vom Mittelalter bis zur Romantik* (Halle: Niemeyer, 1928), p. 371.

15 *SG,* p. vi.

16 Ibid.

17 In 1914 a German regiment had three battalions; each battalion, four companies. The full strength of a company was 250 men.

18 This passage occurs in the third version, i.e., the second revision, *In Stahlgewittern: Ein Kriegstagebuch* (Hamburg: Deutsche Hausbücherei, 1934), pp. 31–32. Hereafter *SG3.* The third and final version, never translated into English, is much longer than its predecessors and is the text readers would have known during the Third Reich. It adorns the narrative structure of the first version and second versions with exfoliating metaphors, softening a once sinewy terseness by impressions and asides.

19 *Die Schleife,* p. 55.

20 *SG,* pp. 13–14.

21 For incredulity on the other side see Louis Ferdinand Céline's *Journey to the End of Night,* trans. Ralph Manheim (London: John Calder, 1988), pp. 16–17: "Maybe our colonel knew why they were shooting, maybe the Germans knew, but I, so help me, hadn't the vaguest idea. As far back as I could search my memory, I hadn't done a thing to the Germans, I'd always been polite and friendly with them." This picaresque naïveté is far from Jünger's tone.

22 In the 1920 version, he admits his nerves broke down completely: "Quite simply, I was afraid, mindlessly afraid." But in the revised version (1934) he aestheticizes the experience of others wounded: "Here reigned great pain, and for the first time I gazed as through a demonic fissure into the depths of its realm."

23 *SG,* p. 17 (*SG3,* p. 44). *SG3* includes remarks on the trainees' camp: "You could read on the faces of the hundreds of young people who streamed together here from every German stock, that the land had no shortage of good fighting manhood."

24 *SG3,* p. 45.

25 *SG3,* p. 48, a slightly revised version of *SG,* pp. 19–20.

26 *SG3,* p. 51. This revision was clearly retrospective to the glamorized depictions of the soldier's life in the anti-Remarque war literature of the early thirties.

27 *SG,* p. 22 (*SG3,* p. 55).

28 As Hitler complained in *Mein Kampf,* German propaganda fell far short of the British in rousing troops to hatred or revulsion toward the foe.

29 The fascination of the Jeanne d'Arc episode lies in its hiddenness. Artist that he is, Jünger knows what to leave unsaid.

30 *SG,* p. 36 (*SG3,* p. 82).

31 "The Memoirs of A. B. Russell" (Imperial War Museum, Documents) from the Third Battalion, Queen's Westminster Rifles, offer a down-to-earth and unheroic account of British night patrols around Cambrai (Jünger's vicinity) in late summer, 1917. Fifteen men with a Lewis machine gun were assigned to engage the enemy and gather IDs. "Due to foreshortening of the front lines in one's field of vision, there was a strange impression that, when out in no-man's-land, one was operating in an enclosed circular area. . . . It was very difficult to keep one's bearings and it was nearly always necessary to use a magnetic compass to avoid walking into the enemy's lines, and, eventually, to get back to one's own trenches."

32 *SG3*, p. 102: "ein starkes persönliches Guthaben." There is no mention of this episode in the original version.

33 *SG3*, p. 168.

34 *SG3*, p. 106. In *SG*, p. 50, he remarks only that lying under steady fire was "a test of nerves."

35 On the English capture of Guillemont, we have direct testimony from Major Phillip F. Story of the Ninety-sixth Field Company of Royal Engineers (Twentieth Division), in a letter of September 10, 1916 (Imperial War Museum, Documents): "We fairly pasted the Bosche—six hundred prisoners and a large number of killed and wounded. . . . The Bosches were good specimens, mainly of the 73d Fusilier Regiment. . . . They had Gibraltar embroidered on their cuffs—a prisoner told me they had at one time helped to defend the rock. One of our hireling regiments, I expect. The prisoners fraternised fairly well with our men, and carried back many a wounded man; they were very good stretcher bearers. Guillemont was blotted right out, not one brick standing on another."

36 *SG3*, p. 117. No mention of this spectacular event in the first edition (see *SG*, p. 57) or the first revision (see *SG2*, p. 95). The Homeric coloring obtrudes upon the straight-forwardness of the earlier narratives.

37 *SG*, p. 49. Cf. *SG3*, p. 105: this anonymous soldier seemed "the possessor of a new, mysterious, and hard world."

38 *SG3*, p. 114.

39 *SG3*, p. 123.

40 *SG3*, p. 131.

41 *SG3*, p. 144. Jünger never owns any affinity with the French.

42 *SG3*, p. 146. Lt. Col. J. D. Wyatt, then company commander in the 2/4th Battalion, Gloucestershire Regiment, Sixty-first Division, kept a diary during the Germans' withdrawal to the Hindenburg Line (Imperial War Museum, Documents). March 10, 1917, with a view of Chaulnes from the southwest: "The Boche is certainly burning something behind his lines as dense clouds of smoke can be seen any day at various points and flames at night. Is he burning villages in rear? If so, he is certainly about to retire." March 19, 1917, in the village of Potte: "When we got there we found the

village in ruins. It was not till then that we realized that the Huns really meant to destroy every village they had to evacuate."

43 *SG3*, p. 172.

44 *SG3*, p. 197.

45 *Der Kampf als Inneres Erlebnis* (Berlin: Mittler, 1922), p. 60. Hereafter *KIE1*.

46 *SG3*, p. 208.

47 Friedrich-Georg Jünger's "diary," quoted in *SG3*, p. 202; the account in *SG*, p. 107 (and in *SG2*, p. 170) is much more economical: no mention of tears nor anything "wondrous and shocking" about the meeting. Had Fritz, too, revised his account?

48 *SG*, p. 117 (*SG3*, p. 218).

49 *SG3*, p. 232; cf. *SG*, p. 127.

50 *SG3*, p. 240, a considerably expanded revision of *SG*, p. 132.

51 *SG*, p. 133.

52 *SG3*, p. 251.

53 Herbert Bornebusch, "Kriegsromane," in *Deutsche Literatur: Eine Sozialgeschichte: Weimarer Republik-Dritter Reich*, ed. Horst Glaser and Alexander von Bornman (Reinbek bei Hamburg: Rowohlt, 1983), p. 142.

54 *SG*, p. 143.

55 *Feuer und Blut: Ein kleiner Ausschnitt aus einer grossen Schlacht* (Magdeburg: Stahlhelm Verlag, 1925), p. 54. Hereafter *FB*. Quotations, unless otherwise noted, are from this first edition.

56 *SG*, p. 146.

57 *FB*, p. 108.

58 *FB*, p. 117; cf. *SG3*, p. 260. The phrase beginning "into that vanished world . . ." comes in a later version, in the first collected edition of Jünger's *Werke*, 1:511, published by Klett in 1958.

59 *FB*, p. 123.

60 *FB*, p. 137.

61 *SG3*, p. 267.

62 Liddell Hart, *The Real War*, p. 364, describes this spring campaign as "a tussle between a lean Hercules and a bulky Cerberus."

63 *SG*, p. 179.

64 *SG3*, p. 315. Only in this edition does Jünger mention the cigarette exchange, a relaxing of tension that faciliated his escape.

65 *SG*, p. 181.

66 *SG2*, p. 281.

67 See Bernd Peschken, "Klassizistische und ästhetizistische Tendenzen," in Horst Deukler and Karl Prümm, eds., *Die Deutsche Literatur im Dritten Reich* (Stuttgart: Reclam, 1976), p. 217.

68 *SG*, p. 169. We can only speculate as to why Jünger omitted this passage in preparing

the third version. It is certain that, while recognizing the "dehumanizing" effects of war, he did not concede anything to the clamorous pacifists in the late twenties.

69   *Das Wäldchen 125: Eine Chronik aus den Grabenkämpfen 1918* (Berlin: E. S. Mittler, 1926), p. 238. Hereafter *W125;* all quotations are from the 1926 edition.

70   *W125,* p. 180.

71   In order to write, he was relieved of many duties by his company commander, Captain Trauthig, the first reader of *In Stahlgewittern* in manuscript.

72   *KIE1,* p. 7.

73   *KIE1,* p. 2.

74   *KIE1,* p. 15.

75   For a discussion, see George Mosse, *Fallen Heroes* (New York: Oxford University Press, 1990), pp. 15–50 passim.

76   *KIE1,* p. 26.

77   *KIE1,* p. 40.

78   Sigmund Freud, "Zeitgemässes über Krieg und Tod," in *Gesammelte Werke,* ed. Anna Freud (Frankfurt: S. Fischer, 1946), 10:337, 338.

79   Peter Jansen, "Der Enkel des Atavus," *Streit-Zeit-Schrift* 6, no. 2 (September 1968): 29, contends that "the acidulous smell of sperm" lies over "the Jüngerian landscape of craters, mire, pus, and blood," that the proximity of the combat's adversary prompts Jünger to orgasmic images and clichés. The point in Jansen's rather overdrawn statement is that some reason for fascination with Jünger's war writing may be precisely this eroticism. Nikolaus Sombart submits that French leftists' interest in Jünger is bound up with their erotic romanticizing of the SS (*Streit-Zeit-Schrift* 6, no. 2 [September 1968]: 7).

80   *KIE1,* p. 47.

81   *KIE1,* p. 44. In his latest revision of this essay, *Sämtliche Werke* (Stuttgart: Klett, 1980), 7:47, Jünger adds, "It seemed not unthinkable that one day the best manhood of peoples would climb from the trenches on sudden impulse and moral understanding, extend the hand, and finally conduct themselves like children who had been fighting for a long while."

82   *KIE,* Berlin: Mittler, 1926 (second edition, substantially revised), p. 49. Hereafter *KIE2.*

83   *KIE2,* p. 48.

84   *KIE2,* p. 46.

85   Ibid.

86   *KIE2,* p. 55. This aspersive distinction is polemical; nowhere in the war memoirs does Jünger distinguish soldiers' performance according to their socioeconomic class.

87   *SG,* p. 153 (*SG3,* p. 269).

88   *W125,* p. 19. This passage is omitted from the Klett editions. In his translation, Basil Creighton (p. 21) misrenders "trotzt" as "trusts."

89   *W125,* 2d ed. (Berlin: Mittler, 1926), p. 210.

90   Ibid., p. 213. Basil Creighton's translation of *Copse 125* (London: Chatto and Windus, 1930), p. 221, suggestively but mistakenly renders Jünger's "hundert Menschen" as "a mere handful of men."

91   *W125*, p. 154.

92   *W125*, p. 230.

93   *W125*, p. 52.

94   *KIE2*, p. 74.

95   *W125*, p. viii.

96   *FB*, p. 159.

97   *KIE1*, p. 114. For the second Klett edition Jünger cut substantially or recast the five paragraphs after this statement.

98   *KIE1*, p. 116. In the second Klett edition (p. 103) he celebrates the will to power as an expressed mastery of "the technological wonderworks of might."

99   This is the argument he might have made to English antiwar poets decrying the waste and carnage that wars bring.

100 *W125*, p. 50.

3. Weimar Polemics

1   Letter to Friedrich-Georg Jünger, November 18, 1918, reproduced in *Die Schleife: Dokumente zum Weg von Ernst Jünger,* ed. Armin Mohler (Zurich: Arche, 1955), p. 56.

2   *Annäherungen: Drogen und Rausch* (Stuttgart: Klett, 1970), p. 223.

3   *Annäherungen,* p. 202.

4   Letter to Friedrich-Georg, January 20, 1920, cited in Heimo Schwilk, *Ernst Jünger: Leben und Werk in Bildern und Texten* (Stuttgart: Klett, 1988), p. 89.

5   Letter to Friedrich-Georg, March 17, 1920, in *Die Schleife,* p. 61.

6   Letter to Friedrich-Georg, November 1, 1920, quoted in Schwilk, p. 92.

7   According to Michael Geyer, "The German Officer Corps as Profession," in *German Professions,* ed. Geoffrey Cocks and Konrad Jarausch (New York: Oxford University Press, 1990), p. 196, "In effect, the front-line ideology is nothing but Taylorism for the organization of violence."

8   "Skizze moderner Gefechtsführung," *Militär-Wochenblatt* 105, no. 20 (November 13, 1920): 433.

9   Correlli Barnett, "The Education of Military Elites," *Journal of Contemporary History* 2, no. 3 (1967): 21.

10 "Die Technik in der Zukunftschlacht," *Militär-Wochenblatt* 106, no. 14 (October 1, 1921): 487.

11 Ibid., 487. This essay could be read as Jünger's answer to Spengler's contention in *Der Untergang des Abendlandes* (Munich: C. H. Beck, 1922), 2:526, that the ascendance of machinery in modern war had eliminated personal heroism and the ethos of nobility.

12 "Die Ausbildungsvorschrift für die Infanterie," *Militär-Wochenblatt* 108, no. 3 (August 10, 1923): 53. In a complementary essay on the speed of attack, "Über Angriffsgeschwindigkeit," 107, no. 32 (May 25, 1923): 688, he argues for two kinds of attack on enemy depth zones: one planned step-by-step, another "recklessly lashed forward" which "by the will to victory and one's own planning pulls the foe's last remnants of defense into a backward flowing whirlpool."

A fifth essay, "Auf welchen Grundgedanken beruht die Infanterietaktik?" *Militär-Wochenblatt* 107, no. 22 (1922), is ascribed to Jünger in Hans Peter des Coudres's bibliography of his work, but is almost certainly not his. It is not signed by him and, abundant in quotations and single-sentence paragraphs, is not in his style.

13 The Versailles Treaty's enforced contraction of the army to 100,000 men meant that the new ranks could retain the best men. To the relief of the military establishment, the antimilitary socialists were never able to act upon their prejudices; they needed the army to contain the threat of a Soviet-style revolution. On benefits see Gordon Craig, *The Politics of the Prussian Army, 1640–1945* (New York: Oxford University Press, 1955), p. 395.

14 Letter to Friedrich-Georg, November 22, 1921, in *Die Schleife,* p. 66.

15 "Even today I consider him one of the church fathers of the modern," *Annäherungen,* p. 183.

16 Chief of the German army's High Command, 1934–1938, Fritsch is remembered as the victim of Himmler's "frame-up" charge of homosexuality, which Hitler used to force his resignation.

17 *Annäherungen,* p. 183: "Fritsch probably meant that this kind of literary inspiration is detrimental to service and thus to one's career. He was right: passion is always an index for what one should pursue as well as for what one should let go. 'Reader' is not a favorable predicate on a résumé."

18 Letter to Friedrich-Georg, August 27, 1922, in *Die Schleife,* p. 69.

19 Letter to Friedrich-Georg, March 25, 1923, quoted in Schwilk, p. 94.

20 Ibid.

21 This attractive little work was not included in Klett's first edition of Jünger's works. His bibliographer, Hans Peter de Coudres, came upon it in 1960, and it was reprinted in 1963.

22 In his *Der Krieg und die Schriftsteller: Der Kriegsroman der Weimarer Republik* (Stuttgart: J. B. Metzler, 1986), p. 255, Hans Harald Müller suggests *Sturm* is not a novel about war but about the impossibility of writing a novel about war, meaning that Jünger failed in his supposed attempt to merge the soldier's elementary battle experience and the artist's creative refinements.

An entry from Jünger's Second World War diaries is pertinent here. From Laon, June 12, 1940 (*Gärten und Strassen* [Paris, 1942], p. 161) he notes that while overseeing seven hundred French POWs, he loses the sense for all practical details, even though they admit some intellectual pleasure: "At certain crossroads in our youth

Bellona and Athena might appear, one promising to teach the art of leading twenty regiments into line ready for battle, the other promising us the gift of composing twenty words to make up the perfect sentence. We might choose the second laurel, which blooms more rarely and imperceptibly on the rock slope."

23 *Sturm* (Olten: Georg Rentsch Sons, 1963), p. 31. This first edition was privately printed and limited to 605 copies.

24 Ibid., pp. 16–17.

25 Ibid., p. 93.

26 Ibid., p. 79.

27 In his *Entretiens,* p. 26, Hervier, unjustly characterizing *Sturm* as "uncompleted," asked Jünger if he had "entirely forgotten" it. Yes. "At the time I had such personal problems that it's understandable I no longer thought of it." This response seems incredibly disingenuous.

28 Jünger's lengthy assessment of Hitler in his 1946 diaries refers only to the years after the aborted putsch of November 1923.

29 Hans Driesch, *The Possibility of Metaphysics: A Course of Four Lectures Delivered before the University of London in March, 1924* (London: Faith Press, 1924), p. 56.

30 Passing from zoology to philosophy, Jünger said he went from "the frying pan into the fire." "Briefe eines Nationalisten," *Arminius* 8, no. 10 (March 6, 1927): p. 7.

31 Hervier, p. 63.

32 *AHI,* p. 125.

33 *AHI,* pp. 125, 126.

34 *AHI,* p. 129.

35 *AHI,* p. 131. When visiting Jünger, I recalled from memory the first two sentences quoted here. He answered, "Not bad. If someone else had written that, it would have been applauded."

36 *AHI,* p. 130.

37 Harry Kessler, *In the Twenties* (New York: Holt, Rinehart & Winston, 1971), p. 267.

38 Ibid.

39 On the circulation figures, see Roger Woods, *Ernst Jünger and the Nature of Political Commitment* (Stuttgart: Hans Dieter Heinz, 1982), p. 101, n. 4.

40 Friedrich Hielscher, *Fünfzig Jahre unter Deutschen* (Hamburg: Rowohlt, 1954), p. 122.

41 On the generational differences within the Stahlhelm see James Diehl, *Parliamentary Politics in Weimar Germany* (Bloomington: Indiana University Press, 1977), p. 222.

42 Oberst F. Immanuel, review of *KIE* in *Literarisches Centralblatt für Deutschland* 73, no. 30 (July 29, 1922): 574.

43 See the review by Oberst D. Gaedtke, *Leipziger Nachrichten,* January 13, 1925, p. 15, and the anonymous review in *Militärwochenblatt* 109, no. 21 (December 4, 1924): 595.

44 "Neue Bücher für den Stahlhelm und Jungstahlhelm," *Der Stahlhelm* 7, no. 3 (January 18, 1925): 13.

45 Albrecht Erich Gunther, review of *W125* in *Deutsches Volkstum,* January 7, 1925, p. 84.

46   Gunther, review in *Deutsches Volkstum,* May 8, 1926, p. 182.

47   "Der neue Typ des deutschen Menschen: Aus einem Brief an einem alten Frontsoldaten," in *Stahlhelm Jahrbuch* 1926, ed. Wilhelm Kleinau (Magdeburg: Stahlhelm Verlag, 1925), p. 60.

48   Ibid., p. 62.

49   "Der Frontsoldat und die innere Politik," *Die Standarte* 13 (November 29, 1925): 2.

50   "Der Internationalismus," *Die Standarte* 12 (November 11, 1925): 2.

51   Ibid.

52   "Der Pazifismus," *Die Standarte* 11 (November 15, 1925): 2.

53   "Briefe," p. 64. For "redress" *Steuer* in its old sense.

54   Ibid.

55   *Strahlungen,* May 7, 1945.

56   When I suggested to Jünger that Goebbels might be considered a failed writer, he parried that one could enter politics and remain a writer of integrity. He cited Barrès as his first example.

57   "Die Tradition," *Die Standarte* 10 (November 8, 1925): 2.

58   "Der Frontsoldat und die innere Politik," p. 2.

59   Gordon Craig, *Germany 1866–1945* (Oxford: Oxford University Press, 1981), p. 509.

60   "Grossstadt und Land," *Deutsches Volkstum* 8 (August, 1926): 579, 580.

61   "Der Nationalismus," *Standarte* 1, no. 1 (April 1, 1926): 2.

62   Ibid., p. 6.

63   "Der Aufmarsch," *Standarte* 1, no. 3 (April 15, 1926): 55.

64   Ibid., p. 56.

65   Ibid., p. 130.

66   "Die nationalistische Revolution," *Standarte* 1, no. 8 (May 20, 1926): 173.

67   "Schliesst Euch zusammen!," *Standarte* 1, no. 10 (June 3, 1926): 226.

68   Ibid.

69   Ibid.

70   "Von den Wahlen," *Standarte* 1, no. 21 (August 19, 1926): 488.

71   Friedrich Wilhelm Heinz, "Kampf dem Stahlhelm?" in *Standarte* 1, no. 22 (August 26, 1926), p. 517, scolded this "messiah of a new nationalism" for deserting to a "literary" opposition.

72   Arminius, a Germanic soldier of the Roman army, betrayed Varus and three legions in the Teutoburg Forest, 9 C.E. Tacitus (*Annales* 1.55) calls him "turbator Germaniae" and Velleius Paterculus (*Historia,* 118.2) characterizes him as "ardorem animi vultu oculisque praeferens"—a prototype of Jünger's fiery nationalist.

73   "Das Sonderrecht des Nationalismus," *Arminius,* January 23, 1927, pp. 3–4. Jünger's notion of the contingency of rights has a notably Darwinian aspect. He rejects what he calls "the yammer of the oppressed." Since every right is really only a claim on life and the world a battlefield of rights, the weak have no part in it. But he rejects "survival of the fittest" as a mechanical formula. Defeat is as significant and fruit-

ful as victory because the victor owes "the new form" in part to the defeated. In a review of Albrecht Erich Günther's *Totem,* in *Arminius* 8 (1927): 8–10, he refines his objection to Darwinism: it is the Weltanschauung of the half-educated, who, content with scientific proofs, subordinate will to the understanding. "Schopenhauer couldn't fight enough against this vice."

74 According to Jünger in "Kasernenhof der Idee," *Arminius* 7, no. 45 (1926): 3.

75 "Der Nationalismus der Tat," *Arminius* 7, no. 41 (1926): 11.

76 "Die Zwei Tyrannen," *Arminius* 8, no. 11 (1927): 3–4. As George Mosse has noted to me in private correspondence, Jünger's nationalism was very close to Italian fascism, but the praise Jünger gives it here was as close as he came to an endorsement. He preferred that Germany make its own totalitarian revolution.

77 "Nationalistischer Brief," *Arminius* 7, no. 43 (1926): 7.

78 "Soldaten und Literaten," *Arminius* 8, no. 12 (1927): 10.

79 "Was Herr Seldte sagen sollte," *Arminius* 7, no. 44 (1926): 7. These disclaimers should not obscure Jünger's continued belief in the naturalness, hence inevitability, of war. In "Die Abrüster," *Arminius* 8, no. 28 (1927): 6–7, he admits he feels inclined to war, even calls it a matter of taste (*Angelegenheit der Geschmacke*) comparable to another person's inclination to love or to "other powerful manifestations of elementary life."

80 "Die antinationalen Mächte," *Arminius* 8, no. 5 (1927): 4.

81 "Nationalismus und Nationalsozialismus," *Arminius* 8, no. 13 (1927): 8–10. Two years before, in "Abgrenzung und Verbindung," *Die Standarte* 2 (September 13, 1925): 2, Jünger had reckoned Hitler "a figure that undoubtedly is already, like Mussolini, the stirring presentiment of a wholly new kind of leader."

82 "Unsere Kampfstellung," *Arminius* 8, no. 23 (1927): 10.

83 "Der neue Nationalismus," *Völkischer Beobachter* 40 (January 23/24, 1927). The editor's introduction ineptly refers to the author as Jürgen.

84 *Strahlungen,* April 2, 1946.

85 Ibid. Jünger's excuse for his lack of commitment says a good deal: "Personally I was content with my situation and wanted no change. Work at the desk and in the garden, conversations with friends, now and again a trip to southern valleys. Activities, assignments, posts, honors could only have been disruptive."

86 "Nationalismus und Nationalsozialismus," *Arminius* 8, no. 13 (1927): 10.

87 "Student sein," *Arminius* 8, no. 29 (1927): 5.

88 "Professorales und Nichtprofessorales," *Arminius* 8, no. 36 (1927): 3.

89 "Die Schicksalzeit," *Arminius* 8, no. 1 (1927): 6.

90 "An die Freunde," p. 10.

91 "Die Schicksalzeit," p. 7. See note 50, on "Der Internationalismus." Here, again, a kind of anticipatory exultation in crime is affirmed. Let the world hate us!

92 Lass took a curious turn. Since 1925 he had been codirector of a far-right Schilljugend, then (1927) broke away to form the Freischar Schill. In 1929 Hitler allegedly offered him leadership of the Hitlerjugend (see Schüddekopf, *Links Leute von Rechts*

[Stuttgart: Kohlhammer, 1960], p. 246) but Lass preferred "national bolshevism" and became a member of the German Communist Party.

93 "Feuer," *Eckhart* 4, no. 6 (June 1928): 273, 274. *Eckhart* proclaimed itself a paper for "evangelical edification" (*Geisteskultur*). This article is not listed in the des Coudres-Mühleisen bibliography.

94 In his *Young Germany* (London: Routledge and Kegan Paul, 1962), p. 155, Walter Laqueur summarizes: "Before the First World War, the Wandervogel, tolerated as a curiosity, had little effect beyond its own membership. . . . But after the war had transformed the scene, the whole country suddenly became youth-movement conscious."

95 Wolfgang Zorn, "Student Politics in the Weimar Republic," *Journal of Contemporary History* 5, no. 1 (1970): 132.

96 "Die Opfer," *Der Vormarsch* 1, no. 6 (November 1927): 114.

97 "Die Blindgänger des grossen Krieges," *Der Vormarsch* 1, no. 8 (January 1928): 181.

98 "Die Opfer," p. 114.

99 "German Day of Humiliation," *Morning Post* (London), June 28, 1929, p. 13.

100 See Eberhard Kolb, *The Weimar Republic*, trans. P. S. Falla (London: Unwin Hyman, 1988), pp. 64, 104.

101 "Der unsichtbare Kern," p. 330.

102 Hans-Peter Schwarz, *Der konservative Anarchist: Politik und Zeitkritik Ernst Jüngers* (Freiburg-im-Breisgau: Rombach, Freiburger Studien zu Politik und Soziologie, 1962), p. 104.

103 "Trotskis Erinnerungen," *Widerstand* 5 (1930): 49.

104 Joseph Goebbels, *The Early Goebbels Diaries, 1925–1926,* ed. Helmut Heiber, trans. Oliver Watson (New York: Praeger, 1962), pp. 62, 93.

105 *Strahlungen,* May 7, 1945; this entry a week after Goebbels committed suicide.

106 *Die Tagebücher von Joseph Goebbels,* ed. Elke Fröhlich (Munich: K. G. Saur, 1987), 1:354.

107 "Nationalismus und 'Nationalismus,'" *Die Kommenden* 4, 41 (October 11, 1929): 40–41. All citations are from this issue, a reprint of the *Tagebuch* essay.

108 "Rund um die Rotationsmaschine," *Der Angriff* 3, 47 (October 27, 1929), as quoted in Lina Dornheim, *Vergleichende Rezeptionsgeschichte* (Frankfurt am Main: Peter Lang, 1987), p. 116.

109 In his remarks on Constantin Hird's anti-Semitic and anti-Masonic views, "Die anti-nationalisten Mächte," *Arminius* 5 (January 30, 1927): 4.

110 "Über Nationalismus und die Judenfrage," *Die Kommenden* 5 (September 19, 1930): 446. This essay appeared earlier in a symposium published in the *Süddeutsche Monatshefte* 27 (September 12, 1930) by the editor, Paul Nikolaus Cossmann, who died in Theresienstadt. Another contributor was Rabbi Leo Baeck.

111 Ibid. As George Mosse has reminded me in private correspondence, a group within the early membership of the Nazi Party felt like him, that either Jews should vanish into the German population or go back to Orthodoxy. This minority view disappeared very quickly.

112 "Schlusswort zu einem Aufsatz," *Die Kommenden* 5, no. 8 (February 21, 1920): 90. Jünger could hardly have realized how prophetic these words were: in less than a decade, *Der ewige Jude,* the wartime film of ghetto Jews juxtaposed to swarms of rats, would be shown in theaters. Hitler insisted on the visual equation.

113 Ernst Nolte, *The Three Faces of Fascism,* trans. Leila Vennewitz (New York: Holt, Rinehart, and Winston, 1966), pp. 402–7.

114 "Schlusswort zu einem Aufsatz," 90.

115 Ibid.

116 Leopold Schwarzschild, "Heroismus aus Langeweile," *Das Tagebuch,* September 28, 1929, p. 1590.

117 On Schlageter and the Nazis' exploitation of his "martyrdom," see Jay W. Baird, *To Die for Germany: Heroes in the Nazi Pantheon* (Bloomington: Indiana University Press, 1990), pp. 13–40.

118 *Strahlungen,* May 8, 1945.

119 Schleicher was allegedly inspired by the authoritarian elitism of Hans Zehrer, the dynamic young editor of *Die Tat.* But Schleicher was a veteran authoritarian, a confidant of Hindenburg, and a born intriguer (the very meaning of his name in German). His initiative failed virtually on inception as the labor leaders he courted (and the Social Democrats whom he did not) saw that his intent was not anticapitalist. His failure indicates with empirical eloquence how dismally utopist—a kind of fascist idyll—Jünger's soldier-worker state was. On Schleicher and Zehrer see Joachim Petzold, *Wegbereiter des deutschen Fascismus* (Cologne: Pahl-Rugenstein, 1978), pp. 274–89; Klemens von Klemperer, *Germany's New Conservatism* (Princeton: Princeton University Press, 1957), pp. 129–33.

120 *Blätter und Steine* (Hamburg: Hanseatische Verlagsanstalt, 1934), p. 109.

121 Ibid., p. 112.

122 Ibid., pp. 113–14.

123 I borrow this last point from Volker Katzmann, "Magischer Realismus," in *Wandlung und Wiederkehr: Festschrift zum 70. Geburtstag Ernst Jüngers,* ed. Heinz Ludwig Arnold (Aachen: Georgi Verlag, 1965), p. 103.

4. Beehives in a Botany of Steel

1 Cited from the Westdeutsche Akademische Rundschau, on the back page of *Auf den Marmorklippen.*

2 For a discussion of Hauser's writings, see Helmut Leuthen, *Neue Sachlichkeit, 1924–1932* (Stuttgart: J. B. Metzler, 1975), pp. 68–72.

3 *Der Arbeiter: Herrschaft und Gestalt* (Hamburg: Hanseatische Verlaganstalt, 1932), p. 21. All translations I have made from this second unrevised edition. Hereafter, *A.*

4 Oswald Spengler, *Der Mensch und die Technik* (Munich: C. H. Beck, 1932), p. 58.

5 See John Carey's *The Intellectuals and the Masses: Pride and Prejudice among the Literary Intelligentsia* (London: Faber and Faber, 1990), esp. pp. 3–90.

6   *Deutsches Wörterbuch,* vol. 4, pt. 1, sec. 2 (Leipzig: Hirzel, 1897), s.v.

7   Jünger's *Gestalt* should not be confused with the Gestalt school of psychology in the 1940s, even though that movement's central perceptual creed of whole over parts seems to be suggested here.

8   *A,* p. 35.

9   *A,* p. 40.

10   George Orwell, *Collected Essays, Journalism, and Letters of George Orwell, II: My Country Right or Left, 1940–1943,* ed. Sonia Orwell and Ian Angus (Harmondsworth: Penguin, 1984), p. 29, corroborates Jünger's point in a review of *Mein Kampf:* "Hitler, because in his own joyless mind he feels it with exceptional strength, knows that human beings *don't* only want comfort, safety, short working hours, hygiene, birth control and, in general, common sense; they also, at least intermittently, want struggle and self-sacrifice, not to mention drums, flags and loyalty parades."

11   *A,* p. 56.

12   *A,* p. 58.

13   *A,* p. 63. The phrase serves as title for an essay Jünger contributed to *Die literarische Welt* 6, no. 13 (1930): 3–4. He had apparently borrowed it from Werner Best, who like Jünger had been a member (1925–1926) of the Jungkonservative Vereinigung. Best joined the Nazi Party in 1930, later worked for Heydrich, served in Occupied France till 1942, and ended his fascist career as Reichsbevollmächtiger for Occupied Denmark.

14   *A,* p. 61.

15   *A,* p. 64.

16   The revelation of Arrhenius, for example, that salt, its elements ionized in solution, serves to conduct electricity.

17   *A,* p. 66.

18   Karl Prümm, *Soldatischer Nationalismus der 20er Jahre* (Kronberg Taunus: Scriptor, 1974), p. 409: "Schon die Existenz ökonomischer Interessen geisselt die Ökonomophobie Jüngers als Entartung."

19   *A,* p. 28.

20   See Spengler, *Der Mensch und die Technik,* p. 72. On p. 74, he wails that "a spiritual desolation is taking its grip, a disconsolate uniformity without heights and depths; bitterness awakes against those gifted with creativity. It's no longer realized that the labor of leaders is harder, that one's own life depends upon their success." Jünger indulges in none of this hand-wringing for the old order and its bosses.

21   *A,* p. 29.

22   *A,* pp. 54–55.

23   *A,* p. 34.

24   *A,* pp. 71–72.

25   His terms are "Wille zur Allmacht, Allgegenwart, Allwissenheit." The theme of new frontiers figure in Reinhard Goering's play *Die Südpolexpedition des Kapitän Scott*

(1929) and in Arnolt Broennen's one-man drama *Ostpolzug* (1926), about the conquest of Mount Everest. Concurrent with these ran the so-called "mountain films" of Arnold Fanck, centered upon quasi-heroic attempts to scale peaks: *Der Berg des Schicksals* (1924), *Der heilige Berg* (1926), *Der Kampf ums Matterhorn* (1928).

26 Jünger claims (p. 138) that the tendency of modern science is to seek the infinitely small and infinitely great. Heisenberg's notion of the simultaneous incalculability of electron movements and positions, and Einstein's notion of curved space are instances.

27 Every invention or discovery has someone behind it. Jünger's point is that it may be so momentous in its effects that it *seems* mysterious and unauthored. The explosive power of World War I was largely the work of Wilhelm Ostwald, who found that catalytic oxidation of ammonia produced nitric acid. Says Eduard Farber, in *Nobel Prize Winners in Chemistry, 1901–1950* (New York: Henry Schuman, 1953), p. 40: "The extent and fury of the First World War would have been impossible without this method of manufacturing a basic material from which all important explosives are derived."

28 *A*, p. 102.

29 *A*, p. 152.

30 Crucial to Jünger's thesis is Spengler's paradox in *Preussentum und Sozialismus* (Munich: Beck, 1920), pp. 32 and 33, that in Prussianism freedom and service cohere: "Personal independence and suprapersonal community. Today we call them individualism and socialism. Virtues of the first rank stand behind these words: self-responsibility, self-determination, resolution, initiative in the one; fidelity, discipline, selfless renunciation, breeding in the other." *Preussentum* was their amalgam as a "libertas oboedientiae."

31 *A*, p. 162.

32 Prümm, *Soldatischer Nationalismus*, p. 433.

33 *A*, p. 183. This Homeric remark should be pondered by those who insist that Jünger glorifies death.

34 Wilhelm Stapel, "Der entdeckte Jünger," *Deutsches Volkstum* 15, no. 4 (1933): 178, rightly perceived that in it Jünger had overcome the "new nationalism."

35 See Prümm, *Soldatischer Nationalismus*, p. 438, no. 55.

36 Ibid., p. 439, no. 40.

37 *A*, p. 200.

38 For all his commendation of the Jesuits, an order founded by a soldier, Jünger makes clear that their faith, the content of their discipline, could in no way inform the *Gestalt* he envisages.

39 *A*, p. 218.

40 *A*, p. 219.

41 *A*, p. 223.

42 *A*, p. 227.

43 Hervier, ed., *Entretiens,* p. 85.

44 See Michael J. Neufeld, "Weimar Culture and Futuristic Technology: The Rocketry and Spaceflight Fad in Germany, 1923–1933," *Technology and Culture* 31, no. 4 (October 1990): 725–52.

45 *A,* p. 292.

46 *A,* p. 241.

47 See the entries for April 30, 1943, and November 20, 1943.

48 This is to presume we can trust Hermann Rauschning's polished account in his *Hitler Speaks* (London: Thornton Butterworth, 1939), p. 136.

49 *A,* p. 281. Cf. Plato's plans for a parentless generation of young reared collectively in preparation for guardianship.

50 As H. Stuart Hughes, *Oswald Spengler: A Critical Estimate* (New York: Charles Scribner's Sons, 1952), p. 66, observes of *Decline,* "Long, wretchedly organized books have been the tradition in Germany, and we may wonder whether a shorter, more lucid volume would have achieved the same reputation for profundity."

5. The "Internal Emigration"

1 Armin Mohler, *Die Schleife* (Zurich: Arche, 1955), p. 89: "It is one of Ernst Jünger's paradoxes that from the moment he turned his back on the public he became a kind of public institution."

2 See P. Körbitz, "Ernst Jünger, Der Wegbereiter der deutschen Revolution," *Preussische Lehrerzeitung* 95 (1933), and C. Staiger, "Aus dem Leben und Schaffen eines deutschen Frontsoldaten," *Der deutsche Erzieher* 3 (1934–35): 494–98.

3 As Harry Kessler observed from exile, "That alone has transformed Germany into a negotiating party which has to be taken very seriously and whose offers and proposals have to be heard with respect." *In the Twenties* (New York: Holt, Rinehart, and Winston, 1971), p. 461.

4 Lina Dornheim, *Vergleichende Rezeptionsgeschichte: Das literarische Frühwerk Ernst Jüngers in Deutschland, England und Frankreich* (Frankfurt am Main: Peter Lang, 1987), p. 121.

5 Hans Dieter Schäfer, quoted by Dornheim, ibid., pp. 121–122.

6 Helmut Hoffmann, *Mensch und Volk in Kriegserlebnis,* in *Germanische Studien* 189 (Berlin: Ebering, 1937), pp. 71–72.

7 Hoffmann prescribed as antidote Hans Zöberlein's identification of self with "the German community of fate" in his interminable *Der Glaube an Deutschland* (1931). The Führer wrote the introduction.

8 *Wissen und Wehr* 7 (1934): 488.

9 Quoted in Jacob Wulf, *Literatur und Dichtung im Dritten Reich: Eine Dokumentation* (Gütersloh: Sigbert Mohn, 1963), p. 35.

10 Quoted by Wulf, ibid., p. 91.

11 For the full text, see Mohler, ed., *Die Schleife,* p. 88.

12 For best- and long-seller statistics on the twenties and thirties see Walter Nutz, "Massenliteratur," in *Deutsche Literatur: Eine Sozialgeschichte 9: Weimarer Republik-Drittes Reich,* ed. Horst Glaser (Reinbek bei Hamburg: Rowohlt, 1989), 202–4.

13 M. Duffner-Greif in the *Karlsruhe Tageblatt* (1936), p. 268, quoted by Dornheim, *Rezeptionsgeschichte,* p. A91; see also p. A119. For similar assessments of Jünger see Richard Bie and Alfred Mühr, *Die Kulturwaffen des neuen Reiches: Briefe an Führer, Volk und Jugend* (Jena, 1933); Eugen Schmahl, *Der Aufstieg der nationalen Idee* (Stuttgart, 1933); and H. Bäcker, *Von deutscher Wirklichkeit und ihrer Bahn* (Berlin, 1939).

14 *Illustrierter Beobachter* (hereafter *IB*), Folge (issue, hereafter F.) 12 (March 12, 1934): 444.

15 *IB,* F. 18 (May 2, 1935): 710.

16 See *IB,* F. 41 (October 8, 1936): 1641–43.

17 *IB,* F. 47 (November 25, 1933): 1578; and F. 30 (July 23, 1936): 1172.

18 Letter to Friedrich-Georg from Eidsbygda, Norway, August 5, 1935, in *Myrdun* (Tübingen: Heliopolis, 1949), p. 46.

19 *Myrdun,* pp. 29, 65.

20 *Das abenteuerliche Herz: Figuren und Capriccios* (Hamburg: Hanseatische Verlaganstalt, 1938), p. 32. Hereafter *AH2.* In this work Fischer is caricatured as a nearly inaccessible figure, melancholic and devoted to arcana.

21 *Myrdun,* p. 65.

22 Ibid., p. 64.

23 Ibid., p. 76.

24 Ibid., p. 67.

25 By wretched irony, *Myrdun* was first printed in Oslo, in 1943, for the occupation's troops.

26 It first appeared in London, in 1947, where it was published for German prisoners of war.

27 *Atlantische Fahrt* (Tübingen: Otto Reichl, 1949), p. 40.

28 For a discussion of this phrase see Ian Kershaw, *Hitler* (London: Longman, 1991), p. 8.

29 *Atlantische Fahrt,* p. 23. "You can write passable travel works," Goethe tells Schiller (August 9, 1797), "only about foreign lands where you have no relationship to anyone."

30 Ibid., p. 28.

31 Ibid., p. 54.

32 Ibid., p. 88.

33 Ibid., p. 70.

34 "Die Kiesgrube," *AH2,* p. 9.

35 See Wolfgang Kaempfer's criticisms in his *Ernst Jünger* (Stuttgart: J. B. Metzler, 1981), pp. 85–88.

36 "2. Nachtrag," *AH2*, pp. 147–48.

37 "Nachtrag zur Zinnia," *AH2*, p. 85.

38 "Frutti di mare," *AH2*, p. 51.

39 Karl Widmaier, ed., *Schriften J. G. Hamanns* (Leipzig: Insel, 1921), p. 226.

40 "Der Überfluss," *AH2*, p. 152.

41 "In den Museen," *AH2*, pp. 114–16.

42 "In den Kaufläden," *AH2*, p. 36.

43 "Grausame Bücher," *AH2*, p. 54. Jünger's italics.

44 "Das Entsetzen," *AH2*, pp. 14–15.

45 "Zur Désinvolture," *AH2*, pp. 96, 97.

46 "Historia in nuce: Das Glücksrad," *AH2*, p. 166.

47 "Grausame Bücher," *AH2*, p. 61.

48 *Inselfrühling* (Tübingen: Heliopolis, 1949), p. 36.

49 Ibid., p. 43.

50 Ibid., p. 51.

51 Ibid., pp. 40–41.

52 Letter to A. Frankl, June 1811.

53 For verse see Charles Hoffmann, *Opposition Poetry in Nazi Germany* (Berkeley: University of California Press, 1962).

54 *Consolatio Philosophiae*, 2.4; *Inferno*, 5.121–23. All quotations are from the first edition of *Auf den Marmorklippen* (Hamburg: Hanseatische Verlaganstalt, 1939).

55 *Strahlungen,* April 9, 1939.

56 So complains Hansjörg Schelle, *Ernst Jüngers 'Marmorklippen': Eine kritische Interpretation* (Leiden: Brill, 1970).

57 Peter von Polenz, "Sprachpurismus und Nationalsozialismus," in *Germanistik: Eine deutsche Wissenschaft,* ed. Eberhard Lämmert (Frankfurt: Suhrkamp, 1970), p. 138.

58 In 1992 Jünger showed me this flower in his garden.

59 There is no factual evidence for this statement. Many backroom confidences Jünger has long enjoyed with people in or near to high authority, including the military, have escaped documentation.

60 Quoted by Jünger himself in Hervier, *Entretiens,* p. 89. See note 71; there is no identified go-between for this remark.

61 For a discussion of the mythic uses to which the Nazis, parodying Christian themes, put the deaths of Wessel and Norkus, see Jay W. Baird, *To Die for Germany: Heroes in the Nazi Pantheon* (Bloomington: Indiana University Press, 1990), chapters IV and V.

62 *Annäherungen,* p. 425.

63 Ibid., p. 312.

64 Saul Friedländer, *Reflections of Nazism: An Essay on Kitsch and Death* (1984; Bloomington: Indiana University Press, 1993), p. 135.

65 On his esteem for Boethius, see *Strahlungen,* February 13, 1940.

66 See Hansjörg Schelle's discussion of this point in his *Ernst Jüngers Marmorklippen,* pp. 30–34.

67 *Gärten und Strassen,* August 19, 1939.

68 Hervier, pp. 109–10.

69 Ibid., p. 111.

70 Ibid., p. 111.

71 During the war, *Marmorklippen* had one reissue: twenty thousand copies from the Wehrmacht's press in Paris. There was a Swiss printing in 1943, the year *Stahlgewitter* reached its twenty-fifth edition.

6. In the Golden Cage of Suffering

1 Introduction to *Strahlungen,* p. 11. Most citations from the *Strahlungen* are from the Klett-Cotta edition of Jünger's *Sämtliche Werke* (1978). The dates are given parenthetically within the text in lieu of notes with page numbers. Texts cited other than the 1978 edition are the 1949 edition of the Paris diaries, *Strahlungen* (Tübingen: Heliopolis Verlag), and *Gärten und Strassen* (Berlin: E. S. Mittler, 1942). The latter two are cited only for passages that Jünger omitted or substantially revised for the later edition.

2 Ibid.

3 For contrast, see Walter Bloem's tender remarks on leaving his wife and children, in his account, *The Advance from Mons 1914,* trans. G. C. Wynne (London: Peter Davies, 1930), pp. 9–10.

4 *Gärten und Strassen* (Berlin: E. S. Mittler, 1942), p. 188. Jünger expunged this passage from the Klett edition of *Strahlungen.*

5 *Gärten und Strassen* was issued in the same edition by the "Central Office of Front Bookshops," Paris, 1942. The Luftwaffe ran a nonmarketed special edition of five thousand copies from a press in Riga in May 1943, with three thousand more in October.

6 Jean Guéhenno, *Journal des années noires* (Paris: Gallimard, 1947), p. 102. The date was January 7, 1941.

7 See his report in RW 35/116, Anlage 3, no. 500/40, p. 51, Militärarchiv, Freiburg-im-Breisgau. Hereafter this depository is cited as MA.

8 See RW 35/117, Anlage 67, November 11, 1940, p. 150, MA.

9 Guéhenno, *Journal des années noires,* p. 138 (March 24, 1941).

10 "Beitrag für das KTB (Kriegstagebuch)," RW 35/119, February 11, 1941, p. 73, MA.

11 See "Besondere Anordnungen für die Rückwartigen Dienste, Nr. 25," RW 35/119, January 31, 1941, p. 13, MA.

12 "Aufgabe und Stellung des Quartiermeister des Bez. Chefs und Ihre Bedeutung für den Aufbau einer bodenständigen Versorgung," RW 35/119, February 7, 1941, MA.

13   The italics are Jünger's.

14   "Tagebericht Dezember/Januar," RW 35/286, January 31, 1941, pp. 18, 19, MA.

15   "Richtlinien für die Zusammenarbeit zwischen dem Militärbefehlshaber und dem Beauftragten des Chefs der Sicherheitspolizei und des Sicherheitsdienst in Frankreich," RW 35/32, March 23, 1941, p. 8, MA.

16   Hans Speidel, *Aus unserer Zeit* (Berlin/Frankfurt: Ullstein, 1977), p. 110.

17   Recovered from the ignominy lodged in it, the Majestic, a stately, forbidding specimen of Third Republic architecture (it was opened in 1908) is now the Centre de Conferences Internationales. The Raphael has continued as a four-star hotel to this day.

18   See his entry on women for November 18, 1941, in the 1949 edition, subsequently omitted.

19   Guéhenno, *Journal,* p. 357 (January 12, 1943).

20   These remarks date from the diary entry of May 10, 1945.

21   By the time the Germans left Paris in August 1944, the Majestic's "guests" numbered over a thousand.

22   See his interview with David Pryce-Jones in the latter's *Paris in the Third Reich* (London: Collins, 1981), p. 251. This is an excellent, albeit informal source on the Occupation, especially regarding Heller, whose diaries of 1940–1944 were lost.

23   "Politische Lage in Frankreich," RW 35/238, no. 407/41, January 25, 1941, p. 3, MA. Speidel's emphasis.

24   RW 35/238, no. 3560/41, July 25, 1941, MA.

25   Guéhenno, *Journal,* p. 179 (June 23, 1941).

26   RW 35/238, no. 5300/41, October 30, 1941, p. 3, MA.

27   RW 35/238, no. 6300/41, December 25, 1941, pp. 2, 4, MA.

28   Ibid., p. 7.

29   In his journal for December 7, 1941, Jünger refers to "Merline." His second entry (see *infra*) indicates "Céline." The first French translation of Jünger's Paris journals, published in August 1951, de-coded "Merline" into "Céline." Céline then sued the publisher, René Julliard. "Merline" was a Frenchman in the SS, Philippe Merlen, who had committed suicide in 1944. That Jünger meant Céline in the first instance seems likely from the characterization of a "stone age" mentality in both entries. Complicating matters still further, Jünger wrote a letter to Marcel Jouhandeau stating that "Merline" was not Céline. With that letter he wrote to Céline himself that "this alteration, which I very keenly regret and the hidden motives of which are obscure to me, was done without my knowing it. I do not approve of your views, but nothing is further from my mind than wishing to cause you harm. Should you be attacked on the basis of this passage, I beg you to refer it to me. I shall deny that it refers to you." L.-F. Céline, *Lettres à Texier* (Paris: La Flute de Pan, 1985), p. 111. Jünger had also submitted a letter to Julliard stating that "Merline" *was* Céline. With

this stalemate the proceedings dragged on until Céline's lawyer persuaded him to drop the suit.

30   Several French writers were invited to tour Katyn. Robert Brassilach accepted. Céline did not but must have mentioned the invitation to Jünger, perhaps with boastful enthusiasm.

31   Quoted from the 1949 edition, p. 311; omitted in Klett.

32   In *Aus unserer Zeit*, p. 110, Speidel claims he asked Jünger "at the start of his activity" (spring, 1941) "to investigate the subterranean struggle between the Party and the Wehrmacht . . . particularly the hostage question and its effect upon the political situation." But the hostage issue arose only after the invasion of Russia. Speidel's dating is anachronistic, and Jünger says it was Stülpnagel himself, not Speidel, who ordered him to gather notes.

33   In an entry of January 4, 1942, he remarked a theologian's view that evil first appears bearing light (Lucifer) but ends by annihilating (Satan).

34   On the Germans' efforts to exploit the National Library's archives there are two ample documentary accounts in Freiburg's Militärarchiv, RW/485 and RW/492.

35   "Übergang der polizeilichen Exekutive," RW 35/32, May 29, 1942, p. 35, MA.

36   This is the number given by military historian Earl F. Ziemke, *Stalingrad to Berlin: The German Defeat in the East* (1968; New York: Military Heritage Press, 1985), p. 79. He qualifies that "the exact total was apparently never determined."

37   For a positive assessment of Kleist's service in the east see Samuel W. Mitcham, Jr., "Kleist," in *Hitler's Generals*, ed. Correlli Barnett (New York: Grove Weidenfeld, 1989), pp. 249–63.

38   On December 27, 1942, Jünger inveighs against the loudspeaker's "impious underworld tones," its "demonic brazenness" (*Gekecker*).

39   Joseph Goebbels, *Der steile Aufstieg* (Munich: Zentralverlag der NSDAP, 1944), p. 180. This address offers a kind of *summa* of Nazi ideology. It is remarkable in its bid for a "revolutionary" zeal and an end to "bourgeois sensitivities" (p. 181) as Germany prepares for a life-and-death struggle with Russia.

 For a close analysis of the speech and its composition see Günther Moltmann, "Goebbels Rede zum Totalen Krieg am 18. Februar 1943," *Vierteljahrshefte für Zeitgeschichte* 12 (January 1964): 13–43. As Moltmann indicates, the Sportpalast audience of about fifteen thousand interrupted this two-hour speech over two hundred times with approving shouts and applause.

40   *Kriegsbriefe Gefallener Studenten, 1939–1945*, ed. Walter and Hans Bähr (Tübingen: Rainer Wunderlich, 1952), p. 395.

41   Hans Speidel, *Invasion 1944: Ein Beitrag zu Rommels und des Reiches Schicksal* (Tübingen: Rainer Wunderlich, 1949), p. 85. "In this apocalyptic time with its fearsome stresses Jünger's summons exerted an almost mythic force and created its own agents." Speidel's original, unpublished statement is more temperate: "In the month of May,

Ernst Juenger [*sic*], who served as captain in the staff of General von Stülpnagel, also presented his work on 'The Peace.' This work, the fundamental ideas of which the author had already expounded to me in the winter of 1941–42, made a deep impression on Field Marshal Rommel. He agreed with Juenger's idea of peace and envisaged the publication of the work on a large scale, in due time." See Dr. Hans Speidel, "To the History of Events Preceding 20 July 1944 Ideas of and Preparations Made by Field Marshal Rommel for an Independent Termination of the War in the West and the Elimination of National Socialist Despotism," Imperial War Museum document AL 914, B-271. This work is dated June 16, 1947, from Freudenstadt.

42 For an appreciative essay on this man, see Klaus-Jürgen Müller, "Witzleben, Stülpnagel, and Speidel," in *Hitler's Generals,* ed. Correlli Barnett (New York: Grove Weidenfeld, 1989), pp. 43–72.

43 It was not a complete failure. While Hitler believed his survival providential, Jünger saw it otherwise: "Stauffenberg's bomb took not his life away but his aura; you could even hear it in his voice," he recalled when learning of Hitler's suicide, May 1, 1945.

44 See Speidel's account in *Aus unserer Zeit,* pp. 226–28.

45 ". . . sinnvoler und zweckloser." Jünger likely uses "zwecklos" in Kant's aesthetic sense, "Zweckmässigkeit ohne Zweck," direction without a practical goal and therefore disinterested.

46 So claims Himmler's aide, Wolfram Sievers, who was hanged after the war for selecting people used in "medical experiments."

47 Rolf Hochhuth, "Besuch bei Jünger," in his *Täter und Denker: Profile und Probleme von Cäsar bis Jünger* (Stuttgart: Deutsche Verlags-Anstalt, 1988), p. 377.

48 Hans-Peter Schwarz, *Der konservative Anarchist: Politik und Zeitkritik Ernst Jüngers* (Freiburg-im-Breisgau: Rombach, Freiburger Studien zu Politik und Soziologie, 1962), p. 65.

49 Albert Speer, *Spandau: The Secret Diaries,* trans. Richard and Clara Winston (Glasgow: William Collins Sons, 1977), p. 333.

50 John Ruskin, *Modern Painters,* vol. 2, appendix 2, p. 389 (Library Edition).

51 Ian Buruma, "The Anarch at Twilight," *New York Review of Books,* June 24, 1993, p. 28.

52 Nikolaus Sombart, "Jünger in uns," *Streit-Zeit-Schrift* 6, no. 2 (September 1968): 8.

53 My emphasis.

54 See his conversation with Eckermann, February 18, 1829.

55 See his letter of March 3, 1827, to Christian von Buttel.

56 Letter of January 25, 1813, to Johann Falk.

57 *Maximen und Reflexionen,* 433.

58 All citations in this paragraph are from "Schlachtfeld der Seele," *Der Tag,* no. 21, September 21, 1928 (unpaginated).

59 *Journal de Léon Bloy,* in *Oeuvres* (Paris: Mercure de France, 1963), 12:301. Bloy writes "inventeur," not "découvreur." The former denotes "discoverer" only in terms of a process. It is as though radium, in his mind, was not an element but a contrivance.

60 See his entries of June 26, 1940, November 12, 1941, and March 28, 1942, for these analogies.

61 See RW 35/18, Stabsbefehl 89/42, September 30, 1942, MA.

62 For the notice see RW 35/18, Stabsbefehl 7/43, February 18, 1943 — the day of Goebbels's "total war" address.

63 1949 ed., p. 426 (omitted from the Klett edition).

64 To Eckermann, March 11, 1832. See also *Wilhelm Meisters Wanderjahre* 2:2.

65 When in November 1943 Jünger met the head of the Red Cross, they exchanged "the secret signs by which you recognize each other these days," and discussed desert island reading. She said if there were but two books to choose, the Bible would be the first. Jünger concurred and added the *1001 Nights.* "Thus two Orientalia" (November 13, 1943).

66 *AHi*, p. 57.

67 *AHi*, pp. 49–50.

68 *AHi*, pp. 87–88.

Postlude

1 For a review of its composition, see Gerhard Loose, "Zur Entstehungsgeschichte von Ernst Jüngers Schrift *Der Friede*," *Modern Language Notes* 74, no. 1 (January 1959): 51–58.

2 *AHi*, pp. 88–89.

3 *Strahlungen*, November 23, 1941; December 3, 1941.

4 Ibid., January 5, 1942; January 28, 1942. Both entries come from the 1949 edition. In revising for Klett's first collection of his works, Jünger omitted "Great Man" and added: "In so far as he gives chiefly of himself, he does so for others as well."

5 *Der Friede*, in *Sämtliche Werke* (Stuttgart: Klett, 1978), 7:204. All citations are from this edition.

6 Ibid., 202.

7 Ibid., 203.

8 Ibid.

9 Ibid., 206.

10 Ibid., 225.

11 As Guéhenno's journal is a foil to Jünger's Paris diaries, so is Theodor Haecker's "night books," a diary from within Nazi Germany, a foil to *The Peace.* Haecker, a journalist, was converted to Catholicism in 1920. His diary spans the war, ending with his death a month before Germany surrendered. Limned with near despondence, this writing is pertinent to *The Peace* because Haecker, groping for a theodicy, reckons the war in strictly spiritual terms, precisely those which Jünger misses: a contest between Christianity and an apostate Germany.

12 Ibid., 233.

13   See Arthur A. Cohen, "The Holocaust and Christian Theology: An Interpretation of the Problem," in *Judaism and Christianity under the Impact of National Socialism, 1919–1945,* ed. Otto Dov Kulka and Paul R. Mendes-Flohr (Jerusalem: Historical Society of Israel and the Zalman Center for Jewish History, 1987), pp. 424, 427.

14   Hans Speidel in Armin Mohler, ed., *Freundschaftliche Begegnungen: Festschrift für Ernst Jünger zum 60. Geburtstag* (Frankfurt, 1955), p. 189.

15   The 1979 edition reads: "I constantly swam against the current and never in the undertow of any of the ruling powers."

16   *Strahlungen* (1949 ed.), p. 13.

17   In *Strahlungen,* p. 508 (April 29, 1944), he says the plotters are prompted by moral, not political considerations and would succeed "only if a Sulla appeared, indeed a simple *Volksgeneral,*" by whom he possibly meant Rommel, not yet recruited to the plot.

18   *Strahlungen,* pp. 13–14.

19   A journal entry of October 28: "Germany's fate is in doubt unless a new knightly order arises from its youth, and especially from its workers."

20   In his preface to *The Peace,* translated for the American edition by Stuart Hood (Hillsdale, Ill.: Regnery, 1948), Jünger claims the essay "was ready in its present form in the summer of 1943," but this could hardly be the case. Jünger might mean that in its basic convictions and arguments the essay had reached completion in 1943, but even granting that, summer would have been too early. See Loose, "Zur Entstehungsgeschichte," 57.

21   *Strahlungen,* p. 510. In the 1949 edition Jünger says "Speidel sent me a secret courier who fetched the manuscript," but only in the Klett does he mention Rommel, "who wants to read it." Only in the later text does he part with *The Peace* "reluctantly."

22   March 27, 1944: "The fatherland is now in the greatest danger. The catastrophe isn't to be diverted, only mitigated and modified, since the breakdown in the east is a more terrible threat than that in the west and is undoubtedly tied in with massacres on a grand scale. Consequently, something must be done in the west, and certainly before a landing. . . . A presupposition is the disappearance of Kniébolo, who is to be blown sky high. The best opportunity for that would be during the strategy meeting at headquarters." On this date, Hofacker gave Jünger the names of the conspiracy's inner circle.

23   March 27, 1944 (1949 ed.).

Selected Bibliography

Published Works of Ernst Jünger

There are two collected editions of Ernst Jünger's writings:

Werke. 10 vols. Stuttgart: Klett-Cotta, 1960–64.

Sämtliche Werke. 18 vols. Stuttgart: Klett-Cotta, 1978–83.

In German literary history only four authors have lived to see a second edition of their collected works. The others are Wieland, Klopstock, and Goethe. The definitive bibliography is by Hans Peter des Coudres and Horst Mühleisen, *Bibliographie der Werke Ernst Jüngers* (Stuttgart: Cotta, 1985).

BOOKS

In Stahlgewittern: Aus dem Tagebuch eines Stosstruppführers (SG). Leisnig: Robert Meier, 1920.

Der Kampf als Inneres Erlebnis (KIE). Berlin: Mittler, 1922.

Das Wäldchen 125: Eine Chronik aus den Grabenkämpfen, 1918 (W125). Berlin: Mittler, 1925.

Feuer und Blut: Ein kleiner Ausschnitt aus einer grossen Schlacht (FB). Magdeburg: Stahlhelm Verlag, 1925.

Das abenteuerliche Herz: Aufzeichnungen bei Tag und Nacht (AH1). Berlin: Frundsberg, 1929.

Der Arbeiter: Herrschaft und Gestalt (A). Hamburg: Hanseatische Verlaganstalt, 1932.

Blätter und Steine. Hamburg: Hanseatische Verlaganstalt, 1934.

Afrikanische Spiele (AS). Hamburg: Hanseatische Verlaganstalt, 1936.

Das abenteuerliche Herz: Figuren und Capriccios (AH2). Hamburg: Hanseatische Verlaganstalt, 1938.

Auf den Marmorklippen (MK). Hamburg: Hanseatische Verlaganstalt, 1939.

Gärten und Strassen. Berlin: Mittler, 1942.

Der Friede: Ein Wort an die Jugend Europas und an die Jugend der Welt. Hamburg: Hanseatische Verlaganstalt, 1945.

Sprache und Körperbau. Zürich: Verlag der Arche, 1947.

Atlantische Fahrt. Zürich: Verlag der Arche, 1947.

Myrdun: Briefe aus Norwegen. Zürich: Verlag der Arche, 1948.

Ein Inselfrühling. Zürich: Verlag der Arche, 1948.

Heliopolis: Ruckblick auf eine Stadt. Tübingen: Heliopolis, 1949.

Strahlungen: Der erste Pariser Tagebuch, Kaukasische Aufzeichnungen, Der zweite Pariser Tagebuch, Kirchhorster Blätter (PT). Tübingen: Heliopolis, 1949.

Über die Linie. Frankfurt am Main: Klostermann, 1950.

Der Waldgang. Frankfurt am Main: Klostermann, 1951.

Besuch auf Godenholm. Frankfurt am Main: Klostermann, 1952.

Der Gordische Knoten. Frankfurt am Main: Klostermann, 1953.

Das Sanduhrbuch. Frankfurt am Main: Klostermann, 1954.

Am Sarazenenturm. Frankfurt am Main: Klostermann, 1955.

Rivarol. Frankfurt am Main: Klostermann, 1956.

Gläserne Bienen. Stuttgart: Klett, 1957.

Jahre der Okkupation. Stuttgart: Klett, 1958.

An der Zeitmauer. Stuttgart: Klett, 1959.

Der Weltstaat: Organismus und Organisation. Stuttgart: Klett, 1960.

Sgraffiti. Stuttgart: Klett, 1960.

Sturm. Olten: Georg Rentsch Sons, 1963.

Typus, Namen, Gestalt. Stuttgart: Klett, 1963.

Geheimnisse der Sprache. Frankfurt am Main: Klostermann, 1963.

Grenzgänge: Essays, Reden, Träume. Stuttgart: Klett, 1966.

Subtile Jagden. Stuttgart: Klett, 1967.

Ad hoc. Stuttgart: Klett, 1970.

Annäherungen: Drogen und Rausch. Stuttgart: Klett, 1970.

Sinn und Bedeutung: ein Figurenspiel. Stuttgart: Klett, 1971.

Philemon und Baucis: Der Tod in der mythischen und in der technischen Welt. Stuttgart: Klett, 1972.

Die Zwille. Stuttgart: Klett, 1973.

Zahlen und Götter. Stuttgart: Klett, 1974.

Eumeswil. Stuttgart: Klett, 1977.

Siebzig verweht I. Stuttgart: Klett-Cotta, 1980.

Siebzig verweht II. Stuttgart: Klett-Cotta, 1981.

Maxima-Minima: Adnoten zum "Arbeiter". Stuttgart: Klett-Cotta, 1983.

Aladins Problem. Stuttgart: Klett-Cotta, 1983.

Eine gefährliche Begegnung. Stuttgart: Klett-Cotta, 1983.

Autor und Autorschaft. Stuttgart: Klett-Cotta, 1984.

Zweimal Halley. Stuttgart: Klett-Cotta, 1987.

Die Schere. Stuttgart: Klett-Cotta, 1990.

Siebzig verweht III. Stuttgart: Klett-Cotta, 1993.

Siebzig verweht IV. Stuttgart: Klett-Cotta, 1995.

ENGLISH TRANSLATIONS

The Storm of Steel. Trans. Basil Creighton. New York: Doubleday, Doran, and London: Chatto and Windus, 1929.

Copse 125. Trans. Basil Creighton. London: Chatto and Windus, 1930.

On the Marble Cliffs. Trans. Stuart Hood. London: John Lehmann, 1947.

The Peace. Trans. Stuart Hood. Hinsdale, Ill.: Regnery, 1948.

African Diversions. Trans. Stuart Hood. London: John Lehmann, 1954.

The Glass Bees. Trans. Louise Bogan and Elizabeth Mayer. New York: Noonday, 1960.

Aladdin's Problem. Trans. Joachim Neugroschel. New York: Marsilio, 1992.

A Dangerous Encounter. Trans. Hilary Barr. New York: Marsilio, 1993.

Eumeswil. Trans. Joachim Neugroschel. New York: Marsilio, 1993.

The following essays have been selected and annotated chiefly for their polemical content. Few are neutral; most indicate how Jünger's reputation has been shaped or caricatured since 1945. As an Auschwitz survivor, Jean Améry, wrote of Jünger nearly forty years ago, "Perhaps the strongest evidence for his value as a writer is that he leaves no one indifferent."

General Studies of Jünger

Bohrer, Karl Heinz. *Die Ästhetik des Schreckens: Die pessimistische Romantik und Ernst Jüngers Frühwerk.* Munich: Carl Hanser, 1978. Centers upon the two versions of *Das abenteuerliche Herz* to conceptualize Jünger's "phenomenology of angst": an iconography of horror based upon violent surprise is made normative through stoic contemplation; Jünger ennobles the moment of horror by stylizing it into a harmony. A long, dense study, rich in cosmopolitan literary references, especially to Jünger's precursors in so-called decadence: Poe, Baudelaire, Wilde.

Bullock, Marcus Paul. *The Violent Eye: Ernst Jünger's Visions and Revisions on the European Right.* Detroit: Wayne State University Press, 1992. An excellent series of critical essays on Jünger's aesthetics, concentrated primarily upon brief passages from the second edition of *Das abenteuerliche Herz.* Bullock's critical perspective, however, owes much to Walter Benjamin, from whose Marxism and Jewish mysticism Jünger could not be more distant.

Kaempfer, Wolfgang. *Ernst Jünger.* Stuttgart: J. B. Metzler, 1981. A relentlessly hostile leftist survey of Jünger's writing, ingathering all possible charges against him: sadomasochism, nihilism, solipsism, "bourgeois compromising of truth," etc. Only *Afrikanische Spiele* escapes this critic's harsh verdict.

Loose, Gerhard. *Ernst Jünger: Gestalt und Werk.* Frankfurt am Main: Vittorio Klostermann, 1957. A courageous work that, at a time when Jünger's reputation was at its lowest ebb, evenhandedly surveyed his writing to date. Loose's dispassionate tone and scrupulous attention to the texts, which he reads as the record of an adventurer, prove a welcome antidote to ad hominem attacks upon Jünger by some subsequent writers. Loose has also written a short work on Jünger for the Twayne World Authors series.

Stern, J. P. *Ernst Jünger*. Cambridge: Bowes and Bowes, 1953. A brief but penetrating essay, its arguments insightfully centered upon Jünger's metaphoric language. While commending Jünger's depictions of war for their brilliant accuracy and admitting our common "quasi-erotic" fascination with violence, Stern censures his "radically defective sensibility" for its incapacity to feel. Stern's discussion of Jünger in the posthumously published *Dear Purchase: A Theme in German Modernism* (Cambridge: Cambridge University Press, 1995) adds disappointingly little to this original discussion.

The Wilhelmine Era

Eley, Geoff. "The Wilhelmine Right: How It Changed." In Richard J. Evans, ed., *Society and Politics in Wilhelmine Germany,* pp. 112–35. London: Croom and Helm, 1978. Challenges the historiography which established a continuity between Wilhelmine conservatism and Nazism, and rejects the biographical focus of Fritz Stern's "cultural despair" thesis. It argues that the German Right had to galvanize support from ascendant agrarian and artisan leagues and from the urban white-collar class in order to head off the proletariat's rising power. This article informs us about the "masses" before Spengler and Jünger recoiled from them.

Hermand, Jost. "Germania Germanicissima: Zum präfaschistischen Arierkult um 1900." In *Der Schein des schönen Lebens: Studien zum Jahrhundertwende,* pp. 39–54. Frankfurt: Athenäum, 1972. An exacting view of ground-level racism in the time of Jünger's childhood, this essay examines the viciously emotive chauvinism that Hitler later passed off as his own creation. German unification in 1871 failed to bring national identity because it lacked a *völkisch* movement. This failure bred a hydra-headed irrationalism of quests for "an imperialism of the soul." Hermand reviews antimaterialist neoromanticism in the bunds and the emergence of a bourgeois master-slave ideology to justify repression of workers.

The First World War

Herwig, Holger H. "The Dynamics of Necessity: German Military Policy during the First World War." In Alan Millett and Williamson Murray, eds., *Military Effectiveness: The First World War,* pp. 80–115. Boston: Unwin Hyman, 1988. A well-documented review of politics and economics in Germany's war effort, this essay argues that the Schlieffen Plan was impracticable from the start because Germany did not have the technological resources to match the Allied defense. Its industrial profile in the war shows why Jünger's program of total mobilization would have been impossible.

Höfler, Günther A. "Das neue Paradigma des Krieges und seine literarischen Repräsentationen." In Franz Karl Stangel and Martin Loschnigg, eds., *Intimate Enemies: English and German Literary Reactions to the Great War, 1914–1918,* pp. 277–91. Heidelberg: Carl Winter, 1993. Argues that war technology in 1914–1918 fragmented participants' consciousness into a cinematic disjunction of their combat experience. Jünger is cited as the primary example, but his fragmentary narrative is a function of the daybook accounts he kept, then wrote up in memoirs.

Möser, Kurt. "Kriegsgeschichte und Kriegsliterature-Formen der Verarbeitung des Ersten Weltkrieges." *Militärgeschichtliche Mittleilungen* 2 (1986): 39–51. Reviews in German and English sources the discrepancy between official combat reports and testimony from those "below" like Ludwig Renn and Robert Graves. Notes that Jünger rationalizes his experience in terms of technical-tactical knowledge but does not put staff historiography in question; he writes independently of it. Unlike some late-twenties German war novelists, he does not heroize whole companies.

Müller, Hans-Harald. "Die Verflüchtigung des Sinns des Kriegserlebnisses . . . Ernst Jüngers Frühwerk und das Kriegserlebnis." In *Der Krieg und die Schriftsteller der Weimarer Republik,* pp. 211–95. Stuttgart: J. B. Metzler, 1966. Of particular value for its thorough reading of *Battle as Inner Experience.* Müller finds Jünger's anthropology of barbarism incompatible with *Stahlgewitter*'s heroic model and the war's technology. An excellent discussion of Jünger's *Sturm* and of the Weimar essays; Müller sees naïveté resorting to romantic subjectivism—i.e., Jünger's "magical understanding" is (contra Bohrer) premodern. The odd gap in this otherwise brilliant essay is Müller's negligence of *Stahlgewitter*'s 1926 and 1934 revisions.

———. " 'Herr Jünger thinks war a lovely business,': On the Reception of Ernst Jünger's *In Stahlgewittern* in Germany and Britain before 1933," in Stangel and Loschnigg (see entry on Höfler), pp. 327–40. Argues that English critical reception of *In Stahlgewittern* in Basil Creighton's translation was favorable because it was regarded as a literary and not political text. Müller cynically suggests that Jünger played up to British prejudices by a flattering portrayal of English fighting in the war. He overstates Jünger's popularity in Britain. *Storm of Steel* quickly went through five editions but was reprinted only in 1994; *Stahlgewitter* had an enduring, though less splashy, appeal in Germany for over a generation. From 1920 to 1940 it never went out of print.

Segeberg, Harro. "Regressive Modernisierung: Kriegserlebnis und Moderne-Kritik in Ernst Jüngers Frühwerk." *Wirkendes Wort* 39, no. 1 (1989): 95–111. Argues the cohesion of Jünger's politics and aesthetics. "Regressive modernization" means renaturalizing war, bringing back heroic themes that war technology had made anachronistic. As a work process, war is symbolically elevated; it becomes instrumental in the regression to a primeval elitism. Overstates the bonds of camaraderie and a collective will to aggression in Jünger's early works; they are more evident in *Battle as Inner Experience* than in the memoirs.

———. " 'Letzthin ist der Untergang das einzige Normale': Über Krieg und Technik im Frühwerk Ernst Jüngers." *Der Deutschunterricht* 41 (October 1989): 20–27. Contends that

the elitism of "organic construction" and "an aesthetic metapolitics" of a technoid race
are evident from the first edition of *In Stahlgewittern;* that is, the autonomous *Stahlgestalten* of *The Worker* are already present in Jünger's earliest war writing.

Woods, Roger. "The Conservative Revolution and the First World War: Literature as Evidence in Historical Explanation." *Modern Language Review* 85, pt. 1 (January 1990): 72–91.
Succinctly pleads for restoration of literary contextual studies to counter the predominance of social history. Cites the profound ambivalence about war in Jünger's memoirs
and claims the Conservative Revolution's notions of heroism came from the war's implicit meaninglessness: meaning had to be salvaged and so it was internalized; war and
the courage to wage it became ends in themselves.

The Weimar Era

Bein, Sigfrid. "Der Arbeiter." In Heinz Ludwig Arnold, ed., *Wandlung und Wiederkehr: Festschrift zum 70. Geburtstag Ernst Jüngers,* pp. 107–16. Aachen: Georgi, 1965. A summary
of *The Worker,* arguing it mirrors its time and seeks to expose the sources of that time's
unrest. Of special interest is this essay's antithetical conjunction of *The Worker* with Jünger's 1951 *Waldgang,* where the defenseless individual must protect freedom in the face
of necessity.

Berman, Russell. "Written Right Across Their Faces: Ernst Jünger's Fascist Modernism."
In Andreas Huyssen and David Bathrick, eds., *Modernity and the Text: Revisions of German
Modernism,* pp. 60–80. New York: Columbia University Press, 1989. Makes an ingenious
but overwrought charge that *The Worker* amounts to a fascist bid for the destruction of
writing itself; also, that Jünger, an antipatriarch and therefore fascist, is anti-Semitic.
Suggests Jünger's fascism is prompted by survivor's guilt from the Great War.

Herf, Jeffrey. "Ernst Jünger's Magical Realism." In *Reactionary Modernism: Technology, Culture, and Politics in Weimar and the Third Reich,* pp. 70–108. Cambridge: Cambridge University Press, 1984. Assesses Jünger's romanticization of technology but curiously fails
to discuss *Stahlgewitter,* the indispensable first text, and the essential first essays on technology, in military journals. Herf dismisses *Stahlgewitter* in a phrase, as "a spectacularly
aestheticized version of life in the trenches" (p. 72) without noting on which version
of the work this judgment rests.

Hermand, Jost. "Explosion in the Swamp: Jünger's *Worker* (1932)." In Teresa de Lauretis,
Andreas Huyssen, Kathleen Woodward, eds., *The Technological Imagination,* pp. 123–31.
Madison, Wis.: Coda Press, 1980. A harsh estimate, that *The Worker* is mostly Nietzsche
and Spengler *rechauffée* and Jünger ideologically "more merciless, more bestial" than
the Nazis, "for he was openly steering toward chaos and the end of the world" (p. 130).
Overstatement.

Hielscher, Friedrich. "Ernst Jünger," in his *Fünfzig Jahre unter Deutschen.* Hamburg: Rowohlt, 1954, pp. 111–17. With Jünger in Leipzig during the twenties. Hielscher forgets
his then Nietzschean fanaticism, contrasting his "scholastic, yet extroverted" character

with Jünger's, distant and observant. He claims to favor grace and mysticism to Jünger's conjury and magic.

Kahler, Erich. "Nihilism and the Rule of Technics." In *Man the Measure*, pp. 567–602. New York: George Braziller, 1956. Jünger is important in seeing "with terrible clarity" the masses' role in a world made nihilistic by technology. Kahler finds Jünger's view of technology descriptive, not theoretical, yet he asserts that Jünger "bears the greatest responsibility for preparing the German youth for the Hitler state, between 1920 and 1933" (p. 594). Walter Laqueur's *Weimar Culture* contends that Jünger's influence among Weimar youth groups was slight. Kahler confuses Jünger's articulation with influence.

Ohana, David. "Nietzsche and Ernst Jünger: From Nihilism to Totalitarianism." *History of European Ideas* 11 (1989): 751–58. My objections: (1) Jünger's vitalism is not reducible by *Quellenforschungen;* (2) *The Worker's* organicism owes more to Spengler as mediator than to Nietzsche himself; (3) Jünger's Will to Power issues in a statism Nietzsche would likely have rejected.

Orr, John. "German Social Theory and the Hidden Face of Technology." *European Journal of Sociology* 15 (1974): 312–36. Establishes the seminal influence of Jünger's technology of *Gestalt* on Herbert Marcuse's *One Dimensional Man*. A shrewd assessment of *The Worker's* "anti-humanist and metaphysical" (equivalent terms?) conflation of human and natural energy and its degradation of individual work. Orr caricatures *Stahlgewitter* as "a gospel of sacrifice and death," and errs in saying that Jünger's "perverse and ecstatic pessimism" made him reject technology's role in "historical progress."

Prümm, Karl. *Soldatischer Nationalismus der 20er Jahre (1918–1933)*. Kronberg Taunus: Scriptor, 1974. A magisterial account, thoroughly well-documented and densely argued, of Jünger's writing from *Stahlgewitter* to *Der Arbeiter*. In that Prümm thoroughly researched the materials he discusses, he is entitled to his hostile, one might say historical-polemical, view of Jünger. Two faults require notice: though not a psychologist, Prümm uses clinical terms such as "traumatic-pathological" to characterize Jünger's writing. He also overestimates Jünger's politics in the twenties as though he had a programmatic intent or ambition. As his elitism sat too uncertainly with his vision of a soldier-worker state, the supposition of a Jüngerian ideology seems doubtful. Still, this is one of the best books on Jünger and deserves translation.

Rausch, Jürgen. "Ernst Jünger oder die Qual des Bewusstseins." In *Der Mensch als Martyrer und Monstrum*, pp. 201–23. Stuttgart: Deutsches Verlags-Anstalt, 1957. One of the best essays on Jünger, impartial and insightful. Rausch discusses Jünger's distancing stereoptics, his search for identity between wonder and reality, his "immoral plasticity of conception" that allows him to yoke opposites and to transcend causality in favor of mystery. He sees honestly the hazards in Jünger's Olympian removal, that his ever-refining consciousness tends to instrumentalize experience and subordinate it as a key to some hieratic unity: "He is a suffering man who with all his wealth still is unable to close the wound which the faithlessness of his age has torn" (pp. 215–16).

Reimann, Bruno W. and Renate Hassel. *Ein Ernst Jünger Brevier: Jüngers politische Publizistik*

1920 bis 1933: Analyse und Dokumentation. Marburg: BiWi-Verlag (Forum Wissenschaft Studien, 31), 1995. The documentation from the 1920s polemics is generously quoted but the "analysis" is at times perverse with wildly wrong-headed claims such as "of Jünger's anti-Semitism there can be no doubt."

Struve, Walter. "Ernst Jünger: Warriors, Workers, and Elite," in his *Elites against Democracy.* Princeton: Princeton University Press, 1973, pp. 377–414. Excellent analysis of *The Worker,* Jünger's audience, and his style. Reading *The Worker,* "one often feels in the midst of a dream—or nightmare. Every image, every scene seems precise, but on reflection becomes obscure. . . . [It] moves gracefully from one point to the next but no point ever seems to be completed" (p. 381). Struve finds the style diagnostic rather than programmatic and sees the book's projections and its conceptual failures as derivatives of the war. The claim that "Jünger was obsessed by the need for manipulating people" (p. 412) lacks clinical warrant.

Marmorklippen *and the Third Reich*

David, Claude. "Ernst Jünger: Das abenteuerliche Herz." *Studi germanici* 21–22, nos. 59–64 (1983–1984): 239–54. Contrasts the two versions: preoccupation with political issues in 1929 gives way to Goethean naturalia in 1938. David sees in the second a new theology of cheer amid terror, a sense of the void, and a commingling of beauty with horror. Both versions proclaim the same truths but differently.

Hochhuth, Rolf. "Besuch bei Jünger." In *Täter und Denker: Profile und Probleme von Cäsar bis Jünger,* pp. 347–68. Stuttgart: Deutsche Verlags-Anstalt, 1988. Germany's foremost living dramatist considers Jünger as a target of controversy. Because "among people who judge authors without reading them Jünger is still placed in the vicinity of the Nazis or even of anti-Semites," Hochhuth focuses on facts that set Jünger apart from and against the Hitler regime. He concludes with a vigorous defense of Jünger's continuing value, which lies for him not least in Jünger's Goethean pull against the materialist tendencies of the age.

Kaempfer, Wolfgang. "Das schöne Böse: Zum ästhetischen Verfahren Ernst Jüngers in den Schriften der dreissigen Jahre," *Recherches germaniques* 14 (1984): 103–17. One of the harshest estimates of Jünger's work in the thirties, this essay argues that Jünger's aesthetic does not fuse form with experience; it is a preconceived program, the montage of a postromantic neurosis with an intoxicant, narcissistic rhetoric. Jünger differs from Nietzsche in taking subjective obsessions as objective facts.

———. "Literatur als Alibi: Zum Perspektivismus in den Schriften Ernst Jüngers." *Studi germanici* 21–22, nos. 59–64 (1983–1984): 255–71. Jünger's narrative does not resolve into a corrected or completed perspective but into ambiguity: whose voice are we hearing, the dandy's, the soldier's, the entomologist's? Attacks on the bourgeoisie in *The Worker* reflect "status anxiety," and Jünger "exemplifies the European bourgeois torn to pieces."

Kater, Michael. "Anti-Fascist Intellectuals in the Third Reich." *Canadian Journal of History*

16 (August 1981): 263–77. Why didn't they speak out after Hitler came to power? They ceased to be indispensable because German society's deadlock after 1933 meant there was no dynamic for policy making. Reviews the problems of emigration: fear of losing the native German audience, uncertainty of employment abroad, barriers of language, absence of an exilic tradition—even antifascists preferred the hazards at home. Jünger was safe because of his nationalist credentials. Mann, cautioning against self-righteous attacks on the "internal emigrants," condemned them after 1945.

Kiesel, Helmuth. "Ernst Jüngers *Marmorklippen*." *Internationales Archiv für Sozialgeschichte der deutschen Literatur* 14, no. 1 (1989): 126–64. Includes a useful review of critical estimates of this work, evaluates Jünger's "cold-heartedness" but remarks, too, his postwar position on the concentration camps. Claims Jünger's *dandysme* precluded active resistance to Hitler.

Philippi, Klaus-Peter. "'Versinken im Wirbel': Chaos und Ordnung im Werk Ernst Jüngers." *Deutsche Vierteljahrsschrift für Literaturwissenschaft und Geistesgeschichte* 63, no. 1 (March 1989): 154–93. After reviewing the past generation of Jünger's critics, Philippi puts him in the tradition of romantic idealism, but his notion of hidden harmonies amid apparent chaos suggests succession to Angelus Silesius. A convincing discussion of *Abenteuerliches Herz, I* as the philosophical kernel of Jünger's writing.

Schelle, Hansjörg. *Ernst Jüngers Marmorklippen: Eine kritische Interpretation.* Leiden: Brill, 1970. Argues that *Marmorklippen* does not cohere as an epic because the narrative is entirely determined by a fragmentary sensibility and subjective biases.

Stern, J. P. "Representations of the Self, Singular and Collective, from Kleist to Ernst Jünger." *Comparative Criticism* 12 (1990): 3–24. This too brief essay suggests ways in which modern German literature of "the fragmentary self" reflects the epistemological breakdown of the self in Hume, Kant, and Lichtenberg. Jünger in *The Adventurous Heart* (1938) takes the reduction of the "I" to its extreme limits. Stern faults him for making a point of his metaphysics of meaninglessness, and finds this procedure exemplary of "a validating and consoling explication" in German literature between the wars.

The Second World War

Chatwin, Bruce. "Ernst Jünger: An Aesthete at War." In *What Am I Doing Here?* pp. 297–315. New York: Viking, 1989. An impressionistic essay that reiterates caricatures. Chatwin portrays Jünger as the Occupation's dandy, a self-absorbed courtier of the Parisian demimonde. Some brilliant remarks, though, on the Wehrmacht in Paris: "The atmosphere in which he clothes the Military Command reminds one of a Racine tragedy, in which the central characters are either threatened or doomed, and all numbed into elegant paralysis by the howling tyrant offstage."

de Mendelssohn, Peter. "Über die Linie des geringsten Widerstandes." In *Der Geist in der Despotie,* pp. 123–235. Berlin: Grünewald, 1953. A trenchant attack on Jünger, centered on *Marmorklippen* and the Paris diaries. Granting Jünger's descriptive acuity, Mendelssohn finds him eccentrically incapable of apprehending life's human center. Jünger's self-excusing and disingenuous attempts to moralize so as to secure distance from the SS are far more objectionable than his notorious aestheticizing of catastrophes. One of the best studies of the moral issues raised by Jünger's *désinvolture*.

Guder, G. "Ernst Jünger." *German Life and Letters* 2 (1948–1949): 62–71. Discussion of *The Worker* is warped by the assumption that it is a Nazi tract. Guder overstates the Führer-prinzip at the cost of Jünger's elitism of an ascetic corps. He also erroneously reads into Jünger a Spenglerian futility quite at odds with the predominant theme of "organic construction" in a new world order. Guder is right to score *The Peace* for its "failure to shoulder the guilt of Germany" so far as Jünger did not acknowledge in it a collective guilt for Nazism and the war.

Index

Thomas R. Nevin is Professor of Classical Studies
at John Carroll University.
Library of Congress Cataloging-in-Publication Data
Nevin, Thomas R., 1944–
Ernst Jünger and Germany : into the abyss, 1914–1945 /
Thomas Nevin.
Includes bibliographical references and index.
ISBN 0-8223-1879-2 (alk. paper)
1. Jünger, Ernst, 1895–   .
2. Authors, German—20th century—
Biography.   I. Title.
PT2619.U43Z73   1996
838'.91209—dc20   96-27326   CIP
[B]